FIRE MOUNTAINS OF THE WEST
The Cascade and Mono Lake Volcanoes

THIRD EDITION

STEPHEN L. HARRIS

2005
Mountain Press Publishing Company
Missoula, Montana

Second Printing, April 2006

Cover photo caption:
*July 22, 1980 eruption of Mount St. Helens, with
Mount Rainier (back cover) in the background.*
—James Vallance photo, U.S. Geological Survey

Illustrations are by Chris Hunter unless otherwise noted.

Library of Congress Cataloging-in-Publication Data

Harris, Stephen L., 1937–
    Fire Mountains of the West : the Cascade and Mono Lake volcanoes /
Stephen L. Harris.—3rd ed.
        p. cm.
    Includes bibliographical references and index.
    ISBN 0-87842-511-X (pbk. : alk. paper)
    1. Volcanoes—Cascade Range. 2. Cascade Range. I. Title.
    QE524.H18 2005
    551.2'1'09795—dc22

                                    2005015629

Printed in U.S.A

Mountain Press Publishing Company
P.O. Box 2399, Missoula, Montana 59806
(406) 728-1900

For Doug

Contents

CASCADE RANGE

Mt. Garibaldi
Mt. Baker
Glacier Peak
Mt. Rainier
Mt. Adams
Mt. St. Helens
Mt. Hood
Mt. Jefferson
Three Sisters
Mt. Thielsen
Crater Lake
Mt. McLoughlin
Mt. Shasta
Lassen Peak

PACIFIC OCEAN

Vancouver
Strait of Juan de Fuca
Puget Sound
Seattle
Tacoma
Olympia
Columbia R.
Portland
WILLAMETTE VALLEY
Eugene
Medford
SACRAMENTO VALLEY
Redding

Preface ————————————————————

This new edition of *Fire Mountains of the West: The Cascade and Mono Lake Volcanoes* brings into a single volume the latest research on each of the Pacific Coast's major volcanoes, from California's Mammoth Mountain to British Columbia's Mount Meager, the most recently active peak in Canada. Although nontechnical and easily accessible to the general reader, the book provides a complete geologic biography of Mount St. Helens and of all its fellow fire mountains—including Lassen, Shasta, Mazama (Crater Lake), Hood, Rainier, and Baker—detailing the specific hazards that each volcano represents to human life and property when it next erupts.

Following St. Helens's cataclysmic eruptions in 1980, geologists have focused on learning the history and eruptive potential of every volcano in the Cascade Range and in the Long Valley region that poses a threat to people living nearby. Using newly developed methods for dating volcanic rock, scientists have now been able to discover the approximate ages of lava flows and other eruptive units, enabling them for the first time to discover how often and in what quantity individual volcanoes have erupted. Some Cascade giants, such as Rainier, Adams, and Shasta, have extremely long lives—half a million years or more—and have repeatedly experienced periods of high lava output interspersed with stages of lower magma production. Even moderate eruptions at these high-standing, heavily glaciated peaks, however, have had catastrophic effects on areas downvalley from the volcano. The discovery and dating of newly recognized deposits reveals that most of the volcanoes have erupted far more often—and with more far-reaching effects—than was previously recognized.

Although it is not a field guide, *Fire Mountains of the West* concludes almost every chapter with directions on how readers can enjoy a particular mountain by car, by foot, or, in some cases, by climbing to its summit. The book explains why and how the individual mountains assumed their present forms and distinctive configurations, processes that created the magnificent scenery that draws millions of people to their slopes every year.

Acknowledgments

In acknowledging my great debt to the many geologists and historians whose work is cited in the bibliography, I would like to offer my special thanks to Dwight R. Crandell, formerly of the U.S. Geological Survey in Denver, who edited the original edition of this book for technical accuracy and who contributed many invaluable suggestions. For this edition, I am particularly grateful to Patrick T. Pringle of the Washington State Department of Natural Resources, who reviewed the revised chapters on Mounts Hood, St. Helens, and Rainier, and who also created the new map showing lahar hazard zones in the Puget Sound area that appears in chapter 1.

Many scientists with the U.S. Geological Survey at the David A. Johnston Cascades Volcano Observatory in Vancouver, Washington, and with the USGS at Menlo Park, California, also contributed significantly to this updated edition. Larry G. Mastin expertly reviewed the chapters on plate tectonics and volcanism; Carolyn L. Driedger shared her expertise on glaciers and their behavior; David P. Hill provided new information on volcanic hazards in the Mono Lake–Long Valley area; Michael A. Clynne reviewed the chapter on Lassen Peak, giving many helpful suggestions; Robert L. Christiansen, who was the USGS scientist-in-charge during St. Helens's 1980 paroxysm, reviewed both the Lassen and Shasta chapters; Charles R. Bacon reviewed the chapter on Crater Lake (Mount Mazama), making many helpful recommendations; and Manuel Nathenson shared his recent research on the formation of the caldera lake.

Julie M. Donnelly-Nolan graciously shared the results of her in-progress fieldwork on the Medicine Lake volcano and the Newberry Volcano, offering many valuable suggestions. In addition to patiently answering questions about several of the volcanoes, William E. Scott reviewed the chapter on the Three Sisters.

Wes Hildreth not only offered new data on the ages of the South and Middle Sisters, he also provided detailed reviews of the chapters on Mounts Adams and Baker. Andrew Calvert also kindly shared his ongoing research on the Sisters. Richard P. Hoblitt, now at the Hawaiian Volcano Observatory, offered enlightening comments on the discussion of Mount St. Helens. James W. Vallance, who has significantly enlarged our understanding of Mount Rainier's Holocene eruptive history, generously shared the results of his recent fieldwork. Thomas W. Sisson contributed an indispensable narrative summary of Rainier's Pleistocene growth, as well as a geologic map of the volcano's eruptive products.

James Begét (now at the University of Alaska in Fairbanks) and Richard B. Waitt of the USGS reviewed the chapter on Glacier Peak. Catherine

Hickson of the Canadian Geological Survey offered important information on Mount Meager and other Canadian volcanoes. Scott Lundstrom and Jim O'Connor of the USGS kindly provided valuable data on current glacial trends in the Oregon Cascades, and François Le Guern, a scientist in France, and Slawek Talaczyk of the University of California, Santa Cruz, shared their field research on the glaciers, respectively, of Mount Rainier and Mount Shasta.

In addition to research scientists at the U.S. Geological Survey, I am particularly grateful to Robert Jensen and Lawrence Chitwood of the U.S. Forest Service in Bend, Oregon, who provided much helpful information about Newberry Volcano. Robert Jensen also contributed several Newberry photographs that appear in chapter 12, and Larry Chitwood provided useful review comments.

Other USGS contributors to the earlier edition include James G. Moore, who supplied insight into the mechanism of St. Helens's 1980 debris avalanche and pyroclastic surge; C. Dan Miller, who identified specific hazards at Mount Shasta and the Mono Lake region; Donald Peterson; Wendell A. Duffield; Patrick Muffler; David Frank; Austin Post; Dee Molenaar; and David Sherrod.

Other geologists who helped with the earlier edition include Eugene P. Kiver of Eastern Washington University, Cheney; W. S. Wise of the University of California, Santa Barbara; Edward Taylor of Oregon State University, Corvallis; Alexander McBirney of the University of Oregon, Eugene; Kenneth Hopkins of the University of Northern Colorado; Dean Eppler; John Souther; Kenneth Sutton; and the late LeRoy Maynard, formerly of the University of Oregon, for his unpublished studies of Mount McLoughlin.

I would also like to thank Chris Hunter, a talented artist and cartographer, for the visual appeal of his maps and drawings that illustrate this book, and Chris Aynesworth, who skillfully digitalized all the artwork. David Wieprecht, photo archivist of the USGS Cascades Volcano Observatory, contributed a number of Cascade images to the new edition. The work of several gifted photographers greatly enhances the new edition, particularly that of Ellen Morris Bishop, Phyllis Gray, Ronald Warfield, and Douglas Tustin. Finally, I am grateful to my editors at Mountain Press, Kathleen Ort, Lynn Purl, and Beth Parker, for their guidance in seeing the book through production.

Because *Fire Mountains of the West* is intended for the general reader, its editors decided to eliminate footnotes crediting individual sources. To the many geologists and researchers who graciously made their work available the author expresses his appreciation by citing their publications in the bibliography listed at the end. The glossary, which defines essential terms in volcanism and glaciology, has also been updated and expanded.

CHAPTER 1

Our Western Volcanoes

AN OVERVIEW

After dozing sedately for eighteen years, Mount St. Helens—the most frequently and violently active volcano in the forty-eight adjacent states—abruptly returned to life in the fall of 2004. Following a sequence of shallow earthquakes, a series of mild steam explosions opened a new vent behind the massive lava dome that St. Helens had erected in its mile-wide crater between 1980 and 1986. Glowing tongues of molten rock began to ooze from the vent on October 11, inaugurating a new eruptive phase that may continue intermittently for years or decades to come.

Of the many volcanoes that extend from the Mono Lake area in east-central California through the Cascade Range of northern California, Oregon, and Washington to southwestern British Columbia, Mount St. Helens is perhaps the most volatile and unpredictable. It also has the most varied volcanic repertory: At different times during its relatively brief geologic history, St. Helens has staged huge explosive outbursts that deposited ash over hundreds of thousands of square miles in the Pacific Northwest; on other occasions it has poured out incandescent streams of fluid lava like those at Kilauea and other Hawaiian volcanoes; on still others it extrudes thick, viscous lava, building steep, bulbous mounds like the lava dome now forming.

The renewed activity of St. Helens informs a new generation of Americans that geologic forces are still at work reshaping our western landscape. Older generations are already well aware of the volcano's power to transform a once-familiar scene beyond recognition. Before the catastrophic eruption of May 18, 1980, St. Helens was a classically symmetrical cone surrounded by conifer forests and alpine lakes. Afterward, reduced 1,300 feet in height, it was a horseshoe-shaped wreck. A vast crater gaping open to the north faced a moonscape of gray desolation. At 8:32 that clear Sunday morning, after seven weeks of earthquakes and minor eruptions, the entire north side of St. Helens collapsed, generating the largest debris avalanche in historic time. Sudden removal of the volcano's north flank released the gas-rich magma (molten rock from underground) that had previously been injected into the mountain's interior.

1

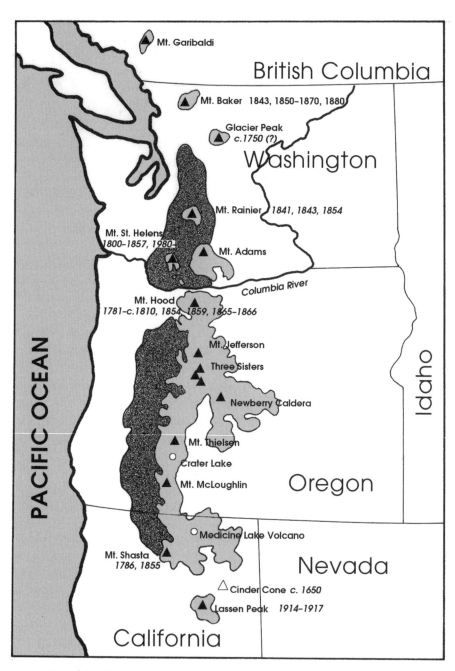

Map of the Cascade Range, showing locations of the principal volcanic cones and the dates of known historic eruptions

During the initial minutes of the daylong eruption, a ground-hugging blast of hot gas and rock fragments swept 17 miles to the north, mowing down an old-growth forest, killing 57 people and thousands of wild animals, and devastating 230 square miles. As the eruption progressed, winds carried an immense ash cloud eastward, turning day into night over a wide swath of eastern Washington, northern Idaho, and western Montana. Within fifteen days, the St. Helens ash had circled the globe.

Between May and October 1980, five additional explosive eruptions occurred, typically sending columns of ash 10 miles into the air. For the next six years, St. Helens erupted more quietly, extruding thick lobes of lava that gradually built a dome 876 feet high and sporadically ejecting plumes of ash-laden steam.

We do not know if the eruptive episode that began in 2004 will produce another paroxysm comparable to that of May 18, 1980, or how long activity will continue. If the recent geologic past is a guide, the volcano may erupt even more violently than it did in 1980 and remain active for decades or centuries. An explosive outburst in AD 1479 was six times larger than that of 1980 and began a cycle that continued intermittently for almost 300 years. St. Helens's most recent eruptive period before its twentieth-century awakening lasted for more than half a century, from 1800 to 1857. It has erupted cataclysmically in the past, at times severely disrupting plant, animal, and human life over vast areas, and it will eventually do so again.

Mount St. Helens is not alone in the volcanic threat it represents to people living on the Pacific Coast. Towering 14,411 feet above the densely populated shores of eastern Puget Sound, glacier-clad Mount Rainier is officially recognized as the single most dangerous volcano in America. Although Hawaii's volcanoes erupt much more often, Rainier is potentially far more dangerous because of its great height, steepness, thick cover of glacial ice, and proximity to the Seattle-Tacoma metropolitan area. Hot rock ejected onto Rainier's extensive ice fields, causing rapid melting, has repeatedly triggered floods and lahars (volcanic mudflows of water and rock debris that flow downslope like torrents of liquid concrete), inundating valleys that originate on the mountain. During the last few thousand years, Rainier has produced dozens of large-volume lahars that have traveled as far as 65 miles from the volcano, emptying into Puget Sound and burying the sites of towns and cities where 150,000 people now live.

Particularly worrisome is Rainier's tendency to produce large mudflows unrelated to volcanic activity. High on the cone, corrosive acidic gases chemically change solid rock into soft, crumbly, claylike material. This weakened, water-saturated rock can collapse without warning. An earthquake, heavy rainfall, or the simple pull of gravity can trigger massive avalanches of such hydrothermally altered rock, without the precursors that

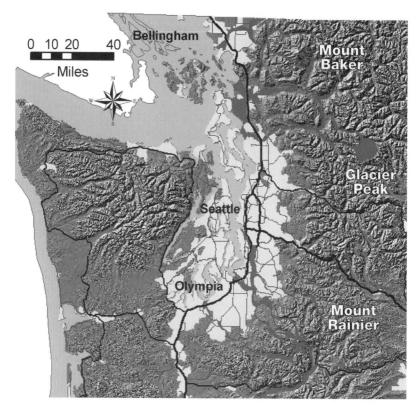

Map of the Puget Sound region in western Washington, showing areas inundated by lahars (volcanic mudflows) from Mount Rainier, Glacier Peak, and Mount Baker. River valleys heading on these volcanoes have repeatedly served as channels for floods and lahars debouching into the eastern Puget Sound lowland. Future lahars will impact the same areas, burying sites that are now densely populated.
—Courtesy of Patrick T. Pringle, Washington State Department of Natural Resources, Division of Geology and Earth Resources

ordinarily precede a volcanic eruption. When large sections of Rainier's cone suddenly collapse, as they have repeatedly in the recent geologic past, the avalanching rock, mobilized by water contained in the porous rock, typically transforms into a lahar that travels tens of miles beyond the volcano's base. About 2,600 years ago, the Round Pass mudflow, moving as a giant wave that temporarily filled the upper South Puyallup and Tahoma Creek valleys to a depth of at least 1,000 feet, traveled well beyond the Cascade mountain front. The Electron Mudflow, which occurred about 500 years ago, buried a forest at the site of present-day Orting before streaming many miles down the now heavily populated Puyallup River valley. Because they have not been unequivocally linked to volcanic deposits, both of these huge lahars may have taken place when the volcano was quiet. Geologists estimate that if a mudflow similar to the Electron—several hundred million cubic yards in volume—were to occur today, downvalley residents would have no more than an hour's warning to evacuate their homes and businesses.

Two particularly deadly twentieth-century eruptions, one in South America and the other in the Carribean, illustrate the kinds of activity that the Cascade volcanoes typically produce—and the possible consequences to nearby communities. In 1985, a relatively small event at Colombia's Nevado del Ruiz triggered a lahar that destroyed the town of Armero, snuffing out the lives of 20,000 people. When del Ruiz spewed hot rock that rapidly melted part of the volcano's summit glacier, a voluminous torrent of mud raced 30 miles down a canyon toward Armero, engulfing the city and entombing most of its inhabitants. Up to 3,000 additional victims died in other valleys that originated on the mountain.

The Nevado del Ruiz mudflow, in terms of human fatalities, was the second greatest volcanic disaster in the twentieth century. The worst occurred in 1902 on the Caribbean island of Martinique, where in mere minutes Mont Pelée reduced the entire city of St. Pierre to flaming rubble, incinerating and/or asphyxiating all but two or three of its 30,000 inhabitants. The victims at St. Pierre were killed by a phenomenon then poorly understood—a pyroclastic flow and surge. From a Greek term meaning "fire-broken," a pyroclastic flow is a swift-moving mixture of hot gas and incandescent rock fragments that speeds along the ground like a seething liquid. At Mont Pelée, the flow, largely confined to a neighboring stream valley, did not actually enter the city. It was the accompanying pyroclastic surge, a less dense, turbulent cloud of gas and fine ash particles that, billowing high above and spreading laterally beyond the earth-bound pyroclastic flow, caused the destruction. Rushing through St. Pierre with hurricane force, the surge (which French scientists called a *nuée ardente*) literally flattened the city, toppling walls several feet thick and igniting fires everywhere in its path, even aboard the ships anchored far out in St. Pierre's harbor.

Most of the deaths and serious injuries at Mount St. Helens in 1980 were caused by a similar pyroclastic surge that easily surmounted ridges 1,200 feet high and traveled up to 17 miles from the crater. Whereas trees growing more than a few miles from the volcano were thrown down like rows of matchsticks, stripped of their limbs and bark by the abrasive surge, areas nearer the crater were scoured down to bedrock, leaving no trace of the evergreen forest that previously existed there. As geologists now know, pyroclastic flows and surges, as well as mudflows much larger and more far-reaching than those that claimed 23,000 lives at Nevado del Ruiz, are common eruptive phenomena at many Cascade fire mountains, including Rainier, Hood, and Shasta. When the volcanoes revive, their eruptions will inevitably affect the lives of millions of people living in their shadows.

Historic Eruptions in the West

The Cascade Range, extending from the Garibaldi volcanic belt in British Columbia to Lassen Peak in northern California, a distance of more than 700 miles, contains a dozen or more large volcanoes that pose potential threats to many Pacific Coast residents. Geologists believe that the most recently active volcanoes are also the most likely to erupt again in the near future. Six of the seven historically active volcanoes—St. Helens, Rainier, Baker, and Glacier Peak in Washington, Mount Hood in Oregon, and Mount Shasta in California—are precisely the six peaks located closest to rapidly growing population centers. Ironically, the same fertile river valleys that attract the most residents also regularly function as transport channels for huge lahars descending from the volcanoes. Stream valleys originating on Baker, Glacier Peak, and Rainier terminate in eastern Puget Sound, where parts of cities such as Seattle, Tacoma, Kent, and Auburn risk inundation. Mounts St. Helens and Hood ultimately funnel their lahars into the Columbia, endangering river towns from Castle Rock, Kelso, and Longview in southwest Washington to Troutdale and Hood River in northern Oregon. Although the seventh historically active volcano, California's Lassen Peak, stands a presumably safe 50 miles from the Sacramento Valley towns of Redding and

Cascade eruptions during the last 4,000 years. Note that St. Helens, Shasta, Glacier Peak, and the Medicine Lake volcano erupted most frequently. —Courtesy of Barbara M. Myers, U.S. Geological Survey

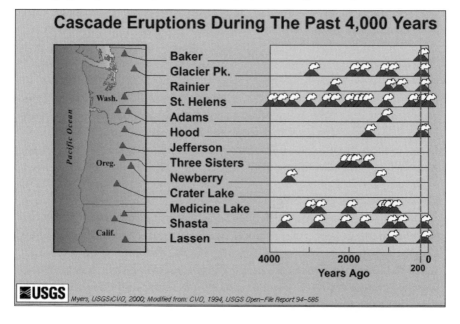

Cascade Eruptions During The Past 4,000 Years

Baker
Glacier Pk.
Rainier
St. Helens
Adams
Hood
Jefferson
Three Sisters
Newberry
Crater Lake
Medicine Lake
Shasta
Lassen

Wash.
Oreg.
Calif.
Pacific Ocean

4000   2000   0
Years Ago   200

USGS *Myers, USGS/CVO, 2000; Modified from: CVO, 1994, USGS Open-File Report 94-585*

Red Bluff, a repeat of its 1914 to 1917 eruptions could nonetheless damage resorts, campgrounds, and other tourist facilities located nearby.

Although the Cascade peaks have produced most of the historic activity in the forty-eight adjacent states, a small island volcano in Mono Lake in east-central California has also erupted during the last two or three centuries. The Mono Lake–Long Valley area remains geologically restless. Beginning in 1978, a series of damaging earthquakes has shaken this region, a volcanic landscape well known for its popular ski village, Mammoth Lakes. After a flurry of 6.0 temblors and measurable ground uplift in May 1980, the U.S. Geological Survey warned of possible eruptions. Although these events, typical precursors of volcanic activity, have not yet culminated in an eruption, continuing quakes, ground deformation, and effusions of carbon monoxide gas that have killed large stands of trees on Mammoth Mountain indicate that magma (molten rock underground) has risen toward the surface. During the last 2,000 years, the region has produced at least thirty significant outbursts. The latest large event occurred at multiple vents during the fourteenth century when a chain of volcanic domes and cones, the youngest part of the Mono-Inyo Craters, was formed. A sequence of smaller eruptions at Paoha Island took place even more recently, spanning several decades of mildly explosive activity between the early eighteenth and mid-nineteenth centuries. Many geologists believe that another eruption is overdue.

Although it is impossible to predict either the date, exact location, or size of the West's next major volcanic eruption, it will almost certainly take place in either the Mono Lake–Long Valley area or in the Cascade Range. During the years since the end of Pleistocene time (which began 1.8 million and ended 10,000 to 12,000 years ago), the Cascade volcanoes have produced an average of one or two eruptions per century. This represents a minimal estimate, as the evidence of smaller events is commonly eroded away or buried under later deposits. During the 1840s and 1850s, observers logged many eruptions at Mount St. Helens, but only two left ash deposits that are still visible. Similarly, none of St. Helens's ash eruptions that preceded the May 18, 1980, explosion were voluminous enough to leave a recognizable layer, although they often formed ash plumes rising 10,000 to 12,000 feet above the volcano's summit. Some products of earlier historic activity, such as the Goat Rocks dome emplaced during the 1840s, were totally destroyed when St. Helens's north side collapsed in 1980. With a few exceptions, such as the pyroclastic flow and mudflow deposits at Mounts Hood and Shasta, much of the material ejected during historic eruptions of roughly the last 250 years is poorly preserved. Even the 1915 layer of gray pumice that formerly mantled a large area east of Lassen Peak is in many places now difficult to detect.

HISTORIC ERUPTIONS IN THE CASCADE RANGE

DATE	VOLCANO	NATURE AND/OR PRODUCTS OF ERUPTION
ca. 1750	Glacier Peak	Ash
ca. 1781–1810	Hood	Old Maid eruptive episode: growth of Crater Rock dome; pyroclastic flows; mudflows
1786	Shasta	Pyroclastic flows from Hotlum Cone; hot mudflows
1800	St. Helens	Tephra (layer T); lava flows
ca. 1820	Rainier	Ash(?)
ca. 1820–1854	Rainier	Pumice (tephra X)
1831	St. Helens	Ash
1835	St. Helens	Ash
1842	St. Helens	Tephra; debris flows
ca. 1842–1847	St. Helens	Goat Rocks dome; hot avalanches
1843	Baker	Tephra; debris flows
1843	Rainier	Ash(?)
1846	Baker	Ash
1846	Rainier	Ash(?)
1848–1850	St. Helens	Intermittent ash
1850	Baker	Ash
1852–1953	Baker	Ash
1853	St. Helens	Ash
1854	Baker	Tephra
1854	St. Helens	Ash
1854	Rainier	Ash(?)
1854–1857	Chaos Crags	Steam(?)
1855	Shasta	Ash, steam(?)
1855	Baker	Small ash clouds
1856	Baker	"Dense smoke"
1857	St. Helens	Ash clouds
1858	Baker	Reported "fire" and "smoke"
1859	Hood	"Fire," ashfall on snow or mudflow
1859	Baker	Reported "flame" and dense smoke
1860	Baker	Ash
1863	Baker	Ash
1865	Baker	"Dense clouds of smoke"
1865–1866	Hood	Ash, "jets of flame," "smoke"
1867	Baker	"Dense volumes of smoke"
1870	Baker	"Great volumes of smoke"
1873	Rainier	"Clouds of smoke from highest peak"
1879	Rainier	"Brown, billowy clouds"
1880	Baker	Reported "flames" and "smoke"
1882	Rainier	"Brown, billowy clouds"
1907	Hood	Temporary increase of heat emission at Crater Rock
1914–1917	Lassen Peak	Tephra; lava flow; pyroclastic flows
1975	Baker	Sudden increase in heat and steam flow
1980	St. Helens	Catastrophic debris avalanche; Plinian ashfall; pyroclastic flows; mudflows; dome elevation
1980–1986	St. Helens	Episodes of dome growth in crater; small explosive bursts; pyroclastic flows; mudflows
2004–2005	St. Helens	Small steam explosions; growth of new lava dome

Because the period of recorded observation in the American West is so brief—contrasted with at least 2,500 years of written records for such old-world volcanoes as Vesuvius and Etna—geologists must rely almost exclusively on studying physical deposits in order to infer the nature and effects of the activity that formed them. During recent decades, university scientists, state geologists, members of the U.S. Geological Survey, and other researchers have found that the Cascade volcanoes have erupted much more frequently, and with far greater disruption of the natural environment, than previously supposed. It is now possible to tell the story of such individual Cascade giants as Rainier, Adams, Baker, Hood, Mazama (Crater Lake), Shasta, and Lassen more fully than ever before. New methods of dating volcanic rock allow us to read a particular volcano's biography, tracing its life history from inception to maturity. Some Cascade volcanoes, such as Mount Rainier, are extremely long-lived, their activity spanning more than a half million years. Others, like St. Helens and Lassen, have existed for only a few tens of thousands of years. Cinder Cone in Lassen Volcanic National Park was born a mere 350 years ago.

The Cascade Landscape

The highest freestanding landforms in the United States, the Cascade volcanoes rise as high as 2 miles above the lesser mountains at their feet. Whereas the loftiest points in the Rocky Mountains or Sierra Nevada tend to be only slightly higher than other nearby summits, the individual Cascade peaks stand in splendid isolation, typically dominating the landscape for 50 to 100 miles in every direction. California's Mount Whitney (14,495 feet), the highest mountain in the forty-eight adjacent states, is almost indistinguishable from the surrounding High Sierra crest, but there is no chance of viewers mistaking the identity of Mount Shasta (14,162 feet), which soars 10,000 feet above its base, the most prominent topographical feature in northern California.

Mount Rainier's dominance is even more impressive, not only because of its permanent snowcap—the volcano hosts 34 square miles of solid ice, the largest glacier system of any single U.S. peak south of Alaska—but also because its visual height nearly equals its actual elevation. Viewed from sea level on Puget Sound, Rainier looks every inch of its 14,411-foot stature and holds undisputed visual sway over the skylines of Seattle, Tacoma, and Olympia, the state capital. To residents of western Washington, Rainier is simply "the mountain."

Three guardian volcanoes flank Portland, the Pacific Northwest's second-largest city. Looming above the eastern horizon, Mount Hood, Oregon's highest peak (11,239 feet), offers the typical Cascade paradox of perilous beauty. A mecca for skiers, hikers, and climbers, Hood is also an active volcano that threatens numerous towns and resorts built near rivers that drain the mountain. Beginning in about 1781, Hood erupted intermittently for almost a century, spewing ash and oozing thick lava that broke into fragments and avalanched down its south flank, generating mudflows that swept down both the Sandy and White River valleys. Some of these lahars were large enough to dam the mighty Columbia River temporarily. Today jets of steam still spurt from Crater Rock, a steep lava dome that formed high on Hood's south side about 200 years ago. When atmospheric conditions are favorable, Hood's heat and steam emission generates plumes visible from Portland, occasionally prompting worried phone calls to the staff at Timberline Lodge, the picturesque alpine hotel on the volcano's south slope.

Located across the Columbia River from Portland in southwestern Washington, Mount St. Helens repeatedly showered the city with ash during its 1980 eruptions. Thirty-five miles to the east, Mount Adams (12,276 feet) has been slumbering for about 1,000 years but still emits heat and sulfurous fumes from its summit crater. As many Portlanders know, these three snowcapped sentinels figured prominently in prehistoric Native American myth, in which Adams and Hood were mountain siblings jealously contending for the love of beautiful St. Helens, which before 1980 displayed the smooth symmetry of an almost perfect cone.

South of Mount Hood, the range is divided into two generally parallel belts, the older western Cascades and the younger (mostly less than two or three million years old) High Cascades. Whereas the western section is extensively eroded into high-standing ridges separated by deep canyons, the eastern belt forms a broad platform of intermingling lava flows and overlapping shield volcanoes—broad, gently sloping edifices built by flows of very fluid lava, which glaciers and streams have not yet had time to dissect. Built atop the elongated platform of coalescing shields and smaller cinder cones (small volcanic hills built of fragmental rock) is a stately procession of Oregon's highest peaks: Mount Jefferson, the Three Sisters (all over 10,000 feet), and Mount Mazama, the decapitated volcano now holding Crater Lake. Despite the abundance of Oregon's geologically young volcanoes, however, there is a noticeable chronological gap in recent activity through most of the state. For more than a millennium, no eruptions have taken place in the 280-mile-long segment lying between Mount Hood and Mount Shasta.

North of Snoqualmie Pass, where Interstate 90 connects Seattle with eastern Washington, the character of the range changes significantly. Whereas the entire range to the south is composed of relatively young volcanic rock, peaks in the North Cascades consist of much older metamorphic and sedimentary formations that display a long and complex geologic evolution. Uplift is greatest in this northern segment of the range, and erosion has been correspondingly severe, removing almost all the overlying volcanic deposits and exposing the ancient foundation rock. Up to 80 miles wide from west to east, the North Cascades have the highest average elevations in the range (7,000 to 8,000 feet) and the highest topographic relief: the vertical distance between valley floors and adjacent summits is commonly 4,000 to 6,000 feet. Although most of the exposed rock is nonvolcanic, the region's two highest peaks—Mount Baker (10,781 feet) and Glacier Peak (10,541 feet)—are youthful volcanoes that have punctured the older metamorphic and sedimentary foundation.

Eroded into a maze of sharp peaks, steep ridges, and twisting glaciated valleys, the North Cascades rank among the most rugged mountainscapes in North America. Except for the recently completed North Cascades highway linking eastern Washington's Okanogan country with the Puget Sound area, the region has few paved roads. Shrouded by frequent storms that nourish hundreds of glaciers, its craggy interior conceals a true wilderness that resists easy exploration.

After a break in the range near the Canadian boundary, where the Fraser River has excavated a spacious valley, the volcanic sequence resumes in southwest British Columbia. Mount Garibaldi (8,787 feet), 40 miles from the cosmopolitan port of Vancouver, British Columbia, and its fellow volcanoes to the north have produced several eruptions during Holocene time (roughly the last 10,000 years). The latest, at Mount Meager (8,790 feet), occurred about 2,400 years ago.

Because of its height, length (almost double that of California's Sierra Nevada), and location, the Cascade Range is an effective climatic barrier. Running roughly parallel to the Pacific Coast on a generally north-south axis, the Cascades intercept moisture-laden winds blowing inland from the Pacific Ocean. As the marine air rises over the mountain front, it cools rapidly and condenses, falling as rain or snow. Although precipitation is less in the southern part of the chain, it can reach over 150 inches annually on the wettest slopes; world-record snowfalls have been recorded at both Mount Baker and Mount Rainier, the two most heavily glaciated volcanoes in the range.

Whereas the western Cascade slopes are thickly forested with Douglas fir, hemlock, and cedar, east of the Cascade crest the scenery and vegetation change abruptly. The pine and juniper forest on the east side is drier, free of the tangled undergrowth of lush ferns and brush that characterize the much damper and greener west side. Because the annual rainfall dwindles to as little as 8 inches east of the divide, the lower east flanks are typically brown in summer, sporting only clumps of parched grass, sagebrush, and other scrub growth. Almost nowhere else in the nation do a few miles mark so complete a transformation of the landscape.

History and Exploration

Although Native Americans had hunted, fished, and built their villages in and near the Cascades for thousands of years, the range was completely unknown to Europeans or Americans until the last decade or two of the eighteenth century, when Spanish, English, and American explorers first sighted individual summits. It was not until the British navigator George Vancouver sailed into Puget Sound in 1792 that the Cascade peaks began to receive their present names. Baker, the northernmost of the U.S. volcanoes, was named for Vancouver's third lieutenant. Rainier honored Admiral Peter Rainier, while St. Helens commemorated an influential diplomat friend of the captain. While exploring the Columbia River, Vancouver's first lieutenant, Broughton, was the first ship's officer to spot Mount Hood. Apparently dazzled by its gleaming white spire, Broughton estimated the

In this aerial view from the north, Mount Hood (11,239 feet) displays some of its nine major glaciers and perennial snowfields (containing 12.3 billion cubic feet of ice). —Austin Post photo, U.S. Geological Survey

peak to be 25,000 feet high, and named it after Samuel Hood, another high-ranking naval officer. At the place where the Sandy River flows into the Columbia, Broughton noted a large bar of sediment extending from the Sandy's mouth into the larger river. Although the Englishman would not have known the cause of this unusual feature, the sandbar represented runout from a large mudflow that had occurred during an eruption of Mount Hood about ten years earlier. Although Vancouver assumed that the individual peaks probably belonged to a continuous chain, he made no attempt to christen the range.

The Cascades originally took their name from a series of white-water rapids in the western part of the Columbia River Gorge, a steep-walled channel that the river cut through the heart of the range. Because it is one of only three places in its entire length where a stream has breached the chain, forming an east-west passage linking the Northwest's arid interior with the well-watered Pacific Coast, the Columbia Gorge became the primary trading route for both prehistoric Native Americans and later Anglo-European explorers and trappers. When Lewis and Clark journeyed to the Pacific in 1805, they followed old trails through the Gorge, encountering the last major obstacle to their quest at the Columbia's notorious cascades. To the pioneers and settlers who came after Lewis and Clark, the precipitous mountains looming above these boat-shattering cataracts were known as "the mountains by the Cascades." Although nothing comparable to the Columbia Gorge exists elsewhere in the range, the pioneers' name was appropriate, for few spots in the Cascades are far removed from the music of running water.

Today, the perilous rapids for which the range is named no longer exist; the site is now submerged beneath the waters impounded behind Bonneville Dam. Until the dam was completed in the late 1930s, however, when the river ran low, boaters could look beneath its surface to see fish swimming through the tree limbs of a spectral forest. Forests bordering the river drowned when an enormous avalanche of basaltic rock—the Bonneville landslide—created the rapids, substantially raising the water level upriver. For a short time before the river breached it, the slide formed a natural causeway spanning the Columbia, giving Native Americans a temporary means of crossing the river dry-shod and inspiring the famous legend of "The Bridge of the Gods" (see sidebar on page 214).

From a vantage point on bluffs above the Columbia, Lewis and Clark sighted another snowy pinnacle 46 miles south of Mount Hood, which they called Mount Jefferson, honoring the president who sponsored their expedition. Oregon's second-highest mountain, Jefferson (10,497 feet) is the only Cascade volcano named by the explorers. The rest of the Cascade peaks received their present names almost casually from later nineteenth-century explorers and settlers. The Three Sisters, central Oregon's most prominent landmarks, were at first christened Faith, Hope, and Charity by early homesteaders. Controversy continues over who first named Mount Shasta, with partisans of both the Spanish and the Russians claiming precedence. During the 1830s, Hall J. Kelley and Thomas J. Farnham led a movement to rename the Cascades the "Presidents' Range." Although the Kelley-Farnham plan failed, two of the presidential names they proposed stuck: Mount Washington in Oregon and Mount Adams in Washington commemorate the nation's first two chief executives. Mount Mazama, the collapsed volcano cradling Crater Lake—which American settlers did not even discover until 1853—was named by an Oregon mountaineering club, the Mazamas, named after a South American mountain goat. Another Oregon peak, Three-Fingered Jack, expresses the pioneers' picturesque vernacular.

National Parks and Monuments

With its dense conifer forests, perennial ice fields, and myriad lakes, streams, and waterfalls, the Cascade Range contains some of America's most remarkable scenery. Although much of the range has been subject to clear-cutting, mining, and other commercial development, Congress has preserved some of its unique attractions in four national parks and three national monuments. Mount Rainier's rare combination of volcanic heat and glacial ice was given national park status in 1899. Washington's North Cascades National Park was created in 1968, although it excludes the region's two conspicuous volcanoes, Mount Baker and Glacier Peak. Mount St. Helens was made a national monument after the 1980 eruptions and is now a living laboratory in which scientists can study the gradual recovery of plant and wildlife after a natural disaster.

The logging industry adamantly opposed the creation of Crater Lake National Park in 1902. Although the industry's opposition was eventually overcome in the case of Crater Lake, it has remained a powerful influence in preventing the creation of other such preserves in Oregon. A small part of the huge Newberry Volcano in central Oregon became a national monument in 1990, shielding some of its many geologic wonders from continued exploitation. Although Mount Shasta, which bears California's largest glaciers, has never received federal protection, Lassen Volcanic National Park was formed in 1916, when Lassen Peak was in the midst of its latest eruptive cycle. Located in the arid northeastern corner of California, Lava Beds National Monument contains hundreds of lava tube caves, long passages or tubes that formed inside fluid basaltic lava flows from the Medicine Lake volcano. One of the West's largest volcanic edifices, the Medicine

Lake shield (about 140 cubic miles in volume) stands 35 miles northeast of Mount Shasta. Efforts to extend national park status to other equally spectacular parts of the range, such as Mounts Baker, Hood, and Shasta, have been consistently defeated by timber and other economic interests.

When Sleeping Giants Wake

Of the almost three thousand individual volcanic vents that geologists have mapped in the Cascade Range, no two are precisely alike. They range in size from small piles of cinders to enormous composite cones—long-lived volcanoes such as Rainier, Hood, and Shasta that repeatedly erupt lava flows and pyroclastic material, gradually constructing a massive edifice high enough to pierce the clouds. The glory of the range, these lofty, glacier-crowned composite cones (also called stratovolcanoes) form a procession of stately peaks, generally spaced about 40 to 60 miles apart, that give this volcanic chain its distinctive character. Although the most deeply eroded cones, such as Oregon's spindlelike Mount Thielsen and Washington's jagged Goat Rocks, are extinct (not expected to erupt again), at least thirteen of the large composite volcanoes are still in the prime of life.

Recent geologic studies show that some of the thirteen composite cones were dormant (sleeping) for many millennia, only to awaken violently and begin a new eruptive cycle. Geologists have found that individual volcanoes vary considerably in their long-term behavior, including their rate of lava production. Long periods of voluminous lava effusion, constructing a large cone over hundreds of thousands of years, can be followed by many thousands of years of little or no activity, allowing glaciers and other erosional forces to tear down the cone. At Mount Adams, for example, recent mapping and dating of deposits reveals that the volcano experienced several episodes of vigorous cone-building, succeeded by long quiet intervals during which glaciers destroyed much of the edifice. Much of Adams's present cone, standing atop its deeply eroded predecessor, was formed between about 25,000 and 15,000 years ago, after which its activity again abruptly declined. Although Adams has erupted only seven or eight times in the last 10,000 years, the volcano's huge size (second most voluminous composite cone in the range) and long life (more than a half million years) suggest that it could increase its eruption rate at any time.

Mount Hood, Adams's rival brother in Native American myth, was quiet for about 12,000 years before beginning a new cycle of activity around AD 500. Hood has had two extended eruptive episodes since. Mount Mazama slumbered almost twice as long—at least 20,000 years—before roaring back to life with a cataclysmic eruption that spread 42 cubic miles of ash over a half million square miles. Even so hyperactive a volcano as Mount St. Helens is known to have napped as long as four thousand years between recurrent episodes of explosive violence. Long interludes of silence do not ensure that a given volcano has entered into permanent hibernation. In the case of many now-dormant composite cones, the volcano may only be gathering energy to stage an earth-shaking comeback.

In addition to the high-standing composite cones that represent its greatest potential dangers, the Cascade Range also contains hundreds of cinder

LIVING, DEAD, OR ONLY ASLEEP?

A popular method of classifying volcanoes labels them as active, dormant (sleeping), or extinct. The first classification is particularly flexible, with some geologists defining an active volcano as one that is now erupting or has erupted very recently; others expand the definition to include volcanoes that are presently quiet but that are known to have erupted during the past few centuries and are expected to erupt again. In the case of the Cascade and Mono Lake–Long Valley volcanoes, where the period of historical observation is brief, several volcanoes are catalogued as active because they have erupted during historic time, currently manifest thermal anomalies, and/or are likely to erupt in the future. Thus not only the currently erupting Mount St. Helens but also Mounts Baker, Rainier, Hood, and Shasta can be considered active volcanoes. All erupted during the late eighteenth and/or nineteenth century and continue to emit heat and steam.

Although inactive for 500 years or more, many other West Coast volcanoes that erupted during Holocene time are merely resting between eruptive cycles. These dormant peaks include Mount Adams, the South Sister, Newberry Volcano, the Medicine Lake volcano, and the Mono-Inyo Craters chain in east-central California. Because large composite cones have eruptive lives that may extend over hundreds of thousands of years—with long silent intervals between eruptions—it is risky to pronounce a long-lived stratovolcano dead. Mount Jefferson and the Middle Sister have slept thus far through Holocene time, but cannot be dismissed as extinct. Jefferson's loftier neighbor, Mount Hood, slumbered for perhaps 12,000 years before coming out of retirement about 1,500 years ago. Since then, Hood has erupted a series of lava domes and numerous pyroclastic flows.

Even the longest-lived volcano, however, eventually dies. The Goat Rocks volcano in the south Washington Cascades had a long history that extended from late Pliocene well into Pleistocene time, but has not erupted in at least a half million years and is safely extinct. Many of the small to midsized Cascade volcanoes are monogenetic—they erupt for a few decades or even centuries, and then shut down permanently, leaving their cones vulnerable to severe erosion. Such dissected cadavers as Oregon's Three-Fingered Jack or Mounts Thielsen and Washington—with their glacier-whittled summit spires—proclaim their demise. Severe erosional scars on long-lived stratovolcanoes, however, do not guarantee against its resuscitation. For people living near a volcano that has not erupted for millennia, misinterpreting sleep for extinction may have unfortunate consequences.

cones that have the propensity to pop up almost anywhere in or near the range. Many cinder cones are clustered together in distinctive volcanic fields, such as central Oregon's McKenzie Pass area or the Indian Heaven field west of Mount Adams, but others are scattered promiscuously along the Cascade flanks, even extending outward into populated areas. Although they are usually associated with established volcanic centers, cinder cones typically appear where no previous volcano existed. Like Paricutin, the volcano born in a Mexican cornfield in 1943, these cinder cones are mod-

Plumes of steam rise from ice-clad Mount Baker's Sherman crater. Repeatedly active between 1843 and about 1880, Baker suddenly intensified its heat and steam emission in 1975. —U.S. Geological Survey

erately explosive and can build a pyroclastic cone several hundred feet high in a few weeks or months. They also pour out lava flows that can travel several miles from the vent, burying many square miles. Although these volcanoes are monogenetic—dying after a single eruptive episode—they can suddenly show up in highly inconvenient locations. In 1973, a new cinder cone threatened to engulf the town of Vestmannaeyjar on Iceland's Heimaey Island. A youthful cinder cone, Lava Butte, stands only 10 miles south of Bend, Oregon, while another, Pilot Butte, occupies a choice position near the center of town. As even a cursory inventory of the range's many vents reveals, the volcanic pulse of the Cascades may be irregular, but it remains persuasively strong.

CHAPTER 2

Plates in Motion

THE RING OF FIRE, HOT SPOTS, AND SUPERERUPTIONS

Volcanoes and earthquakes are worldwide phenomena, but they do not occur evenly all over the globe. The most intense seismic and volcanic activity is largely concentrated in well-defined linear belts, such as the "Ring of Fire" that encircles the Pacific Ocean. Most of the world's earthquakes take place in this circum-Pacific belt, and about 70 percent of the world's 1,511 potentially active land volcanoes are located there. However, even more of the planet's volcanism—approximately 80 percent—takes place invisibly beneath the sea, particularly along midocean ridges, which are submarine volcanic chains that twist around the earth like seams on a baseball.

Plate Tectonics: A Global Overview

To understand the volcanoes of the Cascade Range, which form a major link in the Ring of Fire, as well as others scattered throughout the American West, it is helpful to see them as part of a worldwide geologic process known as plate tectonics. According to this theory, the earth's crust is composed of about sixteen major tectonic plates and several minor ones. Linear belts mark boundaries between plates—huge slabs of rigid crustal rock that carry continents or ocean basins on their backs. These plates are always in motion, pulling apart, rubbing against each other, or colliding together. Their dynamic interaction determines where and when most earthquakes and volcanoes occur. Like giant barges, the plates drift slowly over an underlying zone of hot plastic material, the mantle. Eighteen hundred miles thick, the mantle lies between the earth's heavy metallic core and its brittle outer shell, which is proportionately thinner than the skin of an apple. Together, the crust and solid portion of the uppermost mantle form the lithosphere, the earth's fragmented outer layer of interlocking plates.

Heat circulating through the earth's interior keeps the plates in constant movement. As workers in South Africa's deepest gold mines know, the earth's internal heat becomes progressively more noticeable as the miners descend beneath the surface. The rate at which temperature increases with depth in the crust is known as the geothermal gradient. Although the rate averages about 75 degrees Fahrenheit for every mile below the surface, the

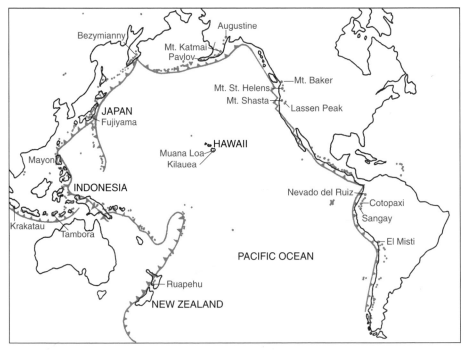

The circum-Pacific "Ring of Fire," with the locations of some major volcanoes, including four in the Cascade Range. Approximately 70 percent of the world's known active land volcanoes are located along the margins of the Pacific Ocean basin.

geothermal gradient varies considerably, with continental interiors generally much cooler than the volcanic zones along their margins. The highest concentrations of internal heat form convection cells, similar to ones in a pot of boiling water. This cycle of currents in the mantle, buoying the crust in one place and tugging it down in others, provides energy for plate movement.

The linear rift zones at which plates separate are called divergent boundaries, or spreading centers, where magma oozes up through long fissures in the crust, creating submarine mountain ranges such as the Mid-Atlantic Ridge and the East Pacific rise. Perhaps the best-studied spreading center, the Mid-Atlantic Ridge began to form about 200 million years ago, a period when all the continents were joined together in a colossal landmass called Pangaea. This ancient supercontinent began to break up when a great rift, a linear system of deep fractures in the crust, split Pangaea apart. As the plates on opposite sides of the rift pulled away from each other, forced apart by upwelling magma, the basin of the Atlantic Ocean began to form.

Submarine eruptions continue today, causing the Atlantic Ocean floor to expand and pushing the Americas ever farther westward. In only a few places has the Mid-Atlantic Ridge broken the ocean surface, notably at Iceland, a volcanic island that is slowly being torn in two as its east and west sections travel in opposite directions.

Although most spreading centers are hidden beneath oceans, the rifting process is clearly visible in Africa. The same forces that opened the Atlantic Ocean split the Arabian plate from the rest of the continent, forming the Red Sea. A new spreading center may be developing within the East African rift system, a site of numerous earthquakes and several active volcanoes. When the crust stretches and thins, tension cracks riddle crustal rock, which is then invaded by magma. Even when the magma does not reach the surface to cause volcanic eruptions, it increases pressure on the crust, producing additional fractures and expanding the rift zone. If the East African rift continues to grow and deepen, the resulting depression will eventually be flooded by the Indian Ocean, transforming Africa's easternmost corner into a large island.

Eruptions along the Mid-Atlantic Ridge represent a divergent plate boundary, where plates on opposite sides of a spreading center move in opposite directions, in this case carrying the Americas on one side and Europe and Africa on the other away from each other. Similar spreading centers in the Pacific Ocean, however, trigger a confrontational geologic process called convergence, in which oceanic and continental plates collide. At convergent plate boundaries subduction zones typically form. As magma issuing from linear fractures in the Pacific plate creates new sea floor, older crustal rock is thrust outward toward the continents. When the dense, relatively thin basaltic seafloor collides with the much thicker and lighter granitic rock composing the continents, the heavier ocean floor is forced downward, gradually sinking into the mantle beneath the continental margins. As the water-saturated oceanic plate plunges deeper into the mantle, the descending rocky slab encounters increasingly high temperatures. The addition of water to subterranean hot rocks lowers their melting point and generates new magma. Hotter and lighter than the surrounding rock, the magma rises into the continental crust, typically forming underground reservoirs of molten rock called magma chambers. When the chemically evolving magma becomes more buoyant than the surrounding rock and migrates to the earth's surface, a new volcano is born or an old one revives.

Plate convergence forms subduction zones around most of the Pacific basin, triggering some of the world's greatest earthquakes and volcanic eruptions, including those in Alaska, Kamchatka, Japan, Indonesia, Central America, and western South America. At the Cascadia subduction zone, two relatively small fragments of the Pacific plate, the Juan de Fuca plate and the even smaller Gorda plate to the south, are currently sinking beneath the northwest margin of North America, moving eastward at the rate of 2 or 3 inches a year. Subduction of these descending slabs generates magma beneath the edge of the continental plate and probably also creates zones of weakness through which magma rises to the surface, forming the Cascade volcanoes from California's Lassen Peak to Canada's Garibaldi and Mount Meager.

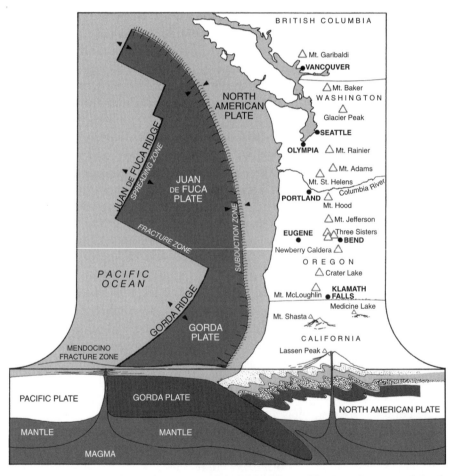

Plate movement along the northwest coast of the United States. The Juan de Fuca and Gorda crustal plates are slowly sliding under the western margin of North America. Subduction generates magma beneath the edge of the continental plate, providing fuel for the Cascade volcanoes. —Adapted from B. L. Foxworthy and M. Hill, *Volcanic Eruptions of 1980 at Mount St. Helens —The First 100 Days* (U.S. Geological Survey Professional Paper 1249 [1982])

A more complex subduction process occurs in the Mediterranean Sea basin, where Africa is gliding northward into southern Europe and southwest Asia. Second only to the Ring of Fire in length and recently active vents, the volcanic belt extending from southern France through Italy, Greece, and Turkey into Armenia and Georgia boasts some of the world's most famous volcanoes. These include Vesuvius, Etna, Stromboli, Vulcano, Santorini, and Mount Ararat, the legendary peak on which Noah's ark reputedly came to rest after the biblical flood. Classical Greco-Roman writers documented eruptions of the volcanoes in Italy and Greece, providing the longest recorded history of fire mountains anywhere in the world. In addition, the particular kinds of eruptions that occurred there were the first to be studied by geologists. As a result, Italian volcanoes such as Stromboli and Vulcano have given their names to distinctive eruptive styles recognized the world over (described in chapter 3).

Although plate movement seems slow in human terms—a few inches per year in most cases—it is swift by geological standards. At this rate a subduction zone can gobble up 30 miles of seafloor every million years. As subducted ocean floors are recycled into new rock deep in the earth's interior, plate relationships can change dramatically.

Such a change has taken place in California, where subduction no longer occurs south of the Mendocino fracture zone, an east-west trending line of faults extending west from the California coast at a latitude about even with Lassen Peak and the southern terminus of the Cascade Range. According to geologists' reconstruction of events that led to this change in plate interaction, subduction took place along the California coast between about 40 and 18 million years ago, when a spreading center, the East Pacific rise, was active offshore of western North America. As the North American plate drifted westward, the slab of seafloor lying east of the spreading center—called the Farallon plate—was eventually consumed. About 30 million years ago, the East Pacific rise collided with the North American plate near northern Mexico, and the zone of collision then gradually migrated northward along the California coast to its present position at Cape Mendocino. After this convergence, which geologists believe destroyed the East Pacific rise spreading center, subduction ceased along most of the California coast. At present, only small remnants of the ancient Farallon plate—the tiny Gorda plate, a Pacific seafloor fragment north of the Mendocino fracture zone, and the larger Juan de Fuca plate off the coast of Oregon and Washington—continue the process of subduction.

To the south of the Mendocino fracture zone, the Pacific plate is no longer being thrust under the continental landmass but is gradually moving alongside it, in a generally northwesterly direction. The boundary dividing this part of the Pacific plate from the North American plate is the notorious

San Andreas fault system, a complex zone of parallel branching fractures up to 60 miles wide. Extending about 650 miles from the Mexican border to north of Point Arena on California's Mendocino County coast, where it passes into the sea floor, the San Andreas system generates most of California's damaging earthquakes.

As the Pacific plate grinds inexorably northwestward alongside the North American plate, sections of the fault temporarily lock together and then break free, releasing enormous seismic energy and setting the ground in violent motion. In 1989 the San Andreas fault slipped about 6 feet, triggering an earthquake that measured 7.0 on the Richter scale and causing billions of dollars in damage from Santa Cruz to San Francisco Bay. In 1906, maximum displacement of the northern San Andreas fault was four times greater—up to 25 feet—and affected a much longer segment of the fault, generating a Richter magnitude 8.2 earthquake that shattered San Francisco and other coastal cities. The earthquake's death toll, including fatalities in the ensuing fire that destroyed most of San Francisco, exceeded 3,000. In 1857, the last major rupture on the southern San Andreas fault severely jolted the greater Los Angeles region where 12 million people now live. Similar high-magnitude temblors are an inevitable part of California's future.

The Mono Lake–Long Valley volcanic area is not related to subduction, or directly to the San Andreas fault. (Some geologists believe that crustal pressures from the San Andreas system may indirectly affect areas as far east as the Mono region.) Lying along the east flank of the Sierra Nevada, it occupies a highly unstable region of active mountain building and frequent earthquake activity. The Sierra consists of huge blocks of crustal granite that have been tilted to the west and lifted to heights of 12,000 to over 14,000 feet above sea level. The east face of the range is a steep fault scarp thousands of feet high that looms above the Long Valley and Owens Valley region, which occupies a large depression formed by the sinking of a crustal block east of the Sierra uplift. This subsidence may have been caused by the stretching and thinning of the continental crust as the North American plate lurches westward toward its encounter with the Pacific plate.

Magma has leaked to the surface at many points along the fractured east margin of the Sierra, but the most recent activity has been largely confined to the Mono Lake-Long Valley area. About 720,000 years ago, this region produced a cataclysmic outburst that shrouded much of North America with ash. Innumerable smaller eruptions have occurred since then, the latest at Mammoth Mountain, at an island in Mono Lake, and at the Mono-Inyo chain of craters. Given the ongoing series of volcanic earthquakes, ground swelling, and gas emissions that began in the 1980s, this area retains a high potential for future activity.

Hot Spots

Although most of the world's land volcanoes occur in well-defined chains paralleling subduction zones—as do the Cascades, the Andes of South America, and the 1,600-mile-long Aleutian Range in Alaska—some volcanoes are located far from plate boundaries. The Big Island of Hawaii, which contains two of the world's most active volcanoes, Mauna Loa and Kilauea, stands approximately 2,000 miles from the nearest margin of converging plates. Geologists believe that Hawaii and similar midocean and midcontinent volcanic centers are caused by hot spots, geographically isolated concentrations of high heat energy resulting from a thermal plume rising from deep in the mantle. Like a subterranean welder's torch, the mantle plume literally burns a hole in the rocky crust above it, allowing magma to erupt on the surface and build volcanoes like Kilauea and those of Iceland and Reunion in the Indian Ocean.

The Pacific plate slides north-northwestward across the Hawaiian hot spot at the rate of about 4 inches a year. As the plate creeps over the mantle plume, one by one the volcanoes form above it and then gradually pass it, losing their magma supply. Like a giant conveyer belt, the plate carries the volcanoes away from their heat source, causing their fires to sputter and die. No longer replenished by infusions of magma, the dying volcanoes are defenseless against unending erosion by storm and stream.

Because this process has been going on for millions of years, it is possible to trace the path along which the volcanoes have traveled, from the presently active Big Island, situated directly above the Hawaiian hot spot, to the island of Midway, 1,500 miles to the northwest. Erosion has worn the northernmost volcanoes of the Hawaiian archipelago to below sea level, allowing coral atolls to form atop the drowned mountains. Midway, millions of years older than Hawaii, represents this late stage of the islands' geologic evolution. Farther north, a line of submarine volcanic cones, known as the Emperor seamount chain, extends into the deep trench between Kamchatka and the western tip of the Aleutian Islands. Volcanic islands that emerged from the sea to host luxuriant tropical growth are thus eventually conveyed to icy Alaskan waters, where they are plunged deep into the mantle, ultimately providing fresh magma for northern volcanoes. Even as the oldest islands meet their doom, a new submarine volcano—the Loihi seamount—is currently rising from the ocean floor about 20 miles directly south of Kilauea. When it finally breaks the ocean surface several thousand years from now, Loihi will provide a new island paradise for our fiftieth state.

Whereas the midoceanic Hawaiian hot spot generates relatively mild effusions of basaltic lava, the mantle plume currently simmering under

Yellowstone National Park concocts a more dangerously volatile brew. Yellowstone's bubbling hot springs, spouting geysers, and brilliantly colored mineral terraces, which draw millions of visitors every year, are but gentle indicators of the powerful volcanic forces at work beneath the surface. America's first national park, Yellowstone is the site of three of the most violently explosive eruptions known. It may, some geologists fear, be evolving toward a fourth.

The Yellowstone hot spot has a long history. Its journey across western North America, many geologists believe, was eastward from the Columbia River plateau, through Idaho's Snake River plain, to its present location under the Yellowstone plateau in northwestern Wyoming. The hot spot's trek from west to east represents the westward drift of the North American plate as it traveled for millions of years over a relatively stationary thermal plume. The oldest evidence of the hot spot's presence are the floods of basaltic lava that inundated eastern Washington and Oregon, beginning in Miocene time about 17 to 15 million years ago. Issuing from fissures many miles in length, enormous torrents of extremely fluid basalt swept over tens of thousands of square miles of the Pacific Northwest, with single flows traveling 300 miles down the Columbia River's ancient channel and emptying into the Pacific. No eruptions of historic time have come near to equaling the vast quantities of molten rock—60,000 cubic miles—that poured out, mostly during a comparatively brief period of 2 or 3 million years. Successive waves of basalt overwhelmed the Columbia's ancestral course, pushing the river ever farther to the north and burying the present sites of Mount Hood and other parts of the Oregon Cascades.

Today, the Columbia has cut a deep gorge through the flood basalts' northern margin, its erosive force keeping pace with the uplift of the modern Cascade Range during Pliocene time (5.3 million to 1.8 million years ago). The Columbia Gorge, which now forms the boundary between Washington and Oregon, was significantly enlarged in late Pleistocene time, when a series of catastrophic floods—released by the repeated failure of an ice-dammed glacial lake in western Montana—surged across eastern Washington and through the gorge to the Pacific. The Glacial Lake Missoula floods rapidly scoured out the Columbia channel, widening the canyon, steepening its walls, and exposing sequences of basaltic flows stacked atop each other like poker chips. When the floods radically reconfigured the gorge, slicing through and removing its former walls, they created a particularly scenic phenomenon—hanging waterfalls, such as the spectacular Multnomah Falls that plunge 600 feet over the gorge rim a few miles east of Portland.

As the Columbia was eroding its way through the flood basalt formations and the rising Cascade barrier, the tectonic plate carrying North America continued its westward movement over the hot spot. While the basaltic eruptions in Washington and Oregon gradually ceased, a series of violently explosive eruptions began to the east. When the solid granitic crust of southern Idaho slowly passed over the mantle plume, pockets of granitic rock were melted to form a highly silicic and explosive magma known as rhyolite. Beginning about 13 million years ago in southwestern Idaho, rhyolitic magma was ejected in a prolonged sequence of huge pyroclastic flows and surges that left thick deposits of light-colored ash smothering the area. Fallout from the towering ash clouds deposited extensive layers of ash east of the Rockies and over the northern plains region.

Supereruptions

About 2.2 million years ago, after the North American plate had moved farther west, eruptions began in the Yellowstone region. Like a subterranean blow torch, the hot spot melted the granitic continental crust, brewing an unusually large gas-rich body of rhyolitic magma beneath the surface. By 2 million years ago, enough magma had accumulated to produce one of the largest explosive outbursts known to have occurred on earth. The first and most voluminous of the three giant Yellowstone eruptions, this event spewed out more than 600 cubic miles of fresh magma, enough to build six mountains the size of Mount Shasta.

Although no eruption of this magnitude has occurred in historic time, geologists who have studied the deposits and observed similar but smaller historic activity can deduce what took place. As the magma rose in the eruption's early stages, escaping gas whipped it to a glassy froth, which burst simultaneously from a series of concentric crustal fractures that had formed above the subterranean magma reservoir. After rising to stratospheric heights, a massive column of gas and incandescent ash collapsed to spread outward in all directions. The turbulent waves of ash traveled enormous distances, sweeping over ridges and peaks and filling valleys with still-molten material. The clouds of ash surged over thousands of square miles so quickly that the incandescent rock lost little heat in transit. Deposited at extremely high temperatures, glassy fragments in the ash surges fused together, welding the ash particles together to form a solid rock called ignimbrite.

So much material was ejected that the roof of the underground magma chamber collapsed, causing the overlying crustal rocks to subside several thousand feet. The resulting collapse depression—called a caldera (from the Spanish word for "cauldron")—covered an area of about a thousand square miles. Extending across the Island Park area in Idaho and the Yellowstone plateau, the caldera outlines have been largely obscured by later eruptive and erosive activity.

The second great explosive episode, which took place about 1.3 million years ago, largely duplicated the events of the first. The smallest of the three eruptions, this event ejected about 70 cubic miles of material and formed the Island Park caldera, about 17 miles in diameter. The third and latest climactic outburst occurred about 600,000 years ago, expelling about 250 cubic miles of ash—approximately 1,000 times the volume of material that Mount St. Helens erupted in 1980. Although not as voluminous as the initial Yellowstone eruption, the ash column reached high into the stratosphere and probably darkened the skies over much of North America. Geologists have found ash deposits in locations as distant as California, Kansas, and Saskatchewan, Canada. Rapid emptying of the magma chamber caused its roof to cave in, forming the present caldera, which measures about 30 miles across and 50 miles long—one of the largest volcanic depressions on the planet.

The Yellowstone volcano continued to erupt intermittently during the next several hundred thousand years, emitting an additional 250 cubic miles of material, mostly in the form of lava flows and domes. Although the most recent eruptions occurred about 70,000 years ago, the hot spot keeps a large body of subsurface magma on the boil, providing enough heat to maintain about 10,000 hot springs, geysers, and bubbling mud pots. The ongoing thermal activity, intermittent earthquakes, and measurable uplift of the caldera floor demonstrate that the volcano is still a potential threat. The last two cataclysmic eruptions occurred about 600,000 years apart, approximately the same interval that has elapsed since the last event. However, unlike Old Faithful, the geyser whose eruptions are famously predictable, the Yellowstone volcano does not adhere to a regular schedule. No one knows whether it will remain indefinitely in repose or whether it is presently generating enough rhyolitic magma to fuel another gigantic outburst.

Living with a Volcanic Threat

Fortunately for humanity, the supereruptions that formed the calderas at Yellowstone and Long Valley are comparatively rare, occurring perhaps at the rate of one or two per 100,000 years or more. The most recent took place on Sumatra in Indonesia, forming the Toba caldera about 71,000 years ago. Like the Yellowstone volcano, Toba erupted on a colossal scale that has been (fortunately) unknown in historic time, ejecting approximately 600 to 750 cubic miles of ash and triggering a volcanic winter that, according to scientific estimates, lasted for six years. That dark period was followed by the coldest one thousand years of late Pleistocene time, resulting in a widespread decimation of plant and animal life, particularly in the northern hemisphere. So severe and prolonged were Toba's wintery effects that, according to some scientists, most humans then living starved to death, reducing the world population of *Homo sapiens* from hundreds of thousands to perhaps a total of 15,000 to 40,000 people stranded in isolated pockets of Africa, Europe, and Asia. Some anthropologists, such as Stephen H. Ambrose, speculate that the Toba-induced population decrease may have caused the widely scattered human groups to differentiate rapidly, stimulating the genetic differences that now characterize various branches of the global population. According to Ambrose's hypothesis, all of today's ethnic groups thus may descend from relatively few ancestors.

Some geologists believe that the Toba event may represent the largest explosive eruption possible on earth, primarily because the crustal rock cannot physically contain a magma chamber much larger than that which supplied the Toba cataclysm; when a magma reservoir's upper limit is reached, it will erupt spontaneously. Because no outburst of Toba's magnitude has ever been observed since the dawn of recorded history, geologists do not know what distinctive phenomena will herald such an event—or whether human civilization will survive it.

Although such colossal events occur infrequently, even moderate-sized eruptions can have a disproportionately severe impact on affected populations. Because volcanic soils are commonly among the most fertile in the world, populations tend to concentrate near volcanoes. As the global population inexorably grows, volcanic eruptions impact increasingly large numbers of people. A recent scientific study by Tom Simkin and his colleagues at the National Museum of Natural History in Washington DC estimates that, in recorded history, volcanic activity has killed about 275,000 people. Most of the fatalities resulted from pyroclastic flows or tsunamis—seismic sea waves generated by submarine earthquakes and/or collapse of island volcanoes. Although volcanoes claim far fewer lives than large earthquakes—single temblors in China have caused a half million fatalities—Simkin's group found a disturbing trend. Because of the world's steadily increasing population, each of the past three centuries has shown a doubling of fatal eruptions. Recent decades have averaged around three deadly eruptions per year.

If we have learned anything from Mount St. Helens (1980), the disaster at Nevado del Ruiz (1985), or the even more violently explosive eruptions at Mount Pinatubo in the Philippines (1991), we should recognize the swiftness and overwhelming power with which a volcano can take human lives and radically alter the landscape. These recent eruptions offer abundant proof that volcanic mountains are not, as some poets would have us believe, changeless or eternal. The lofty glacier-crowned peaks that give much of the West its most impressive scenery also have the largely ignored potential to decimate vast areas, including some of our towns and cities. Just as people in other parts of the nation must learn to cope with natural disasters such as floods, tornadoes, or hurricanes that threaten their particular region, so must residents of the Pacific Coast heighten their awareness of the geologic hazards—earthquakes and volcanic eruptions—generated along this vulnerable region where continent and ocean floor collide.

To help reduce losses from future eruptions, the U.S. Geological Survey operates a program to monitor potentially active volcanoes. In 1980 the USGS established the David A. Johnston Cascades Volcano Observatory in Vancouver, Washington, named in honor of a brilliant young geologist killed in the 1980 eruption of Mount St. Helens. The observatory maintains an interdisciplinary staff of geologists, geophysicists, chemists, and seismologists to monitor St. Helens and other western volcanoes and to warn the public of any impending activity. Using a variety of seismic, ground-deformation, and geochemical techniques, the observatory scientists were able to predict all of St. Helens's post–May 18 eruptive activity, several hours to three weeks in advance.

During the mid-nineteenth century, several Cascade peaks, including Baker, Rainier, St. Helens, and Hood, produced eruptions of varying size and intensity; it would surprise few geologists if the twenty-first century were to witness a similar volcanic renaissance. Accordingly, the U.S. Geological Survey has installed various monitoring devices at other Cascade volcanoes and in the Mono Lake–Long Valley region. The monitoring system includes electronic distance meters and tilt leveling stations to measure changes in ground level, the tumescence that typically signals the rise of magma into a volcanic cone. In cooperation with the USGS, the University of Washington monitors seismicity at most of the Washington volcanoes, as well as at Mount Hood in Oregon. Other seismometers have been set up at Shasta, Lassen, Mammoth Mountain, and Long Valley.

Drawn by their scenic beauty and the many recreational facilities on their forested slopes, millions of tourists annually flock to the national parks, monuments, wilderness areas, and commercial resorts lying in the shadow of our western volcanoes. Rising majestically above popular campgrounds, ski lodges, trout streams, and lakes crowded with fishing boats and swimmers, the snowy cones look permanent and serene, reassuring monuments to earth's assumed stability. It is too easy to forget that they are subject to violent change that may drastically affect millions of human lives. As an integral part of the Ring of Fire, the Cascade volcanoes embody one of nature's most deadly forces.

CHAPTER 3

Magma and Mountains

HOW VOLCANOES ERUPT AND THE LANDFORMS THEY BUILD

In classical mythology and Native American tradition, volcanoes were typically seen as the abode of gods. According to the Greek playwright Aeschylus, Mount Etna, Europe's highest and most active volcano, was the prison of Typhoeus, a primordial dragon of chaos whom Zeus, king of the Olympian gods, had defeated by dropping Etna on top of him. Whenever Typhoeus struggled to escape, the mountain roared and spewed fountains of rock melted by the monster's fiery breath. In Roman mythology Vulcan, god of fire and the forge, set up his subterranean workshop on the Mediterranean island of Vulcano, the name from which our word *volcano* is derived. In the *Aeneid,* an epic of imperial Rome, Virgil placed the entrance to the underworld at a cavern on Lake Avernus, a water-filled crater near the Bay of Naples. Expanding on Virgil's vision in the *Inferno,* the medieval poet Dante portrayed the nine levels of hell as nine concentric craters, the lowest of which—at the center of the earth—contained Satan himself.

Tale-spinners in the New World similarly interpreted volcanoes as the residences of supernatural beings. In prehistoric Klamath lore, the sky-god Skell descended from heaven to inhabit the region's most impressive earthly landmarks, including Mount Shasta. Skell's intermittent presence was marked by the fires he kindled in his mountain residence, illuminating Shasta's summit with a ruddy glare and sending columns of smoke wafting high into the air. Skell's rival Llao, an underworld deity, dwelt under Mount Mazama (Crater Lake). The Klickitat tribes near the Columbia River explained the eruptions of Wy'east (Hood) and Pahto (Adams) as a battle between brothers for the love of the beautiful alpine deity Loowit (St. Helens). (See "Geomythology and 'The Bridge of the Gods'" on page 214.)

Although modern science has stripped the volcano of its mythical trappings, volcanoes still make terrifying neighbors. Paradoxically, however, they are creators as well as destroyers, building new land for human cultivation and enriching old soils with volcanic nutrients. Over eons of geologic time, volcanoes have contributed significantly to a long process that has made the earth inhabitable. During the planet's early history, volcanic eruptions emitted vast quantities of water vapor and other gases, helping to create the earth's oceans and atmosphere. Many regions across the globe, from New Zealand to Iceland to California, harness subterranean volcanic heat in the form of geothermal energy to generate electricity and to power industry.

The Products of Eruption and the Edifices They Form

A volcano is both an opening in the earth's crust through which gas and hot rock are emitted and the hill or mountain formed by the ejected material. Molten rock underground is called magma; erupted on the earth's surface it is lava.

Geologists usually divide modes of eruption into two broad categories: effusive and explosive. Relatively quiet, effusive eruptions produce streams of molten rock—lava flows—that typically travel a few miles downslope before cooling and solidifying. Except near their source vent, where they can be extremely hot (up to 2,200 degrees Fahrenheit) and fluid, most lava flows move more slowly than a healthy human can run and seldom cause fatalities. They do, however, crush, bury, and/or burn everything in their path. Far more dangerous to human life, as well as property, are explosive eruptions. When gas-rich magma rises to the surface, where confining pressure is released, it typically explodes into fragments, forming pyroclastic rock.

The most common form of pyroclastic material is tephra, consisting of solid or semisolid fragments that are blown into the air above a volcano. Tephra fragments are generally classified according to their size or other physical characteristics. When tephra particles are 0.1 inch or less in diameter—the size of silt or sand grains—they form clouds of volcanic ash that can blanket large areas downwind from the volcano. Larger fragments, measuring about 0.1 inch to 2.5 inches in diameter, are called lapilli (Latin for "little stones"). Solid angular fragments ranging from 2.5 inches to many feet in diameter are known as blocks. When erupted in a plastic, or molten, state, fragments of this dimension are called bombs, because of the streamlined shape they assume when projected through the air.

In addition to size, tephra can also be characterized by texture. If tephra fragments are glassy and have a high gas content, the rapidly escaping gas leaves behind empty spaces, or vesicles, in the rock (60 percent or more of the fragment's total volume), forming pumice. Lightweight and vesicular (porous), this frothy volcanic glass, which can range in size from lapilli to blocks, is buoyant in water. Masses of floating pumice are frequently sighted after midoceanic eruptions. Scoria, another form of vesicular tephra, resembles pumice but is typically somewhat less porous and darker in color.

Volcanoes built entirely of tephra are called cinder cones, so named because the rock fragments composing them resemble cinders from a furnace.

Among the smaller volcanic landforms, cinder cones rarely stand more than 1,200 feet above their base. With steep slopes of about 35 degrees (the normal angle of repose), they typically have truncated summits containing a circular, funnel-shaped depression called a crater (in Greek, a bowl for drinking wine). A crater contains the vent through which hot rock erupts; it is the surface expression of a volcano's central conduit—the internal pipe through which the underground supply of magma travels upward. Cinder cones are monogenetic volcanoes, built during a single eruptive phase that typically lasts weeks, months, or decades, after which all activity permanently ends. Although constructed of loosely consolidated tephra, cinder cones also commonly erupt lava flows, usually from a vent at the base of the cone rather than from the summit crater.

Abundant throughout the western states, cinder cones are particularly numerous in the Three Sisters area of central Oregon. Lava Butte, a cinder cone located about 10 miles south of Bend next to U.S. 97, takes its name from the extensive lava flows surrounding it. A paved road leads to the summit, from which, on a clear day, a dozen of the snow-capped Cascade volcanoes are visible, from Mount Scott near Crater Lake to Mount Adams in Washington. Directly west of Bend, the McKenzie Pass Highway traverses some of the freshest lava flows in the range, offering unobstructed views of several youthful cinder cones that produced them.

Cinder Cone, in the northeastern corner of Lassen Volcanic National Park, formed about AD 1650, making this steep pile of tephra the youngest volcano in the Cascade Range. —Douglas Tustin photo

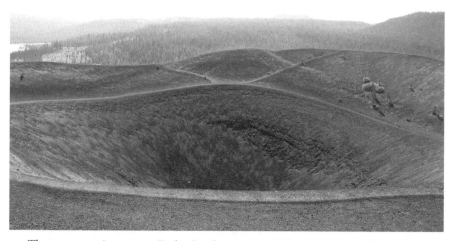

The two concentric craters at Cinder Cone's summit probably represent two different phases of the same eruptive cycle that produced both the 700-foot-high cone and its series of lava flows about 350 years ago. Contrary to some nineteenth-century claims, the volcano did not revive in 1850–1851. —Douglas Tustin photo

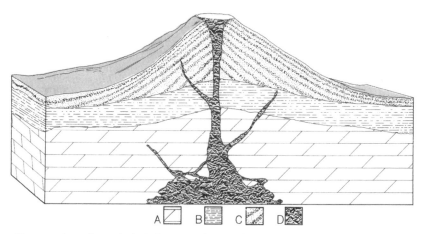

Cross-section of a typical cinder cone, showing basement rock (A), pre–cinder cone deposits (B), pyroclastic material (C), and magma chamber and feeder pipes (D)

Lava flows from most Cascade volcanoes, including the many cinder cones at McKenzie Pass in central Oregon, display a rough, jagged crust resembling a heap of black slag or clinkers from a smelter. Called aa after its Hawaiian prototype, this kind of lava surface is extremely difficult to traverse. Even more inhospitable is the surface of a blocky flow, where the crust is broken into huge jumbles of angular lava blocks. A massive blocky flow from Mount Shasta, with margins 300 to 500 feet high, borders U.S.

97 just north of Weed. In contrast, a pahoehoe flow (another Hawaiian term) is generally much thinner and has a smooth, ropy surface that commonly hardens into billowy, wavelike undulations that, when solidified, are comparatively easy to walk on. Erupted at slightly higher temperatures and with a somewhat higher gas content than the aa or blocky variety, pahoehoe flows may contain in their interiors long, hollow tubes called lava tubes, horizontal passageways through which the molten rock advanced.

Whereas cinder cones are essentially mounds of tephra, shield volcanoes, a second type of volcano found in the Cascades, are built almost entirely by fluid lava flows that typically spread out in thin sheets to form a very broad, gently sloping edifice. This low-profile volcanic landform receives its name from its supposed resemblance to a Roman warrior's shield when placed flat on the ground with its convex side upward. All of the Hawaiian Islands are giant shield volcanoes rising from the Pacific Ocean floor. Two of the largest Hawaiian shields, Mauna Loa and Mauna Kea, are actually the world's tallest mountains, standing more than 30,000 feet above their submarine foundations. Although they are rarely explosive, the magma

A typical blocky lava flow surface. Cinder Cone, Lassen Volcanic National Park. —Douglas Tustin photo

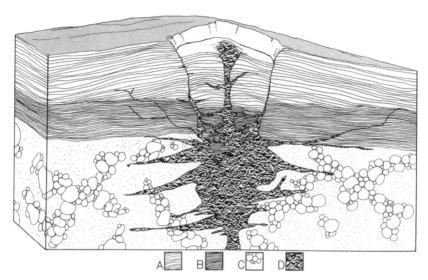

Cross-section of a typical shield volcano, showing lava flows (A), ancestral deposits (B), nonvolcanic rock (C), and magma chamber and feeder pipes (D)

erupted at shield volcanoes typically contains enough gas to spray blobs of molten rock high into the air, forming spectacular "lava fountains" that feed extensive lava flows. The most recent Hawaiian eruption, at Kilauea's east rift zone, began in January 1983 and has continued sporadically into the twenty-first century, its lava flowing into the sea and creating many acres of new land on the Big Island.

Most of the High Cascade platform in Oregon is built of overlapping lava flows from shield volcanoes formed at various times during the last two million years. Notably smaller than their Hawaiian counterparts, the Cascade shields are also somewhat steeper and, like Pelican Butte on the west shore of Klamath Lake in southern Oregon, are typically capped with a cinder cone at the summit. Visitors to Lassen Park can see several midsize Cascade shields, including Prospect Peak (8,338 feet), whose bulk dwarfs the comparatively tiny Cinder Cone (about 700 feet) at its southeast foot.

By far the youngest Cascade shield, Belknap shield (formerly called Belknap crater—a misnomer) at McKenzie Pass erupted large volumes of aa lava about 1,000 BC and again about 1,500 years ago. Its bare and rugged lava fields contrast sharply with the older, thickly forested shields in the range. Subject to repeated glaciations that scoured deep canyons in their slopes, most of the older shields, such as Mount Washington just north of Belknap, and Union Peak south of Crater Lake, are now so deeply eroded that the solidified rock filling their inner conduit is exposed. Glaciers stripped away the material surrounding the interior lava plug, whittling the shields' formerly rounded summits into sharp spires.

The third, and most impressive, volcanic landform found in the Cascades is the composite cone, which typically produces both effusive and explosive eruptions. Also called a stratovolcano because it is built of alternating layers (strata) of lava flows and pyroclastic deposits, the composite cone has a more varied eruptive style than any other kind of volcano. Although the loftiest Cascade peaks—Baker, Rainier, Adams, Hood, Jefferson, the Three Sisters, and Shasta—are constructed primarily of lava flows, most of them have also erupted significant quantities of tephra, as well as domes, pyroclastic flows, and pyroclastic surges. Because of their height, steepness, and ice cover, the large composite volcanoes also generate large debris avalanches and lahars that can travel great distances from their source, inundating valley floors and threatening areas that are now densely populated.

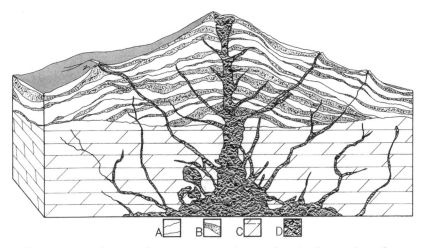

Cross-section of a typical composite cone (stratovolcano), showing lava flows (A), pyroclastic and mudflow deposits (B), basement rock (C), and magma chamber and feeder pipes (D)

A fourth kind of volcano, found in the Cascades and in the Mono Lake–Long Valley region, is the lava dome. Unlike the shield or composite cone, the lava dome is not composed of distinct layers of material added during successive eruptions. Instead, it is a largely undifferentiated mass of lava extruded during one or more pulses of activity. Too stiff and viscous (resistant to flow) to travel far from the vent from which it emerges, the lava oozes out like toothpaste from a tube, forming a steep pile above the eruptive opening. The craggy lava dome that rose in St. Helens's crater between 1980 and 1986, 925 feet high, was erupted in discrete stages, sometimes by lava emerging through cracks to add fresh lobes to the dome, sometimes by the infusion of new magma into its interior, causing it to swell and expand.

Perhaps the world's largest lava dome, Lassen Peak (10,457 feet) formed about 27,000 years ago. The last extensive advance of Pleistocene glaciation began shortly afterward, forming glaciers that eroded away most of the jagged spires and angular blocks that typically characterize a lava dome's surface, leaving behind the aprons of fragmental material, called crumble breccia, that now mantle the dome's solid interior. About 1,100 years ago, a series of steep-sided domes called Chaos Crags erupted immediately north of Lassen. In contrast to Lassen's glacier-smoothed slopes, the Chaos Crags retain their original surfaces, bristling with sharp, spiny protrusions. Black Butte, a somewhat older cluster of extremely steep Holocene domes at Mount Shasta's west foot, borders Interstate 5 between the towns of Weed and Mount Shasta.

Magma Composition and Modes of Eruption

The size, shape, and eruptive behavior of a given volcano are largely determined by the chemical composition and gas content of the magma it erupts. Gas dissolved in the molten rock underground is the driving source behind all volcanic eruptions. Composed primarily of steam, volcanic gas also includes other volatile elements such as carbon dioxide, carbon monoxide, sulfur dioxide, and hydrogen sulfide, the latter giving volcanic emissions their unpleasant "rotten egg" odor. As gas-rich magma, hotter, lighter, and more buoyant than the surrounding mantle rock, rises to the surface, confining pressure from the surrounding rock is effectively decreased, allowing the entrained gas to expand rapidly. When the magma ascends into the uppermost mile of the earth's crust, its gas volume increases about 900 times. Upon reaching the surface, gas escaping the magma blows it to bits, generating violent explosions that can send immense columns of tephra soaring 20 miles or higher into the stratosphere.

In addition to the level of gas content, the magma's chemical and mineralogical components also play an important role in determining a volcano's mode of eruption. The four most common magma types—basalt, andesite, dacite, and rhyolite—are all found in the Cascades, and each type tends to produce a distinctive style of eruption. The constituents are virtually identical in all kinds of lava—silica (SiO_2, silicon dioxide) and oxides of calcium, sodium, aluminum, potassium, magnesium, and iron—but they vary considerably in their proportions. It is primarily the silica (SiO_2) content that determines the group to which a particular lava belongs.

Basalts, rich in iron and magnesium, which give them their dark color, are low in silica, less than 54 percent by weight. A high percentage of silica increases viscosity, and the low silica content of basalts makes them fluid and able to spread out in thin sheets over large distances. The most abundant lava type on earth, basalts make up all the oceanic plates and midocean ridges and volcanic islands, such as Hawaii and Iceland, forming about 70 percent of the planet's crust. Basaltic flood eruptions also formed the Columbia lava plateau, as well as numerous cones in the western United States. In addition, most shield volcanoes consist of basalt or basaltic andesite.

Devil's Homestead basalt flow, a clinkery black aa flow from the Medicine Lake volcano, viewed from a partly vegetated older flow in Lava Beds National Monument. —Courtesy of D. W. Hyndman

The most characteristic Cascade lava—that of which most of the high composite cones are built—is andesite, so named because it is plentiful in the Andes Mountains of South America. Andesite has an intermediate silica content of about 54 to 62 percent. Less fluid than basalt, it flows shorter distances and thus piles up to form a moderately steep cone. Varieties of andesite are generally named from the iron and magnesium minerals they contain; the most common in the Cascades is pyroxene andesite, typically dark gray or brown in color. Some Cascade peaks, such as Baker, Rainier, Adams, and Shasta, are constructed almost exclusively of this kind of lava. Others, such as St. Helens, South Sister, and Mazama, demonstrate a much greater range in the chemical composition of their lavas; during different eruptive cycles they produced basalts or basaltic andesites and dacites, as well as andesite.

Although less abundant than andecite, dacite, with a silica content of 62 to 68 percent, is also found in the Cascades. Usually light colored, dacite has a low melting point, about 850 degrees Celsius, and is viscous when molten. It tends to produce short, thick tongues of lava or bulbous, steep-sided domes such as Lassen Peak and Chaos Crags. Both Glacier Peak in Washington's North Cascades and Mount Garibaldi in British Columbia are built of dacite. Most of Mount St. Helens's voluminous tephra eruptions, as well as the domes growing in the crater, also consist of dacite.

Rhyolites, the fourth type of Cascade lava, have a silica content of 72 percent or more. Although normally very light in color—light gray, beige, or pink—rhyolites are sometimes unexpectedly dark. Perhaps the most striking form of rhyolite is obsidian, a glistening black volcanic glass that Native Americans prized for its usefulness in fashioning projectile points and other sharp tools. Exceptionally large obsidian flows erupted about 1,300 years ago on the floor of Newberry caldera and about 1,000 years ago atop the Medicine Lake shield, providing material for a widespread prehistoric trade.

Some Cascade volcanoes have also produced rhyodacites, silicic lava intermediate between dacites and rhyolites. About 2,000 years ago, a series of rhyodacite domes and flows erupted along South Sister's southeast flank. This chain of domes, which also features crags of glittering black obsidian, extends downslope as far as the edge of Cascade Lakes Highway south of Bend. The largest Holocene outpouring of rhyodacite, however, took place about 7,700 years ago when Mount Mazama discharged many cubic miles of rhyodacite tephra that blanketed more than a half million square miles of western North America.

The silica content in different kinds of lavas determines not only their relative fluidity, but also their explosive potential. When basalts are gas poor, they usually erupt quietly, forming streams of liquid rock that seldom directly threaten human life. Hawaiian-style eruptions, named for their frequent occurrence in Hawaii, are typically gas poor and low in silica, and thus nonexplosive. Tourists—from a reasonable distance—can visit the Big Island's "drive-in" volcanoes and watch lava fountains gush torrents of molten basalt without fear of harm. Some gas-rich basalts or basaltic andesites, particularly those in which rising magma encounters groundwater, causing it to flash into steam, are explosive enough to produce quantities of tephra even though they are relatively low in silica. Even basalts, with low viscosity but with a relatively high gas content, can trigger moderately explosive activity, such as that which builds cinder cones. This type of eruption is called Strombolian after Stromboli, a volcanic island off the coast of Sicily in the Tyrrhenian Sea, known as the "Lighthouse of the Mediterranean" for its almost continuous but mildly explosive eruptions.

Whereas basaltic explosive activity tends to be comparatively mild, volcanoes that erupt lava with both a high gas and high silica content, such as dacite or rhyolite, are much more dangerous. Because highly silicic magma is extremely viscous, the gases remain trapped in it until all confining pressure of the overlying rock is removed, which happens the instant the magma reaches the surface. The abrupt release of pressure allows the gas to expand explosively, shattering the magma into millions of fragments.

Highly explosive eruptions that produce towering ash clouds are called Plinian, after Pliny the Younger, the Roman author who composed the world's oldest surviving account of this type of volcanic phenomenon. In two letters to the historian Tacitus, Pliny described in vivid detail the AD 79 eruption of Mount Vesuvius, which entombed the cities of Pompeii and Herculaneum. Plinian eruptions are also characterized by extensive pyroclastic flows and surges. An extremely large Plinian event can destroy an entire mountain. When a composite cone, such as Mount Mazama, suddenly ejects an exceptionally large quantity of pyroclastic material, the subterranean magma chamber is rapidly depleted, causing its roof to collapse and removing support from the volcano's superstructure. As the volcano's former summit disintegrates and sinks inward, it forms a caldera, by definition at least a mile in diameter, occupying the truncated cone. During the last 13,000 years, Glacier Peak, St. Helens, and Mazama have produced catastrophic Plinian eruptions, but only Mazama suffered a major collapse, forming the caldera holding Crater Lake.

After most of the gas in a given batch of magma has escaped, a quieter phase may ensue in which the remaining silicic material emerges quietly to pile up in thick flows or domes. This explosion-followed-by-extrusion sequence characterized St. Helens's 1980–1986 activity, as it did the formation of the Mono-Inyo chain of domes and flows near Mono Lake about 600 years ago.

Explosive eruptions that are moderate to strong are known as Vulcanian, after Vulcan, the Roman god of fire and metalcraft. A typical Vulcanian event blasts volumes of ash into the air, forming dark "cauliflower" clouds, and hurls out old rock from the volcano's interior with little or no new lava. Violently explosive events commonly discharge ballistic projectiles, rock fragments of various sizes and shapes that, ejected like artillery shells on a ballistic arc, can crush objects on impact. Although this volcanic shrapnel is typically thrown no farther than about three miles from its source vent, ballistic projectiles occasionally travel greater distances. During a rare explosive eruption, Mount Rainier hurled a lava block 4 feet in diameter 8 miles from the summit.

Peléan eruptions, named for the Caribbean island volcano Mont Pelée, typically produce the growth of silicic domes that crumble or collapse to generate pyroclastic flows and surges, such as those that destroyed St. Pierre in 1902 or that decimated a forest on Mount Hood's south flank about 1781 (see image 16 on plate 9). In 1991, the partial collapse of a new dome growing atop Japan's Mount Unzen generated a pyroclastic flow that took the lives of forty-one people, including French volcanologists Katia and Maurice Krafft and American geologist Harry Glicken, who had come to study the eruption. The Unzen pyroclastic flow, though deadly, was relatively small. The largest pyroclastic flow event in the twentieth century created the famous Valley of the Ten Thousand Smokes when Novarupta, a new vent at the foot of Alaska's Mount Katmai, erupted violently in 1912.

HOW OLD IS THE ROCK? ▬▬▬▬▬▬▬▬▬▬▬▬▬

When fragments of charcoal, wood, grass, roots, or seeds are found in a volcanic deposit, scientists can use the carbon-14 method to discover their age. Because all plants and animals absorb carbon during their lifetimes (a process that ends with death) and because carbon-14 decays at a known rate, it is possible to measure how old a sample is by the relative amount of radioactive carbon (C-14) it contains. Radiocarbon dates are commonly expressed as years BP ("before the present," which is arbitrarily set at AD 1950). Thus a dated charcoal sample permits geologists to state that Mount Mazama's climactic eruption occurred about 6845 BP. To arrive at more precise dating, which includes compensating for past fluctuations in the levels of carbon-14 production, geologists commonly employ such techniques as tree-ring dating, which enables them to arrive at a calendar age of about 7,700 years for Mazama's destruction.

With its short half-life (about 5,730 years), however, radiocarbon dating does not work for determining ages greater than about 40,000 years (although some new techniques are extending this range). For igneous rocks more than 100,000 years old, the potassium-argon (K-40) method is employed, a technique that measures the quantities of radioactive potassium and its product, a form of argon (Ar-40) in rock samples. Like the potassium-argon method, the more recently developed argon-argon dating technique relies on measuring radioactive decay in volcanic rock, but has the advantage of greater precision and the capacity to date younger rock, from a few tens of millions to a few thousands of years old. This method has been found reliable in determining the ages of different lava flow sequences at several Cascade volcanoes, including Rainier, Adams, and Baker.

A Plinian eruption column boils 12 miles into the air above Mount St. Helens, May 18, 1980. During an earlier phase of the eruption, a colossal anvil-shaped ash plume towered almost 100,000 feet into the stratosphere.
—Don Swanson photo, U.S. Geological Survey, Cascades Volcano Observatory, Vancouver, Washington

Only after studying the effects of pyroclastic flows from Pelée, Katmai, and other volcanoes did geologists begin to understand the nature of the phenomenon—a hurricane of incandescent rock fragments—that had created vastly larger pyroclastic deposits in volcanic zones all over the world, from Indonesia and New Zealand to the American West. The Katmai-Novarupta eruption ranks as the most voluminous of the twentieth century, but it is dwarfed by past pyroclastic flows from the Yellowstone, Long Valley, and other western volcanoes. During the last two million years, these huge eruptions blanketed hundreds of thousands of square miles of the United States under thick layers of rhyolitic ash, some of which was emplaced at such high temperatures (about 1,800 degrees Fahrenheit) that molten glassy particles in the ash were fused together, forming welded tuff. Although originally composed of discrete fragments, welded tuff solidifies into a dense rock that may be difficult to distinguish from ordinary lava;

such is the case with the Bishop tuff in Long Valley and the yellowish deposits that gave Yellowstone its name. Large pyroclastic flow deposits are known as ignimbrites—literally "fiery rain-cloud" rocks, a term that graphically suggests their origin in the fallout from monstrous waves of ash that sweep over the landscape with cyclonic force.

Volcanoes and Climate

The immense quantities of ash lofted into the stratosphere from the Yellowstone and other caldera-forming eruptions in Wyoming, Colorado, and New Mexico would have smothered much of the continent, killing vegetation and

HOW BIG WAS THE BLAST?

Although volcanologists do not have the instruments to measure the relative magnitude of volcanic eruptions, they can calculate the relative strength of individual eruptions by considering such factors as the volume of material ejected, the distance to which large rock fragments are hurled, and the height of the ash cloud. To compute the comparative size of explosive outbursts (both prehistoric events for which there are no written records and events reported by eyewitnesses), scientists have devised the volcanic explosivity index (VEI). Like the Richter scale for measuring earthquakes, the VEI has a simple numerical rating system, ranging from zero to eight, with each successive full number representing an increase of about a factor of ten. The higher the number, the more voluminous and violently explosive the eruption. As is the case with earthquakes, small events occur much more frequently than large ones.

In a recent edition of the Smithsonian Institution's *Volcanoes of the World*, a comprehensive listing of the world's 1,511 known volcanoes, the editors assign no eruptive event during the last 10,000 years a VEI rating as high as 8. Only four, including the Tambora eruption of 1815 and that at Mount Mazama (Crater Lake) about 5,700 BC, receive a rating of 7. Even Tambora, the Indonesian volcano that produced the most voluminous ejecta of modern times—about 20 cubic miles of dense magma—is easily overshadowed by another Indonesian volcano, Toba, which ejected more than 600 cubic miles of magma approximately 71,000 years ago, forming enormous pyroclastic flows and surges that smothered at least 10,000 square miles in deposits up to 1,000 feet thick. Toba's ash clouds may have created near-global darkness and caused a severe worldwide cooling, perhaps, as some geologists believe, precipitating a new pulse of the ice age. Some scientists think that Toba's outburst, at a VEI of 8, was also responsible for creating a "bottleneck" of the earth's human population, reducing it to a few thousand individuals scattered throughout Africa, Europe, and Asia, and thus influencing the course of human evolution.

North America's Yellowstone volcano produced a comparable eruption about two million years ago; another Yellowstone outburst, almost as large, occurred about 1.2

contaminating rivers and lakes. The air-borne ash also would have triggered a volcanic winter, cooling the global climate for years afterward. Buoyed by superheated gas, ash columns can rise 20 or 30 miles into the air, spreading as a vast downwind canopy over continents and oceans and permeating the stratosphere with sulfuric aerosols.

Although fine volcanic ash usually falls out of the atmosphere and settles after about three months, small droplets of sulfur dioxide can remain in the stratosphere for several years, efficiently reflecting sunlight into space and keeping the sun's rays from warming the earth. When Mount Pinatubo in the Philippines erupted in 1991, it slightly lowered world temperatures for the next two years.

million years later. Cataclysmic events of this magnitude occur only once or twice per 100,000 years; none has occurred in historic time.

During recent decades, the world's volcanoes have produced about 60 eruptions per year. Of these, one eruption every few weeks rates a VEI of 2, meaning that it generates about 1.3 million cubic yards of rock fragments, or tephra. A VEI-3 eruption producing about 13 million cubic yards of tephra, such as the 1985 Nevado del Ruiz event, occurs several times a year. This event's comparatively modest quantity of ejecta had an unusually lethal effect, melting summit ice fields to trigger large mudflows that killed about 25,000 people. The del Ruiz event demonstrated that even moderate eruptions at volcanoes located near heavily populated areas can cause more fatalities than much larger outbursts at remote sites.

Only once in a decade do VEI-5 events, such as the 1980 eruption of Mount St. Helens, which ejected about 0.25 cubic mile (about 1.4 billion cubic yards) of dense magma, take place. An outburst like that of Krakatau in 1883, which had a volume of 2.4 cubic miles—ten times that of St. Helens—rates a VEI-6, and occurs about once in a hundred years. As the Smithsonian editors point out, St. Helens, which devastated more than 200 square miles of prime timberland and killed 57 people, created a local catastrophe, whereas Krakatau was a regional catastrophe, generating massive tsunamis and killing 36,000 people, one as far away as India. A VEI-7 event, like that at Tambora, can cause significant global cooling and justifiably be regarded as a major disaster from the perspective of New England farmers who lost all their crops in the "year without a summer," but a VEI-8 event, such as the prehistoric outbursts at Yellowstone, Toba, and Long Valley, probably had an almost unimaginably severe impact on the world environment.

It is a sobering thought that eleven out of the eighteen largest eruptions during the last two centuries, including those at Tambora in 1815, Alaska's Katmai in 1912, and the Philippines' Pinatubo in 1991, took place at volcanoes for which there had been no previous record of historic activity. One of the world's most voluminous Holocene eruptions—that at Mount Mazama about 7,700 years ago—was preceded by a quiet interval that lasted at least 20,000 years. Other sleeping giants in the Cascades, some quiescent for tens of thousands of years, may one day awake to produce similarly cataclysmic outbursts.

Other historic eruptions have had much more severe cooling effects, a link between volcanoes and climate that Benjamin Franklin was perhaps the first to note. Following the voluminous lava fountaining and basaltic flows from Iceland's Laki volcano in 1783, Franklin and other observers reported a "dry fog" spreading over Europe, reducing temperatures, causing extensive crop failures, and resulting in economic losses that may have helped to spark the French Revolution. Franklin shrewdly deduced that a volcanic eruption was the culprit.

The mightiest explosive eruption in recorded history—that of Indonesia's Mount Tambora in 1815 (with a VEI magnitude of 7)—produced even greater climatic changes. It was also one of the most deadly: of the 12,000 inhabitants of Sumbawa, the island on which Tambora stands, only 26 people reportedly survived the outburst. Another 80,000 people were killed by the ash fall or the famine that followed the disaster. So dense was Tambora's ash plume that the area within 200 miles of the volcano experienced three days of total darkness. Even people halfway around the globe suffered its chilling effects: 1816 became known as "eighteen hundred and froze to death" or "the year without a summer." From New England to western Europe, average temperatures plunged 1.8 to 4.5 degrees Fahrenheit below normal. With snow and frosts occurring every month of the year in New England and a similarly abnormal growing season in Europe, wheat became scarce and prices rose accordingly, making it more expensive in 1816 than at any other time in the nineteenth century.

Representing almost every variety of volcanic landform—from the vast depression of the Long Valley caldera in east-central California to the towering composite cones of Mounts Shasta and Rainier—the many volcanoes of the Pacific Coast states have also produced virtually every imaginable kind of eruption. As of this writing (February 2005), Mount St. Helens is extruding a second lava dome in its 1.2-mile-wide crater, a relatively quiet process that could change at any time to another violent explosive eruption. Although mudflows from glaciated Cascade volcanoes pose the greatest hazard to densely populated areas in the Pacific Northwest, explosive outbursts, such as those St. Helens typically stages, have affected even larger areas. Since the last Pleistocene glaciers melted between about 10,000 to 12,000 years ago, St. Helens, Glacier Peak, and Mount Mazama (Crater Lake) have ejected immense volumes of tephra that blankets hundreds of thousands of square miles from California to Montana to British Columbia, Alberta, and Saskatchewan. The more we know about the volcanoes that have repeatedly devastated the sites of some of the West's most populous towns and cities, the better prepared we will be to face an inevitable volcanic crisis.

CHAPTER 4

Glaciers on CascadeVolcanoes

MIXING FIRE AND ICE

The Cascade volcanoes were built by volcanic fire, but they were largely sculptured into their present rugged shapes by glacial ice. From Mount Shasta north, most of the higher peaks still support sizable glaciers—flowing rivers of ice that keep their summits white and glistening throughout the year. Only one long segment of the range, between Shasta and the Three Sisters, presently lacks permanent ice cover, partly because of generally lower elevations in this area and partly because of the prolonged warming trend that began about 1850. Until about 1900, even Mount McLoughlin (9,496 feet), Oregon's southernmost composite cone, could boast of at least one active glacier, the Sholes, which has since completely disappeared. By the beginning of the twentieth century, however, most of the small perennial snowfields in the southern Oregon Cascades had vanished, although observers report that two very small glaciers may still exist on Mount Thielsen's shaded north side.

In general, the farther north a Cascade peak is, the heavier its burden of glacial ice. Blasted by the fierce heat of California's long summers, Lassen Peak (10,457 feet) is mostly snow free by late July or August. Oregon's South Sister, approximately the same height as Lassen but 275 miles farther north, supports half a dozen small glaciers and remains snowcapped all year. The Cascades of Washington have approximately 1,000 glaciers, more than any other state except Alaska. Four of Washington's five large stratovolcanoes—Rainier, Baker, Glacier Peak, and Adams—bear the most voluminous glaciers, a number of which extend downslope far below the tree line. The champion glacier-bearer, Rainier is sheathed in 1 cubic mile of ice, a volume equal to that mantling all the rest of the Cascade volcanoes put together.

The range's second most heavily glaciated peak, Mount Baker, presently holds the North American record for annual snowfall—1,140 inches in the 1998–1999 season. Baker's record only slightly surpasses that of Rainier, established in 1971–1972 at 1,122 inches. Throughout the entire chain from British Columbia to northern California, the Cascades are whitened down to about the 2,500-foot level from autumn to late spring. As far south

Before 1980, the Nelson, Forsyth, and Loowit glaciers covered the north face of Mount St. Helens. The May 18, 1980, eruption removed the entire area shown here, including the volcano's summit and north flank. —Austin Post photo, U.S. Geological Survey

as Crater Lake, the seasonal snowfall averages about 50 feet, but because of lower altitudes and warmer temperatures most of it melts by midsummer.

Although important in maintaining glaciers, enormous annual snowfalls are not the primary cause of glacier formation. All that is required for creating these flowing ice streams is a rate of snow accumulation that, over many years, significantly exceeds the rate of melting. As successive layers of snow fall, compressing those underneath, the aging snow loses its light, fluffy texture. Gradually the air is forced out as the tightly compacted snow changes into granular ice. Impelled by gravity and its own weight, the ice mass begins to slide downward over the underlying bedrock. If winter storms regularly supply more snow than can melt in the summer months, the glacier will continue to grow and advance. Conversely, if the annual precipitation decreases or the climate turns warmer to the extent that more snow melts than accumulates, the glacier will diminish in size and may disappear.

The elevation above which snow persists throughout the year is called the annual snowline. On a glacier, it is also known as the firn line. These lines of demarcation may vary with fluctuations in the weather from year to year. That portion of a glacier below the firn line, where melting exceeds accumulation, is the ablation zone. In the Cascade Range of California and southern Oregon, this zone lies much higher than it does farther north, primarily because the low sun angle at northerly latitudes provides less solar energy to thaw the ice. Whereas the glaciers of Mount Shasta (14,162 feet) do not descend below about 9,000 feet, some glaciers on Rainier, which is only about 250 feet higher but much farther north, extend into canyon floors as low as 3,200 feet. In general, the largest and longest glaciers tend to form on a mountain's north and northeast slopes, where they are more protected from solar radiation.

How Glaciers Work

The presence of glaciers gives the loftiest Cascade volcanoes much of their aesthetic appeal, but the grinding ice eventually has a destructive effect on the host mountain. Given favorable conditions, such as abundant snowfall and short, cool summers, the glaciers ultimately will wear the mountain down to elevations so low that the glaciers themselves disappear. Volcanic cones are particularly vulnerable to a glacier's erosive power. Some parts of a stratovolcano, such as the solid rock forming dikes and the interiors of most lava flows, are comparatively erosion-resistant, but much of the edifice is composed of unconsolidated fragmental material. Such accumulations of volcanic rubble offer little resistance to glacial scouring.

As a glacier flows, it scoops out chunks of bedrock and transports them downslope. The underlying rock surface is also ground down by the abrasive action of the debris frozen into the glacier's base. The glacier thus sinks ever deeper into the trench it cuts for itself, polishing and smoothing some surfaces it passes over, gouging grooves and furrows into others. When the glacier base is laden with fine-grained sediment, it typically produces glacial polish; when it contains coarser particles, it etches long parallel scratches in the bedrock called glacial striations.

The mechanics of glacial erosion are aided by numerous fractures in rock joints. These fractures form prior to glaciation and are enlarged by frost action. Ice moving over such a surface is able to quarry, or extract, these joint blocks and incorporate them into its base. Although the quarrying action at the base of the glacier cannot be observed, it may be initiated when water enters these cracks, freezes, expands, and pries the joint block up where the moving ice can exert its tremendous force. Large boulders as well as small stones thus become embedded in the glacier; as it moves forward, the loosened rock is plucked from place and carried away in the moving ice stream. The rock subsequently becomes a tool of the glacier, used to scrape out other fragments from the glacier's bed.

Besides plucking and scouring their beds, glaciers also cut into the margins of the canyons containing them. When a glacier enters a winding stream valley, the ice typically broadens it by scraping deeply into the valley walls, steepening them and planing off projections. Widened, deepened, and straightened, the valley becomes a classic U-shaped glacial canyon, with sheer, precipitous sides and a rounded bottom. In the North Cascades, where glaciation has been particularly intense, examples of these spacious glacier-cut canyons abound. At Crater Lake, visitors can even see U-shaped glacial

MOUNTAIN BUILDING AND ICE AGES

GEOLOGIC TIME	SOME MAJOR EVENTS IN THE CASCADES
HOLOCENE (last 10,000 years)	Little Ice Age (ca. AD 1350–1850). Glaciers reach their Holocene maximum extent; intermittent eruptions at most Cascade stratovolcanoes. Glaciers advance and retreat several times in early and mid-Holocene.
PLEISTOCENE (1.8 million to 10,000 years ago)	Repeated formation of continental ice sheets and extensive alpine glaciers; construction of large composite cones in Cascade Range.
PLIOCENE (5.3 to 1.8 million years ago)	Growth of many overlapping shield volcanoes and deposition of erosional debris along mountain fronts; elevation of modern Cascade Range.
MIOCENE (23.7 to 5.3 million years ago)	Explosive volcanism, followed by erosion of mid-Miocene composite cones; deposition of sediment along flanks of range; eruptions of flood basalts cover much of eastern Washington and Oregon; basaltic flows extend west to Pacific coast; intrusion of molten granitic rock into older strata, forming Snoqualmie batholith in North Cascades; Tatoosh pluton at site of Rainier.

valleys in cross-section. When the former summit of Mount Mazama collapsed, it took with it the tops of the glacier-carved trenches on Mazama's south slopes, leaving only the canyons' lower portions, which now appear as deep notches along the southeast caldera wall.

Many glaciers heading at high altitudes on a volcano's flanks carve deep, semicircular recesses in the mountainside, called cirques. The largest cirque in the range still occupied by a glacier is located on Rainier's north flank, where the Carbon glacier has cut an extremely steep headwall—the Willis Wall—rising about 4,000 feet above the glacier's deck to the summit icecap. Other conspicuous cirques are found on Baker, Adams, Hood, Jefferson, and the North Sister. Although now devoid of glacial ice, even Lassen Peak sports a shallow cirque on its northeast slope, the work of a since-vanished late Pleistocene glacier.

According to some geologists, glacial ice functions as a perfectly plastic substance: it is brittle and capable of cracking like a solid and, when subjected to a critical degree of stress, is also capable of deformation, enabling it to flow. As the ice mass flows downslope, it typically encounters uneven terrain that causes different parts of the glacier to move at different speeds. (Under most conditions, the center region of the upper part of the glacier travels faster than either the margins or base, usually at the rate of a few inches per day.) When sliding at varying speeds over obstacles in the bedrock, the glacier typically forms crevasses, gaping fissures in the ice surface that may be many tens of feet deep. In places, the glacier surface may appear blistered with networks of crevasses, produced by its movement over irregular knobs or ridges. Seracs are pinnacles or vertical blocks of ice that form when the glacier surface is broken by sets of crevasses. When a coherent ice stream plunges over a cliff or some other exceptionally steep grade, icefalls are formed, such as those of the Tahoma glacier as it tumbles down Rainier's west face, or the Adams glacier as it ripples northward from Adams's summit icecap. Up close, these precipitous ice masses resemble huge frozen waterfalls.

When a glacier descends to low elevations where melting exceeds replenishment of the ice from above, it dumps its load of rock. Containing rock fragments ranging in size from large boulders to a gray flourlike substance, this unsorted aggregation of debris is called glacial till. Whereas till is deposited directly by the glacier, the term glacial drift also encompasses material distributed by meltwater or streams issuing from the glacier. The long ridges of till and other debris that form along a glacier's side margins are known as lateral moraines—loose material that was shed there from its rounded, convex surface. The piles of rocky debris at the glacier's downvalley end are terminal moraines, which commonly form a long mound parallel to

After cascading down the north face of Mount Adams in a spectacular icefall, the Adams glacier spreads out in a broad fan of ice. —Robert Krimmel photo, U.S. Geological Survey

the glacier's front or terminus. Some moraines stand hundreds of feet above the valley floor, indicating the thickness of the glacier that deposited them.

Although glaciers are commonly viewed as nature's bulldozers, pushing aside quarried rock to form lateral moraines, the implied analogy is misleading. As Carolyn Driedger of the U. S. Geological Survey explains, the amount of material—usually only soft sediments—that glaciers actually shoulder aside is minimal. Instead, lateral moraines typically form at Cascade volcanoes in ablation zones, where melting predominates, causing rocks and other debris strewing the glacier's surface to roll from its convex middle to its margins. As the glacier's edges thin, the rock melts out, accumulating in elongated ridges at its sides and snout. In some cases, where the ice contains an exceptionally high percentage of rock, the moraines form from the outside in: as the glacier thins and recedes, it first drops rocks on its outer margins, and subsequently rock deposits are made progressively closer to its retreating tongue.

The presence of U-shaped valleys, glacial drift, cirques, or moraines even on cones that no longer sustain perennial snowcaps, such as Lassen Peak, Mount McLoughlin, or Mazama (Crater Lake), offer unmistakable evidence that Cascade glaciation was once far more widespread than it is now. At Crater Lake, terminal moraines are found 17 miles down Munson Valley southeast of the caldera rim. Today's glaciers on Mount Rainier, extending a maximum of 5 or 6 miles from the summit, are puny compared to glaciers of Pleistocene time, one of which flowed from the base of the mountain

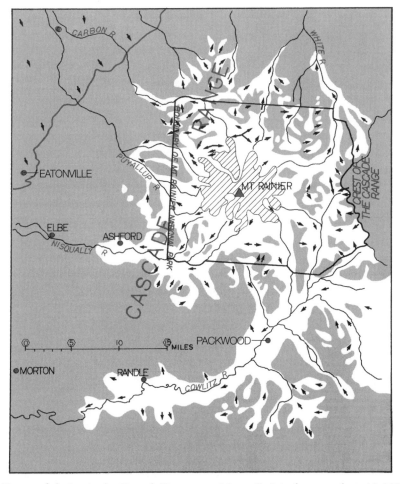

Extent of glaciers in the Cascade Range near Mount Rainier between about 18,000 and 25,000 years ago. Arrows indicate the direction of ice movement; striped area represents contemporary glacier on Rainier. —Adapted from Crandell, 1969

as far as 65 miles down the Cowlitz River valley. Innumerable moraines and other glacial deposits far distant from existing ice fields are distributed throughout the range, indicating that in the past Cascade glaciers covered many thousands of square miles that are presently ice free.

Pleistocene Glaciation

Pleistocene time, during which huge glaciers repeatedly developed in the northern latitudes, began about two million years ago with a worldwide cycle of cold, wet weather. A global drop in temperature, coupled with intense precipitation, resulted in the formation of vast continental ice sheets that eventually covered millions of square miles in North America, Europe, and Asia. At least four and perhaps as many as ten times during the Pleistocene ice age, enormous ice caps grew rapidly during cold cycles, temporarily retreated as the climate warmed, and then readvanced during renewed cooling. In North America, massive continental ice sheets repeatedly formed and spread southward into the present state of Washington. During the last glacial advance, the Cordilleran ice sheet—an ice mass flowing from Canada—not only filled the Strait of Juan de Fuca and overrode the North Cascades, but also pushed through the Puget lowland to a point south of Olympia, smothering the site of Seattle under an ice mass 4,000 feet thick. The giant Puget lobe melted only about 13,500 years ago.

During peak Pleistocene glaciations, when the Cascade Range was buried under ice up to a mile thick, alpine glaciers of the North Cascades flowed many miles downvalley to merge with tongues of the Cordilleran ice sheet that extended southward on both sides of the chain. In Oregon, an unbroken ice cap stretched from Mount McLoughlin northward almost to Mount Hood, which was itself the center of a large ice cap. In California, Mount Shasta was subjected to intense glacial erosion, which carved out the large trenches now visible on the volcano's south side, where no ice fields now exist. At its maximum extent, Pleistocene ice, thousands of feet thick even in the southern part of the range, buried all but the highest peaks and ridges. With a large percentage of the world's fresh water locked up in glaciers, global sea level dropped about 400 to 500 feet, exposing large areas of the continental shelf that are now under water.

Because later glaciations obliterated deposits from most of the previous ones, geologists are not sure how many there were. We do know, however, that the glaciers' cumulative effect on the landscape was tremendous, grinding billions of tons of rock to powder, stripping away the outer surfaces of the older volcanoes, and transforming narrow stream valleys into wide, flat-bottomed canyons. When the glaciers made their final retreat between 10,000 and 12,000 years ago, they left vast lowland areas stripped of topsoil or buried under gravelly till. Only recently relieved of its stupendous burden of ice, the earth's crust in many places is still slowly rebounding.

Volcanic Fire and Glacial Ice

Most of the Cascade composite volcanoes were built during and between episodes of intense glaciation. For most of their history, the cones of Baker, Rainier, Adams, Hood, Jefferson, the Three Sisters, Mazama, and Shasta were almost entirely sheathed in grinding ice. When the volcanoes erupted, the interaction of volcanic heat and glacial ice dramatically increased their destructive potential: hot rock fragments showering down on snowfields caused rapid melting, triggering floods and mudflows that extended many tens of miles downvalley, devastating lowlands far beyond the reach of even the longest lava streams. As demonstrated at Mount St. Helens in 1980, Nevado del Ruiz in 1985, and Alaska's Mount Spurr in 1992, pyroclastic flows are particularly effective in melting snow and ice, spawning floods that, mixed with both old rock and freshly erupted material, swiftly pour into adjacent valleys, burying large areas far from the volcano.

By contrast, a coherent lava flow moving ponderously over snow or ice ordinarily causes only limited melting. When it plunges over steep cliffs high on the cone, however, the flow commonly breaks up into thousands of molten fragments that avalanche downslope. Transformed into a pyroclastic flow, the disintegrated lava produces similar wholesale melting. Because Mount Rainier was built high astride deep intersecting canyons, its mudflows traveled many tens of miles away from the cone, repeatedly inundating the Puget lowland. The mudflows from Mount Shasta, which grew atop a less rugged mountainscape, did not drain as far from the volcano, but piled up in massive aprons around the volcano's base.

Besides generating innumerable destructive mudflows, the presence of glaciers on the Cascade volcanoes throughout most of their history also significantly determined their present shape and form. Biting deeply into their cones, scraping away their original surfaces, and excavating broad cirques, deep trenches, and other erosional scars, the glaciers reconfigured the volcanic edifices into the ruggedly irregular forms that most of them have today.

On some peaks, such as Mount Rainier, glaciers also influenced the path of lava flows. During periods of maximum glacial extent, lava flows emitted directly onto the surface of thick ice streams probably shattered and, reduced to hot rubble, avalanched downslope as lithic pyroclastic flows. Incorporating meltwater from ice and snow, the pyroclastic flows were transformed into mudflows, which then swept debris from the disintegrated flows far downvalley.

Extent of glaciation (white) in the Cascade Range in Oregon, approximating the area covered during the last maximum Pleistocene ice advance (ca. 18,000–25,000 years ago). —Adapted from Crandell, 1965

By contrast, when a lava stream oozed along ridge tops bordering glacier-filled canyons, it remained a coherent flow, adding to the height and size of the ridge. As voluminous lava flows traveled first down one ridge crest and then another, they gradually built ever-higher walls along the edges of glacier-occupied canyons. Shaded by these massive lava ridges constructed along their margins, the glaciers continued sinking their beds ever deeper into the mountain's flanks.

Cascade Glaciers Today

Although today's glaciers are much smaller than their ice-age predecessors, the quantity of snow and ice mantling a particular volcano still significantly determines its potential to wreak havoc at great distances from the mountain. Recognizing that floods and mudflows will probably represent the single greatest hazard when a Cascade volcano next erupts, the U.S. Geological Survey recently measured ice volumes on half a dozen major peaks located near populated areas. Carolyn Driedger and her USGS colleagues found that Shasta's five major glaciers and adjacent ice fields have a volume of about 4.7 billion cubic feet, more than enough potential meltwater to generate large mudflows that could overwhelm nearby highways, railways, reservoirs, and the town of McCloud.

In central Oregon, the Three Sisters, a cluster of composite cones each more than 10,000 feet high, have a total ice volume of 5.6 billion cubic feet. Middle Sister, the smallest of the volcanic trio, has the most ice cover, including the Hayden and Diller glaciers, which mantle most of its steep east face. The Collier glacier, the region's largest, descends from Middle Sister's north slope and cuts across the west flank of North Sister. Containing 0.7 billion cubic feet of ice, the Collier glacier is also the thickest in the region, with a depth of 300 feet. The North Sister's several glaciers are negligible; those on the South Sister, especially the Prouty, the Lewis, and the Lost Creek, are somewhat larger.

With a combined volume of about 12.2 billion cubic feet, Mount Hood's nine major glaciers feed several rivers and streams, all of which ultimately empty into the Columbia River. Poised above the orchards and villages dotting the Hood River valley, the Eliot glacier is Hood's largest, with a volume of 3.2 billion cubic feet and a thickness of 361 feet. The Coe-Ladd glacier has the largest surface area—23 million square feet. All the stream valleys draining Mount Hood, especially those of the White, Zig Zag, and Sandy Rivers, have been repeatedly overwhelmed by massive floods and mudflows during recent eruptions, including one that occurred only about 200 years ago.

Subject to heavy precipitation and prolonged freezing temperatures at higher altitudes, two of Washington's volcanoes, Baker and Rainier, not only hold continental records for annual snowfall, but also support the largest ice volumes in the Cascade Range. Containing 155.8 billion cubic feet of ice (more than a cubic mile), Rainier's glaciers, covering 34 square miles, have as much ice as the total on all other Cascade volcanoes. (The aptly named Glacier Peak ranks third in ice volume.) Rainier also has the most voluminous glacier, the Carbon, which extends to a lower elevation (3,200 feet) than any other ice stream in the lower forty-eight states. The Emmons glacier, which occupies much of Rainier's east flank, has the largest surface area—120.2 million square feet. Fifty percent of Rainier's snow and ice lie between elevations of 6,000 and 9,000 feet, while 30 percent is above an altitude of 9,000 feet.

Rainier's twin snow-filled summit craters tilt toward the east, indicating that eruption-induced meltwater may flow first in that direction, down the Emmons and Winthrop glaciers and into the White River valley. The volume of ice poised above the White River drainage totals 47.2 billion cubic feet, while that above the Cowlitz River drainage area to the south totals 20.2 billion cubic feet. During the last few thousand years, most streams originating on Mount Rainier—including the White, Cowlitz, Puyallup, and Nisqually Rivers—have repeatedly channeled voluminous mudflows toward the Puget lowland, burying the sites of numerous cities and towns that now contain large populations, including Sumner, Puyallup, Orting, Enumclaw, Auburn, south Seattle, and the Port of Tacoma. Streams draining the slopes of Mount Baker and Glacier Peak have similarly directed enormous mudflows onto the now-populated shores of northern Puget Sound, while St. Helens and Hood have frequently sent mudflows pouring into the Columbia River, sweeping over the sites of several cities and towns.

Even cones without a perennial ice cover, such as Lassen Peak or Oregon's Mount Bachelor, sustain heavy snowpacks during winter and spring. If an eruption occurs when the volcano is still shrouded in snow, extensive mudflows typically occur. When Lassen erupted explosively in May 1915, pyroclastic flows and surges melted much of the snow cover, generating mudflows that streamed down both the east and west flanks of the mountain. Runout from these lahars traveled at least 20 miles down Lost and Hat Creeks, flooding areas where several resorts and many vacation homes are presently located. Eruptions as far south as the Mono Lake–Long Valley region have also triggered numerous mudflows.

Although most Cascade glaciers have been retreating, with some irregular advances, since about 1850, they continue to erode their alpine hosts, steepening cliffs, carving some summits into sharp horns, and transporting eroded material downslope. The history of most Cascade volcanoes embodies an unending battle between two opposing forces of nature: eruptions of lava and pyroclastic material that build their towering cones and the erosive power of glacial ice that tears them down, eventually reducing even the loftiest peaks to rubble. Many scientists believe that the warm period in which we are now living is only another interval in a long cycle of recurring glaciations, and that in another 10,000 to 20,000 years much of the range will again be submerged in grinding ice. Even while the present warming trend continues, however, we can expect innumerable future eruptions to transform summit ice fields into raging torrents of water-mobilized debris that will race down valleys to crush and bury thousands of houses, bridges, shopping malls, industrial plants, and other businesses, disrupting countless human lives.

CHAPTER 5

The Mono Lake–Long Valley Region

CALIFORNIA'S RESTLESS CALDERA

When Mark Twain first sighted Mono Lake in the 1860s, he was appalled at its apparent desolation, dismissing it as "a lifeless, treeless, hideous desert . . . the loneliest spot on earth." Today's visitors to this still sparsely populated region, which lies on the dry side of the Sierra Nevada directly east of Yosemite National Park, are likely to have a far more positive reaction. Viewed from the north, where U.S. 395 crosses Conway Summit (8,138 feet), Mono Lake forms an almost perfect azure circle, its sky-reflecting waters offering a welcome oasis of color in a largely unforested tableland lying between the White Mountains to the east and the Sierra to the west. (See image 1 on plate 1.)

Twice as salty as the ocean, Mono Lake is an infertile beauty, supporting virtually no marine life except the minuscule brine shrimp. Like the biblical Dead Sea, which it strikingly resembles in its austere grandeur, the lake has no outlet. The alkaline remnant of a much larger body of water, during Pleistocene glaciations of the nearby Sierra it was up to 900 feet deep and extended over many square miles of now-arid flatlands. The lake's postglacial shrinkage was escalated drastically during the early 1940s as water from streams flowing into the lake basin was diverted to supply the demands of ever-growing Los Angeles. Not until 1985 was the rapidly evaporating lake made a natural preserve, providing a refuge for waterfowl and wildlife, including the loon, whose plaintive cry now echoes again through the Mono basin.

U.S. 395, California's principal north-south artery east of the Sierra, leads travelers through the heart of the Mono Lake–Long Valley volcanic region. After skirting the lake's western shore with clear views of Mono Craters, a miniature mountain range of young volcanic cones extending southward from the lake, U.S. 395 winds among even younger vents of the Inyo Craters. Passing by the foot of Mammoth Mountain (12,000 feet) and near the prosperous ski resort of Mammoth Lakes, the road then traverses Long Valley, a caldera 20 miles long and 10 miles wide, formed about 760,000 years ago by a colossal Yellowstone-style eruption. Since that outburst,

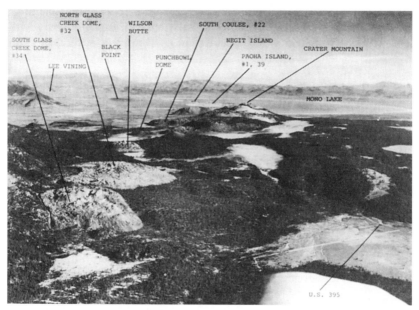

View northeast along the Mono Craters chain, with Mono Lake in the distance. This young line of obsidian domes, flows, and cinder cones has produced numerous eruptions during the last 2,000 years. —Courtesy of the California Department of Mines and Geology

which deposited ash as far east as Nebraska, volcanic activity has continued intermittently on a smaller scale, with the Mono-Inyo chain erupting explosively about 600 years ago. The most recent activity occurred between about AD 1720 and 1850, a series of small eruptions on Mono Lake's Paoha Island, which was steaming as late as 1890.

Residents of Lee Vining, Mammoth Lakes, and other small settlements in the area inhabit one of California's most geologically active regions, where they are frequently shaken by two different but often interrelated kinds of earthquakes—tectonic and volcanic. Tectonic quakes in this region are associated with crustal deformation resulting from the movement of the North American and Pacific plates, an interaction that produces crustal stress at least as far inland as the eastern Sierra. The largest historic tectonic temblor occurred on March 26, 1872, when the Owens Valley fault, which parallels the steep east face of the Sierra, abruptly shifted, cutting a deep furrow in the ground surface for at least 100 miles from Haiwee Reservoir south of Olancha to Big Pine. Horizontal movement was dramatic, particularly between Lone Pine and Independence, where relative displacement on opposite sides of the fault was as much as 20 feet. In Lone Pine, which then had about 250 to 300 inhabitants, 52 of its 59 adobe houses were leveled, killing 23 people. Although the Owens Valley earthquake probably approached a magnitude of 8.0 on the Richter scale, it claimed only about 60 victims, primarily because the affected area was so thinly settled. Despite a low population density even today, a repeat of the 1872 event, which triggered massive rockfalls and avalanches in Yosemite Valley and other parts of the Sierra, could endanger thousands of people who hike, climb, camp, ski, fish, or otherwise explore this region every year.

Whereas large tectonic quakes commonly involve an initial powerful jolt followed by a series of aftershocks of gradually diminishing intensity, volcanic earthquakes tend to occur in an array of minor quakes, typically focused beneath a volcano, that continue over an extended period at roughly the same intensity. These seismic swarms may also involve the sudden breaking of crustal rock along faults, but in addition they include the movement of subterranean fluids—magma or magmatic brine—into or through fractures in the crust. Beginning in 1978, after decades of relative quiet, a long sequence of volcanic temblors has disturbed the Long Valley area. On May 25, 1980, exactly one week after the catastrophic eruption of Mount St. Helens, a succession of four magnitude 6.0 shocks—three on the same day—alerted scientists that this region of young lava flows, domes, and active hot springs again faced a volcanic threat. The U.S. Geological Survey soon discovered other signs of the earthquakes' volcanic origins: besides new vents at the Casa Diablo Hot Springs about 1.5 miles east of the epicenter, geologists detected a significant uplift in the central caldera floor. Between the summer of 1979 and mid-1980, a broad dome-like area had risen approximately 1 foot. The rate of subsurface magma intrusion has apparently slowed, however; as of the end of 2004 the swelling, which now affects 100 square miles, totaled 2.6 feet.

Perhaps a more ominous indication of magma's upward movement is the ongoing emission of volcanic gas that is killing hundreds of trees at Mammoth Mountain. A large pile of overlapping silicic domes and thick lava flows constructed between about 100,000 and 50,000 years ago, Mammoth Mountain is the southernmost volcano in the Mono-Inyo chain. Banked against the east flank of the Sierra, the steep-sided cone offers some of the best skiing in California, attracting tens of thousands of winter enthusiasts to the extensive lifts that transport skiers to its slopes. Although it has not had a major eruption in 50,000 years, about 700 years ago a series of steam explosions blasted the north slope about two-thirds of a mile west of the Mammoth Mountain ski lodge.

Following a swarm of moderate quakes centered beneath Mammoth Mountain in 1989, U.S. Forest Service rangers began to notice areas of dead and dying trees on the mountain. After eliminating such causes as drought and insect infestations, USGS scientists discovered that the roots of the trees are being killed by exceptionally high concentrations of carbon dioxide (CO_2) in the soil. CO_2, which kills trees by depriving roots of oxygen and interfering with nutrient uptake, makes up about 20 to 95 percent of the soil's gas content in affected areas (it is normally less than 1 percent). By the late 1990s, the steady emission of 300 tons of CO_2 per day—compared to an emission rate of 9,000 tons at a constantly active volcano like Kilauea—has killed trees on more than 100 acres. Because this invisible gas seeping from a body of magma beneath Mammoth Mountain is heavier than air, it tends to collect in depressions or inside storage sheds or other unventilated structures on the mountain. This creates a potentially fatal hazard for both hikers and wild animals, as CO_2 displaces atmospheric oxygen and causes rapid asphyxiation.

The Long Valley Caldera

Volcanic activity in the Mono Lake–Long Valley region began about three to four million years ago, roughly contemporaneous with the onset of extensive faulting and uplift of the White Mountains and Sierra Nevada. Two distinct but interrelated volcanic systems dominate the region's volcanic history: the Long Valley caldera and the Mono-Inyo volcanic chain. The older of the two is centered at the Long Valley caldera. Beginning with the eruption of basalts and andesites about 3.8 million years ago, the Long Valley magma became increasingly silicic over time. Some early lava flows, which originally spread over relatively level terrain, have been dramatically displaced by the rising Sierra front, with one section of a flow uplifted as high as 3,300 feet above the other part of the same flow in the valley below. Between about 2.1 and 0.8 million years ago, rhyolite lava erupted, forming Glass Mountain on the northeast rim of the present caldera.

The transition from low silica lavas to the viscous rhyolites of Glass Mountain indicates that the Long Valley magmas were chemically evolving, creating a gas-rich silicic brew in a shallow magma chamber. By about 760,000 years ago, an enormous quantity of rhyolitic magma had accumulated only 4 miles beneath the surface. In a climactic release of pressure, about 150 cubic miles of frothy rhyolitic magma then burst through a series of concentric fractures to the surface. Buoyed by escaping gas, towering waves of incandescent ash swept outward in every direction at speeds exceeding a hundred miles an hour. So great was the volume of ejected pumice, and so high its velocity, that one arm of the frothing mass surmounted the steep east face of the Sierra—a barrier thousands of feet above the

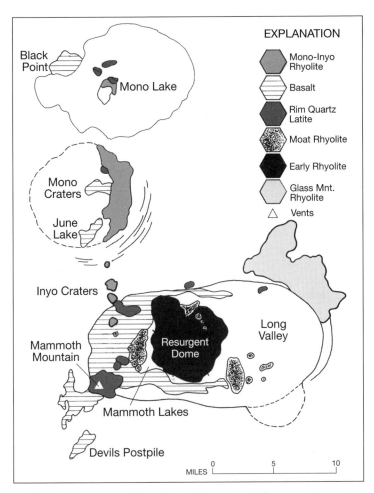

EXPLANATION

Mono-Inyo Rhyolite

Basalt

Rim Quartz Latite

Moat Rhyolite

Early Rhyolite

Glass Mnt. Rhyolite

△ Vents

Black Point

Mono Lake

Mono Craters

June Lake

Inyo Craters

Mammoth Mountain

Resurgent Dome

Long Valley

Mammoth Lakes

Devils Postpile

0　　　　5　　　　10
MILES

Simplified geologic map of the Mono Lake–Long Valley area in east-central California. Note the general north-south alignment of vents from Mammoth Mountain in the south to the volcanic islands in Mono Lake in the north.

erupting vents—and, overtopping the crest, raced westward down the San Joaquin River drainage, perhaps as far as California's Central Valley.

Another pulse of the rhyolitic ash flows traveled at least 50 miles southward down the Owens Valley past the present site of Bishop. The airborne tephra and pyroclastic flow deposits, known as the Bishop tuff, completely buried at least 580 square miles of central California and southwestern Nevada. Seventy-five miles from the volcano, ash fell to a depth of more than 4 feet; at a distance of 125 miles, it was 16 inches thick. Fallout from the turbulent clouds generated by the pyroclastic flows darkened skies over most of the western states and blanketed the Midwest with a layer of ash identifiable even today. As was the case with comparable eruptions at Yellowstone, so much magma was ejected that the roof of the magma chamber collapsed, causing the ground surface to sink about 1 mile and creating the oval-shaped Long Valley caldera. Geologists estimate that the magnitude of the eruption was about 2,000 times that of Mount St. Helens in 1980.

After the collapse basin formed, activity on a smaller scale resumed on the caldera floor. Explosive eruptions of tephra were followed by black, glassy flows of obsidian. Pressure from rising magma eventually arched the caldera floor, creating a phenomenon known as a resurgent dome. Beginning about 100,000 years ago, Mammoth Mountain, at the caldera's southwest

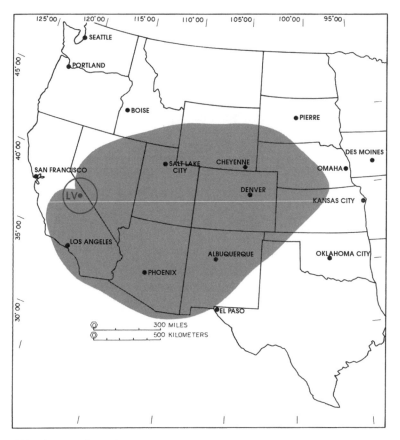

Distribution of ash fall from the Long Valley caldera (LV). Many feet thick near its source, the ash layer thins to about half an inch at its eastern extremity. A future eruption comparable to that of 760,000 years ago would deposit ash downwind to a depth of 3 feet within a 75-mile radius of the Long Valley vent. —Adapted from Miller et al., 1982

rim, produced massive dacite flows on the average of every 5,000 years for a span of about 50,000 years. Although geologists do not expect another outburst comparable to that of 760,000 years ago in the foreseeable future, it is possible that Long Valley's magma chamber will eventually evolve toward another silicic supereruption. In the meantime, many small-to-moderate eruptions will again occur in or near the caldera, perhaps at Mammoth Mountain.

The Mono-Inyo Volcanic Chain

Much younger than the Long Valley volcanic center, the Mono-Inyo volcanic chain extends from just south of Mammoth Mountain northward 25 miles to the north shore of Mono Lake. During the last 40,000 years, the Mono-Inyo volcanoes have erupted frequently and sometimes simultaneously, forming a "chain of fire" as a series of vents spouted ash or oozed lava. During the last 5,000 years, eruptions have occurred somewhere in the chain every 250 to 700 years. During the last 1,000 years, at least twelve eruptions took place, including those that formed the Inyo Craters (about 600 years ago) and the South Deadman Creek Dome. Rather than the product of a single large magma chamber, such as that which fueled the Long Valley cataclysm, the Mono-Inyo activity is probably fed by a number of small, discrete bodies of magma.

A Future Chain of Fire?

If a volcano's recent eruptive history is an indication of its future behavior, the next activity along the Mono-Inyo Craters chain may produce a whole series of new vents erupting at the same time along a zone several miles in length. This simultaneous activity is exactly what happened between about AD 1325 and 1365 (according to tree-ring dating), when the chain produced a closely spaced sequence of both explosive and effusive eruptions, perhaps within a period of a few weeks or months. Activity began at the north end of the Mono chain when a dike—a thin tabular sheet of rising magma—encountered groundwater, causing it to flash into steam and blast open a line of vents 4 miles long. Because gas entrained in the rising magma is concentrated at the top of the magma column, the initial eruptions were the most explosive, discharging clouds of tephra that mantled approximately 3,000 square miles of the Mono Lake area. The winds repeatedly shifted direction during this phase, depositing ash to the north, northeast, east, and south of the volcanoes. Twenty miles downwind, ash accumulated to depths of 8 inches; 50 miles away, it was 2 inches thick.

During the second phase of the eruptions, pyroclastic flows and surges swept in narrow tongues as far as 5 miles from the vents, burying about

38 square miles, a small fraction of the area mantled by the air-fall tephra. With the magma's gas content largely depleted, the eruption's third stage was much quieter: sticky masses of rhyolite magma oozed from the vents to form thick lobes of lava and steep-sided domes. Of the several domes emplaced, the most prominent is Panum Dome, which rises above an encircling ring of pyroclastic material at the north end of Mono Craters. The largest single mass of lava forms Northern Coulee, which contains well over half the total volume of material erupted.

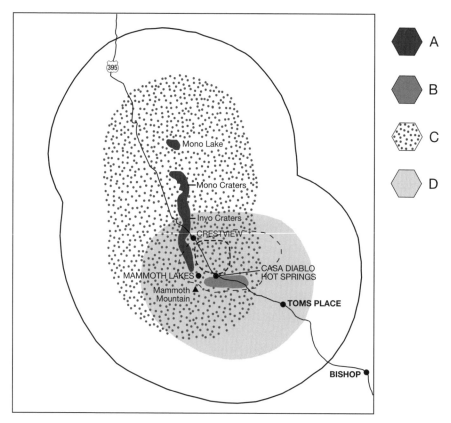

Potential hazard zones of future eruptions in the Mono Lake–Long Valley region. The hazard zones are based on the nature and size of eruptions that occurred in this area during the last 10,000 years. (A) Chain of explosive silicic vents active during last 10,000 years. (B) Potential sites of new vents indicated by seismicity since 1980 and by proximity to the Long Valley ring-fracture system. (C) Area subject to pyroclastic flows and surges around existing explosive vents. (D) Area subject to pyroclastic flows and surges around possible future explosive vents inferred by seismicity. —Adapted from Miller et al., 1982

About a year or two after the eruptions at Mono Craters, an almost identical sequence of events took place at Inyo Craters, a few miles to the south. A similar dike of rhyolitic magma, perhaps 4 to 8 miles long, rose to within about 700 feet of the surface before erupting. Again, a chain of new craters was ripped open, some of which discharged columns of tephra that drifted over the present site of Mammoth Lakes, mantling it in ash an inch thick. Some vents produced only phreatic (steam-blast) eruptions, leaving deep craters now occupied by lakes. During the final quiet eruptive phase, pasty rhyolite emerged like putty from a tube to form massive domes at the South Deadman Creek, Glass Creek, and Obsidian Flow vents.

According to a recent study, the latest activity in the region took place on two islands in Mono Lake. Investigating fluctuations in lake level during the past 3,500 years, Scott Stine of the University of California at Berkeley found that features on Negit Island, which consists of a cinder cone, five blocky lava flows, and a central area of pyroclastic material, were formed after a high-water level of 6,456 feet above sea level was reached less than three centuries ago. Two of Negit's stubby lava flows do not have shorelines carved by wave action at that elevation.

Even younger is Paoha Island, which was formed when a shallow intrusion of magma pushed up a large block of lake bottom sediments. Spires of viscous rhyolite lava protruded through the sediment block on the north part of Paoha, while eruptions of dacite magma built a cluster of seven cinder cones and a lava flow on the island's northeastern corner. As Stine noted, the absence of a shoreline at 6,456 feet, the lake's most recent high mark, is "strong evidence that the island did not exist" only two or three centuries ago. The presence of twenty distinct layers of ash lying atop the tephra erupted from Mono Craters about 600 years ago indicates that the Paoha vent was intermittently active for perhaps a century, between about AD 1720 and 1850. When pioneering geologist Israel C. Russell visited Paoha in the early 1880s, he observed active fumaroles at Hot Spring Cove on its eastern margin, one of which registered temperatures of 150 degrees Fahrenheit. In cold, clear weather, Russell noted, "columns of steam hundreds of feet in height have been seen to escape from these orifices." Although Paoha's thermal display has now faded, the kind of magma intrusion into Mono Lake that formed the island is so geologically recent that it could be repeated in the near future.

Since the current swarms of volcanic earthquakes began, the U.S. Geological Survey, in cooperation with the California Department of Emergency Services, Mono County, and other governmental agencies, has maintained a network of seismometers and other devices to monitor the Mono Lake–Long Valley area for signs of an impending eruption. The USGS has compiled a response plan that coordinates four levels of volcanic activity with four stages

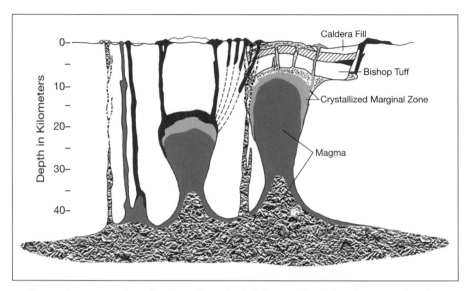

Composite cross-section showing a hypothetical form of the inferred magma chambers underlying (from left to right) Mono Lake, the Mono-Inyo Craters, and the Long Valley caldera. —Adapted from R. A. Bailey, "Other Potential Eruption Centers in California: Long Valley–Mono Lake, Cosco, and Clear Lake Volcanic Fields," in *Status of Volcanic Prediction and Emergency Response Capabilities in Volcanic Hazard Zones of California*, edited by R. C. Martin and J. F. Davis (California Department of Conservation, Division of Mines and Geology, special publication 63, 1982)

of official response, represented by four different colors. Code green encompasses several states of unrest—ranging from weak to strong—that occur with regularity and require no action other than routine monitoring and keeping local agencies informed. Yellow signifies intense unrest, such as an increase in seismic swarms, rapid ground deformation, and/or increased heat and steam emission, and requires the USGS to alert all state and county agencies and to activate the Long Valley Observatory field office for intensified on-site observation. An orange alert indicates that an eruption is likely to occur within hours to days, and the USGS director will issue a specific warning to the general public. Code red means that an eruption is in progress. In 2002 a USGS team headed by seismologist David Hill published *Response Plan for Volcano Hazards in the Long Valley Caldera and Mono Craters Region, California*, which provides detailed lists of the kinds of geologic events associated with each stage of the color code.

Although events justifying an orange or red alert are expected to occur only once every few hundred years, geologists regard future eruptions in

the Mono Lake–Long Valley area as virtually certain. The region's volcanoes have been erupting intermittently for four million years and show
no sign of stopping in the foreseeable future. Judging by events of the last
5,000 years, eruptive activity is likely to center along the Mono-Inyo Craters chain and/or in Mono Lake and may involve multiple vents erupting
simultaneously. The potential destructiveness of future eruptions depends
largely on such unpredictable factors as wind direction, precise location of
active vents, and the season of the year when the eruptions occur (a sudden
eruption of snow-shrouded Mammoth Mountain during the height of the
ski season, increasing the risk of floods and mudflows, will be particularly
threatening to life and property). Whatever form future eruptions take,
authorities responsible for warning the public or even evacuating local residents and tourists will have their hands full.

Visiting the Mono Lake-Long Valley Region

A viewpoint on U.S. 395 at Conway Summit offers unobstructed views of
Mono Lake and Mono Craters. A network of dirt roads running east of U.S.
395 between Lee Vining and the turnoff for Mammoth Lakes approaches
the Mono Craters, with California 120 coming close to Panum crater at
the north end of the chain. Because they are located in a forested area, the
Inyo Craters are harder to see, but a few signs on U.S. 395 mark turnoffs
to several of the vents near the highway. U.S. 395 also crosses Long Valley
from northwest to southeast; the resort of Mammoth Lakes is located in the
central western part of the caldera.

CHAPTER 6

Lassen Peak

CALIFORNIA'S MOST RECENTLY ACTIVE VOLCANO

The southernmost major volcano in the Cascade Range, Lassen Peak (10,457 feet) stands a full 2 miles above the floor of the northern Sacramento Valley. As the only Cascade volcano more than 10,000 feet high that is not a composite cone, Lassen—rising only about 2,500 feet above its immediate surroundings—is perhaps less visually impressive than its fellow fire mountains. Located too far south to maintain a perennial snow cover, Lassen's earth-colored plug dome stands so close to Mounts Brokeoff and Diller, eroded remnants of a much older composite volcano, that summer travelers driving north on Interstate 5 may have difficulty distinguishing Lassen from its near neighbors. The jagged crests of Chaos Crags, a cluster of young domes rising directly north of Lassen, also help to diminish its visual impact.

After leaving Interstate 5 and driving eastward on California 36 through the arid, oak-studded Cascade foothills to the southwest entrance to Lassen Volcanic National Park, visitors discover that Lassen is actually located in a setting of remarkable alpine beauty. But east-bound travelers must first cross the sparsely vegetated Tuscan Formation, which borders the western margin of this part of the range, traversing an uninviting accumulation of ancient rock debris washed down from the volcanic highlands to the east. A few thousand feet above the valley floor the scenery changes dramatically: The bleak, rock-strewn grasslands dotted with scrub growth give way to thick stands of pine and fir. From California 89, the north-south two-lane road bisecting Lassen Park, visitors discover a rugged mountainscape where numerous winding streams and sparkling lakes punctuate the evergreen forest cover. Although Lassen itself may not compete with grander peaks like Shasta or Hood, its surroundings live up to the best Cascade standards.

Turning its most attractive profile toward tree-shaded Manzanita Lake at its west foot, where the park visitor center and museum are located, Lassen's talus-mantled dome manifests some of the majesty characterizing its companions to the north. It also has one unmistakable distinction: a tongue of glassy black dacite 1,000 feet long—the youngest lava flow in California—clinging to its west face. (See image 2 on plate 1.)

A tongue of dark dacite lava, erupted in May 1915, clings to Lassen Peak's western summit. From 1914 to 1917 Lassen produced lava, tephra, pyroclastic flows, and mudflows. —Robert Krimmel photo, U.S. Geological Survey

Lassen's Reawakening

In the years 1914 to 1917, Lassen emerged from obscurity to become a center of national attention—the first volcano in the conterminous United States to erupt during the twentieth century. When Lassen suddenly began puffing steam in the spring of 1914, it also became the first mainland volcano to be photographed in action. Attracting hoards of newspaper reporters as well as photographers, Lassen's eruptive behavior was far better documented than that of the northern Cascade volcanoes, such as Baker, Rainier, St. Helens, and Hood, that had erupted during the first half of the nineteenth century, when West Coast settlers were few and frontier camera-owners almost nonexistent.

Lassen's first recorded outbreak occurred late in the afternoon of May 30, 1914, when local resident Bert McKenzie was looking directly at the peak. Between about 4:30 and 5:00 PM, McKenzie watched incredulously as a column of what he called black smoke—steam laden with ash from pulverized rock—shot several hundred feet into the air above Lassen's summit. Although McKenzie is generally regarded as the first to witness Lassen's reawakening, the volcano may have sent up some preliminary steam puffs the day before. In the 1970s Anna Scharsch of Scharsch Meadows, a ranch

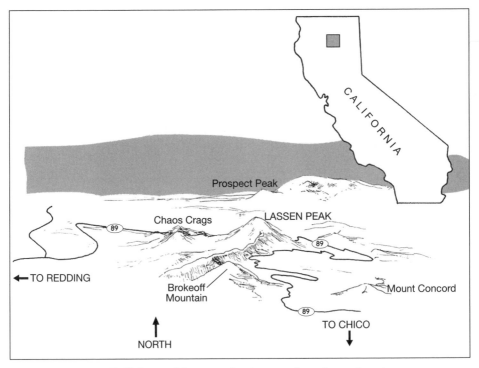

Relief map of Lassen volcanic center from the southwest

near Lassen Volcanic National Park, told the author that during the evening of May 29, when she was nineteen years old, she saw a "column of smoke" issuing from Lassen. She and her family concluded that the fire lookout station on Lassen's summit had caught fire. At ten o'clock the next morning they saw a larger cloud rise from the peak.

Although most volcanic eruptions are heralded by swarms of minor earthquakes, generated by a column of magma that fractures underground rock as it rises toward the surface, people living in the Lassen vicinity reported no seismic activity either before or during the volcano's awakening. If temblors too small to be felt by humans did occur, in 1914 there were no seismographs in Lassen's vicinity to record them. At least one eyewitness account, however, states that the initial activity was accompanied by a noticeable earthquake. In his valuable compilation of oral history, *The Lassen Peak Eruptions and Their Lingering Legacy*, Alan W. Willendrup states that on the afternoon of May 30 Gladys Brown (later Gladys King) and her father felt the ground swaying beneath their feet just as Lassen began to spout steam. Because their farm near Pittville, 30 miles north of Lassen, is so far from the volcano, geologists doubt that the Browns experienced a volcanic earthquake.

On May 31, forest ranger Harvey Abbey climbed through heavy snow to Lassen's summit. Abbey found that a new vent, measuring about 25 by 40 feet, had ripped open on the northeast side of a shallow depression about 1,000 feet in diameter. Probably scooped out by a long-vanished ice-age glacier, the depression at that time held a small lake. Filled with lava in May 1915, it is no longer visible.

Abbey observed a stream of hot water pouring from the new vent into the lake, cutting a channel in the snow. He also noted that the mountaintop was littered with rock fragments blown out during the first eruptions. Mud and rocks up to 18 inches across covered an area about 200 feet in diameter; a thin layer of fine ash about a mile wide extended across the summit and down Lassen's flanks. None of the ejecta was hot enough to melt the snow it fell on. It would take an entire year before the magma rising slowly through Lassen's plumbing system would reach the surface.

The new crater atop Lassen Peak, June 2, 1914. The fragments of old rock blown out of the new vent were too cool to melt the snow they fell on. —Courtesy of Mary Hill

Like most of the opening eruptions at Mount St. Helens sixty-six years later, Lassen's initial activity consisted of relatively small phreatic (steam-blast) explosions that blew out old material from the volcano's interior. As heat from the upwelling magma caused more groundwater within the cone to flash into steam, the phreatic eruptions gradually increased in intensity. As explosive activity continued, projecting ash plumes thousands of feet into the air, the new vent expanded until it eventually occupied all of the older summit depression.

On Saturday, June 13, ash fell for the first time over Mineral, a village 11 miles southwest of the volcano and now the location of Lassen Volcanic National Park headquarters. The next day a group of local millworkers climbed Lassen to view the action—a venture that almost cost them their lives. The climbers were resting on the edge of the crater, which at that point was about 450 by 125 feet in diameter, when another violent explosion occurred. Benjamin F. Loomis, a local resident, later described the event: "Without a warning . . . a huge cloud of black smoke shot upward with a roar, such as would be caused by a rushing mighty wind, and, in an instant the air was filled with smoke, ashes, and flying rocks from the crater." Running for their lives, one member of the summit party found shelter beneath an overhanging rock, while another, pelted by a hail of rock fragments, slid as far as he could down a steep snowbank and then buried his face in the snow to keep out the blinding smoke and ashes. Caught in Lassen's eruption cloud, the Sunday adventurers found themselves enveloped in darkness "black as the darkest night." The most severely injured climber, Lance Graham, was struck by a flying rock, which cut his shoulder and broke his collarbone. At first Graham's companions left him for dead, but they later revived him when the eruption was over.

While Graham and his friends were engulfed in stygian darkness, Loomis, who was not a member of the climbing party, photographed the June 14 eruption from Manzanita Lake about 6 miles west of the volcano. Recorded on glass plates at intervals of several minutes, this series of photographs documents a phenomenon common during explosive eruptions—a phenomenon that also occurred at St. Helens in 1980. After explosive outbursts sent vertical columns of dark ash roiling thousands of feet above the summit, the ash clouds then rapidly descended to roll downslope and enshroud the entire cone, presenting a hazard even to hikers far from the crater.

By mid-July, the eruptions grew notably more violent, scattering tephra over an ever-widening area. On the morning of July 18, Lassen's ash clouds reached an altitude of 11,000 feet above the mountaintop, causing people at nearby ranches to prepare to hitch their horses for a retreat from this increasingly dangerous mountain. A month later on August 19, huge clouds

of ash attained similar heights, and on August 22 Lassen gave a clear warning of its lethal potential when the ash column shot up obliquely and rushed down the mountainside, a forerunner of the laterally directed pyroclastic flows and surges that would devastate the volcano's northeast flanks less than a year later.

By the close of 1914, Lassen had produced at least 110 observed phreatic eruptions. (Others may have gone unnoticed because of cloudy weather.) Accompanied by strong vibrations and rumblings, probably caused by prolonged and violent venting of steam from small openings in the crater, eruptions were particularly frightening that fall. The outburst of September 21, which one observer described as probably the most violent to date, produced billowing ash clouds that darkened almost the entire sky over Mineral. Viola, Chester, and other hamlets on all sides of the mountain also reported increased ash fall. In late September witnesses sighted "luminous bodies" hurled high into the air and flashes of light from the crater. Because magma did not reach the surface until the next May, however, the reported

West end of Lassen's newly formed summit crater, June 28, 1914. The new vent expanded along an east-west trending fault. —Courtesy of Mary Hill

Clouds of ash-laden steam rise from Lassen's crater, September 29, 1914.
—Jack Robertson photo, courtesy of Mary Hill

flares were probably caused by static electricity, common during volcanic eruptions.

Following a two-hour eruption on October 22, Charles York of Drakesbad, a popular summer resort east of the volcano, climbed the mountain and found that the newly ejected tephra was so hot that his dog's feet were burned. By that date, falling tephra had severely damaged the recently constructed fire lookout, located on a rocky pinnacle about a quarter mile from and approximately 200 feet above the active crater. It would soon be leveled to its foundation.

Bad weather obscured many of Lassen's eruptions during the winter, but at least sixty additional events were observed during the first four and a half months of 1915. When E. N. Hampton climbed Lassen on March 23, 1915, he noted that the crater had expanded to a diameter of 1,000 feet.

The winter of 1914–1915, an El Niño year, deposited a record-breaking 33 feet of snow on the northeast flank of Lassen Peak, setting the stage for a spectacular interaction of molten rock with Lassen's snowpack the following spring. Clouds hid the peak from May 7 until the morning of May 14, when brief clearings revealed almost continuous activity that introduced a new phase of the eruption. On the fourteenth, Alice Dines, postmistress at Manton, 20 miles west of the peak, began to telephone her friends that, for the first time, "fire" was visible. Observers saw a ruddy glow emanating from Lassen's summit that night, and again on May 15 and 17. Benjamin Loomis and Alice Dines were the first to see—in daylight—a small black mass pushing up above the western rim of the crater, the top of an incipient dome of dacite lava that now filled Lassen's crater.

The night of May 19 brought the first of two climactic events. As glowing magma rose above the crater rim, it looked as if the volcano were boiling over. In a letter to J. S. Diller, the USGS geologist who later investigated the eruption, G. R. Milford described a deep red glow that illuminated the entire mountaintop. "The whole rim of the crater facing us," Milford wrote, "was marked by a bright red fiery line which wavered for an instant, and then, in a deep red sheet, broke over the lowest part of the lip and was lost to sight for a moment, only to reappear again in the form of countless red globules of fire about 500 feet below the crater's lip." From Milford's vantage point about 21 miles west of Lassen, some of the incandescent "globules" seemed as large as "about three feet in diameter." Milford compared the erupting crater to a "titanic slag-pot being slowly filled by molten slag" and repeatedly overflowing, causing the slag crust to break open and expose deep-red molten material.

Late on the night of May 19 a powerful steam explosion shattered the growing summit dome, ejecting large blocks of hot lava, some weighing 20 tons, onto the snow-covered northeast flanks of the volcano. Avalanching down Lassen's steep northeast face, the mixture of hot rock and snow a half mile wide surged over a low ridge at Emigrant Pass into Hat Creek. As they cascaded downslope, the lava blocks broke up into smaller fragments, rapidly melting the snowpack over which they passed and triggering a large mudflow that cut a wide swath through the forest on Lassen's northeast slope. Carrying freshly erupted debris, downed timber, and large boulders picked up en route, most of the mudflow was deflected northwestward by Emigrant Summit and poured 7 miles down Lost Creek. After coming to rest, both the avalanche and mudflow released large volumes of water, flooding lower Hat Creek valley during the early morning of May 20.

Many of the settlers living along Hat Creek, including Harvey Wilcox, were saved from the inundations by their dogs. Racing barefoot uphill after his dog's barking alerted him, Wilcox watched the flood sweep away his log house, as well as two iron stoves and other household goods. Elmer Sorahan, who was then homesteading near the ranch of his friend Wid Hall, also was awakened by his dog. Sorahan peeped out of his tent to see what he described as a "mudflow coming like a wave twelve feet high. . . . The flood made a roar something like a gale of wind in the trees, with a crash and boom of the logs and rocks as they came tumbling along in the flood." Leaving his possessions behind, Sorahan ran at top speed to Hall's ranch, reaching it only five minutes ahead of the torrent.

While Mrs. Hall telephoned neighbors farther downstream, Sorahan raced across Hat Creek to warn a man who was sleeping in Hall's barn. He made it across the bridge only minutes before it was washed away. All the settlers managed to reach high ground before the flood arrived, but they could not escape its deafening sounds. According to Hall, "The crash and roar of the flood was so intense that you could hardly hear one yell even at a short distance." When the Halls tried to return to their house about 3:00 AM, they found that it had been pushed over 50 feet off its foundations and had lodged against a tree. The floods also wrecked four other

A giant mushroom cloud rises an estimated 7 miles above Lassen's summit, May 22, 1915. View from Anderson, 45 miles west of the volcano. —Courtesy of the National Park Service

ranches, including the prophetically named Lost Camp. Hat Creek residents described the flood as "looking more like mortar than water" and leaving a thick residue as "slick and smooth [as] pavement."

After the May 19 steam explosion destroyed the rising summit dome, unplugging the central vent and triggering the northeast-side hot avalanche and mudflow, less viscous masses of dacite filled Lassen's crater. One arm of the flow spilled through a gap in the west crater rim, where it now forms a conspicuous tongue, about 300 feet wide at the crater lip and 1,000 feet long, of dark, scoriaceous lava clinging to Lassen's west face. Another lobe of lava, flowing through a larger notch in the crater's east rim, oozed 1,000 feet down the northeast slope. This part of the flow was destined to meet the same fate as the incipient dome.

The Great Eruption

The eruptive climax occurred on the afternoon of May 22, after two days of relative quiet. That morning, Benjamin Loomis had hauled his bulky camera and tripod to the east side of the volcano, photographing the devastation caused by the avalanching hot rock and mudflow of May 19 and 20. Loomis's photograph shows Lassen steaming vigorously, with a clear contrast between the dark area buried by the mudflow and the untouched white snowfields bordering it. Although the eruption had swept away a wide band of forest, thick groves of trees remained standing on both sides of the mudflow. Loomis's photo also shows the northeastern lobe of the new lava flow still in place at the summit, a scene that was soon to change radically.

The photographer had fortunately made his way out of the danger zone by 4:30 that afternoon, when Lassen exploded with tremendous violence, sending an enormous column of ash and gas about 35,000 feet into the air. Churning and rolling into a clear blue sky, the mushroom cloud was visible over most of northern California, even from the coastal town of Eureka, 150 miles to the west. As the giant umbrella unfurled, winds carried the ash eastward, where it fell along a narrow lobe at least 200 miles in length.

The Reno Evening Gazette of May 24, 1915, reported that the Nevada villages of Imlay, Elko, Winnemucca, Golcanda, and Gerlach were covered with a fine white ash. The paper also noted that two Western Pacific overland trains arrived late in Oakland, California, "plastered with ashes and a film of mud thrown out by Lassen Peak." Crew members said that they first noticed the falling ash at Winnemucca, about 200 miles east of the volcano; at a distance of 100 miles, the train was enveloped in an ash cloud so dense that they were forced to reduce speed because the train's headlights could not penetrate the darkness. Winnemucca's Humboldt Star recorded that ash began to fall about 8:00 in the evening of May 22 and continued for about

Viewed from Mineral, 11 miles southwest of Lassen, the May 22, 1915, eruption plume soars skyward.
—E. N. Hampton photo, courtesy of the National Park Service

two and a half hours, covering the clothing of people outdoors with a "grayish substance resembling soapstone."

Photographs taken from Red Bluff, Anderson, and other Sacramento Valley towns 40 to 45 miles west of Lassen show only the vertical eruption cloud. On the northeast side of Lassen, however, dense masses of pumice and other incandescent tephra falling on the volcano's precipitous northeast face were transformed into a laterally moving pyroclastic flow that devastated an area of 3 square miles. Following the same path as the earlier hot avalanche and mudflow, but cutting a much broader swath through Lassen's forest, the pyroclastic flow and surge traveled about 4.5 miles downslope, mowing through stands of virgin timber that had survived the previous eruption. According to Mike Clynne of the USGS, trees downed by the May 19 avalanche and mudflow were ripped out of the ground, roots and all, and incorporated into the mudflow. By contrast, trees destroyed by the May 22 eruption typically were broken off several feet above the ground and thrown down hundreds of feet from their original locations, their severed trunks pointing away from the volcano. These trees, as much as 6 feet in diameter, were felled by the blast wave that traveled slightly in advance of the pyroclastic flow, so that they were already lying on the ground when the pyroclastic flow passed over them. Like the downed trees at Mount St. Helens, those at Lassen were commonly stripped of their limbs and bark. According to a forest service estimate, approximately 5.5 million board feet of timber were destroyed.

Rapidly melting much of Lassen's remaining snowpack on the northeast slope, the pyroclastic flow triggered another, highly fluid mudflow that raced nearly 10 miles down Lost Creek to the village of Old Station. Water running out of this new mudflow brought yet another inundation to the lower Hat Creek valley. Battered by two destructive floods in only three days, even the tenacious Wid Hall family decided to move to safer ground.

Lassen's northeast face before 1914, with Jensen Meadow in the foreground.
—Courtesy of the National Park Service

Lassen's northeast face after the mudflow of May 19–20, 1915, and before the May 22 pyroclastic flow. Note the wide swath that the mudflow cut through the forest on Lassen's flank. The large lava block in the left foreground is part of the dacite flow erupted on May 19. —B. F. Loomis photo, courtesy of the National Park Service

The climactic explosions removed the lobe of lava that had poured down the northeast flank, then blasted out a new crater in the lava that had spread over much of the summit following the May 19 dome-shattering explosion. Heat from the shattered lava fragments and fresh tephra sent additional mudflows streaming down the flanks of Lassen Peak, including a few on the west side. According to Mike Clynne, only two of these small mudflows entered Manzanita Creek, and none traveled as far west as Manzanita Lake.

Lassen's Declining Activity: 1915–1921

Although it is probable that no fresh magma erupted after May 22, 1915, Lassen Peak continued to produce a series of moderately explosive phreatic eruptions for another two years, and to steam visibly for several more. J. S. Diller, a geologist who previously had mapped the Lassen region and accurately predicted that it would see future volcanic activity, returned to the area that summer and correctly surmised that the worst was over and that

Lassen would not stage another outburst as large as that of May 22. The presence of a still-hot body of magma inside Lassen's dome, however, indicated that the volcano was not yet ready to go back to sleep. Throughout the summer and fall of 1915, intermittent explosive episodes, some lasting several hours and sending ash columns 10,000 to 12,000 feet into the air, continued to rack the mountain. Much of this declining activity may have been triggered by groundwater trickling into Lassen's hot interior and generating phreatic explosions similar to those of 1914. Flashes of static electricity in ash clouds caused some viewers to think they were seeing molten rock. During October, observers again reported seeing a glow over the crater and "luminous bodies." From Chester, 20 miles east of Lassen, George W. Olson allegedly saw large flashes of light and "bombs" soaring high over the top of the mountain.

The spring of 1917 brought a particularly violent series of explosive eruptions, although these too were probably caused by water from melting snow

View of the area on Lassen's northeast flank devastated by the May 22, 1915, pyroclastic flow. Compare this 1939 photo with the previous one, taken by B. F. Loomis just hours before the hot blast swept the area clean. Although the devastated area had not then begun to recover, today reforestation is well underway. —Courtesy of the National Park Service

coming in contact with hot rock inside the volcano. On April 5, George Olson reported the heaviest eruption he had seen since the big one of May 22, 1915. This was exceeded by a larger event on May 18, 1917, when loud rumblings accompanied an ash cloud 10,000 to 12,000 feet high. Eruptions were nearly continuous for the next two days.

Twenty-one explosive events were reported during June, when the renewed activity reached its height. According to Day and Allen, who published a detailed study of Lassen's historic activity, the June explosions were strong enough to displace large masses of material at the top of the mountain and alter the appearance of the crater. The major change was the blasting out of a new vent on the extreme northwest corner of Lassen's summit. Separated by a thin vertical wall from the much larger bowl-shaped vent that produced the climactic 1915 eruptions, this vent was still issuing tiny wisps of steam as late as the 1970s.

After June 29, 1917, observers noticed no further activity until June 9 and 10, 1919, when Alice Dines noticed "small smoke" rising from the peak. Two more steam emissions were logged on the following April 8 and 9. A year and a half later, in October 1920, Lassen was again seen steaming for ten to twelve hours at a time. The last recorded activity visible at a distance occurred on February 7, 1921, when Dines reported great clouds of white steam issuing from eastern fissures. Climbers reported active steam jets in the two summit craters for decades thereafter. In the 1950s, Paul Schulz, a former Lassen Park naturalist, counted about thirty steam vents still active at the summit. Even these have since diminished so that any thermal activity is now difficult to detect.

Volcanic Evolution of the Lassen Region

Lassen Volcanic National Park, created in 1916, is named after the region's most recently active volcano, but the park encompasses a wide variety of other volcanic landforms, including cinder cones, steep-sided shields, numerous lava domes, and several deeply eroded composite cones. During the last three million years, a sequence of at least five large andesitic stratovolcanoes, including Mount Maidu, formed in the park area, each constructing a massive cone before becoming extinct and undergoing extensive erosion. This series of composite cones produced voluminous mudflows that repeatedly inundated the lowlands west of the Lassen area. The eroded remnants of these ancient mudflows now form the Tuscan formation, an arid deposit littered by large angular lava blocks that is traversed by California 36 on its way to the park's south entrance.

The Lassen region also hosts one of only three calderas known to exist in the Cascade Range (the others are Crater Lake and the Kulshan caldera near Mount Baker). About 614,000 years ago a huge explosive eruption from a vent south of the site of Lassen Peak ejected at least 20 cubic miles of pumice and ash, which blanketed California as far south as Ventura. Known as the Rockland tephra, this deposit lies several inches thick in the San Francisco Bay Area and extends as far east as northern Nevada and southern Idaho. The large collapse depression formed in this paroxysm has since been filled in by later eruptive activity.

A group of closely spaced volcanoes called the Lassen volcanic center began to form shortly after the Rockland tephra erupted, and their lava flows have almost completely obscured the caldera formed by that eruption. Between about 600,000 and 400,000 years ago, the Brokeoff volcano (also called Mount Tehama) built a large composite cone approximately the same size as Mount St. Helens. Standing atop a thick accumulation of deposits from older volcanoes, the Brokeoff cone probably attained a maximum altitude of about 11,000 feet. Subject to repeated Pleistocene glaciations, the Brokeoff cone is now deeply eroded, its dissected remnants forming an irregular semicircular amphitheater open to the southeast. The highest remaining points include Brokeoff Mountain, Mount Conrad, Mount Diller, and Diamond Peak.

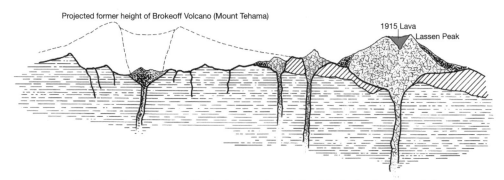

Cross-section of Lassen Peak, showing its relationship to the deeply eroded Brokeoff volcano. The dotted line indicates Brokeoff's profile before erosion.

The demolition of Brokeoff's cone was facilitated by the volcano's extensive hydrothermal system, the steady emission of heat, steam, sulfurous gases, and acidic fluids that percolated through the edifice, chemically transforming once-solid rock to a soft, crumbly mass. Hydrothermal alteration of the volcano's interior continues today; many sections of Brokeoff's erosional caldera display large splotches of white, yellow, orange, and rust-colored rock that are so fragile that a fragment of it crumbles in the hand. Glacial and stream erosion have removed most of the altered material, leaving the mostly unaltered layers of lava as steep cliffs that partly encircle Brokeoff's vanished core. California 89, which winds through the caldera, passes directly by the Sulphur Works, an area of colorful altered rock and odoriferous hot springs and steam vents thought to mark the site of a former Brokeoff conduit. The nearby Bumpass Hell, named for a pioneer who lost a leg from severe burns incurred there, offers an even more extensive thermal

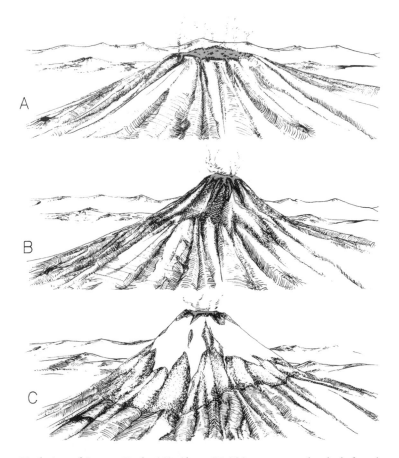

Evolution of Lassen Peak. (A) About 27,000 years ago, shortly before the most recent Pleistocene glacial advance, a dome of viscous dacite lava rose into an old "pre-Lassen" crater. (B) The dome eventually filled and overflowed the original vent. (C) Crumbling fragments from the sides of the plug dome formed aprons of debris around the solid core. Hot avalanches from the sides of the elevating dome created pyroclastic flows. After the Lassen dome formed, Pleistocene glaciers then removed much of the fragmental material, carving a shallow cirque on Lassen's northeast flank.

display, complete with dozens of hot springs, roaring steam vents, and bubbling mud pots—miniature volcanoes that mimic the shape of their larger brethren. (See image 5 on plate 3.) Along with the Devil's Kitchen to the east, these manifestations of continuing volcanic heat comprise the most extensive thermal area in the United States outside of Yellowstone.

Later in the history of the Lassen volcanic center, after activity at Brokeoff's central cone had ceased, flank eruptions of increasingly silicic magma produced a series of more than thirty lava domes on its north slopes. Lassen Peak, about half a cubic mile in volume and one of world's largest lava domes, was born about 27,000 years ago as masses of viscous magma oozed through an older crater, piling up more than 2,000 feet above the vent. When it first emerged, Lassen's dome bristled with spiny protrusions and angular blocks of dacite, most of which have been removed by erosion. About 2,000 years after Lassen appeared, ice-age glaciers again formed, surrounding the dome on three sides (west, south, and east) up to an elevation of about 9,000 feet. Originating on the upper north face, another glacier carved a broad cirque on the north and northeast flanks. When the last glacial advance ended in

View north from the summit of Brokeoff Mountain, the highest remnant of ancient Mount Tehama, toward Lassen Peak. Glacial and stream cutting hollowed out Tehama's hydrothermally altered interior, excavating an erosional caldera (right center).
—Douglas Tustin photo

this part of the range about 15,000 years ago, Lassen's dome was left mantled in layers of rocky talus. Only on the south side, near the parking lot adjacent to the summit trailhead, do several sheer pinnacles still rise above the aprons of crumble breccia that cover the rest of the dome.

Chaos Crags and Chaos Jumbles

Standing about 1,800 feet above their surroundings immediately northwest of Lassen Peak, the cluster of smaller domes known as Chaos Crags erupted about 1,100 years ago, which makes it the youngest part of the Lassen volcanic center dome field. The sequence of eruptive events that produced the Crags—moving from violently explosive to quietly effusive—resembles that of the most recent activity at Mono-Inyo Craters. When a gas-rich column of rising dacite magma broke the surface, it produced powerful explosions, blasting a vertical column of pumice and ash several miles into the air and shooting pyroclastic flows outward from the vent. Even after most of the gas had escaped from the magma, the rising dacite domes were extremely

Aerial view southeast toward Chaos Crags and Chaos Jumbles. The rockfalls compos-ing the Jumbles (lower center) dammed the local drainage, forming Manzanita Lake. Lassen Peak (center) looms above the younger Crags domes, with remnants of Brokeoff volcano on the right. —Robert Krimmel photo, U.S. Geological Survey

unstable, their steep sides partially collapsing to form additional pyroclastic flows of incandescent blocks and lithic ash. Of the six domes emplaced, the oldest was blown away during one of the pyroclastic eruptions, leaving only five still standing.

Even after they had cooled, the Chaos Crags remained dangerous. About 350 years ago, one of the northern domes collapsed, generating three huge rockfalls and creating the area called Chaos Jumbles. The first and largest of the rockfalls traveled 4 miles downslope and had enough energy to climb 400 feet up the side of Table Mountain before being deflected and continuing on to the west. The series of rockfalls radically changed the local topography, burying about 4.5 square miles under a thick layer of angular blocks and damming Manzanita Creek to form Manzanita Lake. What triggered the rockfalls is unknown, though it may have been an earthquake. When the Brewer survey party visited the Lassen area in 1864, some local settlers reported that the northern dome was still steaming, a claim that has not been verified.

As with all of the higher Cascade volcanoes, sudden rockfalls remain a potential threat to visitors in the Lassen vicinity. In the summer of 1993, a rockfall of 13,000 cubic yards (which geologist Mike Clynne compared to the volume of about 500 minivans) swept partway down the northeast flank of Lassen Peak. Fortunately there was no one in its path. Not only climbers heading for the summit but also backpackers and hikers at lower elevations must recognize the inherent instability of many volcanic edifices—even when the volcano is completely dormant—and the multiple hazards they may represent.

Cinder Cone

Rising about 700 feet above its base in the northeast corner of Lassen Park, Cinder Cone is dwarfed by the much more imposing bulk of Prospect Peak, the timber-covered shield volcano that towers more than 1,400 feet above it. Almost perfectly symmetrical, surrounded by masses of mostly unvegetated blocky lava, and boasting two fresh-looking concentric craters (one nested inside the other) at its top, Cinder Cone has the unmerited reputation of being one of California's most recently active volcanoes. (See image 3 on plate 2.)

Several observers attested that they had seen it erupting in 1850 and 1851, all from a distance of 40 miles or more. According to the San Francisco *Daily Pacific News* (August 21, 1850), however, one unidentified witness actually ventured "as near to the base of the cone as the heat would permit" and saw "burning lava running down the sides of the volcano," an assertion geologists consider highly unlikely because lava almost invariably erupts from vents at the base of a cinder cone. Similar reports printed in other newspaper articles and even in later scientific journals contributed to a tradition that Cinder Cone's last lava flow, which extends in a long narrow tongue over the rugged surface of earlier flows to the shores of Butte Lake, erupted in 1850–1851. In 1875, Harvey W. Harkness, a medical doctor and amateur scientist, delivered a paper describing Cinder Cone's alleged eruptions at a meeting of the California Academy of Sciences. Afterward, an Academy member told him of two gold prospectors who, in the spring of 1851, claimed to have seen the volcano eject "fire up to a terrible height," adding that they had walked 10 miles over rocks so hot that their boots were destroyed.

Although these reports and several earlier geologic studies seemed to confirm Cinder Cone's mid-nineteenth-century activity, they conflict with the physical evidence. A team of USGS scientists who recently studied the volcano's history concluded that it has not been active since the cone was originally built, about AD 1650. Several methods used to date its deposits, including the magnetic orientation of its lavas, radiocarbon measurements,

Built only 350 years ago in the northeast corner of Lassen Park, Cinder Cone is the youngest volcano in the Cascade Range. —Doug Tustin photo

and calculations of the age of trees killed or damaged by the eruptions, all agree that Cinder Cone was formed about 350 years ago, perhaps within a few decades of the rockfalls that formed Chaos Jumbles.

Perhaps the most eloquent testimony indicating that Cinder Cone had not erupted in 1850–1851 is the presence of a long-lived willow bush growing near the summit crater. Conspicuous even today because it is one of the few spots of green visible on the cone's charcoal gray slopes, the solitary willow was already thriving in 1853. When he made his reconnaissance study of Lassen's geology in the 1880s, Joseph S. Diller interviewed settlers who had traveled past the cone on the Nobles Emigrant Trail in 1853 and found that they distinctly remembered sighting the shrub, which was almost as large then as it is now. Growing near the crater rim, it could not have survived the showers of hot tephra that supposedly occurred only two years earlier.

Although erected during a single eruptive episode that may have lasted only a few months to a year, Cinder Cone has a complex history. An older cone was mostly destroyed by two streams of basaltic andesite lava that poured south to dam Grassy Creek, forming Snag Lake, named for the drowned trees submerged by its rising waters. Ash falling on the flows while they were still hot were brightly oxidized, forming smooth ash blankets splotched in reddish brown, rust, and orange—and giving this lava the name Painted Dunes (see image 4 on plate 2). After Strombolian eruptions built the present scoria cone, two more lava streams largely free of ash cover—the Fantastic Lava Beds flows—traveled to the north, where they entered Butte Lake, filling much of its former lake basin. Although Cinder Cone, like other monogenetic volcanoes, is not expected to erupt again, future eruptions will construct similar new cones almost anywhere in the eastern section of Lassen Park, where basalt and basaltic andesite magmas predominate.

Other Volcanism in the Lassen Park Vicinity

Throughout most of its history, volcanism in the Lassen region has been strongly episodic, with clusters of eruptions followed by long intervals of quiet. This irregular pattern of eruptive activity has continued into the late Pleistocene and Holocene. Although about 26,000 years elapsed between the formation of Lassen Peak and the Chaos Crags eruptions, the last millennium has witnessed a flurry of activity that radically changed the Lassen landscape: the sudden rise of six dacite domes accompanied by ejections of tephra and pyroclastic flows; the construction of Cinder Cone and its extensive lava fields; the rockfalls creating Chaos Jumbles; and the early-twentieth-century eruptions of Lassen Peak.

During the last 50,000 years, the Lassen area produced a total of about seven major episodes of silicic volcanism (dacite domes, tephra, and pyroclastic flows) and five additional episodes of basaltic and andesite lava flows. During the same time span in nearby areas outside the park, about thirty smaller volcanoes erupted basaltic magma, some of them as part of a single eruptive event.

One of the more spectacular eruptions occurred in Hat Creek valley immediately north of Lassen Park. An elongated north-south depression, or graben, the valley was formed when a block of crustal rock sank more than 1,000 feet below the steep ridge bordering its eastern margin. About 25,000 to 30,000 years ago, a fissure opened on a hillside near the valley's southern end, a short distance south of the present village of Old Station. Fire fountains jetted from numerous vents, building a chain of spatter cones (formed by accumulations of plastic lava globs blown into the air) and feeding torrents of molten basalt that flooded the valley floor for 16 miles to the north. Erupted at temperatures of at least 2,200 degrees Fahrenheit, the pahoehoe lava advanced through long tubes that formed beneath the flow's solidifying outer crust. As the production of magma dwindled and the eruptions ended, the liquid rock, insulated inside the flow, drained out, leaving behind a series of lava tube caves similar to those at Lava Beds National Monument. When the solidified rock roofing the tubes collapsed, these openings in the flow's surface provided a "skylight" entrance to the tubes inside. One of the largest and most accessible of the lava tubes is Subway Cave, located just north of Old Station. Although open to the public, this spacious basaltic cavern has not been wired for electricity; visitors wishing to explore the interior of this pahoehoe flow, which contains stalactites formed by liquid basalt that dripped from the ceiling, must bring their own flashlights.

Visiting Lassen Peak

Of all the major Cascade volcanoes, Lassen Peak is the easiest and safest to climb. Take California 89, the main route through Lassen Volcanic National Park, to the point where it crosses the mountain's southeast shoulder, a few miles north of the Sulphur Works thermal area. The summit trail begins at a parking lot on the north side of California 89, a location watched over by Vulcan's Eye, an icon carved by nature on the face of a massive dacite protrusion on the south side of Lassen's dome. Starting at an elevation of 8,500 feet, the well-graded trail is a 2.5-mile series of switchbacks, taking about 3.5 to 4 hours round trip for people in good condition. At the top the trail branches: the right-hand (northeast) path leads to the highest crag at 10,457 feet. From the northeast summit, climbers can look down the path of the 1915 mudflow that flooded Hat Creek valley. Prospect Peak, with Cinder Cone crouching at its foot, is visible to the northeast. The other branch at the top of the trail, which is less well marked, veers northwesterly across the jagged masses of dark dacite which flowed over the summit area in 1915. After scrambling over the lava's angular crustal blocks, the hiker will find two bowl-shaped craters, the smaller of which was blasted open at the northwest summit in 1917. In clear weather, Shasta is visible 80 miles to the north.

The summit trail is usually open in late June—though it is partly covered with snow until mid-July—and remains in use until the first heavy snows of October or November.

CHAPTER 7

Mount Shasta

MOUNTAIN OF MENACE AND MYSTERY

Glacier-crowned Mount Shasta (14,162 feet) is the largest composite cone in the Cascade Range, its huge bulk containing 85 to 90 cubic miles of lava. It is also the highest landform in the continental United States when measured from base to summit. An exceptionally long-lived volcano, it began to erupt almost 600,000 years ago and has remained active into historic time. It was almost certainly the "flaming" peak that the explorer La Perouse observed in 1786 while sailing a Spanish ship off the coast of northern California. "Only four leagues" from shore, La Perouse "perceived a volcano on the top of a mountain, which bore east of us; its flame was very lively, but a thick fog soon deprived us of this sight." Through radiocarbon dating of its deposits, geologists have confirmed that Shasta's most recent eruption, which generated pyroclastic flows, mudflows, and a conspicuous layer of gray ash blanketing some areas east of the peak, took place about 200 years ago. It was probably one phase of this eruptive episode that La Perouse briefly glimpsed.

Mount Shasta is second only to St. Helens as the most frequently active volcano in the Cascades. During the last 10,000 years, Shasta has erupted on the average of once every 600 to 800 years, a pace that seems to have accelerated in recent centuries to an average of once every 200 to 300 years. Many of Shasta's Holocene eruptions were extremely voluminous, radically altering the shape and appearance of the volcano. In one particularly active period, between about 9,700 and 9,400 years ago, copious outpourings of andesite lava built Shastina on Shasta's west flank. If it stood alone, Shastina would today rank as the third-highest peak in the range, with only Rainier and Shasta itself exceeding its altitude of 12,300 feet. Shortly after Shastina's phenomenally rapid construction, eruptions of thick lava flows from a vent high on Shasta's north side built the present summit cone. Named the Hotlum cone after the large glacier on its north face, this youthful edifice—the site of all later Holocene activity on Shasta—is almost untouched by erosion.

Around the time of the construction of Shastina about 9,700 years ago, another vent near Shasta's summit produced the volcano's largest Holocene explosive eruption, discharging a large quantity of pumiceous tephra over a broad area to the northeast. The Red Banks tephra, named for a layer of reddish orange pumice almost 200 feet thick at the head of Avalanche

Mount Shasta from the northwest, with Shastina on the right and the Hotlum cone on the left. The Bolam glacier mantles the Hotlum's north flank, while Whitney glacier occupies the saddle between the main summit and Shastina. Shasta hosts the only glaciers in the lower forty-eight states that are significantly growing. —Lyn Topinka photo, U.S. Geological Survey, Cascades Volcano Observatory

Gulch on Shasta's south side, makes a useful time marker for dating other Holocene deposits. Extruded after the Red Banks event, two of Shasta's most conspicuous lava flows directly overlie this widespread tephra sheet. The massive Lava Park flow, which emerged from a fissure just below the present terminal moraine of the Whitney glacier (which postdates the flow by several millennia), traveled 4 miles or more down Shasta's northwest flank. At least 360 feet thick at its terminus, with a surface of huge, angular blocks, the Lava Park flow can be viewed from U.S. 97 a few miles north of Weed. Approximately 9,500 years old, the flow surface supports little vegetation—typically scrub juniper and clumps of sagebrush—although a few Douglas fir trees up to 3 feet in diameter grow near the vent area.

Shasta's longest Holocene lava stream, the Military Pass flow, issued near the summit of the Hotlum cone and streamed about 5.5 miles down the volcano's steep northeast slope. The youngest known flow on the mountain, it too lies atop the Red Banks pumice layer and its associated fan of pyroclastic flow deposits. Almost 500 feet thick at its snout, this blocky flow remains mostly vegetation free. Other lava flows from the summit vent were usually shorter, rapidly stacking up to form the steep Hotlum cone. Silicic lava domes extruded at or near Shasta's summit, including those forming the present summit crags, were commonly disrupted or shattered as they rose, forming pyroclastic flows of incandescent dome fragments and ash that swept down the volcano's flanks.

The frequency and nature of Shasta's recent eruptions is of more than academic interest to the thousands of people living in the nearby communities of Dunsmuir, Mount Shasta, Weed, and McCloud, or to the hundreds of thousands of travelers and truckers who regularly depend on access to the three crucial highways that partly encircle its base. Skirting the broad apron of pyroclastic and mudflow deposits underlying Shasta's smooth west flank, Interstate 5 is the Pacific Coast's main north-south transportation corridor, connecting southern California with southwestern Canada. U.S. 97, which branches northwest from Interstate 5 at Weed and traverses the volcano's north flank, forms the principal route through central Oregon to eastern Washington. California 89, linking Interstate 5 with McCloud, Lassen Park, the northern Sierra Nevada, and U.S. 395, crosses some of Shasta's youngest mudflow deposits. When Shasta next erupts, disruption of these essential arteries—not to mention the railroad line that daily conveys Amtrack passengers and millions of dollars worth of freight through the area—could result in crippling economic losses.

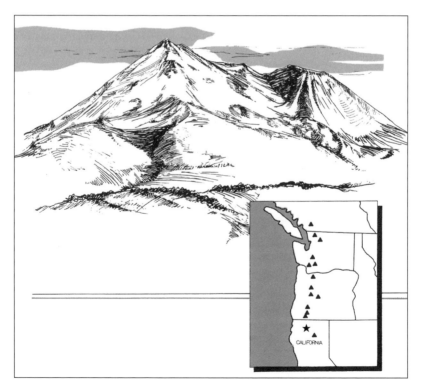

Mount Shasta from the north, with its location in the Cascade Range

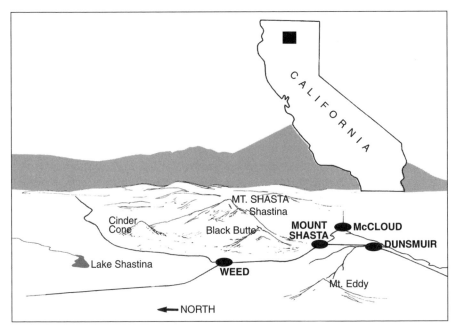

Relief map of the Mount Shasta area

Shasta's Volcanic History

The poet Joaquin Miller famously described Mount Shasta, rising in isolated, snow-mantled splendor above lesser mountains, as "lonely as God and white as a winter moon." Since its inception midway through Pleistocene time, Shasta has reigned supreme over its surroundings, during quiet intervals as a benign white sentinel and during eruptions as a frightening force of nature.

Shasta's most catastrophic impact on the landscape occurred between about 380,000 and 300,000 years ago, after it had already erected an ancestral cone perhaps as large as the present Mount Shasta. At that time, the entire northwest side of the mountain collapsed, creating what is probably the largest landslide in the geologic history of North America. In a series of massive debris avalanches that cut progressively deeper into the cone, approximately 11 cubic miles of water-saturated rock plunged into the Shasta Valley, a broad depression between the Klamath Mountains to the west and the Cascade Range to the east. Today, the valley, though which the Shasta River flows north to join the Klamath River, is characterized by hundreds of mounds, hills, and ridges formed by the avalanche deposits, which extend 28 miles from the mountain. Separated by hollows or flat areas, the hills and ridges are formed by enormous blocks of andesite lava, some several hundred feet in diameter. The flat areas between the hills, some of which are 600 to 700 feet high, consist of deposits of sand, silt, clay, and rock fragments derived chiefly from the volcano, material deposited by the avalanches' more fluid components. (See image 7 on plate 4.) It was only after geologists studied the similarly hummocky terrain formed by the 1980 debris avalanche at Mount St. Helens that they recognized the origin of the material filling Shasta Valley.

Although the cataclysmic collapse of Shasta's northwest side probably left a huge horseshoe-shaped crater resembling the one now present at Mount St. Helens, lava flows and pyroclastic material from subsequent eruptions have completely refilled the depression. The only visible remnant of the ancestral volcano consists of some andesite lavas exposed east of McBride Spring on Shasta's west flank. The oldest known rock on the mountain, these flows erupted about 593,000 years ago.

The modern Mount Shasta is composed of four large overlapping cones, each formed during a separate eruptive episode lasting from a few centuries to several thousand years. Each cycle of cone building followed a similar sequence, beginning with voluminous effusions of andesite lava, mostly from a central vent, that erected the main edifice. As the magma gradually became more silicic over time, the final part of the cycle produced dacite domes at the summit, some of which collapsed while still hot to form lithic pyroclastic flows. After the cone-building eruptions declined, both of Shasta's two older cones underwent extensive erosion, with smaller eruptions occurring sporadically both at the main crater and along the volcano's outer flanks. The flank eruptions typically produced cinder cones, small lava cones, and domes, a profusion of which lie scattered across Shasta's lower slopes.

The Sargents Ridge cone, the largest and oldest of the four main cones built after the ancestral volcano's collapse, is no more than 250,000 years old. Exposed primarily on Shasta's south side, the Sargents Ridge cone—named for the long jagged ridge extending down the south flank—underwent two extensive Pleistocene glaciations, which carved deep glacial trenches, such as the canyon now containing Mud Creek, and removed much of the volcano's original constructional surface.

After a long period of little or no activity, a new vent opened on the deeply eroded north flank of Sargents Ridge, building the cone known as Misery Hill, named for the long slope of dark, hummocky material across which climbers toil on their way to the present summit. The Misery Hill cone, which forms much of the upper part of Mount Shasta, is younger than about 130,000 years, but was severely eroded during the latest Pleistocene glaciation, which cut deeply into the structure, dissecting the dacite dome intruded into its summit crater during its last stages of activity. Shortly after the Pleistocene glaciers dwindled, moderately explosive eruptions built a small pyroclastic structure on the west face of Misery Hill, about a mile and a half from the summit. The well-preserved east rim of this cone contains Sisson Lake in its crater; younger lavas from Shastina have buried the western part.

Postglacial eruptions erected the two youngest of Shasta's four principal cones, Shastina and the Hotlum cone. Rising about a half mile west of Sisson crater, Shastina largely duplicated the eruptive cycle at Misery Hill. The bulk of the cone is formed of pyroxene andesite, but the four or five overlapping domes that largely fill Shastina's broad summit crater are composed of pyroxene-hornblende dacite. The volcano's steep upper slopes are heavily mantled in rocky talus derived from partial collapse of the rising domes. Explosions and hot avalanches accompanying the growth of Shastina's summit domes probably helped carve Diller Canyon, the deep V-shaped gash in the crater's west rim that extends far down Shastina's flanks. About a quarter of a mile wide and as much as 400 feet deep, this ravine may largely have

MAJOR VOLCANIC EVENTS AT SHASTA DURING THE LAST 10,000 YEARS

APPROXIMATE AGE (YEARS)	EVENT	AREAS AFFECTED
200	Pyroclastic flows; hot mudflows; several cold mudflows from Hotlum cone	East, southeast, north, and northwest flanks
700	Block-and-ash flow from Hotlum cone; one hot and six cold mudflows	North and east flanks
750	Hot and cold mudflows	East side
1,800	Several pyroclastic flows and mudflows from Hotlum cone	North, northeast, and east flanks
2,000–3,000	Pyroclastic flows; andesite lava flows, mudflows from Hotlum cone	Almost all flanks
3,400	Pyroclastic flow from Hotlum cone	Northeast flank
4,500–5,000	Hot mudflow; andesite lava flows from Hotlum cone	Lava flows traveled 3.5 miles down north flank
6,000	Pyroclastic flows; mudflows	North and south flanks
9,000–10,000	Intense cone-building activity at both Shastina and Hotlum cone: andesite lava flows, domes, pyroclastic flows, mudflows; Red Banks pumice eruption and pyroclastic flows; extrusion of summit domes at Shastina and Black Butte	All flanks of the mountain. Pyroclastic flows from Shastina and Black Butte covered a wide area along Shasta's west flank

Source: Adapted from Miller, 1980

Aerial view of Shastina's summit crater. The crater rim is breached on the west (left) by a deep cleft that heads Diller Canyon. The snow-covered mounds partly filling Shastina's crater are plug domes blocking the volcano's central conduit. —Courtesy of Mary Hill

been excavated by the erosive power of extremely abrasive pyroclastic flows, which were generated by the repeated partial collapse of domes rising in Shastina's half-mile-wide crater. Subsequent erosion has further modified the canyon.

At the end of the few centuries during which Shastina's cone was built, a cluster of steep dacite lava domes erupted from a vent at its western foot. Standing about 2,500 feet above Interstate 5, which cuts across its western base, Black Butte's elevating domes also repeatedly shattered, producing a series of pyroclastic flows that traveled several miles from the vent. Altogether, pyroclastic flows from Shastina and Black Butte buried 43 square miles, including large portions of the town sites of Weed and Mount Shasta.

The Hotlum Cone

The youngest and highest part of Mount Shasta, the Hotlum cone began to form on the north side of Misery Hill following the Red Banks tephra and pyroclastic flow eruptions of about 9,700 years ago. Built primarily of andesite lava flows, the Hotlum edifice contains some flows that are notably thick and stubby. From a distance, these high-sided lobes, prominent on the north and northeast flanks of the mountain, resemble eroded ridges. They are, however, original constructional features that form step-like terraces just below the summit.

As with its three predecessors, the Hotlum cone was invaded by a silicic dome, the highest crags of which form the present summit. The latest eruption, about 200 years ago, probably shattered part of a rising lobe of the summit dome, generating a hot pyroclastic flow, a hot mudflow, and three cold mudflows that swept about 7.5 miles down Ash Creek, the deep canyon eroded on Shasta's east flank. Another mudflow traveled at least 12 miles down Mud Creek, burying areas now inhabited. Ash clouds accompanying partial collapse of the summit dome and the resulting pyroclastic flows probably contributed to the sandlike charcoal gray ash blanketing open surfaces east of the volcano, a composite layer formed incrementally during numerous eruptions throughout the Holocene.

Shasta's poorly defined summit crater, a shallow, snow-filled depression about 600 feet long, lies between the highest pinnacles bordering it on the northeast and a much lower rim on the west. It is distinguished by a hot, acidic sulfurous spring that emerges near the foot of the topmost spires, staining the adjacent snow and ground surface a dirty yellow. A second

Aerial view showing three of Shasta's main cones. The largely uneroded Hotlum cone (top) occupies the north flank of the older Misery Hill cone (right). Whitney glacier (center) descends between these two edifices and Shastina, whose wide crater appears in the right foreground. —Austin Post photo, U.S. Geological Survey

group of small fumaroles is located on the north side of the summit crags. Earlier and more intense hydrothermal activity has altered much of the summit rock.

A feeble steam eruption may have occurred as late as the mid-nineteenth century. In 1855 Nelson Harvey Eddy reported seeing "three puffs of smoke" rise from the summit and drift southward. The son of a tribal chieftain from the Shasta area recalled that his father, as a young man in the 1850s, had also seen "smoke" issuing from the top of the volcano. An account of the first ascent of Shasta, made in August 1854, also suggests that thermal activity at the summit was then more vigorous than it is today. According to a climbing party from Yreka, "a cluster of boiling hot sulphur springs, about a dozen in number, emitting any amount of steam, smoke, gas, etc.," was sputtering on the edge of a snowfield just below the summit pinnacle. Captain I. D. Pearce, who led the ascent, added that "the ground for fifty yards around [was] considerably settled and completely covered with sulphur, and the rocks [were] hot enough to cook an egg in five minutes." Today, thermal activity in the crater has been reduced to a single active spring, which in dry weather produces only about a pint of sulfurous hot water per minute. Infrared images taken during aerial surveys of Shasta's summit detected several thermal abnormalities, which may correspond to the sites of active steam vents reported by early climbers.

Mount Shasta's Glaciers

During Pleistocene time, Mount Shasta was repeatedly enveloped in ice. Alpine glaciers then extended downslope many miles from the peak, thoroughly scouring the volcanic edifice. Even on the south slope, glaciers rose to within 100 feet of the summits of the domes and cinder cones dotting Shasta's flanks. Although later eruptions buried most glacier deposits on the north, northwest, and northeast sides of the mountain, the large gullies and cirques carved in the Sargents Ridge and Misery Hill cones are clearly visible on the south and southeast flanks. Several glacial moraines form long ridges along the Everett Memorial Highway as it winds up Shasta's southwest side to campsites near timberline.

The nine or ten glaciers mantling Shasta today, including Whitney, Bolam, Hotlum, Wintun, and Konwakiton, are much smaller than their ice age predecessors, with none extending below an elevation of 9,500 feet. Rather than shrunken remnants of Pleistocene glaciers, they were probably formed during recent Holocene cool phases, such as the Little Ice Age of about AD 1350–1850. Although most of Shasta's perennial ice fields occur on the Hotlum cone, they have not yet had time to carve cirques or deep trenches on its slopes. Glacial deposits on the Hotlum cone older than a few centuries are

largely buried by younger volcanic deposits. The total absence of erosional
gullies and the lack of significant soil oxidation on Hotlum's unweathered
lava flows indicates the geologic youth of both the cone and some of the
ice streams mantling it.

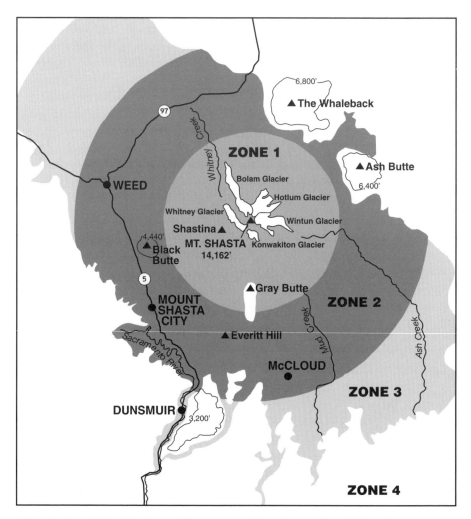

*Volcanic hazards in the Mount Shasta area reflect degrees of risk from future eruptions
involving pyroclastic flows and surges, lateral blasts, and mudflows. Zone 1 areas are likely
to be affected most severely and frequently during future activity. Zone 2 areas are at intermediate risk from pyroclastic flows. Zone 3 areas are likely to be affected by mudflows
and ash clouds accompanying pyroclastic flows in zones 1 and 2, or by exceptionally large
pyroclastic flows. Zone 4 areas (mainly valley floors and other depressions) are likely to
be affected only by mudflows. Lava flows may erupt on any side of the volcano but are not
likely to extend more than about 9 miles from the summit.* —Adapted from Miller, 1980

A USGS study of Mount Shasta's glaciers in the mid-1980s revealed that the volcano's ice cover totals about 4.7 billion cubic feet (about 0.1 cubic mile), only a tenth of that shrouding Mount Rainier. More than a quarter of the ice is contained in the main lobe of the Hotlum glacier, which covers an area of 19.4 million square feet and has a volume of 1.3 billion cubic feet. The Whitney glacier, which occupies the saddle between the Hotlum cone and Shastina and extends over 14 million square feet, is the source of Whitney Creek, the main stream on the volcano's northwest flank. Although its volume is only 0.9 billion cubic feet, it has the greatest thickness of ice measured on Mount Shasta—126 feet. Ninety-four percent of Shasta's permanent snow and ice cover lies above 10,000 feet, with the largest ice masses perched above the drainages of Mud, Ash, Gravel, Bolam, and Whitney Creeks and the valleys of the Sacramento and McCloud Rivers.

When Slawek Tulaczyk and Ian Howat of the University of California, Santa Cruz, began a new study of Shasta's glaciers in the early 2000s, they found that these ice streams—unlike those on most other Cascade volcanoes—are vigorously growing. Between 1951 and 2002, the Hotlum and Wintun glaciers approximately doubled in area, while the Bolam grew about 50 percent, and the Whitney and Konwakiton by about a third (see chapter 22). Tulaczyk ascribes the expansion of Shasta's ice cover to a climatic cycle of increased precipitation.

Tulaczyk also noted that Shasta's present glaciers typically lack well-defined lateral moraines, primarily because they generally extend along the margins of thick lava flows. Constrained by lava ridges, the ice cuts into and erodes the high-standing flow margins, the source of the rock debris that litters much of the ice surface. As Tulaczyk observes, the large quantity of debris covering or imbedded in glacial ice significantly increases the potential for hazardous debris flows when the glaciers recede—or suddenly melt during an eruption.

Eruptive activity melting glacial ice has caused most of Shasta's numerous mudflows, but some have occurred even when the volcano was dormant. Heavy rains or rapid melting of snow during unusually hot summers can also generate destructive mudflows. In 1924 the Konwakiton glacier, which now terminates at a high cliff at the head of Mud Creek canyon, virtually broke in half when floods of meltwater pouring downslope from the summit area permeated the glacier's interior, causing the lower section to collapse. A torrent of water bursting from the glacier's truncated snout poured down Mud Creek canyon, which is 1,500 feet deep, carrying blocks of ice and rock fragments that undermined the canyon walls, temporarily damming the stream. When the impounded floodwaters broke through the barrier, they raced down Mud Creek valley, finally spreading out as thick sheets of liquid mud and rock debris near the town of McCloud.

Runoff containing finer silt drained into the McCloud River and eventually into the Pit and Sacramento Rivers. Because Shasta Dam, which now holds back the Sacramento River, forming the huge reservoir of Shasta Lake, did not then exist, floodborne sediments were carried all the way to San Francisco Bay. Similar floods occurred in 1926 and 1931.

Drought and hot summers in the mid-1970s initiated another series of small mudflows. In the summer of 1977, after a light winter snowfall, rapid melting of Shasta's ice cover sent mudflows traveling down almost every canyon heading at a glacier. Bouldery mudflows, some 15 to 18 feet thick, streamed more than 12 miles down Ash Creek, Mud Creek, and the Bolam and Whitney Creek valleys. Confined to deep ravines until they reached the mountain's base, the mudflows spread out over broad fans of older debris flows. In 1997, additional debris flows down the Bolam-Whitney Creek drainage buried about a third of a mile of U.S. 97.

Although sufficient to supply countless future floods and mudflows, Shasta's present ice fields are relatively modest, partly because of the volcano's southerly location, where average temperatures are higher and periods of sunshine longer than they are farther north in the range, keeping the permanent snow level at about 11,000 feet. In addition, annual rain and snowfall on Shasta is considerably less than it is on Mounts Baker, Rainier, or Hood. The nearby Klamath Mountains intercept the moisture-laden air moving inland from the Pacific before it can bring precipitation to Shasta. As a result, Shasta is much drier and has a much scantier tree cover than either the Cascade peaks to the north or the Sierra to the south. After logging companies stripped the mountain of its old-growth forest in the late 1800s, little of the timber has grown back. Expanses of wiry manzanita and isolated clumps of stunted juniper have replaced the once-thick conifer forest encircling Shasta's base.

The Magic Mountain

Late-nineteenth-century lumber barons so thoroughly denuded the mountain that even the Sierra Club subsequently has made few sustained attempts to preserve Shasta as a national park or monument (concluding that there is relatively little left to save). However, the volcano remains almost irresistibly attractive to thousands of New Age devotees and members of various mystical cults. Adherents of many disparate groups flock to the town of Mount Shasta, giving an almost bewildering variety of reasons for their fascination with the mountain. With little in common except a conviction that Shasta is a "holy place"—a view they share with many Native Americans, both past and present, who also lived under Shasta's spell—such esoteric organizations as the Knights of the White Rose, the Rosicrucians, the Gathering of the

Ways, the Association Sanandra and Sanat Kumara, the Radiant School of the Seekers and Servers, and the I AM Foundation have made Mount Shasta a kind of holy grail that lures pilgrims from all over the world.

One of the most persistent legends about Shasta presents it as the home of the Lemurians, mysterious survivors from the lost kingdom of Mu, an ancient continent now submerged beneath the Pacific Ocean. Reputed to be 7 feet tall, the Lemurians are distinguished by a special eye in the middle of their foreheads, which apparently gives them extrasensory perception, as well as the ability to materialize or vanish at will. Although ordinarily unapproachable, these elusive creatures have permitted a few privileged souls to tour the elaborate tunnel system they have created within the mountain.

The most famous instance of Lemurian-related apparitions on Shasta allegedly took place about 1930, when Guy W. Ballard, a Chicago paperhanger, had a life-changing experience high on the mountain's slopes. In his book *Unveiled Mysteries,* Ballard describes meeting an entity he called St. Germain, "a majestic figure, God-like in appearance, clad in jeweled robes, eyes sparkling with light and love." Responding to this encounter with the numinous rather like Moses on Mount Sinai, Ballard came down from the sacred mountain to found a new religion, the I AM movement, the largest of Shasta's many occult groups.

According to some other sects, the Lemurians are not the only beings to inhabit Shasta's honeycombed interior. The Secret Commonwealth, which dwells in the subterranean cities of Betheleme and Yaktayvia, are also sequestered inside the mountain. According to "authoritative sources," the Yaktayvians have used the technique of ringing specially cast bells to excavate vast underground caverns in which to build their cities. Supersonic vibrations from mighty Yaktayvian bells and chimes not only hollowed out spacious caverns, but also supply those who live in them with heat and light. Producing eerie, high-pitched sounds, the bells also serve to frighten off intruders who might otherwise invade the Yaktayvians' treasured privacy. How these populous folk manage to share their space with the Lemurians, Atlanteans, and several other lost tribes who have set up housekeeping inside Shasta is not known. Nor is it understood how such denizens of the underworld have survived the repeated infusions of molten rock into the volcano's internal plumbing.

While some believers view Shasta as a secret refuge for lost terrestrial cultures, others see the mountain as a landing field for visitors from outer space. Given the mountain's reputation as a sacred place, it is not surprising that some observers report sighting UFOs hovering near the peak. Perhaps stimulated by the luminous disc-shaped clouds that frequently form over the summit, many eyewitnesses claim to have seen spaceships congregating there from distant planets in the galaxy. Like the ancient Babylonians who built lofty ziggurats as pedestals for the gods to descend to earth, thus bringing the divine into the human sphere, many contemporary believers see Mount Shasta as a unique point of intersection between the world of spirit and our familiar material world.

Visiting Mount Shasta

In clear weather, California's highest stratovolcano is easily visible from many points in the northern Sacramento Valley and from as far north as the south rim of Crater Lake. Although Interstate 5 passes directly by Shasta's west base, it does not always afford the most flattering views of the peak, particularly when the west and south sides of the mountain are largely bare of snow (usually from early summer to midfall). Even in summer, Shasta shows its best profile to travelers heading south on U.S. 97; from this perspective, the Hotlum, Bolam, and Whitney glaciers mantle the summit in glistening white. (See image 6 on plate 3.)

Starting in the town of Mount Shasta, the Everett Memorial Highway winds 15 miles across Shasta's southwest side to an elevation of 7,703 feet at the Mount Shasta Ski Park. From this location on the old Sargents Ridge cone, however, neither Shastina nor the actual summit is visible.

To see the seldom-visited east side of the mountain (in a car that can safely negotiate a rutted dirt byway), take the Military Pass Road, which branches from U.S. 97 about 15 miles north of Weed; the turnoff is marked by a bronze tablet commemorating the Emigrant Trail. This little-traveled route continues for 32 miles, connecting with California 89 immediately east of McCloud.

The most frequently climbed route to the summit is Avalanche Gulch, which begins at the Sierra Club's Horse Camp on the southwest side. A 2-mile trail from the Everett Memorial Highway crosses Bunny Flat to the Sierra Club's Alpine Lodge, a small stone building that is usually overflowing with campers. Typically crowded on weekends during the climbing season, the Avalanche Gulch route wends over Olberman's Causeway, a well-marked stone pathway leading from the lodge partway up the gulch; then the trail rises steeply over long expanses of glacier-broken rock fragments interspersed with snowfields. Standing at the head of Avalanche Gulch are the Red Banks, 200-foot cliffs of crumbling pumice. Crampons are recommended for climbing this formation, the most dangerous part of the ascent. The long ridge of Misery Hill leads north to the crater and summit crags of Hotlum cone. Although the vertical distance from Horse Camp to the summit is only 7,100 feet, it is a long and arduous climb demanding considerable stamina. Because of unpredictable rockfalls, snow avalanches, and steep, slippery ice fields, injuries and fatalities are not uncommon.

CHAPTER 8

Medicine Lake Volcano

CALIFORNIA'S LARGEST VOLCANIC EDIFICE

In sharp contrast to Mount Shasta's bold vertical profile, that of its larger neighbor 35 miles to the northeast—the Medicine Lake volcano—is virtually horizontal. Sprawling over an area of almost 800 square miles, this enormous shield rises less than 4,000 feet above its base to a height of 7,913 feet above sea level, little more than half of Shasta's elevation. What the Medicine Lake volcano lacks in height, however, it more than compensates for in sheer bulk. Although its profile is long, low, and undramatic, with a volume of at least 140 cubic miles it may well be the largest Pleistocene-Holocene volcanic edifice of the Far West. (Only the Newberry Volcano in central Oregon exceeds it in volume, and only the Long Valley caldera in east-central California rivals it in length and width.)

Positioned between the Cascade axis to the west and the Basin and Range province to the east, the Medicine Lake shield has qualities characteristic of both volcanic zones. Like the much smaller volcanoes of the Basin and Range region, it erupts primarily basaltic lava, which makes up the largest part of its shield. But it resembles the Cascade composite cones in its great size, its longevity (a half million years), and its production of more silicic magma, including andesite and dacite, on its upper slopes. It also has erupted impressive quantities of rhyolite, including the massive obsidian flows of Glass Mountain, formed less than 1,000 years ago.

Because of its colossal size and the chemical diversity of its erupted magma, this generally unknown behemoth offers a wide variety of volcanic landforms. On its lower slopes, effusions of fluid basaltic lava shaped an environment reminiscent of the goddess Pele's fiery domain on the Big Island of Hawaii—largely barren surfaces of ropy pahoehoe and slaggy aa, cinder cones, deep fissures splitting broken lava crusts, spatter ramparts, and an extensive system of lava tube caves. Near the summit, however, fans of basaltic lava gradually give way to a radically different mountainscape, where highly silicic magmas have constructed jagged domes and thick, blocky flows of glittering black obsidian that overlie massive andesite ridges. An oval-shaped caldera about 4 by 7 miles in diameter indents the shield volcano's broad summit, which contains the shallow waters of Medicine Lake (average depth about 26 feet).

Aerial view southwest over Medicine Lake volcano, with Medicine Lake in the left foreground and the Holocene Medicine Lake glass flow in the right foreground. The late Holocene Little Glass Mountain rhyolite flow is in the middle distance on the upper west flank of the volcano, with Mount Shasta on the far skyline. —Courtesy of Julie Donnelly-Nolan, U.S. Geological Survey

Lying in Mount Shasta's rain shadow, the Medicine Lake edifice is notably arid, particularly on the lower flanks, which support little besides sagebrush interspersed with scattered clumps of juniper. Both annual rainfall and the presence of vegetation, however, increase with elevation, from mountain mahogany near the south edge of Lava Beds National Monument, which occupies part of the volcano's gentle northern slope south of Tule Lake, to groves of pine, with occasional stands of fir, cedar, and hemlock near the summit.

A hike up the steep slopes of Schonchin Butte, the monument's most prominent cinder cone, capped with a fire lookout, affords a panoramic view of the shield's north flank, with its bleak, sagebrush-dotted surface of dark basaltic lava. A drive to the top of Little Mount Hoffman, a glaciated cinder cone high on the volcano's west side, offers visitors—on exceptionally clear days—spectacular views of the southern Cascades, including Lassen to the south and Shasta to the southwest, with Little Glass Mountain in the foreground. Observers knowing what to look for can even spot the rim of

Crater Lake far to the north. Both Little Glass Mountain and Glass Mountain are composed of rhyolite, a highly silicic viscous lava strikingly different from the flows of fluid basaltic lava that pave the lower slopes.

For most visitors, the Medicine Lake volcano's chief attraction lies at its northern foot, in the Lava Beds National Monument. Although the monument, established in 1925, covers only 10 percent of the shield's total area, it provides a wonderful outdoor laboratory displaying the kinds of features associated with the Hawaiian mode of volcanism. At Fleener Chimneys, near the Devil's Homestead flow, gas-driven jets of molten rock soared high into the air, blobs of cooling lava fell downwind, and the sticky particles fused together in thin vertical walls of plastic spatter around the erupting vent. Hawaiian-style "curtains of fire"—multiple jets of fluid basaltic lava closely spaced along a fissure—produced Lava Beds' linear ramparts and, when concentrated at vents with higher fountaining, its hollow chimneys. If hikers follow the lava stream downhill from the Fleener Chimneys picnic area, they can see the undulating surfaces of pahoehoe lava gradually grade into a clinkery aa crust near the paved road. As it traveled farther from its source and moved over uneven surfaces, the flow lost gas and heat, transforming from sinuous pahoehoe to rough aa.

Lava Tube Caves

Lava Beds National Monument is famous for its hundreds of lava tube caves, subterranean tunnels that typically occur in pahoehoe flows, although they also occur in some aa flows. Recently a concentrated effort to provide a more complete inventory of the cave system turned up many previously unknown caves. In 1997 monument rangers had documented 297 lava tubes, with a combined length of 99,000 feet. By 2001, the official count had grown to 436 caves, and their cumulative length to 144,237 feet.

Created primarily during effusions of extremely hot basalt (about 2,150 degrees Fahrenheit), lava tubes typically form in two different ways: either plastic spatter from an open channel of flowing magma gradually constructs a roof over the molten stream, or the outer crust of an active flow thickens and solidifies, insulating the fluid material within. When the eruption ebbs, the molten lava inside its protective rocky shell continues to flow downslope and drains out through the internal tubes, advancing the flow front and leaving long hollow tunnels in its wake. After the lava has cooled, some thinner portions of the tubes collapse, providing entryways to the tubes inside.

Although a few similar lava tubes exist in pahoehoe flows on the flanks of Oregon's Newberry Volcano and at Mount St. Helens, Lava Beds National Monument has by far the largest number of such caves in the continental

United States, and it also has the greatest variety, including large underground chambers, multilevel caves, interconnecting caves, and caves filled with perennial ice.

INFLATING LAVA AND LAVA TUBE CAVES

Although no flows of basaltic lava have occurred in the mainland United States during historic time, geologists observing flows of aa and pahoehoe streaming from vents at Kilauea and Mauna Loa in Hawaii have been able to study some of the processes that took place when the flows at the Medicine Lake volcano were formed. According to a recent report by Lawrence Chitwood, a geologist with the U.S. Forest Service, the behavior of Hawaiian lava flows can be correlated with features occurring in similar but much older basaltic flows in the Lava Beds National Monument. A phenomenon that plays a crucial role in lava flow movement, including the formation of lava tube caves and other structures, is known as inflation, the swelling and thickening of basaltic lava as it advances.

Beginning as thin flows perhaps only 8 inches to a foot thick, pahoehoe lava commonly inflates in complex ways to thicknesses of 5 to 60 feet. As the flow front travels farther from its source vent down a gradual slope, the lava stream slows down and fans out, forming a crust that may be strong enough temporarily to halt forward movement. When molten rock continues to pour into the flow through its inner tube system, the lava stream inflates, swelling from within and pushing up the brittle crust, which rises, cracks, and tilts to form the jagged, uneven surface we see on solidified aa or blocky lava today.

As pressure from inflowing magma renders the flow tumescent, the flow front's outer crust ruptures in various places and the molten material pours out in a flood, creating a new lava tongue and causing the flow to continue its advance. If the lava then moves over level ground, spreading out in wide sheets, its velocity decreases and smaller ruptures from its liquid interior occur. Instead of advancing by flooding, the flow now advances through budding, a process in which small toes or lobes of rounded lava burst or "bud" through the crust of the flow front. Emerging with a thin, plastic skin that stretches as they elongate, these lava toes quickly develop a crust that soon hardens enough to stop the toe from advancing farther. But as magma continues to inflate the flow interior, the increasing pressure again ruptures the lava crust, producing new fluid toes and allowing the lava to ooze forward. Flow advancement through budding is slow, averaging only 10 to 100 feet per hour.

A lava flow's forward movement and inflation occur in two different styles, continuous or discontinuous. When flows advance through the budding process, in which small tongues branch out in all directions, overriding and overlapping each other so that they coalesce, movement is continuous. As molten rock continues to pour through the flow's interior, hydraulic pressure lifts the solidifying crust upward, causing the flow to inflate. In a typical basalt flow, both inflation and advance involve the formation of lava tubes inside the flow. In Chitwood's multipurpose definition, a lava tube is a "tube-shaped conduit within a solidified lava flow that is actively transporting lava, is plugged with solidified lava, or is open because lava drained away." Lava tubes, insulated by the thickening crust, channel streams of molten rock to advance the flow front. When parts of the flow interior eventually stagnate and cool, the inner tube system may be modified so that magma is funneled into only one or two main tubes, which can then reinflate, arching their roofs to form long narrow pressure ridges or a chain of circular or oval mounds (tumuli) on the flow's fractured upper surface. If a large area with a generally horizontal surface of crumpled lava is uplifted, a pressure plateau is formed. These broad uplifts, ranging from 3 to 70 feet high and measuring up to a mile in diameter, commonly form conspicuous surface features on many large basaltic flows.

In discontinuous movement, a lava flow advances at irregular intervals through a succession of halts and outbreaks. As the front of an active flow solidifies enough to stop the advance and the flow interior continues to fill with molten rock, ruptures of the crust produce new units of lava emanating from the stalled front. Depending on the terrain over which they travel, lava flows at different times can advance through both continuous and discontinuous movement, the latter typically occurring when the flow encounters topographic barriers that cause it to thicken and pond to great depths. If the molten rock filling an inflated flow's interior is suddenly drained away through a rupture in the crust, it can precipitate sudden collapse of the flow's uplifted outer shell.

Many basaltic lava flows at Lava Beds National Monument show distinctive forms and structures resulting from the lava's swelling, or inflation, during emplacement. Most of the monument's subterranean passageways and chambers are classic lava tube caves that typically form in two ways: In the first, which typically occurs on steep gradients, fluid torrents of lava pouring downslope eject splatter that constructs a roof over the active lava channel, sometimes leaving openings, or "skylights," that expose the flowing lava. After the eruption is over and the lava has solidified, the skylights provide access to the interior tubes from which the lava has drained. In the second mode, common on gentle slopes, tubes form unseen inside the flow. Fields of inflated lava commonly develop a complex labyrinth of multiple, interconnected lava tubes in the flow's interior, some of which drain and then are repeatedly refilled or partly refilled by fresh surges of erupting magma, creating benchmarks representing different levels of lava on the tube cave's interior walls.

At Lava Beds National Monument, which has the highest concentration of lava tube caves in North America, other types of caves also formed during the process of lava flow inflation. When inflation occurs at a concave flow margin (a flow edge that appears curved inward as the viewer faces it), the fractured blocks and slabs of solidifying crust on pressure ridges and plateaus may be raised up as a coherent unit, forming a rigid, arching mass of rock. The space between the uplifted crustal mass and the underlying rock creates an uplift cave. A slightly different process—the draining out of molten rock from beneath a pressure ridge or plateau that is sufficiently solid to remain in place—forms a deflation cave. Unlike lava tube caves, the deflation cave lacks benchmarks marking high lava tides, smooth walls, and floors of ropy pahoehoe.

The Cave Loop Road

Located immediately southwest of the Lava Beds visitor center, the Cave Loop Road offers easy access to a variety of lava tube caves. Only the Mushpot Cave is wired for electrical illumination, but visitors equipped with powerful flashlights and reasonable caution can explore many other caves on the loop, as well as hundreds of tubes in different parts of the monument.

Entering the dark subterranean world of these cool, hushed sanctuaries brings cavers into direct contact with a region of frozen lava (and in some cases real ice) that differs strikingly from the "marble halls" found in typical limestone formations, such as those at Oregon Caves National Monument. Former conduits of molten lava heated to 2,200 degrees Fahrenheit, the tubes offer abundant evidence of their incandescent past.

Liquid rock dripping from cave ceilings typically forms a network of "lavacicles" overhead, while hot lava dribbling onto cave floors forms miniature lava stalagmites. During the millennia since the formation of the monument caves, with their many levels and tributaries branching out from the main passageways, groundwater filtering through cracks deposited a variety of minerals on the cave ceilings and walls, typically creating intricate patterns of caliche (calcium carbonate) in a lacelike filigree on the dark lava. If cave walls are entirely veneered in this "white lace," they can, when wet, radiate a silver or pale blue sheen, inspiring such names as Silver Cave and Blue Grotto. When a mixture of caliche, iron oxides, and "lava tube slime" (a growth of bacteria and primitive fungi) mantles cave walls, it can gleam like gold when light shines on it. This effect inspired the naming of Golden Dome Cave.

Although the caves along the Loop Cave Road, such as the Labyrinth, Catacombs, and Natural Bridge, occur in the voluminous flows that issued from Mammoth crater, additional fascinating lava tube caves are found in several other flow complexes in the monument. Located in a flow southeast of Schonchin Butte, the capacious Skull Cave is worth visiting, as is the Merrill Cave, part of the same tube system. The Valentine Cave and Bertha's Cupboard occur in the Valentine lava flow, younger and less voluminous than those that issued from Mammoth Crater.

According to official records, the Valentine Cave was "discovered and named by Ross R. Musselman on Valentine's Day, 1933," but most of the caves in the monument were first explored and named by J. D. Howard, a local settler and spelunker who devoted much of his time between 1917 and 1933 to cataloging the wonders of the northeastern part of the Medicine Lake shield. The most complete current guide to the major caves and volcanic features of the area is *Selected Caves and Lava-Tube Systems in and*

Near Lava Beds National Monument, California, a USGS publication by Aaron C. Waters, Julie Donnelly-Nolan, and Bruce Rogers. Besides being a superb text providing authoritative descriptions of the various caves and instructions on how to find them, it offers a collection of detailed maps of cave systems. (For further information on this publication and on Chitwood's study, see the bibliography at the end of the book.)

Most of the lava tube caves thus far discovered occur in the flows issuing from Mammoth crater and other nearby vents that were active at the same time. Exceeding a quarter mile in diameter and 360 feet in depth, the appropriately named Mammoth crater vent erected a secondary shield on the north slope of the Medicine Lake volcano. Torrents of basaltic magma pouring from this source flooded most of the larger shield's northeast flank, ponding to form a lake of seething lava when the molten streams encountered a cluster of older cinder cones. Pouring through gaps in this obstacle, the flows traveled many miles downslope, with several arms of a complex lava fan pushing into the south edge of Tule Lake, where some flow fronts shattered in contact with lake water. (The lake level formerly stood much higher than it does today; after 1900 it was partly drained to provide arable land for local farmers.)

Although some of the tubes conveyed liquid rock underground for 15 to 20 miles from the erupting vents, today the farthest distance one can walk (or crawl, in narrow, low-roofed passages) along a single sequence of interconnected cave tubes is about 4 miles. In some tubes, roof collapse obstructs an entrance, and in many others rock falling from the interior ceilings completely clogs the passageways, forming impassable barriers of tightly packed blocks.

Seeing only the lower flanks, where Hawaiian-style eruptions produced wide sheets of basaltic lava honeycombed with caves and chambers, visitors may miss other salient features that distinguish the Medicine Lake volcano. Besides the young rhyolite lava flows comprising Glass Mountain and Little Glass Mountain, the broad summit area encompasses a caldera formed during violent explosive eruptions. Unlike that of Crater Lake, the Medicine Lake caldera was not created by a single large outburst that destroyed the volcano's former summit. Caldera formation at Medicine Lake may have begun about 180,000 years ago when an explosive paroxysm—the largest known in the volcano's entire history—produced about 2.5 cubic miles of tephra and pyroclastic flows, depositing a thick layer known as the Antelope Well tuff over much of the shield. But most of the summit depression, elongated along an east-west axis, probably results from other processes. Charles Anderson, the first geologist to publish a detailed study of the volcano, suggested that the caldera grew slowly as copious andesite flows issued from

With its long, low shieldlike profile, the Medicine Lake volcano sprawls over 800 square miles. Seen from the northeast, the edifice—bristling with scores of subsidiary cones—stands nearly 4,000 feet above the Tule Lake basin in the foreground. —Courtesy of Julie Donnelly-Nolan, U.S. Geological Survey

numerous vents near the present caldera rim and on the outer flanks. This periodic draining of magma from the volcano's interior gradually undermined the summit area, causing it to sink inward along concentric fractures. Recent studies indicate that subsidence of the caldera floor continues today at an average rate of about a quarter inch per year.

As Julie Donnelly-Nolan of the U. S. Geological Survey has pointed out, at this rate the caldera floor would have dropped about 265 feet during Holocene time and almost 5,000 feet since the Antelope Well tuff was erupted. Cores taken from holes drilled in the caldera, however, show that the Antelope Well layer is found only about 1,376 feet beneath the present surface, indicating that caldera subsidence has probably been intermittent, with alternating phases of inflation and deflation as magma rose and fell in the volcano's subterranean plumbing.

The Evolution of the Medicine Lake Shield

Studies by Donnelly-Nolan and her colleagues at the USGS recently added some surprising facts to the Medicine Lake story. Instead of gradually evolving from a low-silica basalt to a high-silica rhyolite over time, the Medicine Lake magmas have fluctuated widely in their silica content during different stages of the volcano's history. The oldest recognized lava formation, dated at about 475,000 years, is a rhyolite dome. In studying drill cores collected during explorations for geothermal energy, Donnelly-Nolan discovered that during its early history the volcano produced mainly silicic domes and flows, although it also erupted some basaltic lava streams along with the rhyolitic magma. Beginning about 300,000 years ago, production of rhyolite stopped, and much less silicic magma dominated. In mapping the volcano's eruptive deposits, Donnelly-Nolan found that 60 percent of the surface area consists of basaltic flows and 26 percent is composed of basaltic andesite and andesite. Although silicic lavas—dacite and rhyolite—cover only about 5 percent of the mapped area, analyses of rocks from drill cores indicate that up to 30 percent of the shield's interior (as opposed to its surface) may consist of such silicic material.

Pleistocene Glaciation

Compared to the high-standing composite cones such as Shasta or Hood, the Medicine Lake volcano suffered relatively little significant erosion during Pleistocene time, although an ice cap repeatedly covered most of the upper shield. During the most recent glacial advance, ice sheets formed on the summit ridges and flowed into the caldera, with long ice tongues extending both northward and southward through low points in the caldera rim to an elevation of about 6,200 feet. Ice mantling the summit area was apparently thick enough to override Little Mount Hoffman (7,310 feet), as well as most other edifices along the caldera margins, such as the cinder cones of Grouse Hill (7,200 feet) and Badger Peak (7,354 feet). On the north rim, glaciers cut a well-defined cirque on the north face of Mount Hoffman. The presence of only a few small cirques, combined with the general absence of U-shaped glacial valleys or a large volume of glacial till, indicates that glacial erosion was minimal.

In general, Pleistocene glaciers at Medicine Lake simply scraped and scoured lava flow crusts, planing away craggy projections and polishing the underlying rock, with meltwater streams depositing gravel and other outwash on some of the lower slopes. Holocene eruptions, which produced extensive lava flows and several layers of pumice blanketing much of the shield, have since obscured many glaciated areas.

The mid-Pleistocene Plinian eruption that deposited the widespread Antelope Well tuff apparently occurred while the summit was covered in ice, triggering rapid melting and severe flooding downslope. Although channels cut by the Antelope Well event reveal that at least one catastrophic flood took place on the Medicine Lake volcano, stream-cutting or other forms of water erosion have typically played a minor role here. Despite receiving a heavy snow pack every winter, rendering many vacation homes at Medicine Lake accessible only by snowmobile from late fall to late spring, the shield has almost no flowing water on its surface. A single creek located below Paynes Springs runs little more than a mile before disappearing into the porous ground.

Holocene Eruptions

The prevailing aridity in this region accounts for only part of the bleakness of the shield's lower flanks. During the last 11,000 years, the Medicine Lake volcano has been one of the three or four most active Cascade fire mountains, erupting at least seventeen times and producing almost 8 cubic miles of fresh lava. Most of the large events, however, are clustered into two distinct episodes of multiple eruptions—all from separate vents—that are closely spaced in time. The first episode occurred about 12,850 years ago during a span of a few hundred years, during which eight separate eruptions from different vents produced well over a cubic mile of basaltic lava.

A large portion of this volume is contained in a single enormous flow that covers about 15 percent of the volcano's surface. Issuing from Giant crater and nearby vents on the south flank, this extremely fluid lava, which contains extensive tube caves, traveled about 28 miles downslope. Viewed from the air, the Giant crater flow strikingly resembles the extensive sheets of basalt veneering the flanks of Mauna Loa. (Good ground-level views are available from a paved road running between Bartle and Medicine Lake.) Flows erupted during the same eruptive sequence on the lower north side of the volcano include the Devil's Homestead flow and the Valentine Cave flow. After these voluminous outpourings, the volcano was apparently dormant for about 6,000 years.

Broken roof of a lava tube cave at Lava Beds National Monument.
—Courtesy of D. W. Hyndman

Only one significant outbreak occurred during the mid-Holocene, when a northeast-trending line of pit craters located near the southeast rim of the caldera erupted explosively, producing quantities of andesite tephra. Charcoal taken from beneath the tephra layer, which had buried and carbonized the nearby vegetation and forest duff, revealed an age of about 4,900 years. At about the same time, according to geologist Jake Lowenstern's studies of lake sediment, a viscous pancake-shaped mass of dacite—the Medicine Lake Glass flow—issued on the caldera floor just north of Medicine Lake.

After another long quiet period, Medicine Lake staged its most recent eruptive cycle, a sequence of seven eruptions beginning approximately 1,200 years ago and culminating in the formation of Little Glass Mountain (about AD 1000) and Glass Mountain (about AD 1200). This episode produced both basaltic lava on the outer flanks and highly silicic magma in the summit area. Highly fluid basalt was emitted on the far north side, forming an alignment of spatter cones and a number of small overlapping pahoehoe flows in Lava Beds National Monument. Notably more silicic lavas were erupted on the shoulder of Mount Hoffman near the caldera's northeast rim, while about the same time the andesitic Burnt Lava flow emerged on the south flank. The Callahan flow resembles the Burnt Lava flow in appearance and chemical composition, except that it was erupted on the north side. Dated at about 1,100 years, it is the youngest lava flow in the monument. Another mildly explosive basaltic vent, the Paint Pot crater, opened high on the west flank, building a red scoria cone and producing a tongue of hummocky lava. Paint Pot crater takes its name from the contrast between its reddish oxidized cinders and the slightly younger white tephra from nearby Little Glass Mountain that partly mantles the cone.

Located between Paint Pot crater and the caldera's west rim, Little Glass Mountain began life about 1,000 years ago with a violent discharge of white rhyolite pumice that now blankets every neighboring surface. Atypical easterly winds blew the ash plume as far west as Mount Shasta, where Dan Miller of the USGS identified pumice fragments from the Little Glass Mountain eruption. Following the explosive phase, a large mass of viscous rhyolite magma surged into multiple vents along a northeast trend, forming glassy, steep-sided domes and the Crater glass flows. About 200 years after Little Glass Mountain formed, a significantly larger mass of rhyolite magma issued from thirteen different vents just outside the caldera's east rim, producing a similar sequence of explosive action followed by effusions of viscous lava. Thick tongues of silicic lava from three adjacent craters coalesced to form the massive Glass Mountain flow, which has a volume of about a quarter of a cubic mile and covers more than 5 square miles.

A classic example of a zoned lava flow, the first part of the Glass Mountain lobe that oozed down the steep east flank of the shield is made of dacite.

As the eruption continued, however, the magma changed to rhyolite, which comprises the bulk of the formation. Portions of the rhyolite lobes quickly chilled to form obsidian, a black, shiny volcanic glass that gives the peak its name. Ten additional domes of rhyolite or rhyodacite erupted along a northwest trending line north of Glass Mountain, and one to the south. Radiocarbon dating of a dead cedar tree killed by the eruption yielded an age of about 900 years, but some geologists think that date may be too old and that Glass Mountain formed about a century later. A single steam vent remains active at the hot spot near Glass Mountain.

In 1910, a local rancher reported that he had felt mild earthquakes and seen ashes of "blue mud" coating the vegetation near Medicine Lake. Investigators have been unable to find any vent that could have been a source of the ash, and concluded that no eruption has occurred in historic time.

Future eruptions are inevitable, but there is no way to predict whether they will produce fire fountaining and fluid basalt flows on the lower shield, violent explosions of silicic magma near the summit, or both at the same time. Because the Medicine Lake shield has produced extremely large volumes of pyroclastic material only once in its known history, when it deposited the Antelope Well dacite tuff about 180,000 years ago, geologists

Glass Mountain from the south. The massive rhyolite lava flows composing Glass Mountain erupted only 800 years ago, representing the Medicine Lake volcano's most recent activity. —Julie Donnelly-Nolan photo, U.S. Geological Survey

do not think that it is likely to stage a comparably large explosive eruption in the foreseeable future. Despite the recent rhyolitic eruptions at Glass Mountain and Little Glass Mountain, it does not appear that a large silicic magma chamber now exists beneath the volcano. In the opinion of those who have studied its volcanic history in detail, it is much more probable that the Medicine Lake volcano will continue erupting on the same scale as it has thus far in the Holocene, intermittently emitting fluid streams of basalt on its flanks and ejecting moderate quantities of rhyolitic tephra and pasty lobes of obsidian in or near the caldera. Considering its isolated position in a very sparsely populated region east of the Cascade crest, the Medicine Lake volcano is not as likely to cause major problems as are some of the loftier, glacier-bearing composite cones in the range, especially Shasta, Hood, and Rainier.

The great diversity of its magma, ranging from fluid basalts to extremely viscous rhyolite, indicates that the Medicine Lake volcano is not fueled by a single large magma chamber. Instead, the volcano probably taps a number of chemically diverse pockets of magma located at different levels in the crust. Julie Donnelly-Nolan and her colleagues suggest that the voluminous basalt that intruded into the shield about 10,500 years ago may have chemically evolved to produce the highly silicic magma forming Little Glass Mountain and Glass Mountain about 1,000 years ago. A second intrusion of hot basalt into the volcano's interior about 1,250 years ago may have triggered the most recent eruptive events. Additional infusions of basaltic magma, characteristic of the Basin and Range province, are likely to produce similar eruptive episodes in the future.

In his analysis of eruption probabilities at the Medicine Lake shield, Manuel Nathenson of the USGS notes that thirteen of the seventeen identified Holocene eruptions were separated by dormant intervals of less than 780 years (about the same period that has elapsed since Glass Mountain was formed). Two of the Holocene's quiet intervals have been much longer, however, indicating that the volcano does not follow a prescribed schedule. As with other volcanoes, smaller eruptions occur more frequently than large ones, with a voluminous effusion of lava (about a quarter of a cubic mile) taking place only once every 10,000 years.

Captain Jack's Stronghold

One of the West's most dramatic confrontations between Native Americans and the U.S. Army took place amid Lava Beds National Monument's bleak flows and uneven terrain. In 1872–1873 the Modoc Indians, resisting a war of extermination, made their last stand here, in what they called the "land of burned out fires." For months "Captain Jack," a Modoc leader, and his men held out against a disproportionately superior military force, camping in the innumerable crevices and crannies of the basalt formations bordering Tule Lake. Repeatedly successful in outwitting his opponents, Captain Jack was captured only after other Modocs revealed his hiding place, exchanging their leader for a promise of their own safety. At a later period in our history, thousands of Japanese-Americans were forcibly interned near Tule Lake for the duration of World War II. Some German prisoners of war were also incarcerated in the area.

Visiting Medicine Lake Volcano

If traveling from the south, take Interstate 5 north from Redding about 63 miles to Weed and turn right on U.S. 97. Follow U.S. 97 for 52 miles to California 161, then turn right and drive 16 miles to Hill Road, where you turn right again. At the "T" intersection 12 miles later, turn right once more and drive 6 miles to the visitor center and Cave Loop Road on the right. Besides exploring the lava tube caves and other volcanic formations in the monument, travelers may wish to visit Tule Lake and the Lower Klamath National Wildlife Refuge. In early winter, this region hosts millions of waterfowl and other birds on the Pacific flyway as they head south from western Canada and the Pacific Northwest. Attracted by ample food, an estimated 2,000 bald eagles spend the winter here.

Although there are paved roads from the south and east to Medicine Lake, approaching from the north or northwest requires some travel on gravel roads. From the west, an unpaved road from McCloud, just east of Interstate 5, leads to the summit caldera holding Medicine Lake. Glass Mountain is accessible via dirt roads from the caldera to the east flank. For a spectacular panorama of the region, including a view of Shasta's rarely seen east side, follow a Forest Service road to the fire lookout at the top of Little Mount Hoffman. Available for overnight stays, the lookout can be rented from the Shasta–Trinity National Forest ranger station in McCloud.

CHAPTER 9

Mount McLoughlin

SENTINEL OF SOUTHERN OREGON

The highest Cascade peak between Shasta and the Three Sisters, Mount McLoughlin (9,496 feet) became the twelfth-loftiest peak in the range on May 18, 1980, when Mount St. Helens lost 1,300 feet of its summit. Although little known even to most residents of the Pacific Northwest, McLoughlin's slim pointed cone is clearly visible from both Interstate 5 near Medford and U.S. 97 near Klamath Falls, rising just north of Oregon 140. Formerly Mount Pitt, in 1905 the volcano was renamed for John McLoughlin, the Hudson's Bay Company factor who generously helped American settlers during the 1830s and 1840s, when both Britain and the United States claimed Oregon territory.

Despite the mountain's general anonymity, several lakes nestled amid the thick conifer forest girding McLoughlin's base draw numerous fishermen and campers to the area. The poetically christened Lake of the Woods is reputedly the most popular attraction for anglers, but the road to Fourmile Lake offers the best point of departure for a summit climb. The energy expended to clamber up McLoughlin's steep slopes, over sharply angular blocks of basaltic andesite lava, is well rewarded at the top by a 360-degree view of southern Oregon. To the west rolls a mighty sea of forested peaks and valleys—deep green close at hand, smoky blue where they meet the horizon. The most distant ridges are part of the western Cascades, deeply eroded remnants of volcanoes many millions of years old. McLoughlin belongs to the much younger High Cascade volcanoes that grew in a north-south trend along the eastern margins of the older chain.

East of McLoughlin, somber forests extend to the curving shores of Klamath Lake, the largest body of fresh water in Oregon. Beyond it stretch the flat dry plains of Oregon's central plateau. About 70 miles to the south rises the snowy double cone of Shasta. To the northwest looms the truncated cone of Mount Mazama (Crater Lake). On an exceptionally clear day, the white peaks of the Three Sisters appear dimly against the farthest northwest horizon.

From the southwest on Interstate 5 or the southeast from the shores of Klamath Lake, the volcano has a generally symmetrical shape. But to a climber facing northeast from McLoughlin's extremely narrow summit,

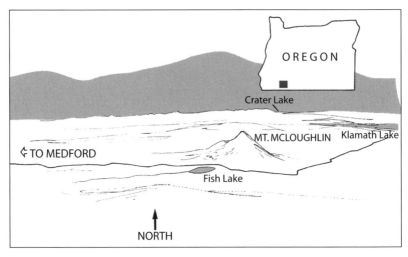

Relief map of the Mount McLoughlin area

it is apparent that the entire northeast sector of the cone is missing, a vast hollow amphitheater in its place. Pleistocene glaciers bit so deeply into McLoughlin's cone that they exposed the volcano's interior, including two solidified conduits that once piped magma to the now vanished summit crater. Between about 25,000 and 12,000 years ago, glaciers descending McLoughlin's north face merged with an icecap up to 500 feet thick at its base. Farther north in the range, the ice cap was thousands of feet thick, smothering almost the entire length of the Oregon High Cascades. Until about 1900, Sholes glacier, a small glacier probably a few centuries old, occupied part of the northeastern cirque, but even the stagnant ice fields that persisted for several decades have since disappeared. From midsummer to early autumn, McLoughlin is now mostly snow free.

In the 1970s LeRoy Maynard, then a graduate student at the University of Oregon's Center for Volcanology, produced the most thorough study of McLoughlin's geology now available. The following summary of the volcano's history is based largely on Maynard's work, supplemented by the work of James Smith of the U.S. Geological Survey, who later mapped the area. Maynard found that McLoughlin grew in at least three distinct stages, each involving a different mode of eruption. Because glaciers have cut deeply into the volcano's interior, its biography is easier to read than that of some less-eroded peaks.

McLoughlin is one of the smaller Cascade volcanoes, with a volume of about 3 cubic miles. Its cone stands high because it is built on top of older

(Pleistocene and Pliocene) shields of basaltic andesite. Although commonly classed as a typical andesite volcano, McLoughlin is composed primarily of basaltic andesite (ranging from 53 to 57 percent silica). During its early growth, probably in the relatively late Pleistocene, the volcano was frequently explosive, producing tephra and other pyroclastic material that comprises roughly a third of its total bulk. Some flows of molten rock accompanied the pyroclastic eruptions, but they seem to have been confined to the lower flanks of the cone. Copious streams of black clinkery lava poured from flank vents on the northwest side and filled the ancestral valley of Fourbit Creek for 4 miles beyond the mountain's base, stopping at the present site of Big Butte Springs. Today, large volumes of water gush from the flow's terminus, providing the domestic water supply for Medford and other towns in the Bear Creek Valley.

Other early flows extend east beyond McLoughlin's base for at least 6 miles; several crop out along Oregon 140 about 3 miles east of its junction with the road leading to Lake of the Woods. Another dark aa flow issued from about the 5,000 foot level and, filling a stream valley for more than 6 miles, descended to an elevation of less than 3,000 feet. Despite its exceptional length and blocky crust, this flow is little more than 500 feet wide for more than 2.5 miles of its length.

Cross-section of Mount McLoughlin, showing the large pyroclastic core that occupies much of the volcano's interior. McLoughlin's most recent eruptions (late Pleistocene) have been andesite flows from vents low on its flanks.

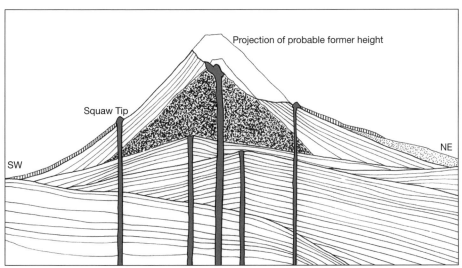

Although erosion has exposed the volcano's pyroclastic core, no lavas from this early period are apparently present in the upper part of the cone. During this initial phase of its development, McLoughlin may have resembled Belknap shield, a much younger basaltic andesite shield located at McKenzie Pass between North Sister and Mount Washington. With a large central pyroclastic cone entirely surrounded by blocky and aa lava flows, Belknap may now have the same general appearance as Mount McLoughlin did early in its history.

In the second stage of McLoughlin's growth, activity at the central vent changed radically, switching from the ejection of fragmental material at the summit crater to the eruption of coherent lava streams. As numerous thin flows of lava—perhaps fed by fountains of liquid rock—coursed down every side of the cone, the pyroclastic interior was completely encased in clinkery basaltic andesite. McLoughlin thus became an "armored cone," with a hard outer shell of solid lava concealing a soft inner core of loosely compacted lava fragments. If glaciers had not cut so deeply into the cone, we would not know of its dual nature.

Mount McLoughlin from the west. The highest peak between Shasta and the Three Sisters, McLoughlin marked the southern end of a Pleistocene ice cap that shrouded the Oregon Cascades northward almost to Mount Hood. Despite the volcano's apparent symmetry when viewed from Interstate 5, glacial erosion has removed its former summit and north side.
—David Wieprecht photo, U.S. Geological Survey, Cascades Volcano Observatory

After activity at the summit ceased, McLoughlin began its third phase of development, erupting from new vents on the flanks of the cone. Flows of blocky lava issued from vents below the summit, while fine-grained dark lavas poured from fissures near the base. Two conspicuous crags high on the west flank of the volcano, North and South Squaw Tips, now mark the vents from which exceptionally large blocky flows emerged. These two flows coalesced to spread over most of the southwest slope below an elevation of 7,800 feet. A much smaller but prominent flow of the same blocky variety, the Rye Spring flow, erupted just south of the Squaw Tip flows, but at a lower elevation. A fourth blocky stream poured from a vent inside the northeastern cirque and flowed over glacial moraines and landslide deposits, suggesting that it probably erupted after the latest Pleistocene glaciers had largely melted.

Although most of the flows underlying McLoughlin's south and west slopes are remarkably well preserved, their rugged surfaces of jagged lava blocks unmodified by glacial scouring, the youngest are probably about 20,000 to 30,000 years old. (The flow covering glacial till in the northeast cirque may be an exception.) The main cone, which probably attained a maximum altitude of 10,000 feet, was essentially complete before Pleistocene glaciation demolished the northeast sector and lowered the summit by several hundred feet.

Brown Mountain and Pelican Butte

Mount McLoughlin has two close neighbors that resemble it in structure and in the chemical composition of their lavas. A small shield with a volume of about a cubic mile, Brown Mountain stands immediately to the south-southeast. Although its basaltic andesite flows, like those of McLoughlin, are bare and unweathered, ice streams that formed during the most recent Pleistocene glacial advance eroded the cinder cone capping its summit, carving out a bowl-shaped cirque on the northeast side. Because evidence for an older glaciation is lacking, geologists estimate that Brown Mountain formed between about 60,000 and 12,000 years ago.

Pelican Butte (8,036 feet), the most prominent shield volcano in the southern Oregon Cascades, stands considerably to the east of McLoughlin, its long gentle slopes forming the eastern margin of the range where it borders Klamath Lake. Containing about 5 cubic miles of basaltic andesite, the cone has a volume about a third greater than that of McLoughlin. Like Brown Mountain and many similar shields in Oregon, Pelican Butte has a large cinder cone at the summit. The bowl-shaped cirque and deep canyon gouged into the northeast part of the shield expose beds of pyroclastic material interspersed with lava flows, indicating that a significant portion of Pelican Butte is constructed of fragmental rock. After mildly explosive eruptions built the summit cone, it was encased in thin flows of aa and blocky lava. Glaciation subsequently excavated the large ravine on the northeast flank and removed most of the lavas veneering the summit area, lowering the edifice by many tens of yards.

Visiting Mount McLoughlin

Although not technically difficult, the 6-mile trail to McLoughlin's summit is most easily hiked after mid-July, when it is largely snow free. Be sure to carry water, as there is none along the trail. From Klamath Falls, take Oregon 140 west about 33 miles to Fourmile Lake Road, just west of milepost 31. Turn north here and proceed 2.5 miles over the unpaved road to the trailhead located on the left, where a sign designates the McLoughlin Trail (3716).

After crossing an open meadow and a clear stream (the last source of water), the trail climbs through evergreen forest. It is a long 4.5 miles to timberline over increasingly steep grades and another 1.5 miles over bare blocky lava and loose rubble to the top. Above timberline there is no easily discernible trail, only red crosses and circles painted on some of the angular blocks. The summit view is well worth the exertion required to enjoy it, encompassing the range from Crater Lake to Mount Shasta. When lingering snowdrifts obscure the red trail markings on trees or lava surfaces, it is easy to get lost, particularly on the descent.

Pelican Butte provides a view that demands less physical effort. Take Oregon 140 about 4 miles east of the Lake of the Woods highway maintenance station. Turn north onto the dirt road, which leads to the summit. The last few miles are steep and narrow.

CHAPTER 10

Crater Lake

BEAUTY BORN OF FIRE

The calm of Crater Lake belies the cataclysmic violence that led to its creation. The enormous lake basin, 5 by 6 miles across and almost 4,000 feet deep, occupies the heart of an ancient volcano, Mount Mazama. (See image 8 on plate 4.) Until about 7,700 years ago, Mazama rose more than a mile above the present lake level, its summit reaching an altitude of about 12,000 feet, surpassing Mount Hood as Oregon's highest peak. A violent explosive eruption—perhaps the most powerful to occur anywhere in the western hemisphere during the last 10,000 years—then ejected so great a volume of material from the magma chamber beneath the volcano that the former summit collapsed inward. In perhaps a matter of only hours or days, a towering snow-clad mountain suddenly metamorphosed into a vast depression.

During the next few centuries after Mazama's self-destruction, smaller eruptions inside the caldera built Wizard Island, the almost perfectly symmetrical cinder cone that now stands about 800 feet above lake level, the only postcaldera edifice to break the surface of Crater Lake. The tiny Phantom Ship, which pokes its rocky sails above water near the southeastern caldera wall, is a picturesque fragment of an older volcano buried during Mazama's growth and then exhumed during its collapse. (See image 12 on plate 6.) Far beneath the lake surface are other postcaldera edifices, including Merriam cone, which rises about 1,300 feet above the caldera floor, although its summit remains submerged at a depth of 640 feet.

Water from rain, snow, and infilling groundwater apparently began to collect in the caldera shortly after it had formed, creating a network of ponds and smaller lakes that eventually expanded to fill the basin to its present depth of 1,949 feet (an official measurement made in 2000). The lake level rose rapidly, even before Wizard Island had finished building its cone. Some of the island's andesite flows contain pillow lava, with rounded or tubular pillow-shaped features, which form only when molten rock flows underwater. Because of its depth and great purity, Crater Lake absorbs all colors of the light spectrum except blue, which it reflects back, giving the lake its incomparable azure hue. On clear days, particularly when the caldera rim is shrouded in fresh snow, the intensity of sunlight radiating from its blue surface can be dazzling.

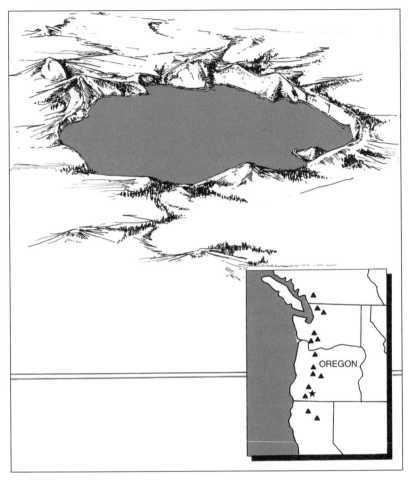

Crater Lake from the northwest. Wizard Island peeps above the caldera rim at the lower right, while Mount Scott, the highest remaining elevation of Mount Mazama, appears at the top left.

The Story of Mount Mazama

With all sides of its interior above lake level fully exposed, Mount Mazama reveals its volcanic history more completely than almost any other Cascade composite cone. From various points on the caldera rim, observers can readily see most of the formations marking Mazama's different stages of growth. Although Crater Lake was well known to native tribes, who have inhabited the region for at least 10,000 years, it was the last major volcanic landform in the range to be "discovered" by Caucasians. In 1853 a gold prospector named John Wesley Hillman accidentally stumbled upon it while looking for the mythical Lost Cabin Mine. Decades later the caldera's

MAJOR EVENTS IN MAZAMA'S ERUPTIVE HISTORY

APPROXIMATE AGE (YEARS)	EVENT OR DEPOSIT
5,000	Extrusion of a small lava dome at the east foot of Wizard Island
7,700–7,200	Postcaldera construction of the Wizard Island edifice, Merriam cone, and the andesite lava platform east of Wizard Island
7,700	Mazama's climactic eruption in three main stages: (1) Plinian outburst at vent north of main summit; (2) ejection of first large pyroclastic flow, forming the Wineglass welded tuff; and (3) multiple large pyroclastic flows from numerous vents accompany collapse of volcano's former summit
7,800?	Explosive and effusive eruptions at two vents on Mazama's north flank: (1) silicic tephra at Llao Rock flow; (2) Cleetwood flow, still fluid when Mazama collapsed
25,000–7,800?	Dormant interval
30,000–25,000	Eruptions of rhyodacite magma: Redcloud Cliff flow and the dome above Steel Bay; Grouse Hill flow and dome
40,000–22,000	Eruptions comingling basalt and dacite erect Williams crater west of Hillman Peak
40,000	Eruption and collapse of silicic domes high on Mazama's southwest flank produces pyroclastic flows and debris flows in Munson Valley and along the southwest flank
75,000–50,000	Numerous lava flows erupted, some probably under glacial ice
70,000	Eruption of Pumice Castle tephra, followed by Scott Bluffs lava flows; construction of Hillman Peak composite cone
140,000–75,000	Lava flows, domes, and pyroclastic flow deposits at Merriam Point
185,000–110,000	Eruption of thin lava sheets at Llao Bay shield volcano
300,000–200,000	Eruption of lava sheets at Cloudcap Bay
300,000	Lava flows at Sentinel Rock vent
340,000	Lava flows at Dutton Cliff vent
340,000	Lava flows at Danger Bay
400,000	Eruption of Phantom cone lava flows and pyroclastic deposits
420,000	Building of Mount Scott composite cone
700,000–600,000	Pre-Mazama rhyodacite flows and exposed domes east of Mount Scott and south of Mazama
Older than 600,000	Basalt lava flows from numerous vents in the High Cascades

unique features began to attract geologic investigators. The first American geologist to recognize that Mazama had collapsed rather than blown apart (as some other scientists then believed) was Joseph S. Diller, who studied the volcano in the 1880s and published his findings in 1902 in one of the first major reports of the U.S. Geological Survey. In 1942 Howel Williams, then a professor at the University of California at Berkeley, published what many regard as the classic study of Crater Lake's geology. Beginning in the 1980s, Charles Bacon and his colleagues at the USGS have issued a series of papers that have further clarified events leading to the caldera's formation. Drawing on the work of these and other geologists, we now have an increasingly clear understanding of Mazama's biography.

Mount Mazama developed not as a single symmetrical cone (like St. Helens before 1980) but as an irregular cluster of overlapping structures, including individual shield volcanoes and small composite cones. The oldest visible part of this volcanic complex is Mount Scott (8,926 feet), a prominent andesitic cone that stands east of the present caldera rim and forms the highest point in Crater Lake National Park. Like most other coalescing edifices that make up Mount Mazama, Scott probably grew during a relatively brief but intense cycle of cone building and became extinct long before the climactic eruptions. Although Scott retains a generally conical shape, repeated Pleistocene glaciations incised a broad cirque on its west face and smaller cirques on its northeast and east slopes, removing all traces of a summit crater. Scott's lavas have an age of about 420,000 years.

Inside the caldera, the oldest exposed rock is that of the Phantom cone (named for its conspicuous outcrop, the Phantom Ship), which is also about 400,000 years old. As Mazama grew, the center of activity gradually shifted westward, with new vents building the slightly younger cones of Applegate Peak and Garfield Peak on the upper south flank. The youngest composite cone in this series, Hillman Peak was constructed on the volcano's southwest side about 70,000 years ago. Now forming the highest point on the caldera rim, almost 2,000 feet above the lake surface, Hillman Peak was sliced in two when Mazama collapsed, exposing its lava-filled central conduit and hydrothermally altered interior in perfect cross-section.

Several shield volcanoes contributed to Mazama's growth, erupting voluminous flows of basaltic andesite that spread out in thin sheets over large areas on the volcano's flanks. Hawaiian-style fountains of fluid lava, similar to those that erupted on the Medicine Lake shield, fed many of these widespread flows, which average only 15 to 20 feet thick. As molten bombs and other incandescent fragments from these lava sprays showered down, they accumulated to form streams of liquid rock. Today, these flows appear as solid bands on the south, west, and east caldera walls. Discharging thin lava

View northeast across the mirror-still water of Crater Lake. The Phantom Ship, the oldest rock exposed in the caldera, appears in the middle foreground; Mount Thielsen's spire rises in the middle distance. —Courtesy of the Oregon State Highway Department

sheets in relatively rapid succession, the individual shields had comparatively brief life spans of only a few hundred to a few thousand years. The Llao shield, which formed on the northwest slope and is clearly visible beneath the dark mass of Llao Rock at Llao Bay, is a typical example.

The eruption of more viscous magma, forming massive flows of andesite lava up to several hundred feet thick, contributed the most to Mazama's bulk. Thick layers of rubble, broken fragments of lava crust, distinguish these more silicic flows, mantling their solid interiors. Like the more fluid lavas, these rubbly flows probably formed from lava fountains and also appear prominently in the caldera walls. Hikers on the trail up Garfield Peak, which begins just east of the Crater Lake Lodge, will find close-up views of andesite flows with typically dense interiors and upper portions composed of chaotic jumbles of angular lava blocks.

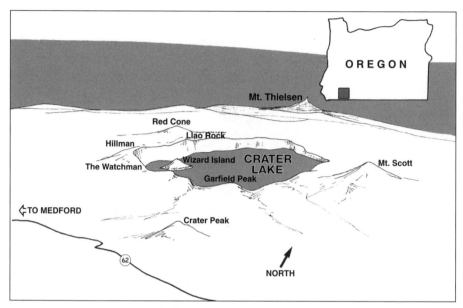

Relief map of the Crater Lake area

Mazama's Glaciers

As Mazama grew by voluminous intermittent eruptions during Pleistocene time, glaciers repeatedly formed, shrouding the asymmetrical complex in masses of ice that extended far down the volcano's slopes, carving deep trenches in its flanks and in some cases filling valleys beyond the base of the cone. These glacier-cut valleys, beheaded (their upper portions removed) when Mazama's summit collapsed, now form conspicuous U-shaped indentations in the caldera rim at Sun and Kerr Notches and the head of Munson Valley. On the northeast flank, glaciers excavated a huge cirque that bit deeply into the mountain, eroding the north face.

When Mazama erupted during periods of intense glaciation, its flows commonly encountered massive streams of ice, which rapidly chilled the lava surface, forming small glassy columns and piles of glassy talus along the flow margins. Between glacial maxima, numerous flows traveled over surfaces that advancing ice had previously scraped and polished; some flows, such as that at Sentinel Rock, poured into glacier-scoured canyons and filled them to great depths. Glacial striations occur at numerous sites around the caldera, including exposed rock surfaces just west of the lodge. Moraines indicating the extent of ice-age glaciers are found as far as 17 miles downslope from the caldera rim.

Although most of Mazama's cone-building eruptions were comparatively quiet effusions of lava, about 70,000 years ago, several vents produced large explosive eruptions of silicic magma, some of which left thick pyroclastic deposits. Pumice Castle, a brilliantly orange feature on the east wall of the caldera, was created when pumice raining down from a nearby vent was so hot that its glassy particles fused together. (See image 11 on plate 6.) The densely welded material of Pumice Castle is more resistant to erosion than nonwelded tephra and survived Mazama's collapse. As Charles Bacon pointed out, the Pumice Castle tephra is visible along the north caldera wall from Cleetwood Cove to Merriam Point. Explosive vents on the north side of Cloudcap and in the wall beneath the east arm of Llao Rock also produced dacite tephra and pyroclastic flows hot enough to weld. The Watchman flow, a thick dacite mass filling a V-shaped notch in the southwest wall, erupted about 50,000 years ago.

By 40,000 to 50,000 years ago, Mazama's cone building was largely complete, although new vents continued to produce both andesite lava flows on the north and southwest flanks and dacite domes high on the south side. Domes rising on the steep south face (the highest part of the mountain) frequently shattered and collapsed, generating a series of pyroclastic flows of hot ash and blocks of dacite lava that swept down Mazama's south flank. Thick deposits of these block-and-ash flows (which early researchers misidentified as deposits of glacial till) are visible in roadcuts on the way from the park headquarters to Rim Village and as far north as the Devil's Backbone: the large craggy dike, exhumed by Mazama's collapse, that extends from lake level up the west caldera wall.

Throughout much of Mazama's development, numerous cinder cones erupted on its outer flanks, at least thirteen of which are included within the boundaries of Crater Lake National Park, with eleven others located outside the park borders. These peripheral cones did not tap Mazama's magma chamber, but probably drew on discrete subterranean bodies of basalt or basaltic andesite, the same "background" sources that supplied most of the smaller volcanoes of Oregon's High Cascades. One partial exception is Williams crater (formerly Forgotten crater, renamed in the early 1980s to honor Howel Williams), a partly eroded cinder cone about half a mile west of Hillman Peak. Unlike the other cinder cones in the area, Williams crater erupted a variety of lava types, mingling the regional basalt with dacite. Charles Bacon has shown that the cone drew its more silicic component from the western end of Mazama's magma chamber, which was inexorably evolving toward the highly silicic, gas-rich mix that produced the climactic outburst.

During most of its long history, Mazama erupted a variety of magma types, ranging from basaltic andesite to andesite to dacite. Beginning about

40,000 years ago, however, the volcano began to produce only rhyodacite, extremely viscous magma with a silica content of about 70 percent. Between about 30,000 and 25,000 years ago, as the final Pleistocene glaciation began, rhyodacite erupted from at least three north-side vents in the form of both pumice tephra and lava flows at Grouse Hill, Steel Bay, and Redcloud Cliff. The thick Redcloud flow, which contains glassy columns indicating contact with glacial ice, now looks like an inverted stone triangle 600 feet high atop the eastern caldera rim. Although its peculiar shape suggests that it occupies an old V-shaped stream valley, it actually fills a funnel-shaped explosion vent. Before the lava was extruded, explosions blasted open an almost vertical-walled crater, ejecting quantities of rhyodacite pumice. The degassed lava welled up to build a steep dome over the Redcloud vent and was later neatly bisected during Mazama's collapse, transforming its south face into a sheer precipice.

A short distance north of the present caldera rim, a similar explosive-effusive sequence formed the Grouse Hill flow and dome (elevation 7,412 feet). Although geologists once believed it was about the same age as Llao Rock, the mass of rhyodacite lava composing Grouse Hill is actually contemporaneous with Redcloud Cliff, about 27,000 years old.

Perhaps just as the last Pleistocene glaciers were withdrawing upslope, well above the elevation of the present caldera rim, the final part of this rhyodacite sequence occurred. A northeast-trending array of rhyodacite domes rose on the northeast flank, including the prominent Sharp Peak. The stage was now set for Mazama's culminating performance.

Mount Mazama before the Great Eruption

Impressed by the fact that a lofty volcanic cone suddenly transformed into a giant hole in the ground, some park visitors try to make a good story even better. Speculating about Mazama's former height, some propose that it was 15,000 to 16,000 feet high, taller than either Shasta or Rainier. To help distinguish hyperbole from probability, Howel Williams compared Mazama with other large Cascade composite cones, superimposing on Shasta, Rainier, Hood, and Adams a hypothetical caldera of the same dimensions and elevation as that at Crater Lake. Williams discovered that if Adams's summit (12,286 feet) were removed at about the 8,000-foot level (the average altitude of Mazama's present south rim), the truncated volcano would accommodate a caldera about the size of the Crater Lake basin. Because Adams most closely matches Mazama in girth at the same elevation, Williams concluded that before its destruction Mazama probably stood about 12,000 feet above sea level—an estimate with which later geologists agree.

Mount Mazama begins its catastrophic eruption at a vent north of the main summit.

Composed of variously eroded edifices stacked closely together, Mount Mazama had a distinctly irregular early Holocene profile. Viewed from the south, a cluster of separate peaks formed a broad ridge of multiple summits, beginning with Mount Scott to the east and ending with Hillman Peak to the west. Since Scott, even after severe erosion, is nearly 9,000 feet high, it is likely that the younger stratovolcanoes farther west, including Garfield, Applegate, and Hillman Peaks, rose considerably higher. Cones and domes erected farther up on the south flanks, well above the present caldera rim, probably added significantly to the volcano's stature. Some features, such as the thick Watchman flow, stood out as glaciated horns. The highest part of the asymmetrical Mazama complex stood somewhat south of the present center of Crater Lake. Because of its height, Mazama may still have supported glaciers, but any that remained were small and confined to cirques near the summit.

Harbingers of the Great Eruption

According to Klamath tribal lore, Llao, god of the underworld, dwelt deep in the earth beneath Mount Mazama, sleeping peacefully for thousands of years in his subterranean abode. When he awoke in a self-immolating fury, Llao rained fire on the surrounding terrain and almost leveled the mountain that housed him.

Appropriately, the site of Llao's reawakening is now marked by a monument befitting a god—an immense mass of dark lava, about 1,200 feet thick and almost a quarter of a cubic mile in volume, that forms the most conspicuous feature of the northwestern caldera rim. With a rounded central section and lateral extensions on each side, this rhyodacite flow, known as Llao Rock, resembles a primordial bird of prey, crouched with wings outstretched as if about to take flight. Violent explosions of gas-rich rhyodacite magma, which sent clouds of pumice and ash high into the air, immediately preceded the erection of Llao's memorial, which took place only a century or two before the climactic eruption. Shifting winds carried the Llao tephra hundreds of miles from the vent in a broad arc extending from northern and eastern Washington, through eastern Oregon, and into western Nevada. After the explosive eruptions had blown out a large crater, pasty rhyodacite lava filled and overflowed the vent. When Mazama later collapsed, opening the vast caldera, it sliced off the upper (eastern) portion of the Llao Rock flow, creating the vertical cliffs that now rise above Llao Bay.

To the east of Llao Rock, another vent, located slightly higher on the north side near the present caldera rim, produced a comparable outpouring of rhyodacite magma called the Cleetwood flow. When Mazama collapsed, slicing through the Cleetwood flow near its vent area, the flow's interior was still hot and plastic enough to ooze hundreds of feet down the newly created northern caldera wall. This rare example of a "backflow" indicates that the caldera formation occurred only a short time—weeks or months—after the Cleetwood lava erupted. This close timing is reinforced by the fact that tephra from the climactic outburst blanketing the Cleetwood surface has been partly welded by heat and gases issuing from the lava. These penultimate eruptions—heralding the main event—were concentrated on Mazama's lower north flank, perhaps because this region lay not far above the roof of the magma chamber.

The Largest Cascade Eruption in a Million Years

The climactic eruption that largely demolished Mount Mazama occurred in three distinct stages, all in rapid succession. The Cleetwood flow was still glowing hot when a vent higher on the north side, but well below the

actual summit, discharged an enormous column of ash that rose an estimated
30 miles into the stratosphere. The height and vigor of Mazama's eruption plume during the initial Plinian phase can be inferred from the vast
area over which southwesterly winds distributed its fallout. Shrouding more
than 500,000 square miles in eight western states and the southern part of
three Canadian provinces, Mazama's ash blankets so vast a territory that it
makes an invaluable time marker, indicating the relative age of objects or
formations found above or below its distinctive orangish deposit. Near the
volcano's base, air-fall pumice accumulated to depths of 20 feet, while 70
miles to the northeast it lay a foot or more thick. Although the succeeding
pyroclastic flows were extremely abrasive, eroding away much of the pumice previously deposited on the volcano's upper slopes, conspicuous air-fall
layers can still be seen today from Hillman Peak around the rim clockwise
to the vicinity of Sentinel Point. Most of the pumice layers exposed in cuts
along the Cleetwood Trail derived from this Plinian stage and from the
slightly earlier tephra from the Llao and Cleetwood vents.

Although fallout from Mazama's buoyant Plinian column created an
ashen desolation for hundred of miles north and northeast of the volcano,

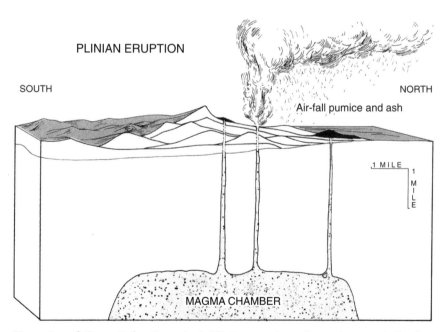

PLINIAN ERUPTION

SOUTH

NORTH

Air-fall pumice and ash

1 MILE

1
M
I
L
E

MAGMA CHAMBER

*Formation of Crater Lake. Stage 1: A Plinian eruption column ejects vertically from
a single vent north of Mazama's main summit. Ash fall extends hundreds of miles to
the northeast.*

the southwesterly winds allowed only a thin sprinkling of pumice to litter areas west of the peak. As Howel Williams noted, an observer standing near Union Peak, only 5 miles away, would probably have enjoyed a relatively safe, if terrifying, view of the event.

In its second phase, the eruption changed radically in character. Perhaps because the main vent widened, or the escaping gas was insufficient to support the immense weight of millions of tons of tephra being ejected, the vertical Plinian column suddenly collapsed. As an enormous volume of incandescent pumice crashed to earth, it sparked a series of pyroclastic flows that cascaded down Mazama's north flank, from Llao Rock on the west to Redcloud Cliff on the east. Emplaced at high temperatures that welded the glassy pyroclastic fragments together, the initial pyroclastic flows—the first of many—formed a prominent deposit on the north caldera wall. Known as the Wineglass welded tuff, it contains large blocks of orange-brown to gray rock, and is well exposed on the Cleetwood Trail. Because they issued from a crater located well north of the summit, the Wineglass pyroclastic flows did not affect Mazama's south slopes.

The situation changed quickly during the eruption's third stage, when all sides of Llao's mountain were bathed in fiery avalanches of incandescent

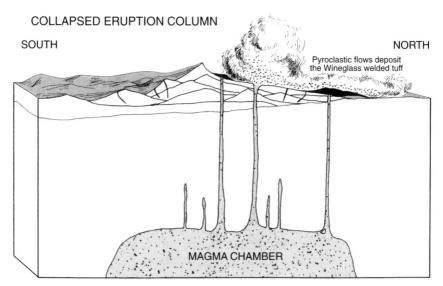

Formation of Crater Lake. Stage 2: Overburdened with fragmental material, the Plinian column collapses, initiating the first major pyroclastic flow (the Wineglass welded tuff).

pumice. Such vast quantities of material ejected from Mazama's magma chamber during the Plinian phase and initial pyroclastic flows that the volcano's summit began to sink inward, like a piston. As the roof of the magma chamber subsided and the mountaintop floundered, a series of concentric fractures opened around the summit area, creating a chain of new vents that encircled the entire cone. Violent explosions along these ring fractures disgorged masses of frothy pumice, producing monstrous pyroclastic flows that rushed down all sides of the volcano at dizzying speeds. Buoyed by gas escaping from tens of thousands of molten particles and by the superheated air trapped beneath and inside them, the pyroclastic flows easily surmounted high ridges, even the summit of Mount Scott, before plunging headlong into the glacier-cut canyons radiating away from Mazama. Divided into many branches after reaching Mazama's base, they raced outward for many tens of miles beyond the volcano.

Highly abrasive, the pyroclastic flows eroded most of the surfaces over which they passed, removing much of the air-fall pumice from Mazama's upper slopes. After thoroughly scouring Mazama's flanks, the flows filled adjacent valleys almost to the brim. Although the flows were largely confined to topographic depressions beyond Mazama's base, turbulent ash clouds

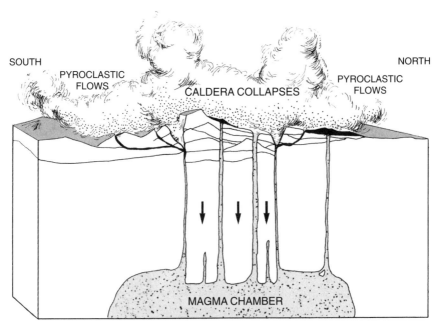

Formation of Crater Lake. Stage 3: As the underground magma chamber drains, Mount Mazama's summit collapses. New vents open along ring fractures, discharging voluminous pyroclastic flows that sweep down all sides of the volcano.

boiled upward along the flow fronts and margins, projecting hot ash over neighboring ridgetops. Following the twisting valley of the Rogue River, one pyroclastic flow traveled westward for at least 40 miles from its source, mowing down and incinerating thick stands of timber before coming to rest. Another flow, carrying pumice bombs and dense rock fragments torn from Mazama's interior, descended to the north, sweeping across Diamond Lake and depositing its rocky burden in the valley of the North Umpqua River. One arm of this flow branched westward down Lava Creek and the Clearwater River, leaving a stratum of pumice 20 to 30 feet thick.

Pyroclastic flows traveling eastward sped over 25 miles of level ground beyond Mazama's base. Although most of the rock fragments have a diameter no more than 1 to 2 feet, some pumice blocks 6 feet in diameter traveled 20 miles from the top of the volcano; at least one lump 14 feet long settled at Beaver Marsh, near U.S. 97. Similar pumice flows moved south down Annie and Sun Creek canyons, filling them to a depth of at least 250 feet. Even after 7,700 years, stream cutting has not yet fully exposed the base unit of these flows, consisting of old andesite fragments ripped from vent walls. Southeastward, the pyroclastic flows poured down Sand Creek, continuing for more than 10 miles across the adjoining flatlands. Some flows reached into Klamath Marsh, from which masses of floating pumice washed down the Williamson River into the Klamath Lakes.

As this paroxysm drew to a close, Mazama apparently tapped ever-deeper levels of its magma chamber. (During the previous 30,000 years, Mazama's subterranean reservoir had become horizontally layered or "zoned," with the lighter, more chemically evolved rhyodacite rising to the top of the chamber, its gas-rich mixture floating above a lower zone of denser andesite and basaltic andesite.) The final pyroclastic flows carried volumes of smoke-gray scoria, which formed a contrasting dark layer above the pale buff, orange, and yellowish rhyodacite pumice erupted earlier. Although these andesite scoria flows did not spread as far as those transporting the lighter-colored pumice, on the north and northeast flanks of Mazama they created the arid deposit known as the Pumice Desert, a large treeless plain visible from the highway at the park's north entrance. Some scoria flows inundated the wide valley of Pumice Creek, while others spread out to the plains bordering Klamath Marsh. The dark upper stratum is particularly conspicuous in areas where streams have since cut narrow ravines into the layered valley fills.

Long after the pyroclastic flows came to rest, they remained extremely hot. Gases seething from these glassy accumulations, some of which were 250 to 300 feet thick, produced cylindrical vents, or fumaroles, in the deposits. As hot vapors ascended through the fumaroles, these natural flues were cemented and hardened, making them comparatively resistant to

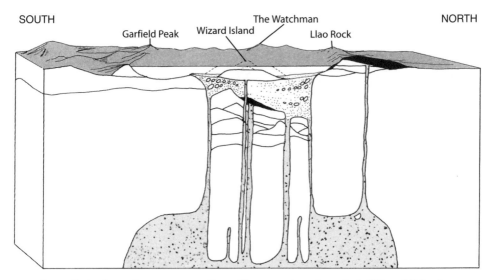

SOUTH   The Watchman   NORTH
                 Garfield Peak   Wizard Island   Llao Rock

Crater Lake formation at present. Postcaldera eruptions have built Wizard Island, a central lava platform, and other features on the now-submerged caldera floor. Groundwater seeping into the depression, along with rain and snowmelt, have half filled the basin, forming Crater Lake.

erosion. When rainfall and streams finally cut through the soft pumice beds, they left the hardened pipes standing as columns and spires. Conspicuous examples of such exhumed fossil fumaroles are visible today along the upper walls of Annie and Sand Creek canyons.

When the volcanic smog around Mount Mazama finally began to clear, the region's surviving inhabitants must have rubbed their eyes in wonder. Not only was the once-green land smothered beneath a sea of tan, orange, and dirty-gray pumice, but Llao's mountain fortress had disappeared. Where a snow-capped peak once towered, there was now only a colossal void, a depression 4,000 feet deep encircled by step cliffs. As Klamath tale-spinners later explained it, Skell, the sky-god residing atop Mount Shasta 125 miles to the south, had dealt his rival Llao such a blow that the defeated god had withdrawn to the depths of his infernal kingdom, where his fallen mountain henceforth imprisoned him.

Considering the enormous quantity of material withdrawn from the magma chamber beneath Mount Mazama, it is no wonder that the volcano collapsed. The volume of the magma ejected during the climatic eruptions roughly equals the estimated volume of Mazama's missing summit, which filled the space vacated in the volcano's underground magma reservoir. In

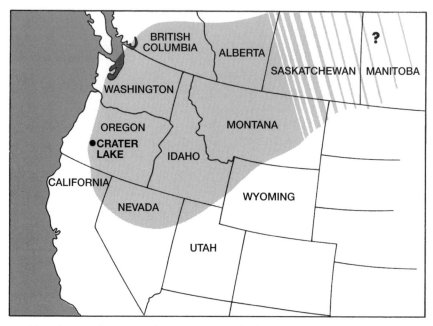

Map showing the extent of Mount Mazama's climactic ash fall, which blanketed virtually all of the Pacific Northwest and extended as far northeast as Saskatchewan, Canada

calculating the difference between the volume of new magma expelled and the volume of the former cone, it is important to remember that magma in its liquid state, before erupting, is much denser and less voluminous than when discharged as frothy, gas-charged pumice. Bacon estimated that Mazama's culminating eruptions ejected about 12 to 14 cubic miles of dense magma, a figure that agrees closely with Williams's estimate of the volume of Mazama's vanished cone.

The Date of Mazama's Demise

Radiocarbon dating of charred conifer twigs taken from several sites within Mazama's climactic pyroclastic flows and other associated deposits has yielded an age of about 6,845 years (plus or minus 50 years) for the eruption. Because the production of carbon-14 in the upper atmosphere does not occur at a strictly constant rate, it is necessary to calibrate the radiocarbon date with other methods, such as dendrochronology (the study of annual tree rings), in order to determine the actual calendar age. Such calibrations made at the University of Washington indicate that Mazama's decapitation occurred about 7,700 calendar years ago, an age confirmed by recent identification and dating of air-fall ash preserved in the Greenland ice sheet. Studies of the chemically distinct Mazama ash found in Greenland ice cores have also revealed that the outburst was not only one of the most violent and voluminous to occur anywhere on earth during latest Pleistocene and Holocene time, but that it also had a significant impact on global climate. A 1999 report indicates that Mazama's outburst created sufficient atmospheric aerosol to lower temperatures in northern latitudes by several degrees Fahrenheit, perhaps having an even more severe chilling effect than the catastrophic Tambora eruption of 1815.

Given that almost eight millennia have passed since Llao's mountain fell, many geologists doubt that native legends about the event represent the preservation of tribal memories, which would have required oral transmission through more than 300 generations. Some researchers suggest that Klamath tales about the eruption were perhaps devised in the relatively recent past to explain Crater Lake's unique topography, the only deep basin in a range of towering peaks. Even so, at least one mid-nineteenth-century Klamath leader, Lalek, came remarkably close to anticipating later scientific discoveries about Mazama's long-ago disappearance. In 1865 William M. Colvig, an American soldier then stationed at Fort Klamath, interviewed Lalek, who said that a great mountain had once stood where Crater Lake is today, adding that it had collapsed during a catastrophic eruption (a concept of caldera formation then unknown to scientists) that threatened to eradicate his entire people. Originally narrated in Chinook, Lalek's story appears in English translation in Ella Clark's *Indian Legends of the Pacific Northwest*.

Mazama's Postcaldera Activity

During and immediately following the destruction of Mazama's summit, the avalanching of unstable rock along the caldera walls greatly enlarged the original collapse depression. The heads of these massive landslides are marked by a series of semicircular coves, or embayments, such as Llao Bay, Steel Bay, and Grotto Cove, that give the caldera rim a scalloped effect. The most conspicuous landslide area visible on the caldera walls, the Chaski slide, significantly postdates the caldera formation. It occurred near Sun Notch on the south rim, where a huge horizontal block, which now has rows of evergreens growing on its upper surface, dropped hundreds of feet. Most of the avalanche debris, containing lava blocks 850 to 1,400 feet long, is deposited underwater across the caldera floor.

Almost as soon as it was formed, the cauldron began to undergo extensive change, filling partly with landslide debris, fresh lava, and a rapidly expanding lake. All of Mazama's postcaldera activity has been concentrated inside the caldera, where a cluster of new cones and lava fields erupted concurrently with the rise of Crater Lake, which has subsequently drowned all but one of them, Wizard Island.

In July and August 2000, a team of government and university scientists conducted an extensive survey of the caldera floor. Using a variety of technologies, including a high-resolution multibeam echo sounder, a vehicle-motion sounder and navigator, and a dual-differential global positioning system (DGPS), the survey team was able to create a remarkably detailed map of both the volcanic edifices and the landslide deposits hidden deep beneath the lake surface. Although the general configuration of the caldera floor was known from earlier soundings and underwater explorations, the 2000 survey provided more accurate and comprehensive information about the exact dimensions and contours of the submerged features, which has led to a more exact knowledge of the formation sequence. (See images 9 and 10 on plate 5.)

Between 7,700 and 7,200 years ago, Mazama's postcaldera activity erected three major volcanic edifices—the central lava platform, Merriam cone, and Wizard Island. In addition, extensive lava flows covered the ash fall deposit, thousands of feet thick, lying beneath the caldera floor. (Judging by erosion-exposed cross-sections of extremely old calderas elsewhere in the world, the layer of tephra and other volcanic rubble lying under the floor of Crater Lake may be well over a mile thick.) In the span of a few centuries, Mazama erupted more than a cubic mile of andesite lava, more than half of which is contained in the Wizard Island volcano. The elegantly symmetrical cinder cone visible above the lake surface is the tip of a submarine "lava-berg"; the cone stands atop a much larger oval-shaped lava pedestal that rises 1,200 feet above the lake floor. Lava pouring from the Wizard Island volcano encountered a rising body of water, an interaction that caused the flow fronts to chill and shatter, forming piles of breccia along their margins. As lava piled above lake level, later flows traveling along narrow channels on the lava surface plunged over the steep margins of their predecessors into the lake, where their fronts were also shattered, forming fragmental underwater "deltas." As the lake level steadily rose, only the uppermost part of the volcano's central cinder edifice—Wizard Island—remained above water.

At the top of the Wizard Island cone, near the lip of the circular crater, is a miniature lava flow apparently formed by a short-lived lava fountain, which sprayed partly molten rock to form the agglutinated lava stream. Extremely thin and narrow, this tiny flow appears as a black, clinkery splotch on the southwest crest of the cone. Another mass of dark lava, forming a small humped dome on the crater floor, represents the top of a plug filling the volcano's conduit.

Crater Lake and Wizard Island. The caldera walls on the left rise almost 2,000 feet above the lake surface. The dark, massive lava flow forming Llao Rock tops the caldera rim on the right. Mount Bailey occupies the middle distance. —Courtesy of the Oregon State Highway Department

Angular blocks of dark lava, measuring 6 or 7 feet in diameter, are perched at several points atop the narrow crater rim. Although these blocks seem too large to have ejected from Wizard Island's small crater, which is only 300 feet wide and about 90 feet deep, they were probably emplaced during the final stages of cone building by weak explosions that blew out fragments of lava already solidifying in the volcano's throat.

Contemporaneous with the formation of Wizard Island, another vent to the east built a similar lava structure, the flat-topped submarine edifice informally known as the central platform. Apparently lacking a fragmental core, the central platform volcano is distinguished by the effusions of lava that traveled far beyond the base of the edifice, forming undulating lava fields to the north and east.

The third submerged structure, Merriam cone, has a classically conical shape rising 1,300 feet above the north floor of the caldera, though it lacks a summit crater. Merriam cone probably was active about the same time as its two much larger neighbors, and probably formed entirely underwater. Mazama's last known activity took place approximately 4,800 years ago at a vent near the east foot of Wizard Island, where a small quantity of viscous

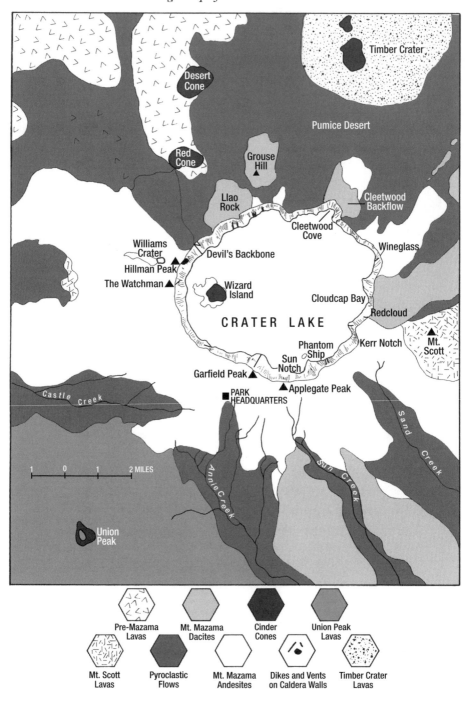

Geologic map of the Crater Lake area

magma oozed out to form a steep-sided rhyodacite dome. After this minor event, which took place 2,400 years after the first cycle of postcaldera activity, Mazama apparently has been silent for almost five millennia.

The 2000 survey of Crater Lake also remeasured its maximum depth, which had previously been established at 1,932 feet (in the east basin). Starting with a lake surface elevation of 6,178 feet, as it appears on U.S. Geological Survey topographical maps, the survey team restated the maximum depth as 1,949 feet. Some other investigators, accounting for seasonal fluctuations, use a mean surface elevation of 6,172.9 feet, giving a maximum lake depth of 1,943.6 feet (give or take a seasonal variation of about 4 feet), a figure that appears on some recent Crater Lake National Park publications.

During the approximately 7,200 years of its existence, Crater Lake's surface level has probably fluctuated often in response to cycles of climatic change. As recently as the first part of the twentieth century, the lake level dropped by about 40 feet. Today, the National Park Service reports that

Aerial view of Crater Lake from the south, with the spire of Mount Thielsen in the distance.
—U.S. Geological Survey

water added by precipitation almost exactly equals that lost by evaporation and subterranean drainage. According to Bacon, most lake seepage takes place near the Wineglass formation on the northern caldera wall, where young rubbly lava flows are most permeable. (Were it not for this invisible drain, the lake would probably have risen until it overflowed the north rim, where the caldera walls are lowest.) Except for minor seasonal variations of a few feet, the lake level now remains almost constant. Crater Lake ranks as the second-deepest body of water in North America after Canada's Great Slave Lake.

The Future of Crater Lake

According to a recent U.S. Geological Survey assessment of volcanic hazards in the Crater Lake region, it is virtually certain that Mount Mazama, which has been sporadically active for at least 420,000 years, will erupt again. Three related factors indicate the probable location of future eruptions:

1. During the volcano's long lifetime, the center of Mazama's activity gradually shifted from the east to the west flanks, where its youngest composite cone, Hillman Peak, developed.

2. Almost all Mazama's cone-building vents and most of the precaldera eruptive centers are encompassed within the present caldera rim or, like Grouse Hill, lie very close to it.

3. All postcaldera activity has taken place inside the caldera, mostly in the western half of the basin. This strongly suggests that Mazama's next eruptions, probably from new vents, will occur in the western part of the lake.

If future eruptions take place underwater, their effects will largely depend on the depth of the eruption, the rate of extrusion, and the volume, viscosity, and gas content of the magma. Eruptions of gas-rich magma in shallow water are likely to be violently explosive, fragmenting the magma into thousands of particles and generating huge clouds of ash, such as those of the Icelandic island volcano Surtsey in the early 1960s. When submarine eruptions occur at greater depth, the pressure and weight of the overlying water tend to inhibit the expansion of steam, making the event more subdued. When lava flows or domes erupt at slow rates onto the caldera floor, they also are unlikely to create an explosive outburst.

The most dangerous effect of a hydromagmatic eruption, in which the rapid mixing of water and a large volume of molten rock produces violent steam explosions, is a pyroclastic surge. Containing relatively more gas and less solid debris than a pyroclastic flow, a pyroclastic surge can transport billowing clouds of superheated ash and rock fragments at hundreds of miles an hour, sweeping over topographic barriers. Although most surges travel less than a mile from their source, others have devastated areas as far as 20 miles distant. Even when they do not generate surges, hydromagmatic eruptions can hurl ballistic blocks—rock fragments measuring many inches to several feet in diameter—several miles from the erupting vent. Hurtling through the air at velocities up to 800 feet per second, such flying objects would have little trouble overtopping the caldera rim.

Unlike the high, steep, glaciated composite cones of Hood, Baker, Rainier, and Shasta, Mazama is not expected to generate extensive mudflows that will threaten settled areas downslope. A vent erupting near the caldera rim in winter or early spring, when a heavy snowpack exists, however, could produce mudflows inundating some low-lying areas. A strongly explosive eruption inside the cauldron, particularly in shallow water, may trigger large waves, but they are not likely to overflow the rim. Geologists do not expect the low northern caldera walls to fail and release large volumes of water to neighboring lowlands, nor do they expect another climactic eruption like Mazama's for many thousands of years.

Visiting Crater Lake

Although much of Crater Lake can be viewed from Rim Drive, the 33-mile-long two-lane road encircling the caldera, a variety of relatively short hikes provide closer contact with some of Mazama's volcanic features. From Crater Lake Lodge, a short hike (1.5 miles) eastward up the Garfield Peak Trail offers a fine vantage point almost 1,900 feet above the lake. On clear days Mount Shasta's distinctive double cone is visible 125 miles to the south.

A longer (2.5 miles) trail leads from the eastside Rim Drive to the summit of Mount Scott (8,926 feet), the highest elevation in the park. The summit offers a 360-degree panorama of southern and central Oregon, including the Three Sisters about 80 miles to the north. This is the best location from which to view the entire Crater Lake region, including Mazama's prominent volcanic neighbors such as spindle-like Mount Thielsen to the northwest.

Cleetwood Trail, a mile in length, descends the north caldera wall to Cleetwood Cove, from which launch trips to Wizard Island and around the lake run during the summer season, beginning in late June or early July, depending on snow conditions. Signs on the north Rim Drive mark a parking lot where the trail starts.

On Wizard Island, a steep climb up the 763-foot cone rewards the hiker with an opportunity to inspect one of the most interesting and best preserved craters in the Cascades—the perfectly circular vent for which the entire lake was named by an Oregon newspaper editor in 1869.

Both the lodge and the park headquarters (located in Munson Valley about 4 miles south of the rim) distribute maps and trail guides to numerous other points of interest in the park.

CHAPTER 11

Oregon's Matterhorns

MOUNT THIELSEN AND ITS CASCADE PEERS

Unique to the Oregon Cascades is a series of volcanic pinnacles whose sharp pointed summits remind travelers of Switzerland's Matterhorn. The most prominent of these spires is Mount Thielsen (9,182 feet), visible from many points along the rim of Crater Lake 12 miles to the south. Farther north in the range, between the Three Sisters and Mount Jefferson, are the similarly hornlike peaks of Mount Washington and Three-Fingered Jack. Rising from gently sloping bases to extremely steep crests with no trace of a summit crater, all these mountains appear utterly unlike any other volcanoes in the High Cascades. Although their summits are less precipitous, Mount Bailey and Diamond Peak, Thielsen's close neighbors, also belong to this picturesque group of Oregon volcanoes.

Several geologic processes account for the striking differences between these sharp spires and the more conventional-looking cones of composite volcanoes such as Hood, Jefferson, and the Three Sisters. The nature of the eruptions that constructed them and the degree to which erosional forces stripped away their upper cones are two important factors. The age and early extinction of these spiked peaks also explain their peculiarly irregular shapes. Thielsen, Mount Bailey, Diamond Peak, Mount Washington, and Three-Fingered Jack had much shorter eruptive lives than many of the large Cascade stratovolcanoes, and most of them died much earlier. All the Cascade "Matterhorns"—those with the steepest summit spires—stopped erupting at least 100,000 to 250,000 years ago, producing no fresh material to repair the ravages of repeated glaciations. All were probably extinct before the last two or three major ice advances, so they are far more deeply dissected than their peers that remained active longer.

Because its geologic evolution resembles that of similar peaks in the range, Thielsen is a good example of this particular kind of High Cascade volcano. Rising above the east shore of Diamond Lake, Thielsen stands atop a broad pedestal of older shield volcanoes. Built of basaltic andesite, the magma type that forms most of the Oregon Cascade shields and cinder cones, Thielsen's eroded cone has a volume of about 2 cubic miles. Pleistocene glaciers have demolished much of the upper cone, exposing spectacular bedded pyroclastics and lava flows, some of which have been hydrothermally altered. Some

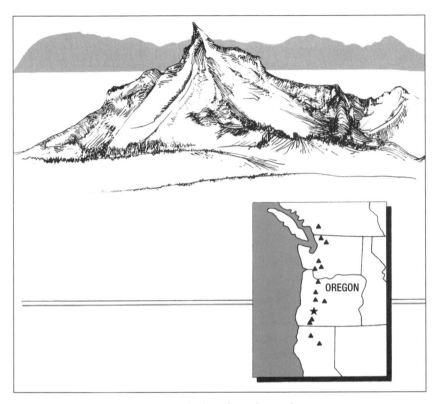

Mount Thielsen from the south

tephra layers banked against the central plug have a distinctive yellowish color, while others range from reddish orange to buff or gray. Mazama ash 12 to 65 feet thick blankets much of the lower slopes, making it difficult to interpret Thielsen's earliest activity. Potassium-argon dating of Thielsen's deposits gives an age of about 290,000 years. Because of its advanced dissection, Thielsen is a reference point for assigning ages based on degrees of physical erosion to other Cascade volcanoes; those under about 250,000 years are said to be "younger than Thielsen," while those from 250,000 to 730,000 years are classed as "older than Thielsen."

In the most extensive published study of Thielsen's life story, Howel Williams divided the volcano's growth into three main stages, details of which have since been modified by the more recent work of David Sherrod of the U.S. Geological Survey. In Williams's interpretation of Thielsen's three-part history, the volcano first erupted fluid lavas to form a broad, gently sloping shield. In the second stage it became more explosive, building a steep pyroclastic cone inside the wide summit crater. In its final phase, the volcano

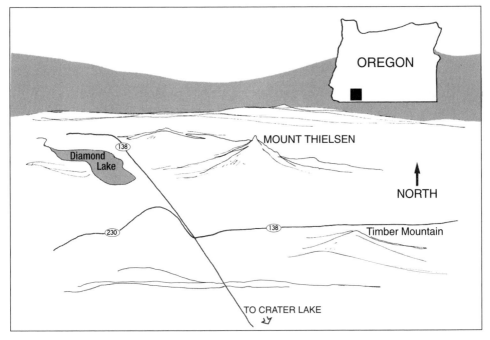

Relief map of the Mount Thielsen area

extruded a massive lava plug into its pyroclastic summit cone, which by then had filled and overflowed the original crater. According to Sherrod's later investigations, Thielsen erupted pyroclastic material and lava flows simultaneously, forming a fragmental core surrounded by extensive flows. In investigating the narrow zone of contact between the central pyroclastic edifice and the encircling lava flows, Sherrod concluded that these deposits resulted from lava fountains that erupted around the margins of the growing pyroclastic core, primarily because the tephra and lava flows can be seen to intermingle. Single flows are as thin as a few inches near their sources, but thicken to more than 30 feet downslope. Fountaining from vents at the edge of the central cone produced molten splatter that coalesced to form many of the flows.

Climbers who reach Thielsen's increasingly steep upper cone are treated to superb views of the volcano's inner structure. Although glaciers have stripped away most of the pyroclastic core, compacted layers of fine-grained tuff interspersed with coarser fragmental deposits radiate in narrow ridges away from the central plug. During its final eruptive sequence, an enormous cylinder of basaltic andesite lava intruded into the central vent, pushing aside layers of tephra and breccia, tilting some at radically steep angles and even overturning others. Almost half a mile across at the lowest exposures, but narrower farther up, this massive plug now forms Thielsen's pointed summit.

In the 250,000 or more years since its construction, glaciers have repeatedly scoured all sides of the peak, stripping away most of the pyroclastic summit cone and exhuming the central plug, eventually bringing Thielsen

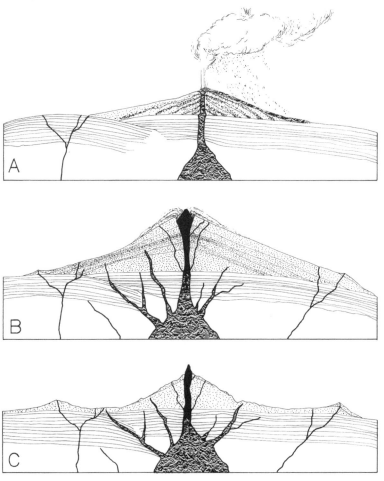

Evolution of a Cascade Matterhorn. (A) During Pleistocene time, explosive eruptions erected a pyroclastic cone on top of a late Pliocene or early Pleistocene shield volcano. (B) After lava flows from the central and peripheral vents largely covered the pyroclastic cone and partly buried the older shield, a swarm of dikes and a massive plug invaded the cone. (C) Glacial erosion cut deep into the edifice, demolishing much of the summit cone and exhuming the central plug as a free-standing spire.
—Adapted from Williams, 1933

to its present needlelike state. Particularly on the north and east sides, ice streams excavated broad glacial basins separated by thin rocky spurs. As climbers discover, the summit pinnacle's north face is dizzyingly precipitous, requiring technical skill to ascend the final 100 feet. On the shadowed north cirque a small perennial snowfield survives, the southernmost permanent ice field in Oregon. A new quadrangle map optimistically identifies it as the Lathrop glacier.

Thielson's lofty spire attracts countless lightning bolts. It has been struck so often that the mountain is known as the "lightning rod of the Cascades." Over the years, innumerable electrical charges have infused the summit rocks with an unusual substance called fulgurite. Derived from the Latin term for "thunderbolt," fulgurites form coatings on rock surfaces or small carrot-shaped tubes inside the rocks, the product of intense heat fusing glassy elements in the lava. On Thielsen, the fulgurites appear as brownish green glass that resembles greasy splotches of enamel paint.

Mount Bailey

Facing Thielsen across the shallow waters of Diamond Lake is broad-shouldered Mount Bailey (8,363 feet), a somewhat younger and less eroded basaltic andesite volcano. Bailey is the southernmost peak in a 6-mile-long north-south trending volcanic chain that stands west and north of the lake. This series of cones is probably late Pleistocene in age, more than 11,000 but less than 100,000 years old. Like Thielsen and other shield volcanoes in the region, Bailey consists of a pyroclastic core surrounded by lava flows. In a 1978 study Calvin Barnes described the 2,000-foot-high main cone, which has roughly the same volume as Thielsen (slightly over 2 cubic miles), as resting on a shield, elongate to the north. Most of Bailey's early effusive activity produced flows of basaltic andesite about 7 feet thick, although the steep upper part of the cone contains stubbier tongues of more silicic andesite lava. A secondary vent north of the present summit covered the volcano's crest with black scoria, which contrasts with the reddish orange fragmental material of the central core. Several late flows issued from a vent on the south flank, while the last of Bailey's summit eruptions formed an explosion crater, approximately 350 feet wide and 100 feet deep, about two-thirds of a mile south of the actual summit. One of the final eruptions of the Bailey chain built Rodley Butte, a cinder cone near Bailey's north base that produced at least ten flows of basaltic andesite.

Diamond Peak

Visible from many points along the rim of Crater Lake, Diamond Peak (8,750 feet) stands about 20 miles north of Bailey and Diamond Lake. The most prominent landform in the Willamette Pass area, Diamond Peak has a volume of almost 4 cubic miles, about twice that of Bailey or Thielsen. Like its neighbors, the volcano is a dual structure: a pyroclastic central core surrounded and partly veneered by flows of basaltic andesite. It consists of two overlapping cones, the older part of which forms the volcano's lower northern summit. A second major vent located slightly to the south later built a higher summit cone, partly burying its predecessor under glassy lava and tephra. Glaciation has significantly modified Diamond Peak's broad serrated crest, indicating that cone building was complete well before the last glacial advances.

A deeply eroded volcanic neck poking out of Diamond Peak's north flank is Mount Yoran, the remnant of a much older volcano. Potassium-argon dating suggests that Yoran is at least 400,000 years old.

Mount Washington

Drivers lucky enough to cross the barren lava wastes at central Oregon's McKenzie Pass on a clear day cannot fail to notice the towering summit pinnacle of Mount Washington (about 7,796 feet), a volcano that strikingly resembles Thielsen in both form and structure. (See image 14

Like the similarly precipitous Mount Thielsen, Mount Washington shows the effects of repeated glaciation, which has removed most of the cone and left the volcano's solidified central conduit as a free-standing spire. —Lyn Topinka photo, U.S. Geological Survey, Cascades Volcano Observatory

on plate 8.) From some angles Washington's spire is pointed enough to be another Cleopatra's Needle; from others, it bears a general resemblance to Sugarloaf Mountain, the famous landmark guarding the harbor of Rio de Janeiro. Edward Taylor of Oregon State University describes it as a composite cone rising about 4,000 feet above an older Pleistocene shield. According to Taylor, the volcano first erupted extensive basaltic andesite lavas that formed a platform atop which the summit cone, comprised of thinner lava flows and pyroclastic material, then formed. Culminating activity included the intrusion of a huge lava plug into Washington's central conduit, after which successive cycles of glaciation demolished most of the upper cone, exposing the sheer obelisk of its central plug. Narrow, ridgelike outcrops separating glacial cirques radiate from the plug, much as they do at Thielsen.

Like Thielsen, Washington has probably not erupted in more than 250,000 years. It stands near recently active volcanic fields at McKenzie and Santiam Passes, however, and a series of aligned small basaltic andesite cinder cones formed on its northeast flank only about 1,400 years ago. Although Washington will not erupt again, other new volcanoes may form near its base.

Three-Fingered Jack

Northernmost of the Matterhorn volcanoes, Three-Fingered Jack (7,841 feet) is as distinctive as its name. Williams's reconnaissance of the mountain suggested that its development almost exactly paralleled that of Oregon's other eroded volcanic necks, which it resembles from some angles. Unlike the summits of Washington and Thielsen, however, Three-Fingered Jack's summit—a long sawtoothed ridge with a generally north-south axis—does not consist of a central plug, but of loose tephra deposits underlain by a 10-foot-thick vertical dike. Even with the near absence of glaciers, Three-Fingered Jack's summit pinnacles are rapidly disintegrating, so precarious that climbers say the mountaintop shudders in the wind.

The informally named Jack glacier, too tiny to appear on U.S. Geological Survey maps, is a body of ice (probably stagnant) that survives in a deeply shaded cirque on the northeast flank. Protected from the sun by high ridges to the south and west, the Jack glacier is one of the lowest-lying glaciers in the central Oregon Cascades. During the Little Ice Age of AD 1350–1850, the Jack was large enough to build moraines almost 200 feet high. At least twice since 1960, however, a meltwater lake has breached the moraines, releasing floodwaters that deposited a large debris fan downslope.

Pleistocene glaciers cut so deeply into the volcano that its eruptive history is clearly displayed. A 1980 report found that Three-Fingered Jack, built on older shield lavas, consists of several overlapping cinder and composite cones that, with their associated lava flows, cover an area of about 34 square miles. The main edifice, about 1,000 feet west of the initial tephra cone, is built of massive light-gray flows of basaltic andesite interbedded with layers of multicolored pyroclastics. Late in its growth, the volcano became increasingly explosive, producing a larger proportion of tephra so that the upper part of the cone consists mostly of unconsolidated material interspersed with progressively thinner lava flows, the last averaging only 3 feet thick.

Another cone rose about 350 feet south of the main vent, while several secondary craters on the flanks erupted both lava and pyroclastics, extending the long axis of the volcano to the north and south. Radial dikes and viscous plugs repeatedly invaded the summit cones and now form the volcano's exposed core.

Cone-building eruptions had probably ceased before Three-Fingered Jack experienced the first of three Pleistocene glaciations that subsequently ravaged the peak. Beginning about 200,000 years ago, glaciers excavated large basins on all sides of the structure, particularly the east and northeast flanks. The northeast face now presents an almost vertical wall of rotten, crumbling rock.

Black Butte

Degree of erosion commonly indicates a volcano's age relative to other nearby peaks; however, a volcano's lack of obvious erosional scars does not always guarantee its relative youth. Although they are extensively dissected, Three-Fingered Jack and Mount Washington are younger than their symmetrical neighbor Black Butte (6,415 feet). Rising 3,200 feet above the eastern margin of the High Cascade plateau, at the southern end of the Green Ridge fault zone, this basaltic andesite cone has a youthful appearance partly because it is in the rain shadow of mountains standing farther west. Not enough snow accumulated on its slopes during the Pleistocene to form glaciers. But despite Black Butte's generally youthful profile, its forested slopes are etched with deep ravines, its surface rock bears thick weathering rinds, and its lavas possess reverse paleomagnetic polarity, indicating that it was built sometime before the earth's last magnetic reversal about 730,000 years ago.

It may be a relief to know that geologists have not prepared evaluations of potential volcanic hazards for any of the Oregon volcanoes discussed in this chapter. All of them are extinct.

Visiting Oregon's Matterhorns

Mount Thielsen is approached via Oregon 138 north of Crater Lake National Park. A trail (1456) begins at the east side of the Diamond Lake parking lot (at the southeast corner of the lake) and leads up a steep ridge on Thielsen's west flank. Novice climbers should not attempt the precipitous summit pinnacle.

Driving through McKenzie Pass (on Oregon 242, closed in winter) offers distant views of Mount Washington, particularly at Windy Point. Another route, U.S. 20 over Santiam Pass, connects with trails up the north flank. Follow U.S. 20 to the Hoodoo Ski Area 20 miles northwest of the town of Sisters, then take Forest Service Road 2690 2 miles south to Big Lake. According to mountaineer Jeff Smoot, just before reaching Big Lake, turn left onto Forest Service Road 500 (Old Santiam Wagon Road) for 0.5 mile to the junction with the Pacific Crest Trail. Hike south 3.5 miles up the Pacific Crest Trail to a path snaking up Washington's north ridge.

Presiding over the Diamond Peak Wilderness (52,737 acres) in south-central Oregon, Diamond Peak is not accessible by paved roads, although the Pacific Crest Trail borders its eastern flank. No well-marked trails lead to the summit.

Three-Fingered Jack, set in the Mount Jefferson Wilderness, also has no paved access roads, although it can be approached on foot. Follow U.S. 20 to the Pacific Crest Trail a short distance west of Santiam Pass, then hike about 5 miles north to the volcano's southern shoulder for close views of the peak.

CHAPTER 12

Newberry Volcano

THE WEST'S LARGEST FIRE MOUNTAIN

Combining the azure beauty of Crater Lake with the colossal size of the Medicine Lake shield, Newberry Volcano is so large and topographically distinct that many people living nearby regard it as a separate mountain range. By volume it is the largest volcanic edifice in the West. Thirty-five miles long from north to south and 22 miles wide, the central part of the volcano is located about 20 miles south of Bend, central Oregon's most populous city, and its lava flows extend through the city and many miles beyond. Standing approximately 35 miles east of the Cascade crest, Newberry resembles California's Medicine Lake volcano in its enormous size and wide variety of eruptive styles. Although Newberry rises little more than 3,500 feet above the surrounding lava plains and has the horizontal profile typical of a shield, geologists now, because of its complex intermixture of lava flows and voluminous pyroclastic deposits, categorize it as a composite cone. Like the beheaded Mount Mazama, Newberry's truncated summit holds a broad caldera, 4 by 5 miles in diameter, in which nestle not one but two sparkling lakes—Paulina and East Lakes. Its gentle slopes bristling with extended chains of cinder cones, domes, and other lava formations, Newberry has more individual vents—at least 400—than any other volcano on the U.S. mainland.

In 1990, the U.S. Congress recognized Newberry's special features by establishing the Newberry National Volcanic Monument. Encompassing more than 50,000 acres, the monument is irregular in shape, covering a generally circular area around the summit caldera and a long narrow corridor extending down the shield's northwest flank across U.S. 97 to the Deschutes River. The monument corridor was drawn to include the northwest rift zone, a linear fracture stretching from the caldera's north wall 14 miles downslope to Lava Butte, a prominent cinder cone standing about 10 miles south of Bend.

Approximately 7,000 years ago, a series of fissure eruptions along this rift zone produced twelve separate lava flows covering a total area of 23 square miles; some of these basaltic flows poured through groves of ponderosa pine, enveloping the trees and forming molds, or casts, around their trunks, producing the Lava Cast Forest, which has paved interpretive trails. Marking the

Aerial view of Newberry caldera with Paulina and East Lakes. The Big Obsidian flow occupies the foreground. —Robert Jensen photo, U.S. Forest Service

rift zone's northern terminus, Lava Butte and its associated lava field along the edge of U.S. 97 are the focal point of central Oregon's Lava Lands Visitor Center, which has a museum showcasing the region's many volcanic phenomena.

Although Newberry lacks the height and perennial snow cover of the nearby Three Sisters, it more than makes up for it with its vast size and fascinating diversity of eruptive products, including two very different, but almost equally spectacular, sets of lava flows. Representing the more silicic variety, the Big Obsidian flow is a black glittering mass of rhyolite that covers more than a square mile of the caldera floor immediately southeast of Paulina Lake. Accessible via a well-maintained trail across its surface of jagged glassy blocks, the Big Obsidian flow is the product of Newberry's most recent eruption, which occurred about 1,300 years ago. Some writers have described the Big Obsidian flow as the nation's—or even the world's—largest Holocene obsidian formation, but it ranks fifth in area covered (about 1.09 square miles) and seventh in volume (0.031 square mile). Three Medicine Lake obsidian flows—the Glass Mountain (which covers 5.2 square miles and has a volume of 0.148 cubic mile), the Little Glass Mountain (2.78 square miles and 0.105 cubic mile), and the Hoffman (2.17 square miles

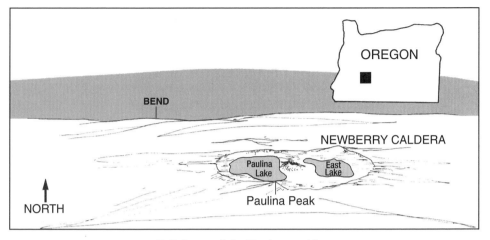

Relief map of the Newberry caldera

and 0.041 cubic mile)—exceed it in both area and volume. Two similar late Holocene flows at nearby South Sister—the Rock Mesa and the Newberry— are also larger, with areas, respectively, of 1.69 and 1.05 square miles and volumes of 0.12 and 0.040 cubic miles. (Ranking sixth in estimated volume is the Obsidian flow in the Inyo Craters chain, south of Mono Lake.)

Less well known but far more voluminous were a series of late Pleistocene flows of exceptionally fluid basalt that issued from multiple vents on Newberry's north flank and streamed northward across the sites of Bend and Redmond, some filling ancestral canyons of the Deschutes and Crooked Rivers, many tens of miles from their source. (Stream erosion has since recut these canyons to their original depth.) The latest in this series of enormous basaltic outpourings covered the Bend area about 78,000 years ago, encircling Pilot Butte, the prominent Pleistocene cinder cone near the city's eastern edge, and filling the Deschutes River bed, forcing it to erode a new channel farther to the west, where it now runs through downtown Bend.

Visitors can explore the interior of this prodigious flow in Lava River Cave, Oregon's longest continuous lava tube cave. From the cave entrance, located a short distance to the east of U.S. 97 about 12 miles south of Bend and 1.2 miles south of Lava Lands Visitor Center, it is possible to hike more than a mile to the north and west, passing under U.S. 97, where the arching cave roof is 45 feet thick. The immense volumes of molten rock pouring northwest through the Lava River Cave and other tubes in the same flow flooded the Deschutes basin and traveled as far as the southern edge of the present city of Redmond.

If lava flows with volumes comparable to those of the late Pleistocene basalts erupted today, they not only could bury the largest settlements in central Oregon, but also could wipe out long stretches of U.S. 97—the area's main transportation corridor—as well as vital gas pipelines and power lines carrying electricity to California.

The walls encircling Newberry's oval-shaped caldera are extremely varied in height, lowest (a few tens of yards) where Paulina Creek, draining Paulina Lake, rushes through a notch in the west rim. By contrast, the south rim rises about 1,500 feet above the caldera floor, where a massive rhyolite flow forms Paulina Peak (7,985 feet), the highest elevation on the cone. A recently improved gravel road climbs steeply to the summit of Paulina Peak, which affords a stunning 360-degree view of the entire region, revealing that Newberry stands near the intersection of four major geologic provinces: the Cascade Range, with the glaciated cones of Mount Bachelor, Broken Top, and the Three Sisters, to the west; the juniper and sagebrush dotted High Lava Plains to the east; the arid Basin and Range province to the southeast; and the ancient (partly volcanic) Blue Mountains to the northeast. During the last ten million years, silicic volcanism in the High Lava Plains has moved progressively from east to west along the Brothers fault zone, a complex system of crustal fractures trending west-northwest from the eastern margin of Harney Basin to the Cascades. The High Lava Plains' youngest silicic domes, less than a million years old, erupted immediately east of Newberry.

The Caldera

Although frequently called Newberry Crater, the large summit basin is really a collapse depression. Except for the bare surfaces of lava flows and pumice deposits erupted during the last few thousand years, much of Newberry's caldera is forested, indicating that it formed much earlier than that of Mount Mazama. Newberry seems to have staged a series of caldera-forming pyroclastic eruptions, each outburst creating a somewhat smaller collapse area than its predecessor and resulting in the concentric or nested calderas we see today. The oldest and largest caldera probably formed about 300,000 years ago, when the volcano ejected an estimated 2.5 cubic miles of pyroclastic material, bathing the shield in voluminous ash flows hot enough to weld. These ash flow deposits, the Tepee Draw tuff, shroud most of Newberry's east flank. Newly obtained argon dating reveals that the most recent collapse event took place about 80,000 years ago, when another violently

Newberry's long, undramatic profile resembles that of the Medicine Lake volcano. —Courtesy of Robert Jensen, U.S. Forest Service

explosive outburst ejected a huge quantity of pyroclastic material, perhaps as much as 2.5 cubic miles. According to Julie Donnelly-Nolan and her USGS colleagues, who began mapping Newberry's deposits in the early 2000s, different phases of the caldera-forming eruption produced rhyodacite pumice and the more widespread basaltic ash flow deposit known as the Black Lapilli tuff, which now mantles much of the volcano's west flank. This eruption blanketed tens of thousands of square miles with ash, one lobe of which may have extended as far south as the San Francisco Bay Area, where it is a centimeter thick. (Named the Olema ash bed when its source was unknown, this widespread tephra layer is found at locations ranging from Tule Lake, at the northern foot of the Medicine Lake volcano, to the San Francisco region, almost 500 miles southwest of Newberry.) Since that time, Newberry has continued to erupt highly silicic magma in or near the caldera, while typically producing basaltic or basaltic andesite flows on its outer flanks.

Although Newberry has produced several large-volume explosive eruptions, their exact number is open to question. According to Stephen Kuehn's 2002 study, the volcano has erupted up to sixty widespread rhyolitic or dacitic tephras, ten of which can be correlated with ash deposits as far away as Idaho, Utah, and northern California. Observing that no more than six tephra layers can be found at any single location, however, Donnelly-Nolan suggests that many of the widespread tephra deposits probably represent different ash lobes from the same eruptive cycle. Differences in the chemical or mineralogical content of many ash layers may be attributed to the volcano's tapping of different levels of a compositionally zoned magma reservoir. Some distinct ash falls do extend over vast areas, such as the Paulina Creek tephra, erupted at least 50,000 to 55,000 years ago, and the Wono tephra, about 20,000 years old, the latter found in both western Nevada and east-central California. The most recent tephra eruption produced the Newberry pumice, ejected just prior to the Big Obsidian flow of approximately

EARLY HUMAN HABITATION IN THE NEWBERRY CALDERA ▬▬

> Thomas Connolly and his colleagues at the University of Utah have recently found evidence that humans have intermittently occupied the Newberry caldera for more than 10,000 years. In 1992, excavations near Paulina Lake revealed remains of what may be North America's oldest dwelling. The archaeological dig uncovered signs of a central hearth and the outlines of a domestic structure, marked by charred support posts and a linear alignment of rocks and measuring about 13 by 16 feet. Radiocarbon dating of charcoal samples from a deeper layer at the site gave a calendar age of about 11,000 years. Although the area's intense volcanic activity—not only Newberry's many outbursts, but also the cataclysmic Mazama eruption that deposited pumiceous ash 2 to 3 feet deep over the caldera—necessarily made human habitation sporadic, Native Americans returned frequently to the caldera to obtain obsidian, prized for fashioning projectile points and other tools. A prehistoric obsidian trade flourished widely throughout much of the Pacific Coast region for thousands of years.

1,300 years ago and extending hundreds of miles to the east. Judging by the great distances that upper-level winds carried Newberry's air-fall material, some of the Plinian eruption plumes may have risen 20 miles or more into the stratosphere.

As a long-lived volcano with relatively recent eruptions and a shallow heat source that still feeds a number of submarine hot springs in both Paulina and East Lakes, Newberry is a prime candidate for supplying geothermal energy. While investigating Newberry's geothermal potential in 1981, scientists with the U.S. Geological Survey drilled a well 3,057 feet deep east of the Big Obsidian flow, where they encountered subsurface temperatures of 509 degrees Fahrenheit. According to Lawrence Chitwood, a geologist with the Deschutes National Forest, in 1995–1996 an energy company drilled two holes 10,000 feet deep, reaching temperatures of 600 degrees, but found no fluids at that depth. Discovering these "dry" wells, without steam or hot water to drive turbines for geothermal power, prompted the commercial explorers to abandon their project. Many scientists, however, believe Newberry is the best geothermal energy prospect in the Pacific Northwest.

In examining drill cores from the 1981 explorations, USGS geologists found that eruptions following the caldera's formation have buried the caldera floor to a depth of 1,640 feet. Core samples reveal that the upper 950 feet of caldera fill contains both air-fall pumice and obsidian flows, as well as basaltic and rhyolitic ash that erupted underwater, indicating that a large lake ancestral to Paulina and East Lakes occupied the caldera thousands of years ago, an inference confirmed by a thick layer of lake-bottom sediments at depths between 950 and 1,180 feet. Core samples from 1,180 to 1,640 feet beneath the surface consisted of pumiceous ash and other pyroclastic material, underlain by deeper layers of rhyolitic to dacitic flows (1,640 to 2,449 feet), and basalt to basaltic andesite flows and breccia (2,485 to 3,057 feet). The transition from pyroclastic fill to solid dacitic and basaltic flows below 1,640 feet probably marks the original caldera floor.

The large volume of pyroclastic material interspersed with silicic lava flows and domes reveals that Newberry, in spite of its shape, is not an ordinary shield volcano of the Hawaiian type. As Stephen Kuehn's recent study points out, Newberry intermittently staged violent Plinian and Peléan eruptions during its long history. Whereas basaltic or basaltic andesite lavas mantle much of its north and south slopes, more silicic tephra and pyroclastic flow deposits shroud much of its east and west flanks. Cores taken from a drill hole 1,200 feet deep on the upper northeast flank showed that Newberry produced more dacite and rhyolite lavas on that part of the edifice than it did basalt. On the west side, deposits of the Black Lapilli tuff cover about 30 square miles up to a depth of 200 feet; exposures are visible along the road leading from U.S. 97 into the monument, about 9 or 10 miles east of the junction on U.S. 97 marked "Newberry Crater." A younger series of ash flow deposits blankets the upper west flank, forming a smooth, gently dipping surface that extends about 2 miles from the caldera rim. Donnelly-Nolan, however, suggests that these deposits result from the same eruption that produced the Black Lapilli tuff. Composed of numerous andesite pyroclastic layers, these tephras and ash flows erupted at high temperatures, forming agglutinates at the caldera rim. Created when molten or plastic lava fragments fuse together, the agglutinates, which grade downward into ash flow deposits, probably erupted from ring fractures bordering both the eastern and western caldera walls. Paulina Creek, the only stream on Newberry, has incised a narrow gorge through this deposit, which forms the 80-foot-high cliffs at Paulina Creek Falls.

In the 1990s, Robert Jensen and Lawrence Chitwood discovered that the channel of Paulina Creek was swept clean of Mazama ash by a large flood that took place between about 2,300 and 4,000 years ago, releasing as much as 12,000 acre-feet of water from Paulina Lake. The geologists also found evidence that the southern part of the caldera floor has tilted upward about 15 feet during the last few thousand years, indicated by wave-cut terraces that now stand above Paulina Lake's present level.

Neither of Newberry's twin caldera lakes has an inlet; both are supplied entirely by precipitation and percolating ground water, including submerged hot springs. Covering 1,530 acres, Paulina Lake, named for a local nineteenth-century Native American resident of the area, has a maximum depth of 250 feet. A narrow isthmus about a mile wide separates it from the smaller East Lake, which covers 1,050 acres and has a maximum depth of 180 feet. The isthmus consists of several rhyolite flows and is surmounted by a conspicuous pyroclastic structure that occupies the center of the caldera, the aptly named Central Pumice cone. About 700 feet high, this broad, flat-topped cone formed during an episode of particularly intense activity about 7,000 years ago, approximately the same period that witnessed the construction of Lava Butte and other effusive basaltic eruptions along the northwest rift zone. Besides the Central Pumice cone and the obsidian flow erupted inside its crater, this eruptive phase also produced the Interlake obsidian flow and the Game Hut obsidian flow, which emerged from a vent at the south side of the Central Pumice cone. Approximately 3,500 years later, an eruption on the East Lake fissure produced both airborne tephra and the East Lake obsidian flows.

Newberry's most recent eruptions, about 1,300 years ago, were confined to the caldera and included both explosive and effusive activity. The sequence began violently with a Plinian outburst, ejecting a towering

The Big Obsidian flow erupted about 1,300 years ago from a vent near the caldera's south wall. —Courtesy of Robert Jensen

column of pumiceous tephra that blanketed the eastern half of the caldera and extended in a straight and narrow lobe hundreds of miles to the east-northeast. Roughly 12 feet thick 5.5 miles from the source vent located low on the southern caldera wall, this layer—the Newberry pumice—diminishes to a thickness of 10 inches at a distance of 40 miles. Winds carried fine particles of this tephra at least as far northeast as Idaho, and perhaps beyond. The gas-rich silicic magma of this eruption also created pyroclastic flows and surges that swept from the vent into Paulina Lake, leaving a deposit of pumice bombs in a matrix of fine, slightly pinkish ash visible from the edge of the Big Obsidian flow to the lake shore. As the gas content of the erupting magma declined, viscous masses of rhyolite then surged from the wall vent, gradually spreading over a square mile of the caldera floor. Oozing northward over the pyroclastic flow deposits for a distance of 6,000 feet, the Big Obsidian flow partly engulfed an older tephra structure, the Lost Lake pumice ring. From a trail over the flow's blocky crust, observers can see many of its features, including flow banding and gradations from pumiceous obsidian to brown streaky bands that contrast with other parts of the black glossy surface. All three phases of the eruption—tephra, pyroclastic flows, and obsidian flow—have the same chemical composition and probably took place in rapid succession.

Vents on Newberry's Flanks

Newberry's shieldlike edifice probably owes its long life and vast bulk to its position at or near the intersection of several geologic provinces and their associated fault zones. Most of the 400 cinder cones, domes, and other vents on Newberry's outer slopes are lined up along three broad zones that join on the upper part of the volcano. The east zone appears to be a continuation of the basaltic volcanism that characterizes the High Lava Plains east of the shield. Most of the cones in this alignment seem to be relatively old. The northwest rift zone, which has produced the most recent basaltic eruptions, parallels a system of fractures near the volcano's base that extends farther northwest along the Tumalo fault zone to Green Ridge in the Cascades. The third line of fractures, a southwest belt, parallels the Walker Rim fault zone. In addition, some aligned cinder cones and fissures near Newberry's summit follow an arcuate pattern that roughly approximates the curve of the caldera rim and are probably associated with the concentric ring fractures responsible for summit subsidence and caldera formation.

Although most of the cinder cones on Newberry's flanks range from about 200 to 400 feet in height, a few rise 500 feet above their bases and have diameters exceeding half a mile. A majority have shallow, saucerlike summit depressions, but some, such as Lava Top and North Kawak Buttes, retain steep-walled craters 200 to 300 feet deep. In most cases, eruptions along fracture zones on the outer shield either concentrated at a single vent and erected sizable tephra cones, or occurred along fissures and built long ridges of overlapping cinder or spatter cones, such as the Devil's Horn a few miles south of East Lake.

Streams of basalt or basaltic andesite commonly broke through the bases of these cones and flowed between or around them, leaving a network of intermingling lava flows. Much of Newberry's north and south flanks are veneered in pahoehoe or aa flows that retain fresh-looking surfaces and sharply defined margins. As their youthful appearance suggests, some of the lava flows erupted late in the Pleistocene. According to Donnelly-Nolan, the Klawhop flow has been dated at about 39,500 years, but is older than several other large flows on the north flank.

One of Newberry's most unusual features is the Badlands shield, visible from U.S. 20 as it crosses the volcano's northeast slope. Defined by Chitwood as a "rootless shield volcano," the Badlands edifice was not built by magma rising directly from an underground source, but is the offspring of a blocked lava tube in a large basaltic lava flow that issued from a vent higher on Newberry's flank. When fluid basaltic lava flowing through the tube reached the blockage, it surged upward and out in successive waves, forming a gently sloping shield about 8 miles in diameter. Paved with a pahoehoe surface, the Badlands shield is dotted with numerous tumuli and topped by a small pit crater.

In addition to its multiple peripheral cones and flows, Newberry has about twenty rhyolitic domes or thick flows on its west, south, and east slopes. At the east base, two large rhyolite or obsidian domes, East Butte and China Hat, are pre-Newberry in age, 850,000 and 780,000 years old, respectively. McKay Butte on the west flank dates to 580,000 years ago. During the Holocene, all rhyolite eruptions have been restricted to vents in or near the summit caldera. Newberry's largest and most prominent rhyolite flow, Paulina Peak, is a mile wide and extends southwestward from the caldera wall about three miles downslope. This elongate mass was extruded about 80,000 years ago, shortly before the most recent caldera-forming eruption.

Standing in the rain shadow of the Cascades, the Newberry edifice is extremely dry, with only one stream—Paulina Creek—flowing on its entire broad surface. It is uncertain whether cooler temperatures and higher precipitation during the Pleistocene allowed glaciers to form on the volcano, as they did on the similarly positioned Medicine Lake volcano to the south. In preparing a detailed geologic map of the volcano, however, Donnelly-Nolan found several glacial erratics—rocks deposited far from their place of origin—on top of cinder cones bordering the caldera's northeast rim. The cones themselves are "boat shaped," with a long northeast axis, suggesting that moving ice modified their forms. In addition, Donnelly-Nolan points out that large quantities of sediment were laid down on Newberry's east and northeast flanks, perhaps the deposits of streams issuing from Pleistocene glaciers higher on the edifice. The long, narrow Potholes lava flow on the east side appears to fill a previously abandoned stream bed, indicating that at one time surface water drained down that slope—and that the Potholes flow is probably postglacial in age.

Lava Butte and Prehistoric Lake Benham

The dozen basaltic lava flows erupted along the northwest rift zone approximately 7,000 years ago were fed by Hawaiian-style lava fountains, geysers of molten rock buoyed up by gas escaping from the fluid magma. At the rift's northern end, eruptions began as a "curtain of fire" along a 1.5-mile-long fissure, forming an alignment of spatter cones and small pahoehoe flows, including the Gas Line flows located immediately east of U.S. 97. As the fissure gradually sealed and activity focused on a single pipelike vent, Strombolian eruptions discharged scoriaceous tephra that rapidly accumulated to build Lava Butte's 500-foot-high cone. Prevailing winds directed most of the ejecta north of the erupting vent, making the cone visibly thicker and the crater rim higher on the north side. Clouds of ash drifted northward, shrouding the landscape in a charcoal gray blanket.

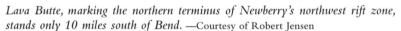

Lava Butte, marking the northern terminus of Newberry's northwest rift zone, stands only 10 miles south of Bend. —Courtesy of Robert Jensen

Copious streams of lava issued through a vent at the south base of the cinder cone but were then diverted westward and northward into topographic low points along the Deschutes River, burying its former channel under lava 100 feet thick. Traveling north for 5 miles and spreading over 9 square miles, a series of overlapping lava flows dammed the river in several places; prehistoric Lake Benham formed behind the uppermost lava dam and eventually extended to a maximum of 30 river-miles upstream. Lake Benham inundated areas as far distant as the present La Pine Recreation Area, completely drowning a forest on the site of Sunriver Resort, now one of central Oregon's most luxurious vacation developments. Displaced from its old riverbed by the Lava Butte flows, the Deschutes was forced to cut a new channel to the west, eventually eroding its way through older rocks bordering the flow and creating a series of picturesque cataracts, including Benham, Dillon, and Lava Island Falls.

Geologists estimate that 90 percent of Lava Butte's magma output took the form of lava flows, with only 9 percent of the total volume forming the cinder cone and 1 percent the thin layer of ash extending to the north.

Visiting Newberry Volcano

The Lava Lands Visitor Center is located 10 miles south of Bend on the west side of U.S. 97. A paved road spirals to the rim of Lava Butte's steep-walled summit crater from the Lava Lands Visitor Center. Walking around the red and black scoria formations at the crater's edge, visitors enjoy a breathtaking panorama that includes both the massive Newberry shield to the southeast and the snowcapped High Cascades to the west. Visitors also can peer directly into a vent through which magma from deep within the earth reached the surface, spraying incandescent showers of molten rock high into the air. Oregon volcanism has produced many cinder cones younger than 7,000-year-old Lava Butte, including the late Holocene cinder cones at McKenzie Pass east of Bend, but none has Lava Butte's easy accessibility—or its ominous proximity to a major urban center.

CHAPTER 13

The Three Sisters

OREGON'S VOLCANIC PLAYGROUND

Throughout most of its length, the Cascade Range is punctuated by large composite cones spaced about 40 to 60 miles apart. This discrete distribution of the major volcanoes allows an individual mountain to reign supreme over its particular domain, as Shasta does in northern California, Hood in northwestern Oregon, and Rainier in Washington's Puget Sound region. In central Oregon, however, the usual pattern is broken: instead of a single snowy peak dominating the immediate countryside, a cluster of closely grouped volcanoes creates an impressively crowded skyline.

Viewed from the hills near Bend, the prominent peaks from south to north include the symmetrical Bachelor; craggy Broken Top; the South, Middle, and North Sisters; and Belknap shield (also called Belknap crater). Farther north are the sharp pinnacles of Mount Washington and Three-Fingered Jack. Several of these peaks remain snowcapped even in summer. The Three Sisters, all over 10,000 feet high, support at least a dozen active glaciers. No part of the Cascade Range can boast a greater number or variety of recent volcanic landforms than the Three Sisters area. From the oldest, deeply eroded spires of Washington and North Sister, to the youthful contours of Bachelor, Belknap, and South Sister, this vista offers a lavish display of volcanoes old and new.

The area's most recent eruptions, at the Belknap shield about 1,500 years ago and the South Sister about 2,000 years ago, produced both explosions of tephra and effusions of lava. After a millennium and a half of silence, however, the region may be reawakening. In 2001 scientists at the U.S. Geological Survey, using a satellite radar technique, detected a new bulge in the crust about 3 miles west of the South Sister. Although the ground swell measures only about 10 inches above previously measured levels, it involves an impressively large area—60 square miles—and continues to rise at the rate of 1 inch per year. Geologists believe that the uplift, which was first accompanied by a swarm of small earthquakes in March, 2004, is caused by an upwelling of magma about 4 miles underground. An eruption may not be imminent, but the USGS keeps a watchful eye on the phenomenon: geologists have installed seismographs in the area and take careful readings of the gas content in local streams and springs.

The Three Sisters seen from the north. Collier glacier (center) still has a maximum thickness of 300 feet, although it has shrunk drastically in recent decades. In about 1900 the ice tongue surmounted the crater wall of Collier cone (bottom center), a youthful cinder cone at the North Sister's northern toe. —Austin Post photo, U.S. Geological Survey

Vigilance is necessary because future eruptions may affect central Oregon's most densely populated areas, including Bend and the town of Sisters, as well as numerous smaller settlements. In addition, the federally protected Three Sisters Wilderness and surrounding area draw tens of thousands of visitors each year to its recreational facilities. During summer and fall, hikers, backpackers, and campers flock to the region's 240 miles of developed trails and many campgrounds, enjoying fragrant pine forests, rushing cataracts, and alpine meadows. Climbing enthusiasts are drawn to the glaciated peaks, which offer a variety of mountaineering opportunities, from the relatively easy south-side ascent of South Sister to the challenging summit crags of the rugged North Sister. In winter, resorts such as the Inn of the Seventh Mountain and the Sunriver Resort regularly attract throngs of skiers and snowboarders. Widely known for its dry, powdery snow, Mount

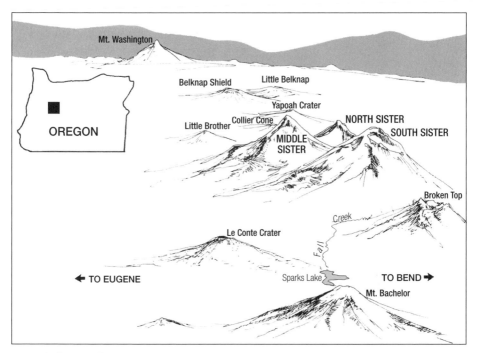

Relief map of the Three Sisters region from the south, with its location in central Oregon. The North Sister, Mount Washington, and Broken Top are among the oldest volcanoes in the region; the Belknap shield and Collier cone are among the youngest.

Bachelor provides lifts that transport skiers all the way to its frosty summit (9,065 feet).

The Cascade Lakes Highway provides access to dozens of alpine lakes, ranging from small tarns to lakes large enough to accommodate multiple sports, including fishing, boating, and water skiing. Many lakes along this scenic drive owe their existence to recently erupted lava flows that dammed streams draining the area. A chain of rhyodacite domes and thick lava flows extruded along the south flanks of South Sister about 2,000 years ago created islands of jagged, barren rock that contrast sharply with the surrounding sea of dense green forest. One of the southernmost domes, rising at the edge of Devils Lake and bristling with angular protrusions, is clearly visible from the highway.

The Geology of the Three Sisters

Over the years, geologists have offered strikingly different interpretations of the Three Sisters' volcanic history, the earliest of which has long since been abandoned, although visitors still occasionally hear of it. When he published the first geological reconnaissance of the region in 1925, E. T. Hodge, then a professor at the University of Oregon, concluded that the present cluster of volcanoes was but the remnant of a once vastly larger volcanic cone that had collapsed in Miocene or early Pliocene time. The broad arc of peaks that runs from Broken Top through Devils Hill, Wife, Sphinx, Husband, Little Brother, and North Sister seemed to outline an ancient caldera rim. Observing the long slopes leading outward from the irregular arc, Hodge imagined them projected upward to an enormous central cone, a vanished edifice he called Mount Multnomah. Hodge concluded that Multnomah had been engulfed, in much the same way that Mazama had collapsed to form the caldera in which Crater Lake lies.

Later investigators, however, have demonstrated that Mount Multnomah never existed. In the early 1940s the late Howel Williams, then a professor at the University of California, Berkeley, thoroughly reexamined the Three Sisters and associated peaks. He concluded that Hodge's supposed arc was a coincidence, that each of the edifices in question is a separate volcano with an individual eruptive history, and that none of the group was ever part of an ancient volcanic colossus.

The Tumalo Volcanic Center

Although Mount Multnomah turned out to be imaginary, the Three Sisters did have some notable volcanic predecessors in the area. Between about 650,000 and 170,000 years ago, a line of silicic volcanoes located east of Broken Top and west of Bend produced a series of violently explosive eruptions, ejecting huge quantities of pyroclastic material that mantled a wide area along the eastern front of the central Oregon Cascades, from the town of Sisters to south of Bend. When David Sherrod of the U.S. Geological Survey, Edward Taylor of Oregon State University, and their colleagues recently mapped the region, they identified and dated three major pyroclastic deposits: from oldest to youngest, the three major units are the Desert Spring tuff, the Bend pumice and Tumalo tuff (two units from the same eruption), and the Shevlin Park tuff. Although their source vents have since been obscured by later eruptions, all apparently originated along a 15-mile-long alignment of silicic volcanoes, extending from Melvin Butte to Edison Butte, known as the Tumalo volcanic center.

Erupted between about 600,000 and 700,000 years ago, the Desert Spring tuff is a widespread rhyodacitic pyroclastic flow deposit up to 100 feet thick. The region's most voluminous air-fall deposit—and more than 42 feet thick about 10 miles from its presumed source—the Bend pumice was ejected about 300,000 years ago; the Tumalo tuff, a pyroclastic flow lying directly atop the Bend pumice, represents the second phase of the same eruptive episode. The most recent of the large Tumalo center pyroclastic flows, that forming the Shevlin Park tuff, took place less than 170,000 years ago and is well exposed at North Fork Squaw Creek. Noting that the Triangle Hill area hosts a cluster of silicic domes and andesite cinder cones similar in composition to the Shevlin Park tuff, Sherrod suggests that both it and the Bend pumice erupted from vents near that site.

In addition to the three dated deposits, other mid- to late Pleistocene pyroclastic layers are also exposed in roadcuts, stream-cut valley walls, and quarries throughout the Bend region, including the pumice of Columbia Canal, an air-fall tephra deposit exposed along the Columbia Southern Canal, and the Century Drive tuff, found in scattered outcrops south and west of Bend. Altogether this explosive sequence, which distributed ash as far south as northern California, ejected several cubic miles of magma and may have formed a caldera, although later eruptions from nearby vents have since buried any collapse depression.

The Shevlin Park tuff, less than 170,000 years old, provides an important time marker limiting the age of the Three Sisters. Because early basaltic lava flows from the North Sister—the oldest of the trio—overlay Shevlin deposits near North Fork Squaw Creek, it is apparent that all three of the Sisters are younger than 170,000 years. The youngest, South Sister, which may have built most of its cone during the last 40,000 years, erupted as recently as 2,000 years ago.

The North Sister

The oldest Sister looks its age. Repeated glaciations have stripped away most of the constructional surface, exposing much of the volcano's internal structure. Erected atop an older, deeply eroded basaltic shield of about the same size—remnants of which form the Little Brother—North Sister (10,085 feet) is a basaltic andesite shield measuring approximately 6 miles in diameter. Williams estimated that the volcano once reached an elevation of 11,000 feet but lost its former summit, along with approximately a fourth to a third of its original bulk, through glacial erosion. It has probably been extinct for at least 100,000 years.

Cirques incised in the summit area reveal that in its later stages of growth North Sister erupted significant quantities of pyroclastic material, forming beds of ash and red and black scoria interspersed with lava flows. A sequence of flat-lying lava flows near the summit suggests that these flows erupted in a large crater or collapse depression, now nonexistent. Compared with the extensive aa flows that compose the lower part of the shield, many of the flows comprising the upper cone are remarkably thin. An exposure south of the Thayer glacier shows that fifty superimposed flows make a cliff only about 120 feet high.

Swarms of dikes invaded North Sister's summit cone, more numerous than those on any similar Cascade peak. Now exhumed by erosion, dozens of vertical or oblique lava walls ranging in width from a few inches to 25 feet radiate away from the volcano's crest. According to Williams, a massive steep-sided plug intruded into the main conduit, thrusting aside and displacing many of the earlier dikes and pyroclastic deposits. Completely filling the volcano's throat, this 300-yard-wide plug now forms the two summit pinnacles, known as Prouty Peak and the South Horn. (Glisan Peak forms a slightly lower subsummit.)

Deeply dissected, the North Sister (foreground) features a large cirque on its north face. The Collier glacier, originating on Middle Sister's northwest flank, appears in the upper right. Mount Bachelor is visible to the southeast (left), and South Sister peeps above North Sister's crest (center). —Austin Post photo, U.S. Geological Survey

Erosion reduced much of the North Sister edifice to rubble, so it now resembles a huge pile of dark lava fragments tentatively held together by an array of dikes and sills, which along with the summit pinnacles seem to be the only solid rock on the mountain. Constant rockfalls from North Sister's steep, crumbly slopes make it one of Oregon's most dangerous peaks to climb. Mountaineers complain that the volcano's upper flanks are so unstable that they offer no secure hand or foothold; so many loose rocks shoot down the gully leading up Prouty Peak that this route is informally known as the "bowling alley." Because of its precipitous, rapidly disintegrating cone and sheer-walled summit crags, climbers have dubbed this Sister "Beast of the Cascades."

Like Thielsen, Washington, and other peaks of comparable age, North Sister probably ceased to erupt long before the last two Pleistocene glacial advances. During its maximum extent, the High Cascade icecap mantled most of the peak, extending north and east to elevations of about 4,000 feet. To the west, some valley glaciers stretched for 15 miles, reaching as low as 1,000 feet above sea level.

Glacial cutting has also effaced most of the original features of North Sister's roughly contemporaneous neighbors, including the Wife, Sphinx, and Burnt Top. Rising to the west of Middle and South Sisters is the Husband, notable for the unusual fluidity of its early lava flows, some of which traveled as far as the western Cascade boundary. The Husband also features two large summit plugs sharpened by erosion. The southern plug measures 200 by 600 yards; the northern plug, standing 800 feet high, is three quarters of a mile long and 300 yards wide.

Broken Top

Although its exact age is unknown, the picturesque Broken Top (9,175 feet), one of the larger stratovolcanoes in the Sisters constellation, is perhaps somewhat older than North Sister. Like its higher neighbor, Broken Top ceased erupting about 100,000 years ago, allowing Pleistocene glaciers to dissect its cone, reducing it to an irregular amphitheater open to the southeast. Its former summit, its entire southeast slope, and much of its interior have entirely disappeared, leaving jagged rocky spurs standing between deep glacial cirques, where small ice streams, including the Bend and Crook glaciers, continue their work of laying bare the volcanic core. In its exposed interior one can see brilliantly colored strata: bands of red, purple, and black scoria alternating with layers of yellow, brown, and orange welded pumice and ash flow tuffs. A conspicuous stratum of white pumice is interbedded with fragments of black lava, giving a vivid salt-and-pepper appearance to the deposit.

In his study of Broken Top, Edward Taylor of Oregon State University showed that the volcano grew by first building a large pyroclastic cone atop a platform of older, glaciated basaltic andesite lavas. The pyroclastic cone was repeatedly invaded by dikes and sills that strengthened the edifice and probably fed lava flows that formed an armor of solid rock covering the original fragmental structure. During this cone-building stage, Broken Top produced a variety of lava types, alternating streams of basaltic andesite with more silicic flows of dacite and rhyodacite. Intermittent explosive eruptions contributed additional tephra and pyroclastic flows.

Partway through its growth, the volcano's former summit collapsed, creating a summit depression about half a mile in diameter. Thin flows of basaltic andesite later filled the crater, spilling down the outer slopes and mantling the cone with a thin veneer of porous lava. In the final stages of development, magma congealing in the central conduit formed a large plug of micronorite, similar to that in Three-Fingered Jack. Acidic hot water circulating through Broken Top's interior then partly altered both the plug and adjacent deposits.

The Middle Sister

Except for its height (10,047 feet) and glacial covering, the Middle Sister has few distinctions. Smallest of the trio of volcanic siblings, it has the outline of a regular cone from which the east face has been stripped away, giving it a general resemblance to Yosemite's Half Dome. Its steep east flank sustains the Hayden and Diller glaciers, which continue to cut into the mountain's interior, enlarging the east-side cirques. Pleistocene glaciations previously removed the former summit and crater.

In the early 2000s, a USGS team including Wes Hildreth, Judy Fierstein, and Andrew Calvert used radiometric dating to determine the ages of twenty glacially eroded dacitic and rhyolitic lava flows erupted by Middle and South Sisters—with unexpected results. It had previously been assumed that the Three Sisters volcanoes were progressively younger from north to south, but the geologists found that Middle and South Sisters, at least in the construction of their upper cones, are roughly contemporaries. Although the basaltic andesite flows and tephra composing South Sister's summit cone are too young to be dated by the radiometric method, many flows along its flanks are coeval with similarly silicic flows from Middle Sister. In addition, the stack of thin basaltic and andesite flows forming Middle Sister's summit edifice are sandwiched by two thick dacite flows. The older of the two flows, which issued from a flank vent near Chambers Lakes and floors the pile of summit cone lavas, yields an age of about 20,000 years. The younger dacite flow, which erupted at an altitude of 8,500 feet on the south side and

REPRESENTATIVE VOLCANIC EVENTS IN THE THREE SISTERS REGION DURING THE PAST 15,000 YEARS

DATE OR APPROXIMATE AGE (YEARS)	EVENT
AD 2001–present	Ground uplift and earthquakes 3 miles west of South Sister
1,400–1,300	Formation of Blue Lake crater and chain of spatter cones near Mount Washington
1,500	Belknap shield lava flows
1,600	Building of Collier cone, Four-in-One cone, Yapoah cone
2,300–2,000	Extrusion of Devils Hill lava flows and domes on southeast and northeast flanks of South Sister; eruption of Rock Mesa lava flow
3,000–2,500	Eruption of Sand Mountain chain of craters, Twin craters
5,500	Lava flows from three vents between Devils Lake and Black Rock Butte
15,000–10,000	Formation of Cayuse crater, Le Conte crater, Sims Butte, Mount Bachelor volcanic chain, and South Sister summit cone

Source: Modified from Scott et al., 1999

extends over the summit lavas, is dated at only 14,000 years, indicating that the Middle Sister—despite its more dissected state—is comparatively little older than her better-preserved sibling.

Collier glacier, descending from Middle Sister's north shoulder, flows north-northwestward directly across the North Sister's west flank, into which it has cut a broad trench. Once the area's largest ice mass, the Collier has been thinning and withdrawing upvalley for many decades. This glacier's former Holocene thickness and extent are indicated by the unusually large lateral moraines bordering its channel. (See chapter 22.)

The South Sister

The highest and most recently active of the Three Sisters, the South Sister (10,358 feet) is the only large composite cone in Oregon to have an intact summit crater, an almost perfectly circular bowl about 1,300 feet in diameter. An ice pack approximately 200 feet thick partly fills the crater, but in spring and summer snowmelt forms a small crater lake, Oregon's highest body of water. Christened Teardrop Pool, on a sunny day its turquoise surface offers a dazzling contrast to the surrounding snow and ice. (See image 15 on plate 8.)

Despite its relative youth and generally conical form, the South Sister has a complex volcanic history, erupting a wide variety of magma types from a number of different vents. The well-preserved summit cone consists of thin flows of basaltic andesite interspersed with reddish scoria and other tephra deposits, probably erupted near the end of the Pleistocene or beginning of the Holocene. In late summer, when snow cover is minimal, the exposed inner walls of the crater reveal colorful strata of black and red scoria, almond-shaped bombs up to a yard long, and dark, porous flows of basaltic andesite. By contrast, the main cone, with a volume of more than 7 cubic miles, is built of more silicic material, primarily andesite and dacite, with only minor

South Sister's snow-filled crater from the south. The Lewis glacier has carved a conspicuous cirque into the young summit cone. —Courtesy of the U.S. Geological Survey

The South Sister from the southwest. The chain of rhyodacite domes and flows (foreground and center) erupted about 2,000 years ago when a dike of silicic magma intersected the volcanic edifice. —Austin Post photo, U.S. Geological Survey

effusions of basaltic andesite. An andesite lava flow underlying the top 1,000 feet of the edifice dates at about 27,000 years, but it overlies silicic flows at least 50,000 years old. Much of South Sister's late Pleistocene activity, between about 35,000 and 15,000 years ago, took place at vents along the lower flanks, where large quantities of silicic magma erupted in the form of both pumiceous tephra and thick flows and domes. One conspicuous flow, a 350-foot-thick rhyolitic lava erupted about 35,000 years ago, issued from a vent low on the northeast flank and poured into Squaw Creek.

During the last 10,000 years, South Sister has produced only two eruptive episodes, both of which resembled the late Pleistocene flank eruptions. Occurring within a few centuries of each other about 2,000 years ago, both the Rock Mesa and Devils Hill episodes produced an initial explosive ejection of pumice, followed by a quieter effusion of thick flows or domes. Light gray or buff-colored pumice fragments from these Holocene eruptions litter the volcano's southeast slopes and can even be found at the summit; bombs and lapilli are abundant along the Fall Creek trail to Green Lakes, which occupy the basin between South Sister and Broken Top.

The first of the two episodes, the Rock Mesa eruptive cycle, centered at two vents at the southwest and south flanks of the cone. Pulsating columns of ash distributed tephra over a broad arc to the south and east: a mile downwind from the vent, the tephra lies 7 feet thick; at a distance of 8 miles, it thins to a depth of about 4 inches; 25 miles south of the vent, at Cultus Lake, and at an equal distance to the east in Bend, it is only half an inch thick. After the gas-rich magma ejected, a sluggish mass of rhyolite lava, flowing over an almost level plain, formed the steep-sided blocky mass of Rock Mesa, as well as several smaller domes.

Perhaps only decades or a century later, South Sister was bisected by a rising dike of silicic magma, which erupted in a linear series of approximately twenty new vents, most located along a zone on the southeast flank, although a smaller line of vents also opened on the north flank near Carver Lake. This second cycle—the Devils Hill episode—duplicated the events of the first: violent eruptions of tephra succeeded by quieter extrusions of viscous rhyodacite magma. The highest vents on the southeast side produced the largest stream of lava, the blocky Newberry flow, which crept down the steep slope to the Green Lakes basin, probably damming Fall Creek and significantly raising the lake levels. Beginning at an elevation of 8,000 feet and extending down the southeast slope for a distance of 3 miles to the 5,500-foot level, the dike fed a chain of vents, producing a sequence of steep-sided domes with black, glassy, deeply furrowed crusts. Bristling with sharp spires, huge angular blocks, and other chaotic surface features, these glistening obsidian domes rear bleakly above the surrounding forest. Travelers on Century Drive will have unobstructed views of the lowest dome near the shores of Devils Lake.

Together, the two eruptive episodes produced about a fifth of a cubic mile of new rock, about 95 percent of it in the form of lava flows and domes. Although extrusion of this relatively small volume of magma radically changed the topography of South Sister's southeast slope, it represents a mere tenth of the quantity of magma erupted during the volcano's similar flank activity during the late Pleistocene.

In compiling estimates of the kinds and volumes of magma erupted during each stage of South Sister's evolution, James Clark, then at the University of Oregon, found that the Pleistocene shield lavas underlying the volcano represent about 14 cubic miles of basaltic material, whereas South

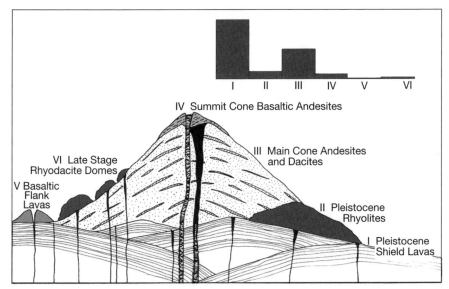

Cross-section of the South Sister volcano, with a bar graph illustrating the relative volumes of lava erupted at the site. The main cone of andesites and dacites (stage III) sits atop an older accumulation of Pleistocene shield lavas (stage I), the most voluminous of the six eruptive cycles in the South Sister area. The basaltic andesite summit cone (stage IV) probably formed during very late Pleistocene or earliest Holocene time, while the rhyodacite domes and flows on the southeast and northeast flanks (stage VI) erupted about 2,000 years ago. —Adapted from Clark, 1983

Sister's main cone, built of andesite and dacite, contains little more than half that volume. The recent summit cone, of basaltic andesite, has a volume of about two thirds of a cubic mile. As at Mount Jefferson and some other Oregon volcanoes, the quantity of andesite and dacite lava that forms the large composite cones is strikingly less than the voluminous basalts—shields, cinder cones, and associated lava fields—that comprise the overwhelming bulk of the High Cascades.

South Sister's Glaciers

Although relatively young, South Sister has been thoroughly scoured by late Pleistocene glaciations. When a vast ice cap smothered the Oregon Cascades between about 30,000 and 15,000 years ago, submerging all but the highest peaks and ridges, ice streams flowing down South Sister's south flanks filled adjacent valleys to a depth of 500 feet. Neither the central ice sheet nor its related valley glaciers, some of which were 19 miles long, extended beyond the High Cascade platform. In the Sisters region, few of the glaciers terminated below an elevation of 3,600 feet. Glaciers cut most deeply into the volcano's north face, where a steep headwall, 1,200 feet high, of layered andesite, dacite, and basaltic andesite flows is exposed below the summit. Three distinct terraces of lava, perhaps representing different cone-building episodes, separate hanging ice fields. (See image 13 on plate 7.)

Although the giant Pleistocene ice sheets disappeared about 12,000 years ago, smaller glaciers formed, advanced, and retreated during various periods of the Holocene, including the recent cooling episode between AD 1350 and 1850 known as the Little Ice Age. This latest neoglaciation deposited fresh moraines and till at elevations between about 7,000 and 9,000 feet on the higher peaks. The shallow cirques on the south flank of South Sister's summit cone were probably incised during this time. Cirques of the Lewis and Clark glaciers, separated by a long ridge of red scoria leading to the

The northwest face of Mount Bachelor, an exceptionally steep basaltic shield built during late Pleistocene and early Holocene time. Except for the small ice-filled cirque just below the summit, this symmetrical volcano is little altered by erosion. A young cinder cone appears at the lower right. A chair lift now carries skiers and sightseers all the way to the summit. —Courtesy of the U.S. Forest Service

crater rim, have significantly steepened, but not yet breached, the crater's outer walls. During the Little Ice Age, the Lewis glacier built an impressive moraine on its south margin, a steep rampart of angular lava blocks plucked from the summit cone. Now drastically thinned and shrunken, the glacier occupies a hollow far below the level of the moraine it constructed during its vigorous prime.

Despite the recency of the Rock Mesa and Devils Hill episodes and the current ground deformation west of South Sister, no active steam vents or other thermal activity now exist in the Three Sisters area. At least one pioneer observer, however, claimed to have witnessed an eruption there. In July 1853, James P. Miller, a Presbyterian missionary stationed in the Willamette Valley, wrote to his home board that on the ninth of that month he saw "one of the Three Sisters belching forth from its summit dense volumes of smoke." Miller stated, "The smoke appears to arise in puffs at intervals, which continued until the mountain was hid from view by the intervening clouds, between sundown and dark; since which, constant cloudy weather has hid the range from view. . . . There can be but little doubt that a crater existed in the peak of the Three Sisters, which issued smoke on Saturday." Miller did not specify which of the three peaks was erupting, but the South Sister is the most likely candidate. Miller's description of the "smoke" issuing in intermittent "puffs" recalls eyewitness accounts of similar minor eruptions at St. Helens and Hood during the 1850s. Geologists most familiar with the Sisters region, however, can find no evidence of historic activity at any of the area's volcanoes.

Mount Bachelor

Formerly called Bachelor Butte, Mount Bachelor (9,065 feet) is a symmetrical shield volcano standing about 3,500 feet above its base just south of Broken Top. Except for a small glacial cirque on its shaded north side, this youthful-appearing edifice of basaltic andesite is little modified by erosion.

The Bachelor, however, is somewhat older than he looks—and he has a family: a long row of similar basaltic andesite volcanoes that formed during an extended eruptive sequence between about 18,000 and 12,000 years ago. The Mount Bachelor chain, 15 miles in length and covering 100 square miles, consists of overlapping scoria cones and shield volcanoes typical of those that make up most of Oregon's High Cascade platform. Bachelor's volcanic kin vary considerably in size and shape: whereas its nearby sibling, Kwolh Butte, has a fairly steep cone, the much larger Sheridan Mountain, near the central part of the chain, manifests a typical shield's long low profile.

The earliest eruptions in the Bachelor chain, between about 18,000 and 15,000 years ago, took place as a Pleistocene glacier covering the area had already begun to stagnate and thin. Located west of Sparks Lake in the northwest part of the chain, the first vents apparently broke through the ice sheet or took place in a meltwater lake bordering the glacier. When water flooded the initial vents, violent explosions discharged large quantities of pyroclastic material, partly filling the lakebed. As the new cones emerged above lake level, milder Strombolian activity built the scoria edifices forming Talapus and Katsuk Buttes. Thick flows of lava from these cones poured into a depression in the receding glacier, banking and chilling against walls of glacier ice on three sides. After the ice melted, the stack of flows was left as a steep-sided plateau. Most of the lava emitted during this early phase, however, was concentrated at the shield forming Sheridan Mountain.

A second pulse of mildly explosive activity erected a series of scoria cones, with associated lava flows, that extends from near Sheridan Mountain to the chain's southern terminus. During the third eruptive episode, extensive flows of basaltic andesite built the broad shield now underlying Mount Bachelor. Subsequent eruptions erected a steep upper cone whose vertical profile distinguishes Bachelor from an ordinary shield. In its penultimate eruptive phase, the volcano discharged long streams of aa lava from vents on its north and northwest flanks. The latest activity built Egan cone, a prominent scoria cone on the north side that erupted lava flows that look deceptively fresh. As Howel Williams observed, "no one who sees the barren flows of basalt which poured from fissures on the north flank and spread in branching tongues into Sparks Lake can doubt that they must have escaped only a few centuries ago." These latest flows, however, have traces of Mazama ash on their surfaces and were thus erupted before 7,700 years ago. Although the lava surfaces are only slightly weathered, some preliminary age tests suggest that they may be as old as the last lavas emitted at the summit, between about 12,500 and 11,000 years ago.

Climbing Bachelor along the edge of the shallow trench excavated by its one surviving glacier reveals on a small scale the glacial processes that sculptured the larger composite cones. Although this unnamed glacier is tiny by Cascade standards, it has done a remarkable amount of damage to the volcano's north face. Furrowed lavas bordering this cirque appear as fresh as if they had just congealed. But where the glacier has flowed over the lava and cut beneath the surface, the ice has ground massive lava blocks into fine, charcoal gray flour, easily carried away by streams issuing from the glacier's snout. The transformation of formerly solid rock into gritty silt is particularly dramatic at the glacier terminus, which is marked by a steep semicircular ridge concave toward the glacier front. Some climbers mistake this formation for a cinder cone; it is actually the glacier's terminal moraine, a testimony to the power of moving ice to reduce solid mountains to drifting dust.

During recent decades, the Bachelor glacier has noticeably shrunk and no longer shows the crevasses that indicate movement. If this trend continues—the result of climatic warming that has diminished glaciers throughout the Oregon Cascades—the now-stagnant ice field will disappear altogether.

Bachelor offers even nonclimbers an opportunity to experience a sweeping panorama of central Oregon, as it is the only large Cascade volcano with a chairlift to its summit (Hoodoo Butte, which also hosts a popular ski resort, is a cinder cone). In summer, well-marked foot paths cross the summit area, providing views far beyond the Three Sisters with their sparkling ice fields, to Jefferson, Hood, and the humped top of Adams in Washington state. Forty miles to the southeast lies the sprawling mass of Newberry Volcano, knobby with its hundreds of peripheral cones and domes.

No large crater occupies Bachelor's summit; instead, its numerous small vents are marked by low, blocky domes or roughly circular depressions that formed as magma sank back into the feeding conduits as the last summit eruptions ended. Fine examples of smooth pahoehoe surfaces are immediately adjacent to several vents, where the erupting lava was hottest and most gas rich. A short distance downslope from their source, the ropy, undulating crusts grade into rough, slaggy surfaces, a transition from pahoehoe to aa resulting from the lava's loss of heat and steam as it flowed away from the vent.

Whether Mount Bachelor will erupt again is an open question. Because it grew rapidly during a comparatively brief time span and produced chemically similar lavas throughout its cone-building, it appears to be monogenetic, constructed by a single batch of magma during a single (albeit extended) sequence of eruptions. Most of the basaltic or basaltic andesite shields and cinder cones found throughout the range are monogenetic; after building their cones and dying out, they do not revive. When fresh magma rises to the surface, it forms an entirely new volcano. Considering its large size and the fact that its last eruptions occurred during Holocene time, however, Bachelor may only be resting between eruptive cycles. If it does reawaken, it will not be good news for the thriving ski industry centered on its slopes.

The Volcanoes at McKenzie Pass

Holocene volcanism has been particularly intense in the segment of the range between North Sister and Three-Fingered Jack, where vast sheets of barren lava cover the mountainscape over many square miles. Since the Pleistocene glaciers withdrew, at least 125 separate eruptive centers in a north-south alignment have blazed and died, most of them in a period of particularly intense activity between about 4,000 and 1,300 years ago. The

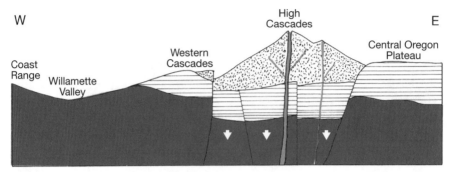

Cross-section of the Cascade Range in central Oregon. The High Cascade composite cones are built atop a graben, a down-dropped block in the center of the range, perhaps a result of the impingement on the Cascades by the Basin and Range province. —Adapted from McBirney, 1978, and E. M. Taylor, "Central High Cascades Roadside Geology, Bend, Sisters, McKenzie Pass, and Santiam Pass, Oregon," in *Guide to Some Volcanic Terranes in Washington, Idaho, Oregon, and Northern California* (U.S. Geological Survey Circular 836, 1981)

Sand Mountain chain alone produced twenty-three cinder cones and extensive lava flows along the western margin of the High Cascades. In the last eruption from this chain, about 3,000 years ago, floods of basaltic andesite inundated the former channel of the McKenzie River, creating Sahalie Falls and Koosah Falls. After the lava blocked the McKenzie River, its impounded waters drowned a forest and formed 1.5-mile-long Clear Lake. Ghostly snags, denuded of bark and branches, are still visible beneath the surface of this popular fishing lake.

Striking views of a lava wonderland are available from the highway at McKenzie Pass (Oregon 242), a narrow, twisting route across the range that links Bend with Eugene in the Willamette Valley. Following the winding course of the McKenzie River, the highway crosses lava fields covering 85 square miles—a forbidding wasteland of black, jagged basalt. Several vents contributed the lava, but the most important were the Belknap shield and Yapoah cinder cone. From the Dee Wright Observatory, a picturesque structure built of lava blocks from these flows, visitors have a good view of several volcanoes responsible for the desolation. To the south looms the black-and-white massif of North Sister, its base dotted with recent cinder cones, including Yapoah cone, which erupted the flow upon which the observatory stands. Northward rises the eroded volcanic neck of Mount Washington, on whose glaciated lower slopes the Belknap shield arose. (Some of the area's youngest vents, unrelated to the older volcano, formed a short chain of spatter cones on Washington's north flank about 1,300 years ago.)

Almost devoid of vegetation, Belknap shield (6,869 feet) is a basaltic andesite shield about 5 miles in diameter, with a pyroclastic core and a volume of 1.4 cubic miles. The youngest volcano of its kind in the Cascade Range, its earliest known eruptions began about 3,000 years ago, discharging tephra over about 100 square miles to the northeast and southeast and erupting lava streams that traveled 6 miles to the east. Only a century or two later, a second eruptive cycle built a smaller shield on the east flank, known as Little Belknap. The third—and most voluminous—phase occurred 1,500 years ago, when torrents of basaltic andesite poured from the central vent (Belknap shield), and from the secondary cone of South Belknap, about a mile to the south. A third active vent, at the northeast base of the shield, issued copious streams of lava that flowed 12 miles westward, plunging onto the McKenzie canyon floor. Spreading over the riverbed, the lava dammed an extensive swamp upstream, Beaver Marsh. Today the McKenzie disappears into the permeable sediments along the flow margins and runs underground until it reappears at Tamolitch Falls.

The large cinder cone, 400 feet high, topping Belknap shield (probably the surface expression of the volcano's pyroclastic core) has three summit

Rubbly surface of an aa lava flow. This Yapoah flow is one of the many late Holocene lava streams at McKenzie Pass in central Oregon. —Courtesy of D. W. Hyndman

craters of varying size, aligned in a north-northwesterly direction. The large southern crater erupted most of the tephra blanketing the area, but the smaller northernmost vent produced both ash and a lava flow that breached the crater rim.

Most of the Belknap lavas have blocky or slaggy crusts, though some manifest ropy pahoehoe surfaces. The collapse of lava tubes, and the breaking up and "peeling back" of cooling lava crusts as the fluid interior of the flow moved forward, make these basaltic andesite surfaces unusually chaotic, jumbled piles of sharp rock fragments. Williams described some of these flow crusts as "reminiscent of a shattered ice jam."

Flows issuing from Little Belknap, about a mile east of the central Belknap crater, surrounded two prominent hills of older rock, leaving them as isolated islands (steptoes) amid a sea of black basalt. Little Belknap's final lavas filled the crater, forming a craggy mound of red clinkery rock, from which collapsed lava tubes diverge radially.

Two recent vents south of Belknap shield at North Sister's base produced notable eruptions. Located a short distance to the west of Yapoah cone, Four-in-One cone, as its name implies, is a row of four closely spaced, almost identical cinder cones. Each of the four had its northwest crater rim breached by lava flows that traveled to the north. Set in an alignment of nineteen similar cones, it probably sits astride a fault zone.

Standing higher than Four-in-One on the North Sister's flanks, directly downvalley from the Collier glacier's terminus, Collier cone formed about 1,600 years ago. Tephra from this well-preserved cinder cone created a mile-square plain of desolation, the Ahalapam cinder field, while its lava flows extended 3 miles to the northwest and 8.5 miles to the west.

Located squarely in the path of Collier glacier, Collier cone blocked the ice stream's advance during several recent glacial expansions. As late as 1924, the Collier glacier snout rode high on the side of the cone. During an earlier advance, when the glacier was at least 200 feet thick at its terminus, water from its melting surface flowed into the crater of Collier cone, covering much of the crater floor with outwash. At the same time, stream gravels were deposited in the lava gutters and flow surfaces surrounding the cone. Today, Collier glacier has retreated far up the North Sister's west flanks (it originates on the Middle Sister), leaving behind extensive lateral moraines bordering the cone.

The Volcanic Future

Although South Sister is the only large composite cone in the area to have erupted in the Holocene—and it had only two brief eruptive episodes about 2,000 years ago—the number and variety of postglacial cinder cones, shields, lava fields, and other volcanic features adjacent to the Three Sisters virtually guarantees future activity. The abundance of youthful volcanoes adjoining McKenzie Pass and Santiam Pass suggests that new cinder cones and lava streams inevitably will be added to this already volcano-rich mountainscape.

The 60-square-mile bulge currently rising 3 miles west of South Sister suggests that magma may be moving toward that volcano and perhaps will trigger an eruption on the west flank, similar to the Rock Mesa episode that generated explosions of pumiceous tephra at a vent low on the cone, followed by the extrusion of a massive lava flow. It is also possible that the magma, if it is basaltic rather than highly silicic like that which formed Rock Mesa or the Devils Hill chain of domes, may produce a new line of cinder cones similar to those at McKenzie Pass. Because we do not know how often in the past such ground uplifts occurred—until the development of satellite technology geologists had no way to detect or measure such a phenomenon—it is possible that similar bulges occur frequently without resulting in an eruption. Eventually, however, fresh magma will reach the surface at some point in the Three Sisters region, with consequences that can only be imagined.

Visiting the Three Sisters

Travelers can enjoy largely unobstructed views of the Three Sisters and adjacent peaks from their cars along U.S. 97 near Bend. The short paved road to the summit of Lava Butte, 10 miles south of Bend, affords an overview of the entire region. Watch for the roadside marker.

Century Drive/Cascade Lakes Highway leaves U.S. 97 at Bend and leads west-southwestward to skirt the base of Mount Bachelor and South Sister before looping through the eastern front of the range southwest of Bend and rejoining U.S. 97 near Sunriver. Although this route provides direct access to Bachelor and the many scenic alpine lakes that dot the sparsely timbered highland, the road does not actually take you on any of the Sisters. The closest approach is to the south flank of South Sister at Sparks and Devils Lakes. Two popular trails lead climbers to the summit. One trailhead at Devils Lake offers a steep hike directly up the south slope. The second, the Fall Creek trail, begins at a meadow near Spark's Lake and leads to the Green Lakes basin at South Sister's southeast foot. From there to the crater rim is an arduous hike. North-side routes require more technical expertise.

Energetic mountaineers in good condition (reputedly) can scale all Three Sisters, plus Broken Top and Bachelor, in a single day. The well-marked Obsidian Trailhead 3528 near Oregon 242 southwest of McKenzie Pass leads 3.5 miles to a junction. Take the left fork (spur 3528A) 1 mile to a junction with the Pacific Crest Trail (PCT), known as Sunshine Junction, former location of the Sunshine Shelter. From there cross-country climbers' trails approach North and Middle Sisters. Seasoned mountaineers advise novices not to risk the rockfalls and exposures of North Sister. (For more details see Jeff Smoot's *Climbing the Cascade Volcanoes*.)

Mount Bachelor, an inviting climb for the beginner, has become almost too accessible. Follow the Cascade Lakes Highway 22 miles west from Bend and turn at the sign for the Mount Bachelor Ski Area. If you choose to ignore the chair lifts, a new trail offers summer hikers a brisk trek to the summit. From the south side of the parking lot east of the lodge, the trail climbs about 2,600 feet in about 4.5 miles of switchbacks to the top.

CHAPTER 14

Mount Jefferson

GUARDIAN OF THE WILDERNESS

Mount Jefferson (10,497 feet), Oregon's second-highest peak, is a paradox. Rarely visible from Portland and many parts of the Willamette Valley, where most of the state's population is concentrated, Jefferson is comparatively little known and completely undeveloped as a tourist destination. With no paved roads approaching the mountain (a gravel logging road, no. 1044, connecting with Oregon 22 over Santiam Pass, comes no closer than 4 miles to the base), Jefferson is accessible only on foot or horseback. Despite its isolation in a largely roadless wilderness, however, the mountain's eco-logical health is threatened by the hoards of seasonal hikers, backpackers, and climbers who flock to savor its alpine charms. The trail leading to the flower-strewn meadows of Jefferson Park, on the volcano's north side, is particularly crowded during summer months, when many weekend moun-taineers make it a point of departure for the summit.

Jefferson is an enigma when it comes to the volcanic hazards it repre-sents. Although capable of violently explosive eruptions—past events have smothered thousands of square miles under thick tephra deposits—Jefferson has not erupted during the Holocene, and glaciation has removed most of the evidence of its late Pleistocene activity, including mudflow deposits. This obliteration of recent eruptive history makes it difficult for geologists to specify the nature and extent of the volcano's potential threat.

Travelers can enjoy good views of Jefferson from U.S. 97 between Bend and Madras, and even better ones from Oregon 26, which runs northwest-ward from Madras through the Warm Springs Indian Reservation toward Mount Hood. Viewed from this perspective, the volcano is a huge pyramid surmounting the Cascade crest, its east flank wrapped in the mountain's largest ice sheet, the Whitewater glacier. From other vantage points, such as the Metolius River area near Camp Shurman or from Oregon 22 west of the mountain, Jefferson rises to a sharp point, as hornlike as the summit pinnacles of Thielsen and Washington.

Early explorers, including Lewis and Clark, who named Jefferson in 1806 after the president who sponsored their mission, were struck by its aloof maj-esty. The mountain's solitary grandeur also impressed Walter Eaton, who, in describing his journeys through the Rockies and central Oregon Cascades,

201

Whitewater glacier on Mount Jefferson's east flank has cut deeply into the volcano's interior. —Austin Post photo, U.S. Geological Survey

praised "old Jefferson" as "the most remote, the most inaccessible and alluring" of Oregon's peaks. Eaton saw Jefferson and Hood as companionable sentinels: "Those peaked white volcanoes, shooting up so far above the level of the blue ranges, seem to hold mystic converse with one another over the canyons between." Mount Jefferson, standing about 46 miles directly south of Mount Hood, may commune inaudibly with its loftier neighbor, but the volcano has remained silent for a long time.

An Incomplete Volcanic Biography

Somnolent for at least 15,000 to 20,000 years, Jefferson is one of Oregon's most deeply eroded composite cones. Pleistocene glaciation erased the volcano's original contours, lowering its former summit by several hundred feet and excavating a broad cirque on its west flank. The West Milk Creek cirque, now containing the two tiny Milk Creek glaciers, penetrates the volcano's interior, revealing that the innermost core consists of tephra and

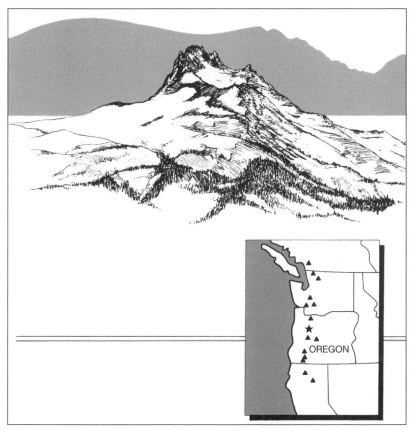

North side of Mount Jefferson

other pyroclastic material. Most of Jefferson's pyroclastic deposits, however, derive from the shattering of lava streams or domes as they disintegrated and avalanched down the volcano's steep slopes.

Built primarily of lava flows erupted atop a rugged terrain averaging 5,500 to 6,500 feet in altitude, Jefferson's cone rises no more than a mile above its base, with some of its longer flows extending up to 6 or 7 miles onto the floors of adjoining canyons. Most of the two hundred or more andesite flows now exposed in the main cone, which began to form about 300,000 years ago, have an average thickness of 10 to 35 feet. By contrast, a massive flow of pink dacite up to 1,000 feet thick occupies part of the volcano's eroded core and is easily seen from the west. About 500 feet below the present summit, a small plug is also visible.

Eroded remnants of lavas emitted during the first major eruptive phase, known as the Main Cone flows, also appear along the west and northwest flanks, in the east wall of the Russell glacier valley, beneath the terminus of Jefferson glacier, in the ridge between the main summit and the North complex, and above Waldo glacier on Jefferson's south flank.

After the volcano reached its maximum size, glaciers stripped away much of its constructional surface, significantly reducing its height and cutting trenches up to 1,000 feet deep in its flanks. Jefferson's latest activity took place during the most recent glacial advance, when it produced thick flows of dacite and silicic domes from vents slightly east of the former main conduit. The presence of a thick ice cover on the mountain during these second-stage eruptions is indicated by the fact that the dacite lava streams, instead of spreading out over the volcano's flanks, piled up on top of each other in thick tongues. Prevented from spreading by masses of ice encasing the volcano, the flows moved down long ridges dividing the glaciers. When they encountered ice barriers, the flow margins were abruptly chilled, forming glassy surfaces and columnar joints or fractures where the flow encountered ice. Some lava flows are now "perched" high on canyon walls, hundreds of feet above valley floors, showing that the valleys were filled with ice at the time the flows were erupted.

Relief map of the Mount Jefferson area

One 150-foot-thick silicic flow oozed down a 25- to 35-degree slope cut in the andesite lavas of the main cone by an ice stream in the Russell glacier valley. An exposure of strata in the wall behind Russell glacier clearly illustrates the sequence of eruptive events: a silicic flow overlies glacial till that in turn lies atop the main cone lavas.

During the second eruptive sequence, which erected a new summit cone high on Jefferson's east side, the repeated growth and collapse of silicic domes generated pyroclastic flows that swept down the volcano's flanks. Cascading masses of rock from lava flows, disrupted as they skidded down icy slopes or plunged over precipitous cliffs, also probably contributed to the fragmental debris mantling the cone, although glaciers have erased almost all of these deposits, including the lahars they presumably triggered.

At some point between about 100,000 and 35,000 years ago, when the Oregon Cascades were buried in a massive ice cap, Mount Jefferson produced an enormous explosive eruption. In the early 1980s Jim Begét, professor at the University of Alaska, Fairbanks, discovered two previously unrecognized layers of air-fall pumice blanketing parts of the Metolius and Deschutes River valleys in central Oregon. An older and thinner deposit, called layer U, is generally covered by a younger, thicker, and more extensive

Mount Jefferson from the east. Severe glaciation has removed the former summit of Oregon's second-highest peak. Although quiet since the late Pleistocene, Jefferson is a long-lived volcano and will probably erupt again. —Lyn Topinka photo, U.S. Geological Survey, Cascades Volcano Observatory

tephra bed, layer E, which forms a stratum 6 to 7 feet thick at a distance of about 12.5 miles from the volcano. Ash from this eruption appears as far away as Arco in southeast Idaho. During approximately the same period, large pyroclastic flows traveled as far as 12 miles down the Whitewater River drainage on Jefferson's east flank and an equal distance down the Whitewater Creek drainage on the west side.

If this violent phase blasted out a large crater, it has been filled in by subsequent eruptions. Geologists estimate that the upper 3,500 feet of Jefferson's cone is less than 100,000 years old, with much of the second-stage lava flows younger than the extensive tephra deposits.

The latest Pleistocene glaciation, between about 25,000 and 12,000 years ago, thoroughly scoured the second-stage cone, leaving only remnants of its flows capping the volcano's main peaks and ridges. A mass of dacite approximately 100 feet thick now forms Jefferson's present summit. Rather than an eroded conduit filling, or plug, like the spires of Thielsen and Washington, Jefferson's pinnacle is part of a lava flow erupted from a now-vanished crater to the west, above the present Milk Creek cirque. Other second-stage lava flows traveled north from the summit area and now cap the cliffs north of the Whitewater glacier. Altogether, the last two Pleistocene glaciations obliterated not only the former summit of the main cone, but also that of the second-stage cone, removing perhaps a third of the volcano's original bulk.

Today the Whitewater glacier on the east side and the small Milk Creek glaciers on the west side continue to carve the mountain, digging ever deeper into the already narrow summit ridge that divides them. A deep cleft will eventually replace the crumbling banks of loose talus between the north and south summit horns—the Red Saddle—perhaps allowing the east- and west-side ice streams to merge.

While the second-stage dacite lavas were erupting, two large peripheral cones formed on Jefferson's flanks. The North complex, located near Jefferson Park, is now deeply eroded, revealing lava dikes that once fed flows. Since the last glacial advance, the creek issuing from the northwest part of the Whitewater glacier has further eroded the complex. A second vent located 2 miles south of Jefferson's summit erupted a dome of reddish brown dacite called Goat Peak.

Additional silicic flows erupted from fissures along the south flank. One such flow moved toward Goat Peak before it cascaded over a ridge and turned southeast. Remnants of this glaciated flow are exposed along the east ridge of the valley north of Shale Lake at an elevation of 7,600 feet. Another part of the same flow underlies the cliffs southwest of Waldo glacier.

The youngest lava flows near Mount Jefferson did not derive from Jefferson's magma chamber, but from a separate reservoir of basaltic magma typical of the central Oregon Cascades. These Holocene eruptions built the Forked Butte cinder cone, which discharged lava flowing down the valley of Cabot Creek, and an unnamed cone south of Bear Butte, which poured lava down the valley of Jefferson Creek. Both of these young flows erupted after the deposition of Mazama ash 7,700 years ago.

In calculating Jefferson's potential hazards in future eruptions, geologists regard mudflows as posing the greatest threat, particularly to large reservoirs in the area. Detroit Lake lies to the west of the volcano and Lake Billy Chinook to the east, both of which are vulnerable to large lahars. As in the Three Sisters region, damaging debris flows occur even while Jefferson is dormant. During the mid-twentieth century, small meltwater lakes impounded behind glacial moraines spontaneously breached their dams, discharging sand, silt, and large boulders downslope. On August 21, 1934, a lake that had recently formed behind the terminus of a lobe of the Whitewater glacier burst through its moraine dam, producing a debris flow that swept across east Jefferson Park and entered the drainage of the Whitewater River. According to a Forest Service report, the park was largely buried under "boulders, sand, and tree trunks to a depth of from 1 to 6 or 8 feet." A smaller, poorly documented debris flow from a similarly ruptured moraine dam streamed through west Jefferson Park about 1957.

Below the snout of the Waldo glacier, which built large lateral and terminal moraines on Jefferson's south flank during the Little Ice Age, a small lake has ruptured its natural dam at least twice. Aerial photographs taken in 1937 show that the lake had breached the moraine a short time earlier. A second debris flow from the lake occurred in 1951, when the breakout carried sediment into the Metolius and Deschutes Rivers.

Age and Volume of Eruptions in the Jefferson Area

Many of the lavas surrounding Mount Jefferson are younger than the last reversal of the earth's magnetic poles, which occurred about 700,000 years ago. The earliest of these, the Minto lavas, formed a broad plateau of coalescing shield volcanoes that were thoroughly glaciated before Jefferson was born about 300,000 years ago. Younger than the Minto formation, the Santiam basalts erupted at some point before the last Pleistocene glaciations. Santiam basalts fill the North Santiam River valley to a depth of 1,800 feet, but because there is no contact between these basalt flows and Jefferson's earliest main cone andesite lavas, it is not possible to determine their relative ages.

The difference in volume of these lava outpourings is instructive. In general, the younger the lava, the less there is of it. Whereas the Minto lavas have a cumulative volume of approximately 23.4 cubic miles, Jefferson's

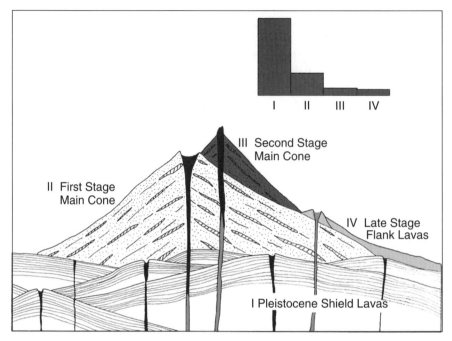

Cross-section of Mount Jefferson, showing the relative volumes of lava erupted during the four eruptive cycles in the Jefferson area. —Adapted from K. Sutton, "Geology of Mount Jefferson" (Master's thesis, University of Oregon, Eugene, 1974); and H. Williams and A. R. McBirney, *Volcanology* (San Francisco: Freeman, Cooper & Company 1979)

main cone andesites total about 5 cubic miles, and the second-stage dacites are less than a cubic mile. The Santiam basalts represent about 2 cubic miles and the Forked Butte lavas only 0.8 of a cubic mile.

Although Jefferson is the most imposing volcano in this part of the High Cascades, its volume is minor compared to that produced by older shield volcanoes and fissure eruptions. This disparity is typical of the central Oregon Cascades, where some individual basaltic flows, with little topographical relief but large areas, have volumes two or three times greater than those of a high composite cone.

Jefferson's Future

Jefferson slept through the culminating glaciations of the Pleistocene and has thus far remained equally comatose in the Holocene. Its denuded cone bears little resemblance to its original form, marking it as Oregon's most deeply eroded stratovolcano and thus a prime candidate for extinction. Given

Jefferson's eroded asymmetry testifies to its long silence; it has not erupted since before the last maximum extent of Pleistocene glaciers. It has been intermittently active for several hundred thousand years, however, and may revive in the future. —Austin Post photo, U.S. Geological Survey

its long lifetime (approximately 300,000 years), however, and its capacity for large explosive eruptions, geologists are not yet ready to strike Jefferson from the list of potentially active volcanoes. Mount Hood dozed for more than 12,000 years before beginning a new eruptive phase about 1,500 years ago; even so vociferous a volcano as Mount St. Helens is known to have napped for several thousand years at a time before blazing back to life, often with catastrophic consequences. Assumptions about Jefferson's demise may be premature.

Visiting Mount Jefferson

The west side of Mount Jefferson is located in the rugged Mount Jefferson Wilderness area and the east side in the Warm Springs Indian Reservation. According to Jeff Thomas's climbing guide, *Oregon High,* the Warm Springs

Tribal Council adamantly forbids public access to Mount Jefferson's east flanks, limiting visitors to west-side U.S. Forest Service roads accessible from Oregon 22, which runs north from U.S. 20 immediately west of Santiam Pass. (U.S. 20, the Santiam Pass route, crosses the range east–west between Bend and Salem, connecting U.S. 97 with Interstate 5.) Scenic Jefferson Park on Jefferson's north slope is accessible only on foot. Thomas recommends taking the Whitewater Trail, which is reached by taking Oregon 22 to Whitewater Road (Forest Service Road 2243), about 10 miles east of Detroit, and then traveling east on Whitewater Road 7.5 miles to the road's end and the Whitewater trailhead. Hike north 1.5 miles uphill to a trail junction and then turn right and go 2.5 miles to the Pacific Crest Trail (PCT); turn left and follow the PCT about a mile to Jefferson Park. Like North Sister, Mount Jefferson is a difficult climb, particularly the sheer pinnacle forming the summit.

CHAPTER 15

Mount Hood

OREGON'S GREATEST VOLCANIC THREAT

Dominating Portland's eastern horizon, Mount Hood (11,239 feet) is not only Oregon's highest peak but also the state's only volcano to have erupted during historic time. Hood belongs to a particularly menacing group of Pacific Northwest volcanoes that, collectively, threaten the residences and businesses of hundreds of thousands of people. Like its more northerly fellow fire mountains, St. Helens, Rainier, Glacier Peak, and Baker, Hood was sporadically active between the late eighteenth and the mid-nineteenth centuries, generating pyroclastic flows and mudflows that streamed down valleys heading on the mountain, inundating the sites of numerous towns, villages, and resorts. With Rainier, St. Helens, and the less frequently active Adams, it forms a quartet of glacier-clad stratovolcanoes that have repeatedly discharged large volumes of debris that ultimately streamed into the Columbia River, in some cases temporarily damming its channel.

Even today, steam jetting from more than a dozen vents near Crater Rock, a prominent lava dome high on Mount Hood's south flank, gives clear evidence of the volcano's inner heat. Erected between about AD 1781 and 1810, Crater Rock is the focus of Oregon's largest thermal area, where heat and gas emission have altered formerly solid lavas to soft, crumbly materials tinted pink, white, orange, and yellow. Some vents leak steam quietly; others on the north side of Crater Rock vigorously spew columns of steam many tens of feet high. Hood's active fumaroles, including those at the nearby Hot Rocks and the base of Steel Cliff, with temperatures approximating that of boiling water, produce a strong sulfur odor that climbers can detect several miles away. On some clear winter days, escaping gas forms a plume curling above Hood's snowy crest, visible in Portland 50 miles to the west. Employees at Timberline Lodge, an elegantly designed alpine hotel located at the 6,000-foot level on the south side, report that they occasionally receive calls from Portlanders worried that the steam cloud may portend an eruption. Intermittent swarms of small earthquakes centered beneath the mountain also serve to remind local residents that molten rock stirs fitfully not far below the surface.

For most area residents, however, this glacier-shrouded cone is far more than a potential geologic hazard: it is a regional icon, a scenic landmark

Mount Hood from the north, with Eliot glacier in the center. The smooth ridge at the left is Cooper Spur. —Austin Post photo, U.S. Geological Survey

intimately associated with Oregon history. In his 1937 classic, *Wy'east, the Mountain*, Fred McNeil wrote: "Mount Hood stands for Oregonians as a monument to their pioneers and a tower of inspiration for their successors." From the earliest days of exploration and settlement, Hood played a major role in the area's development, one that has significantly shaped Oregonians' self-identity. Known as Wy'east to native tribes, it received its present name in 1792, when Captain George Vancouver sent Lieutenant William E. Broughton to investigate the lower Columbia River. Like Baker, Rainier, and St. Helens, Hood was named for an eighteenth-century British aristocrat; in this case, Broughton commemorated Lord Samuel Hood of the Royal Navy. When Lewis and Clark reached eastern Oregon in 1805, Hood's white, glittering spire indicated that the last stages of their arduous trek had begun. Scarcely two generations later, as covered wagons lumbered over eastern Oregon's dry sagebrush plains on their way to the Willamette Valley, the pioneers' first sight of Hood's perennial snowfields promised a welcome respite from the arid desert that stretched between the Rockies and the Cascades. The Cascade barrier had yet to be crossed, via either the

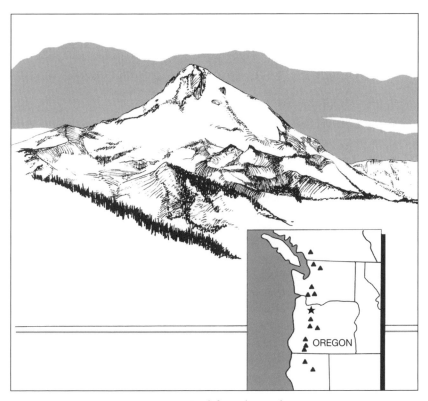

Mount Hood from the north

Columbia Gorge or Barlow Pass, which skirts Hood's southern base, but their journey's end was in sight.

Whereas some early settlers tended to regard Hood's bulk as the final obstacle to completing their overland quest for a new homeland, by the mid-nineteenth century Portlanders began to take considerable pride in its scenic value, manifesting, in McNeil's words, "a reverence that borders on devotion." Known locally as "the mountain"—just as residents of Puget Sound refer to Mount Rainier—Hood attracted climbers aiming for its summit at a surprisingly early date. In 1854, a party led by Thomas J. Dryer, owner and editor of the Portland *Weekly Oregonian*, laid claim to the first ascent, although most historians believe the group stopped short of the actual summit. Honors for the first successful climb, in 1857, went to four men, including Henry Lewis Pittock, an employee of Dryer, and the Reverend T. A. Wood, who wrote a detailed account of the experience. By 1889, Portland entrepreneurs had built an alpine hotel on Hood's remote north slope, Cloud Cap Inn, a rustic log structure that now belongs to a private club from Hood River. In the 1920s speculators planned to construct a cable railway to Cooper Spur on Hood's north flank and a suspended cableway from there to the summit, a fanciful project that was fortunately scrapped when financing fell through. (The friable rock of Hood's summit area would have crumbled under the cableway's weight.) A more appropriate enterprise, designed to blend with the alpine environment, the WPA's construction of Timberline Lodge, with its towering stone fireplace and intricately carved woodwork featuring wildlife and Native American motifs, was completed

GEOMYTHOLOGY AND "THE BRIDGE OF THE GODS"

For countless centuries before Anglo-Americans arrived on the scene, ancient storytellers of the Columbia River region spun imaginative tales about the natural forces that shaped their world, including the area's guardian peaks that intermittently blazed and thundered. As their oral traditions reveal, native peoples typically interpreted geographic landmarks and geologic processes as part of a unified view of the world that blended physical and spiritual components. Mountains were not simply inert piles of rock; they were living presences with distinctive personalities. Rivers, lakes, and other topographical features were inhabited not only by animals, who were kin to humankind, but also by unseen beings who could manifest their power through events that today we are taught to regard as the impersonal working of geophysical laws. In the native worldview, heaven, earth, and human consciousness were bound together in a rhythm of life, a sense of cosmic wholeness in which all things, animate and inanimate, are interconnected.

The relatively new discipline of geomythology studies oral traditions that preserve memories of prehistoric geologic events, such as great earthquakes, floods, and volcanic eruptions. Like native tribes in southern Oregon who interpreted the destruction of Mount Mazama as the result of a titanic power struggle between Llao, god of the underworld, and Skell, lord of the sky, so some Columbia tribes saw their local volcanoes as engaged in a fiery competition that ultimately destroyed the Bridge of the Gods, a natural formation that reputedly once spanned the Columbia River near the present site of Cascade Locks, Oregon. Although it is probably now impossible to disentangle later Caucasian embellishment from the original tradition, a Klickitat account reflects some of the region's actual geologic history.

According to the Klickitat version, long before white explorers appeared in the land, native tribes were able to cross the Columbia via a land "bridge" that was *tomanowos,* a creation sacred to the gods. But when the tribes became greedy and quarrelsome, Tyee Sahale (commonly translated as the "Great Spirit") took steps that eventually led to the bridge's demolition. First, he caused all the fires in their lodges to go out. Only the fire kept by Loowit, an old woman who avoided the violence that divided her people, remained

in 1937. Now a magnet for international skiers, the Timberline resort, with its extensive ski lifts and well-groomed slopes, lures many thousands of winter sports enthusiasts to the mountain every year.

Given Hood's centrality in Oregonians' historic love affair with their natural environment, it was fitting that the oldest and most influential mountaineering club in the Pacific Northwest was founded on its summit. On July 19, 1894, a group of enthusiastic climbers ascended Hood to create the Mazamas, Oregon's leading mountaineering club, and elected William Gladstone Steele, the future architect of Crater Lake National Park, as its first president. Despite squalls and bitter cold on that inclement July day, 193

burning, so all her neighbors had to come to her to rekindle their campfires. When Tyee Sahale asked Loowit to claim a reward for her generosity, she did not hesitate to name her choice: youth and beauty. Transformed into a lovely young maiden, Loowit inadvertently reignited the fires of war by attracting two aggressive suitors, both sons of the Great Spirit. The first, Pahto, ruled over territory north of the Columbia, while the second, Wy'east, led the Willamette people south of the river. When Pahto and Wy'east contended furiously for Loowit's favor, hurling red-hot boulders at each other, Tyee Sahale separated them by overthrowing the *tomanowas* bridge linking their two territories, its fragments creating the cataracts for which the adjacent Cascade Range was later named. The Great Spirit also changed the three principals of this love triangle into volcanic mountains: Pahto became the broad-shouldered giant that white settlers called Mount Adams; Wy'east became Mount Hood; and Loowit, the beautifully symmetrical Mount St. Helens. It was said that Loowit (whom some tribes named Tahonelatclah or Louwala-Clough, "fire-mountain") secretly favored the more graceful Wy'east, who "burned" with passion longer than Pahto, who soon fell asleep under his ermine blanket. Even after Wy'east temporarily banked his fires, Loowit kept her love flame alive, her late-twentieth-century and early-twenty-first-century outbursts continuing the lovers' saga into the next millennium.

An etiological myth explaining the volcanic nature of three sentinel peaks overlooking the mid-Columbia, the Bridge of the Gods tradition evokes memories of an enormous avalanche (the Bonneville landslide) that completely dammed the river only about three centuries ago, forming a rocky causeway that allowed travelers to cross the river dryshod. (Because the local tribes had no word for "bridge," the notion that this formation was a soaring stone arch is a Caucasian invention.) It is possible that some of the large basaltic blocks forming the landslide dam remained in place long after the river cut a new channel through its southern toe, approximately a mile south of its pre-slide course. If so, the famed Bridge of the Gods was in fact a jumbled pile of lava slabs, much as a native leader described it to a French missionary—"a long range of towering and projecting rocks"—before it collapsed, possibly in the Cascade subduction zone earthquake of AD 1700.

For more information on geomythology see Ella Clark, 1952 and 1966.

people, including 39 women, reached Hood's crest. Along with the South
Sister, Hood is now one of the state's most frequently climbed snow peaks.

An Active Volcano

Mount Hood was sporadically active between about 1781 and the late 1860s,
but, as if timing its eruptions to avoid observation by literate witnesses, remained obstinately silent whenever Vancouver's crew or Lewis and Clark's
men had the mountain in sight. Both the British and American exploring parties, however, found ample evidence of the volcano's recent activity.
In 1792, Broughton noted that a long, submerged sandbar extended from
the mouth of the Sandy River across the Columbia, adding that logs were
stranded up to 12 feet above the river's surface. Thirteen years later, Clark
described the Sandy as so full of sediment that it ran only about 4 inches
deep; attempting to wade across, he was astonished to find "the bottom a
quick Sand [sic], and impassable." The Sandy River, which presently runs
through a deep, narrow gorge to the Columbia, was then extremely shallow, choked with debris from a large mudflow originating high on Mount
Hood. By comparing growth rings on trees affected by the mudflow at
different locations, Patrick Pringle, a geologist with the Washington State
Division of Geology and Earth Resources, discovered that the mudflow,
triggered by a massive pyroclastic flow from a vent near Crater Rock, had
occurred in 1781. For decades after the eruption, runoff from the mudflow
continued to deposit sediments in the Sandy, and thence into the Columbia,
much as debris from the 1980 eruptions of Mount St. Helens continues to
filter down the Toutle River, through the Cowlitz, and into the Columbia.

Although the main activity of this eruptive episode, named for its characteristic deposits in Old Maid Flat on Hood's west flank, had subsided
by about 1810, occasional outbursts continued into the period of historic
observation. In 1845, while scouting a route for a wagon train attempting a
first crossing of the Cascades over what became known as Barlow Pass, Joel
Palmer became the first Caucasian to ascend high on Hood's south slope
and obtain a clear view of Crater Rock. Quiescent during Palmer's brief
visit, Hood reawakened only a few years later. Alexis Perrey, the European
historian who kept month-by-month reports of earthquakes and volcanic
eruptions worldwide, noted that Hood was active in 1853; August 1854;
August 15 to 17, 1859; and September 21 to October 8, 1865. Although
Perrey is accurate, his notations are brief and his sources, probably taken
from equally terse newspaper items, are unknown. It is not until 1859 that
we have a local observer's account of Mount Hood in action. On August 20
of that year, the *Weekly Oregonian*, under the heading "Eruptions of Mount
Hood," stated:

On Wednesday last, the atmosphere suddenly became exceedingly hot about midday. In the afternoon the heavens presented a singular appearance; dark, silvery, condensed clouds hung over the top of Mt. Hood. The next day several persons watched the appearance of Mt. Hood until evening. An occasional flash of fire could be seen by every one whose attention could be drawn to the subject. Yesterday, the mountain was closely examined by those who have recently returned from a visit to its summit, when, by the naked eye or a glass, it seemed that a large mass of the northwest side had disappeared, and that the immense quantity of snow which, two weeks since, covered the south

MAJOR GEOLOGIC EVENTS AT MOUNT HOOD DURING THE LAST 50,000 YEARS

DATE OR APPROXIMATE AGE (YEARS)	EVENT	DEPOSITS
AD 1859 and 1865–1866	Minor explosive activity	Scattered ash and pumice
Late nineteenth century	Late neoglacial advance	Prominent, sharp-crested moraines
AD 1781 to ca. 1810	Old Maid eruptive period	Dacite dome (Crater Rock); pyroclastic flow; lahars to south and west; lithic ash
500	Lahars in Zigzag River	Mudflow deposits
1,500	Timberline eruptive period	Avalanche debris from collapse of upper south flank; lava dome; pyroclastic flows; tephra; extensive mudflows south and west
7,700	Eruptions from vent near the site of present-day Parkdale; Mazama ash fall	Basaltic andesite of Parkdale lava flow; layer of Mazama ash
20,000–11,000	Waning stages of Fraser (Evans Creek) glaciation	Glacial moraines
20,000–13,000	Polallie eruptive period	Multiple dacite domes; pyroclastic flows; tephra; extensive mudflows
25,000–20,000	Maximum of Fraser (Evans Creek) glaciation	Complex of moraines in most valleys
30,000–20,000	Dome eruptions	Multiple dacite domes; pyroclastic flows; mudflows
50,000–30,000	Lava flow eruptions	Andesite lava flows of Cathedral Ridge and Tamanawas Falls

Source: Scott et al., 1997

side, had also disappeared. The dense cloud of steam and smoke constantly rising over and far above the summit, together with the entire
change in its appearance heretofore, convinces us that Mt. Hood is
now in a state of eruption, which has broken out within a few days.
The curious will examine it and see for themselves.

The *Oregonian*'s claim that "a large mass of the northwest side had disappeared" is inaccurate; there is no evidence of large rockfalls or avalanches
from this period. The reference to an "immense quantity of snow" disappearing, however, is plausible: phreatic expulsions of lithic ash from vents
near Crater Rock probably blanketed Hood's snowfields, making it seem,
from a distance, that they had vanished.

*Mount Hood from the southeast. Most of the visible cone is thickly mantled in pyro-
clastic flow and mudflow debris from the volcano's last three major eruptive episodes.
Crater Rock, vent site of the Old Maid eruptive cycle, is the dark knob just below the
summit. The White River glacier occupies the foreground, with Newton Clark glacier
on the extreme right.* —Austin Post photo, U.S. Geological Survey

Although published more than forty years after the event, an eyewitness account of the 1859 activity offers a more convincingly detailed report than that appearing in the *Oregonian*. Writing in the *Everett Record* (Washington) of May 17, 1902, W. F. Courtney, an Oregon pioneer, recalled,

> The eruption took place during the later part of September, 1859. . . . We were camped on Tie [Tygh] Ridge about thirty-five miles from Mt. Hood. . . . It was about 1:30 o'clock in the morning . . . when suddenly the heavens lit up and from the dark there shot up a column of fire. With a flash that illuminated the whole mountainside with a pinkish glare, the flames danced from the crater. . . . For two hours we watched, the mountain continued to blaze at irregular intervals, and when morning came Mt. Hood presented a peculiar sight. His sides, where the day before there was snow, were blackened as if cinders and ashes had been thrown out.

Courtney added "That was the only time that I ever saw flames issue from the crater, but I was a member of a party at one time when we encountered hot cinders on the mountainside." The activity Courtney described took place a month after the *Oregonian* article appeared, but was probably a similar incident in the same eruptive phase. He was certainly correct in noting

Relief map of the Mount Hood area

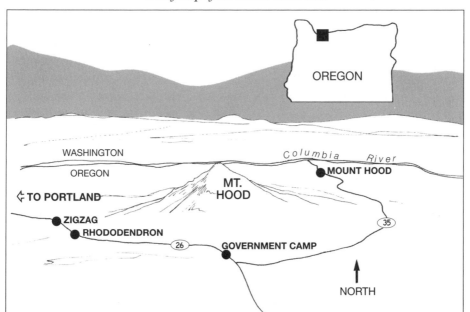

that tephra ("cinders and ashes") from this mildly explosive activity then mantled Hood's snows.

Six years later, on September 26, 1865, the *Oregonian* reported another eruption:"It is some time since we have had an excitement about old Hood belching forth, but on Saturday last the active puffs, in dense black smoke, were witnessed by hundreds of people in this city. The fumes were so thick as to literally obscure the view of the summit at times." Since the source of the "dense black smoke" was a "deep gorge," apparently low on the southwestern flank, it might seem that the *Oregonian* writer mistook a forest fire for an eruption. An eyewitness report published in the same issue of the *Oregonian*, however, confirms that the "dense black smoke" was volcanic in origin. John Dever, of Company E. First Regiment, Washington Territory Volunteers, was stationed at Vancouver during the early morning of September 21. Dever's account offers concrete details:

> Between the hours of 5 and 7 o'clock, and as the morning was particularly bright for this season of the year, my attention was naturally drawn toward the east. . . . Judge, then, of my surprise to see the top of Mount Hood enveloped in smoke and flame. Yes, sir, real jets of flame shot upwards seemingly a distance of fifteen or twenty feet above the mountain's height, accompanied by discharge of what appeared to be fragments of rock, cast up a considerable distance, which I could perceive fall immediately after with a rumbling noise not unlike distant thunder. The phenomenon was witnessed by other members of the guard.

Like Courtney in 1859, Dever reported clouds of smoke and flame issuing from near the volcano's summit, rather than from a "deep gorge," as the *Oregonian* stated. Dever's precise description of flying shards of rock thundering downslope could apply only to a genuine eruption. On November 17, the *Oregonian* noted that Hood was again "steaming voluminously," repeatedly "jetting forth . . . puffs of black smoke." Although the deposits have not been positively correlated with observed historic events, Hood's upper cone is littered with bread-crust bombs, pumice lapilli, and other tephra, some of which may have been erupted in 1859 or 1865.

An unpublished letter by Franklin A. Hinds, who witnessed the 1865 eruptions from Portland, reveals that Mount Hood remained sporadically active into early 1866. Writing on January 28 of 1866, Hinds advised his recipients not to believe versions of the event exaggerated by the press, but to accept his word for it that Hood was actually in eruption. Noting that the volcano had been "smoking" for the previous three months, he added that he had seen it "last eve[ning] just before sundown give unmistakable evidences [sic] of emit[ting] smoke." Laconically, Hinds also observed that

Oregonians were not overly impressed by an active volcano located 50 miles distant, noting that Hood's occasional flare-ups did not "create so much excitement here as you would naturally suppose; the morning paper speaks of it as an item of news and it is soon again forgotten in the hum of business." Hinds's remark about the public's attitude—determinedly ignoring a potential volcanic threat while pursuing business as usual—is still valid and identifies a major social impediment in preparing Pacific Northwest residents for the disastrous effects of a more powerful outburst in the future.

In his list of historic eruptions compiled for Edward Holden's *Catalogue of Earthquakes on the Pacific Coast*, Frederick Plummer states that Hood was again active in 1869, an event of which no written accounts apparently have survived. The only twentieth-century increase in heat and steam emission occurred in August 1907. A. H. Sylvester, a member of the U.S. Geological Survey, was then bivouacked at Government Camp, about 5 or 6 miles south of the summit, when he noticed unusually large clouds of steam rising from Steel Cliff, immediately east of Crater Rock. Later that day (August 28), his companions saw a column of steam rising from Crater Rock and extending high above the summit.

Vigorous steaming continued all day, and after nightfall a member of Sylvester's party, using field glasses, observed a glow from behind Crater Rock which he described as "looking like a chimney burning out." The next morning the White River, which flows from the snout of a glacier occupying the trench between Crater Rock and Steel Cliff, suddenly swelled from a gentle stream to a rushing watercourse triple its usual volume. Because weather conditions could not account for the abrupt increase in the river's flow, Sylvester concluded that volcanic heat had partly melted the White Glacier.

Mount Hood's Holocene Activity

If we had only historical records to go by—mid-nineteenth-century descriptions of mildly explosive activity that apparently had little effect beyond the mountain's immediate flanks—Mount Hood would seem to pose little threat to Oregonians living in its shadow. Investigations of deposits in valleys heading on the south, southeast, and southwest sides of the mountain, however, reveal that the volcano has repeatedly devastated the sites of communities located as far as 50 miles downvalley from its summit. Thanks to the extensive fieldwork of scientists such as William Wise, Dwight Crandell, Patrick Pringle, and Kenneth Cameron, upon whose reports the following summary is largely based, we have an increasingly detailed account of Hood's late Pleistocene and Holocene activity.

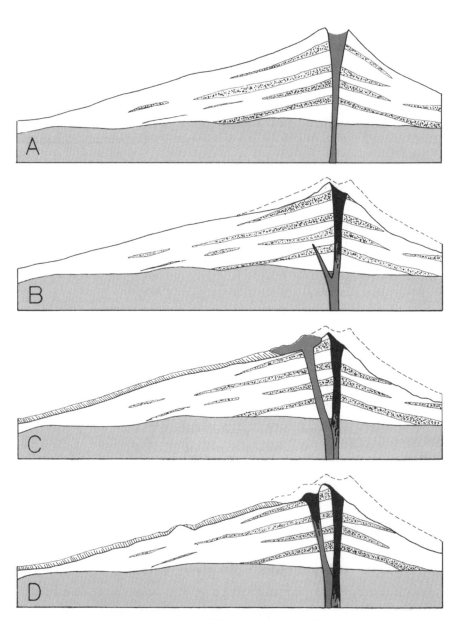

Cross-sections of Mount Hood at four different stages of its development. The darkened vertical areas represent the volcano's then-active main conduit; solid black vertical areas denote solidified magma blocking the conduit. Horizontal dotted areas indicate pyroclastic deposits sandwiched between lava flows. The dotted line above the summit outlines the volcano's former profile. (A) At the time of its maximum height during Pleistocene time. (B) After extensive late Pleistocene glaciations lowered its former summit and scooped out large cirques. (C) Eruption of a dacite dome south of the summit and formation of the large debris fan covering the south flank during the Timberline eruptive episode about 1,500 years ago. (D) Mount Hood today, after another dacite dome, Crater Rock, extruded (at the site of the older Timberline-period dome) during the Old Maid eruptive episode between AD *1781 and 1810.* —Reproduced with permission, William S. Wise, 1966

The Timberline Eruptive Period

After some voluminous eruptions during the Polallie eruptive cycle of the late Pleistocene, Mount Hood entered into a long dormant interval that lasted at least 12,000 years. To a casual observer, the volcano may have seemed extinct, or at least as comatose as Mount Jefferson to the south. About 1,500 years ago, however, Hood was rejuvenated by an infusion of fresh dacite magma, introducing a series of events—the Timberline eruptive episode—that radically changed the contours of its south flank. The Timberline period began with a major disruption of the volcano's south side. Perhaps destabilized by the rising magma column or the phreatic explosions it generated as groundwater within the cone flashed into steam, Hood's south side collapsed, creating a massive avalanche of old rock. Transformed into a huge mudflow, the avalanching rock swept the full length of the Sandy River valley. Depositing lava blocks as large as 8 feet in diameter 30 feet above the present river level where the towns of Wemme and Wildwood now stand, the mudflow gushed from the Sandy's mouth into the Columbia, forcing the larger river's course farther north.

In the next event of the Timberline episode, rising magma blasted open a new vent high on the south side, about 1,000 feet below the summit. Too viscous to flow far, dacite lava welling into the vent piled up to form a large dome, a predecessor of Crater Rock. Pushing through snow and ice, the rising dome shattered and crumbled, initiating hot avalanches of angular blocks as large as 20 feet in diameter, producing pyroclastic flows and surges that rushed as far as 6 or 7 miles from their source. Lithic ash from the collapsing dome and pyroclastic surges mantled Hood's south, east, and northeast flanks to depths of 6 to 24 inches as far as 6 miles from the summit. As it mixed with melting snow and newly erupted ash, the hot fragmental debris also initiated a series of mudflows roiling down the Zigzag and Sandy River drainages, some of which reached the Columbia River. Exposures of these mudflow deposits can be seen today near the town of Troutdale and Interstate 84, 50 miles downstream from the volcano.

Before the Timberline phase began, Mount Hood's south side was perhaps almost as steep and precipitous as the north face is today. By the time the episode concluded, an enormous V-shaped fan of volcanic debris, with its apex at Crater Rock, had reshaped the south flank into the remarkably smooth slope that characterizes it today. William Wise, the first geologist to recognize that the south-side fan originated from collapsing domes and their attendant pyroclastic flows and mudflows, estimated that up to three-quarters of a cubic mile of dacite magma erupted during this period. After two or three centuries of intermittent activity, Hood then slept for another thousand years. If any eruptions occurred during this time, they were small and left no recognizable deposits.

The Old Maid Eruptions

If Lewis and Clark had arrived at the Columbia River about twenty years earlier, they might have witnessed Mount Hood's awesome power in a series of eruptions that buried the valleys of the Zigzag, Sandy, and White Rivers under deposits of fragmental debris tens of feet thick. Although a smaller volume of magma erupted, the Old Maid episode almost exactly duplicated the sequence of events in the Timberline period, producing clouds of lithic ash, extrusions of viscous dacite (forming the dome at Crater Rock), at least one large pyroclastic flow, and numerous large-volume mudflows. The opening volley of throat-clearing phreatic explosions probably destroyed an older dome erected during the Timberline eruptions, blanketing the mountain with thin layers of pink ash. As fresh dacite magma rose to build a new dome—the present Crater Rock—explosions undermined part of the rising dome's north face, causing it to collapse and triggering a large pyroclastic flow of hot dome fragments and ash. Most of this block-and-ash flow descended southeastward onto the White River glacier, where meltwater

Viewed from Frog Butte, the smooth debris fan formed on Mount Hood's south flank during the Timberline eruptive period is clearly visible. The White River canyon (left of center) has been partly refilled by pyroclastic flow deposits from the Old Maid eruptive period (ca. AD 1781–1810). —David Wieprecht photo, U.S. Geological Survey

Ghostly victims of Mount Hood's wrath. Lying like fallen soldiers atop a ridge on Hood's southeast shoulder, these silvery stumps are all that remain of trees that were probably killed by a pyroclastic surge early in the Old Maid eruptive cycle. —Courtesy of Ellen Morris Bishop

generated a series of mudflows that formed the deposit informally known as Mesa Terrace in the White River canyon. Because a number of distinct ash layers are interspersed among these mudflow deposits, it appears that the eruptions took place intermittently, perhaps over a span of several decades, repeatedly triggering mudflows as hot material sporadically cascaded downslope from Crater Rock.

Traveling as far downvalley as the point where Oregon 35 crosses the White River, the pyroclastic flow left deposits tens of feet thick. Pyroclastic surges accompanying the hot avalanches were apparently responsible for killing the trees constituting the Ghost Forest, a stand of bleached snags high on Hood's southeast shoulder. The pyroclastic flow and surge triggered two extensive mudflows, one of which traveled the full length of the White River, inundating Tygh Valley before emptying into the Deschutes River. A somewhat smaller mudflow extended downvalley only as far as the bridge below White River Station.

Because the south face of Crater Rock apparently remained stable as it elevated, relatively little material was directed southward onto the broad debris fan formed during the Timberline episode, sparing the future site of Timberline Lodge from devastation. Some avalanches of hot material, however, were channeled through the gap between Castle Crags and Illumination Rock, plunging down Hood's west flank onto the Sandy glacier, where they produced another series of mudflows that traveled down the Zigzag River valley at least as far as the present-day town of Brightwood.

MOUNT HOOD'S PREHISTORIC BURIED FORESTS ▬▬▬

Although volcanoes are commonly regarded as destroyers, they also can effectively preserve objects they bury. The most celebrated examples of volcanic preservation are found at Pompeii and Herculaneum, ancient Roman cities entombed in AD 79 under airfall tephra and pyroclastic flows from Mount Vesuvius. The Bronze Age town of Akrotiri, on the volcanic Greek island of Santorini (Thera), was similarly engulfed about 1628 BC, sealing up an important outpost of Minoan civilization for posterity. Although they have not—as yet—buried entire cities, some Cascade volcanoes have contributed their share toward preserving human artifacts. In 1972, archaeologists excavated a Native American campsite in the foothills of western Washington, near the present towns of Enumclaw and Buckley, that had been overwhelmed by a huge mudflow from Mount Rainier about 5,600 years ago. Yielding stone projectile points, scrapers, and other tools, the encampment provided evidence of the (then) oldest known human habitation in the Puget Sound region. Ash raining from Mount Mazama 7,700 years ago covered and preserved about seventy pairs of sandals of sagebrush bark that were subsequently found in a cave at Fort Rock, Oregon.

No traces of human settlements have been discovered thus far under Mount Hood's Holocene deposits, but the volcano's recent eruptions have preserved specimens from several prehistoric forests. One stand of trees killed but not buried during the Old Maid eruptive period is visible from a trail a short distance east of Timberline Lodge. Known as the "Ghost Forest," these silvery snags, which line either side of the upper White River canyon, were probably victims of tephra showers or pyroclastic surges that rose above pyroclastic flows descending from Crater Rock. A true buried forest is located at the bottom of the White River canyon; from the Buried Forest Overlook near Timberline Lodge, ten or fifteen snags are visible sticking out of volcanic deposits about 500 feet below. Debris flows of the early Old Maid sequence probably covered these trees, identified as mountain hemlocks, and eventually filled the valley to a depth of about 100 feet. After the eruptions

Mudflows that moved down the Sandy River, burying Old Maid Flat, also dammed two of the Sandy's tributaries, the Muddy Fork and Lost Creek, impounding lakes behind the debris dams. Runout from these mudflows, traveling as far as the Columbia, created the long sandbar extending from the Sandy's mouth that Broughton described in 1792. As noted above, the Sandy's bed was still overwhelmed with sediment when Lewis and Clark visited the river thirteen years later.

Layers of light gray or pink ash from the Old Maid episode cover much of Hood's lower slopes. On Yokum Ridge, about 2.5 miles west of the summit, the tephra lies 5.5 inches thick. On the northeast flank, within a radius

ceased, two streams issuing from the White River glacier cut through the deposit on opposite sides of the valley, leaving a flat-topped remnant in the valley's center (informally known as Mesa Terrace) and exposing the felled timber.

An older buried forest, killed during the Timberline eruptive episode and then partly exhumed by erosion, is located more than 7 miles west of Timberline Lodge, on the south side of Illumination Ridge at an elevation of 5,850 feet. Named for a Portland Judge who discovered it in 1926, the Stadler buried forest is exposed along the upper edge of the deep canyon below Zigzag glacier, where the ends of logs protrude near the top of the almost-vertical canyon walls. According to Kenneth Cameron of the U.S. Geological Survey and Patrick Pringle of the Washington Division of Geology and Earth Resources, who conduct ongoing investigations of Hood's prehistoric forests, between about 20 and 30 logs, averaging 1 to 2 feet in diameter, are in an exceptionally good state of preservation, probably because at this altitude they are frozen most of the year and kept dry in summer. Aligned almost due west and showing signs of intense abrasion, they were mowed down by a series of pyroclastic flows and mudflows about 1,500 years ago.

In addition to the forest relics found high on Hood's cone, Cameron and Pringle have identified several others downvalley from the volcano. These include two buried forests, one above the other, near the Twin Bridges campground on the Zizgag River at the 2,820-foot level, where dead snags remain standing upright, engulfed by a mudflow that was apparently moving comparatively slowly through a dense forest. The upper-level trees were buried in mudflow deposits of Old Maid age, as are the remnants of buried forests occurring all along the upper Sandy River from Old Maid Flat to the town of Brightwood, in the channel of the Zigzag River near Tollgate Wayside, and along the lower Sandy River downstream from Marmot Dam. As Pringle and Cameron noted, these buried forests not only inform us of "past ecological communities," but also "graphically display the far-reaching effects of volcanic activity"—offering silent testimony to the volcano's overwhelming power.

For additional information, see Cameron and Pringle, 1991.

Summit of Mount Hood from the southeast. Bare patches in the snow are sites of fumaroles and hot rocks. Steel Cliff, a massive flow or dome, appears at the extreme right.
—Courtesy of the U.S. Forest Service

of 3 to 4 miles from the summit, the thickness varies from 7 inches at the Tilly Jane Guard Station to about 2.5 inches on Cooper Spur and near Polallie Creek. The presence of ash on all sides of the volcano suggests deposition over a period of years or decades, while winds frequently changed direction. Most of the ash probably derived from collapsing lobes of Crater Rock or from ash clouds accompanying pyroclastic flows and surges.

Crandell also found scattered lapilli of gray pumice on the south, east, and northeast sides of Mount Hood. Generally no larger than pea size, these pumice fragments occur on top of the Old Maid pyroclastic flow deposit in the White River canyon, indicating that they erupted less than 200 years ago, perhaps during the activity of 1859 or 1865–1866.

Mount Hood's Pleistocene History

Like Jefferson, Adams, and other neighboring stratovolcanoes, Mount Hood was born during Pleistocene time, when enormous glaciers repeatedly shrouded most of the Cascade Range. Before Hood began to erupt, at least 500,000 years ago, glaciers and other erosional forces had already sculptured the surrounding mountainscape into the maze of ridges and valleys that characterize the topography today. The average elevation in this area approximately 20 miles south of the Columbia River was—and is—about 4,500 feet, but individual peaks stood at least 2,000 feet higher. The major streams now originating from Hood's glaciers—the Zigzag, Sandy, White, and Hood Rivers—were already present, although they then occupied narrower valleys. The Pleistocene glaciers had not yet finished the job of remodeling them into broad canyons.

As Mount Hood grew, it gradually buried an ancestral volcano that had built a sizable cone during the late Pliocene or early Pleistocene. Now partly exposed beneath the Sandy glacier on Hood's west flank, the eroded remnants of this ancient edifice—the Sandy Glacier volcano—consist of thin lava flows interspersed with layers of tuff. According to Terry White of the U.S. Geological Survey, the pre-Hood deposits are cut by numerous vertical dikes, some of which are visible at the head of the Muddy Fork.

In studying Hood's early eruptive history, Wise concluded that the volcano grew rapidly during its youth, pouring out copious andesite lava flows that traveled as far as 8 miles from the erupting vent. A few individual flows, with volumes approaching half a cubic mile, attained thicknesses of 500 feet and now form long ridges radiating outward from the main cone. As in the case of Mount Rainier to the north, many of these early lava flows probably erupted when Hood was encased in ice. Whereas lava flows emitted directly onto glaciers commonly disintegrated into avalanches of fragmental rock that were swept away in meltwater down glacial canyons, flows that traveled along the tops of rocky divides between ice streams built the massive elongated spurs that are seen on Hood today.

When it erupted while sheathed in ice, Mount Hood generated prodigious mudflows that streamed down every valley heading on the volcano, including the Hood River valley to the north and the Sandy to the west. Portland's east side is partly underlain by a succession of mid-Pleistocene mudflows from its guardian peak, reminders of how far this volcano's reach can extend.

During long periods of warmer weather between glaciations, when glaciers withdrew upvalley to cirques high on the mountain, the more voluminous lava flows typically filled ice-carved trenches, ponding to depths of several hundred feet. Such canyon-filling lava flows formed Barrett Spur and Pulpit Rock, prominent outcrops on Hood's north flank. Four separate flows underlie Lamberson Butte on the east flank, while other thick flows are exposed near Slide Mountain on the southwest flank. Shorter, thinner flows piled up to form Hood's steep upper cone. As it matured, long periods of quiescence, some lasting 10,000 years or more, intervened between comparatively brief episodes—spanning only a few decades or centuries—of intense cone building.

At its zenith, Hood stood approximately 12,000 feet high, a full 8,000 feet above its Cascade foundation. Wise estimates that Hood, with a base covering 92 square miles, attained a volume of almost 45 cubic miles. No other stratovolcano in Oregon except Mazama could match it in bulk or stature. To the north, only Adams and Rainier were larger.

The most catastrophic single event in Hood's long history occurred about 100,000 years ago when the entire north side and summit of the volcano collapsed, sending a gigantic debris avalanche into the Hood River valley. Transformed into a mudflow that was 400 feet deep when it reached the site of Hood River, 20 miles from its source, this tremendous mass had sufficient volume and energy to sweep across the Columbia River and continue for several miles up the White Salmon River valley on the Washington side. At least ten times larger in volume than the south-side partial collapse that later inaugurated the Timberline eruptive episode, this Pleistocene debris flow probably opened a huge U-shaped crater similar to that formed in 1980 at Mount St. Helens.

Like the more recent Timberline-era collapse, the north-side failure may have been triggered during the early stages of an eruption. Subsequent eruptive activity has completely filled in the collapse depression, leaving no trace of the landslide scar. Between about 50,000 and 30,000 years ago, Hood emitted numerous andesite lava flows, including those of Cathedral Ridge and Tamanawas Falls.

When the last Pleistocene ice advance began about 29,000 years ago, Mount Hood may have been much more symmetrical than it is now. As glaciers reformed and expanded to their maximum extent (between about 25,000 and 20,000 years ago), Hood became the center of a massive icecap that extended far down adjacent valleys, particularly on the north and east sides. Burrowing into all sides of the volcano, grinding ice removed much of the constructional surface, lowering the summit by about a thousand feet and transforming the mountain from a comparatively regular cone into the four-faceted horn we see today.

Glaciers scoured the peak so thoroughly that they exposed the original eruptive conduit, now a column of solidified lava visible among the precipices and icefalls of the north face. Wise suggests that Hood's central vent formerly lay significantly north of the present summit ridge, in what is now thin air.

Hood Changes Its Eruptive Behavior

Although andesite lava flows comprise at least 70 percent of its total volume, the upper 4,000 feet of Mount Hood's cone is heavily mantled with pyroclastic debris. With the notable exception of Mount St. Helens, Hood contains a greater proportion of fragmental material than any other Cascade composite cone. Unlike St. Helens, however, Hood is only mildly explosive and typically produces only minor quantities of pumiceous tephra. Hood's abundance of pyroclastic rock probably results from a change in the volcano's eruptive style. After about 30,000 years ago, Hood ceased to produce the andesite lava flows that built most of its cone and instead emitted more silicic magma in the form of dacite domes and pyroclastic flows—a behavior that continued throughout the Polallie, Timberline, and Old Maid eruptive periods.

All of Hood's late Pleistocene and Holocene eruptions are alike in producing domes that emerged from vents high on the mountain and that collapsed to generate avalanches of hot rock, meltwater, and extensive mudflows. Extrusions of viscous magma at or near the summit occurred intermittently during the last glacial maximum, but were particularly voluminous during

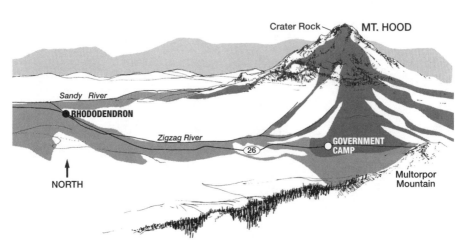

Relief map showing volcanic hazards of the Mount Hood region. Dark gray represents areas likely to be endangered by future pyroclastic flows and surges. Light gray denotes probable courses of lahars. (Ash fallout from pyroclastic flows may affect all sides of the mountain.) Pyroclastic flows derived from dome extrusion and collapse near Crater Rock and accompanying ash clouds and lateral blasts may devastate the south and southwest flanks of the cone, as well as the upper reaches of valleys heading on the volcano. Floods and mudflows may reach tens of miles downvalley, some to the Columbia River. —Adapted from Crandell, 1980

an extended period between about 15,000 and 20,000 years ago, as the Pleistocene glaciers began to thin and retreat. Named for its characteristic pyroclastic flow and mudflow deposits found near Polallie Creek on the northeast slope, the Polallie eruptive period created widespread devastation throughout the region. Whereas effects of Timberline and Old Maid activity were largely confined to the south flank and the valleys of streams that drain it, the Polallie episode affected all sides of the mountain.

As Crandell observed, the Polallie deposits "typically occur in three different topographic positions: ridge top, valley side, and valley floor." The differing locations are a function of the ice cover at the time of the eruption. When glaciers were thick and extensive, material avalanching from domes growing near Hood's summit accumulated along ice-free ridgetops. After glaciers had shrunk, rock fragments cascading from shattered domes was deposited between the valley walls and the margins of the retreating glacier. Fragmental material settled on valley floors beyond a glacier's terminus both during and after glacier expansion and retreat.

Mount Hood from the north, with Mount Jefferson on the horizon. Cooper Spur, the large wedge-shaped apron of pyroclastic debris from the Polallie eruptive episode, appears at the left, bordered by the Eliot glacier at left-center. —Austin Post photo, U.S. Geological Survey

The most conspicuous Polallie-age formation is the enormous triangular deposit on Hood's northeast side that culminates in Cooper Spur. Composed of voluminous pyroclastic flow and mudflow material derived from crumbling domes, Cooper Spur borders the east margin of Eliot glacier and extends to an elevation of 8,500 feet; its apex probably once extended much higher up the mountain. That this huge wedge-shaped accumulation of loosely consolidated rock fragments is present at so high an altitude suggests that the Pleistocene glaciers, which formerly covered this area, had already diminished when the deposit formed. The Polallie eruptions apparently continued intermittently for a long time; intervals of erosion occurred between successive volcanic deposits.

The Parkdale soils, a yellowish brown ash layer as much as 14 feet thick, lies east and north of Mount Hood, particularly in the upper Hood River valley. Renowned for their fertility, these soils probably consist of fallout from ash clouds billowing from massive pyroclastic flows and surges during the Polallie eruptions. Prevailing winds carried the ash to the northeast, where it provides important nutrients for the abundant fruit orchards that now clothe the valley in pastel colors each spring.

By the close of the Polallie eruptive period, Hood presented a grim and gray spectacle. Ash darkened its snowfields and dacite rubble buried formerly timbered slopes. Aprons of fragmental debris surrounding Hood on every side extended miles downslope and merged with mudflows choking every valley heading on the mountain. On the north side, sediment from mudflows filling the Hood River valley repeatedly flushed into the Columbia.

Future Hazards

In his evaluation of Hood's eruptive potential, Crandell noted that the volcano "will almost certainly erupt again, and possibly in the very near future." When Hood joins St. Helens as the second active volcano on the Portland skyline, it will probably behave much as it did during the Timberline and Old Maid episodes. Future eruptions, preceded by swarms of small earthquakes, are likely to begin with phreatic explosions, sending clouds of lithic ash derived from pulverized older rock billowing thousands of feet into the air. If they occur in clear weather, these steam blasts may cause widespread alarm throughout north-central Oregon, conspicuously darkening Hood's snowfields and alerting public officials to the greater dangers that may follow.

The location of new vents will largely determine which areas future eruptions will affect. Since the collapse of Hood's upper south flank 1,500 years ago, all Holocene activity has concentrated at vents located south of the summit. During the Timberline period, material avalanching from a growing dome buried the entire south side of the volcano under pyroclastic flow and mudflow debris. During the Old Maid episode, the main erupting vent was probably located between the summit ridge and Crater Rock, its circumscribed position deflecting pyroclastic flows to the southeast down the White River valley, and to the west down the Zigzag and Sandy River drainages. Very little Old Maid pyroclastic flow material was deposited on the Timberline debris fan, although ash fallout from the flows and surges shrouded the entire cone.

Geologists expect Hood's next eruption to duplicate events of the most recent eruptive periods. After preliminary steam explosions, thick, sticky tongues of dacite lava will ooze from vents near Crater Rock, piling up to form another steep-sided lava dome. Undermined by explosions or the pull of gravity, the dome will collapse, with avalanching blocks of incandescent rock forming pyroclastic flows that will sweep down the upper White and Sandy River valleys. The Old Maid block-and-ash flow, several tens of feet thick, traveled at a calculated speed of 85 miles per hour, overwhelming everything in its path. Future pyroclastic flows can be expected to exhibit the same irresistible energy, with accompanying clouds of hot ash affecting ridgetops high above the flow base and beyond the flow's terminus. As in the late eighteenth century, meltwater will generate mudflows that pour down the White River as far as its connection with the Deschutes and down the Sandy River all the way to the Columbia, perhaps temporarily blocking its channel and closing it to shipping.

It is also possible that Hood will surprise us by opening new vents on the north, east, or west side of the volcano, affecting areas spared since the long-lived Polallie eruptive series ended about 13,000 years ago. Hot rock cascading down Hood's northeast flank onto the Eliot or Newton Clark glaciers, the mountain's largest ice streams, could trigger unusually voluminous mudflows into the Hood River valley, severely damaging innumerable farms, orchards, and towns along the valley floor. Whichever flank of the mountain is affected, economic losses stemming from destruction of highways, bridges, houses, businesses, resorts, forest reserves, and other agricultural investments will undoubtedly exceed the $1 billion lost in the Mount St. Helens eruption of 1980.

Visiting Mount Hood

A drive of about 170 miles encircling Mount Hood, locally known as the Mount Hood loop, offers some stunning views of the peak, as well as of Adams and St. Helens. U.S. 26 from Portland enters the Hood National Forest at Zigzag; much of U.S. 26 west of the mountain parallels the old Barlow Road, the first to cross the Oregon Cascades. Near Government

Camp—named for an American army contingent, the First U.S. Mounted Rifles, who wintered (and abandoned their wagons) here in 1849—take the road to Timberline Lodge, built at an elevation of 6,000 feet near the White River canyon on the east margin of the Timberline debris fan. Although the south flank slopes smoothly upward to Crater Rock, the area behind this steaming dome is icy, crevasse-ridden, and dangerous. Only experienced climbers should attempt the summit.

To see the north side of the mountain, continue east on U.S. 26 past Government Camp, and take Oregon 35 north toward Hood River approximately 22 miles (a few miles beyond the Sherwood campground). Turn left (west) from Oregon 35 onto Cooper Spur Road, toward the well-marked Cooper Spur Ski Area. Look for the small sign to Cloud Cap Road (no. 3512), an extremely narrow gravel road that winds 11 miles to Cloud Cap Inn at the 6,000-foot level. Built in 1889 as an alpine hotel, the rustic log structure (closed to the public) is operated by the Crag Rats, a search and rescue group. A trail leads from the Cloud Cap area eastward to Cooper Spur, affording excellent views of Eliot glacier, Oregon's largest ice stream. North across the Columbia River bluffs toward the Washington Cascades, the magnificent vista includes St. Helens, Adams, and Rainier.

Return to Oregon 35 and proceed to Hood River, from which you take the Columbia River Highway back to Portland and Interstate 5. From Cascade Locks, about 20 miles west of Hood River, look northwest to the prominent scarp on flat-topped Table Mountain, a source of the Bonneville slide that created the legendary Bridge of the Gods. Despite summer crowds, Multnomah Falls and Crown Point State Park are worth a special stop.

CHAPTER 16

Mount Adams

THE FORGOTTEN GIANT OF WASHINGTON

The second-highest peak in Washington state and the third-highest in the Cascades, Mount Adams (12,276 feet) is also the second-most voluminous stratovolcano in the range, exceeded in the sheer bulk of its accumulated lavas only by Mount Shasta. Despite its vast size and ten glaciers, however, its isolation in a rugged mountainscape far from major population centers makes it relatively unknown.

The broad, humped profile of Adams can be glimpsed from various points in the Columbia Gorge, and it looms prominently over the western skyline of Yakima in southeastern Washington, but the higher visibility—and more obvious aesthetic appeal—of its volcanic neighbors tend to divert public attention from Adams's scenic and geologic attractions. With its asymmetrical cone and wide, almost flat summit, Adams lacks the soaring quality that characterizes the pyramidal north face of Mount Hood, its legendary rival across the Columbia. Forty-eight miles to the north, Rainier's greater height and spectacular glacier cover inspire countless admirers in the urbanized Puget Sound area, while Mount St. Helens, about 35 miles to the west, fascinates with its intermittent pyrotechnic displays. As if to emphasize Adams's undeserved obscurity, when it appears in the background of photos showing St. Helens in eruption, the peak is often misidentified as "Mount Rainier."

The tendency to ignore or devalue this somewhat clumsily designed giant is apparent even in the tales of indigenous peoples. When Pahto (Adams) competed with Wy'east (Hood) for Loowit's (St. Helens) affections, Loowit rejected her northern suitor for the more handsome Wy'east. Pahto not only failed to win the fair damsel, but he also suffered the indignity of having Wy'east land so powerful a blow on his head that it was flattened into its present lumpish shape.

Nor did Caucasian settlers always show the respect due an alpine deity. In the 1930s Adams acquired the dubious distinction of becoming the only major Cascade volcano to have its crater invaded by commercial speculators. In 1929 and 1931, Wade Dean, a promoter from White Salmon on the Columbia River, filed sulfur claims covering the 210-acre summit plateau. A horse and mule trail was built on the comparatively gentle south flank

The dual-armed Lyman glacier (center), flowing from the summit ice cap, bites deeply into the northeast face of Mount Adams. Red Butte, a partly eroded cinder cone, sits atop the extensive lava field in the foreground. —Austin Post photo, U.S. Geological Survey

and a diamond core-drilling machine was laboriously hauled to the crater. In 1934, workers drilled through the summit icecap, more than 300 feet thick, to penetrate the hydrothermally altered rock beneath, finding some sulfur in sludge from the drill holes. Despite Dean's aggressive advertising of his project, it seems that no significant amount of sulfur was either mined or sold. By 1959, when the last assessment was done, the cost and trouble of trying to extract marketable sulfur had become prohibitive, and efforts to mine Adams's summit were abandoned.

In the early 1980s, when USGS geologists Wes Hildreth and Judy Fierstein evaluated sixty samples of summit rock, they found that earlier prospectors had overestimated both the quality and the quantity of the crater

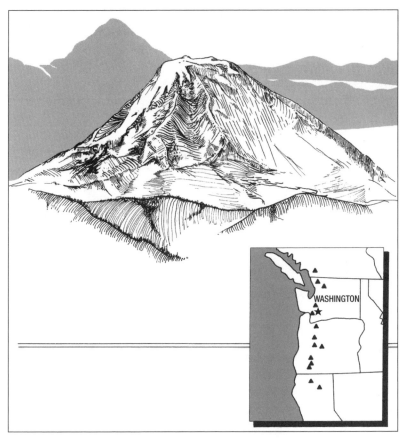

Mount Adams from the south

sulfur deposits. They concluded that while the volcano's sulfur resources had been grossly exaggerated, "the difficulty of recovering it cannot be."

The story relating how Adams belatedly received its present name—through careless error and long after the other High Cascade volcanoes had received theirs—illustrates the somewhat haphazard way in which the mountain too often has been treated. Although Lewis and Clark sighted the peak as early as 1805, at first they confused it with St. Helens and consequently made no attempt to bestow an appropriate name on what they mistakenly thought was "the highest pinnacle in America." Since Vancouver had not seen the mountain during his exploratory voyage of 1792, it did not, unlike Baker, Rainier, St. Helens, and Hood, already bear the name of yet another eighteenth-century British diplomat or naval officer.

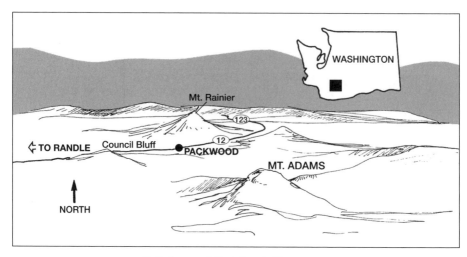

Relief map of the Mount Adams area

Hall J. Kelley, a fervent American patriot and booster of the "Oregon Country," was primarily responsible for the accidental christening of Adams. In the early 1830s, Kelley initiated a movement to call the Cascades the "Presidents' Range," renaming all the major peaks after former U.S. presidents. Oregon's Three Sisters and California's Shasta were to become Madison and Jackson, while Hood and St. Helens were to honor Adams and Washington. It appears that Kelley had no glimmer of Adams's existence, and did not give it a place in his campaign.

Working from inadequate maps, one of Kelley's supporters, Thomas J. Farnham, inadvertently interchanged Kelley's names for Hood and St. Helens and also made a serious error in latitude, placing "Adams" on his map about 35 miles east of St. Helens and north of Hood. As mountaineer Ray Smutek commented, "In what has to be one of geography's greatest coincidences, there was a mountain there to accept the name." Ironically, Adams was the only name in the Kelley-Farnham scheme that took, and it was bestowed on a mountain they did not know existed!

T♭e Mount A♂ams Region

Because of its comparatively remote position, with few paved roads leading into the densely forested area, Mount Adams is not ordinarily besieged by hoards of tourists, as are Hood, St. Helens, and Rainier—although the Forest Service estimates that several thousand climbers reach the summit annually. Undeterred by its lack of celebrity or glamour, many thousands of backpackers, campers, and other summer visitors hike its trails, savoring the views of its deep glacier-cut valleys, peripheral cinder cones, and fresh-looking flows of lava. The Mount Adams Wilderness, part of the Gifford Pinchot National Forest, encompasses about 47,000 acres on the volcano's upper cone, with a section of the Yakama Indian Reservation occupying much of the east flank. Only two small towns, Trout Lake and Glenwood, both located south of the peak, offer accommodations or other amenities for visitors.

The "humped" appearance of Mount Adams, noted by Lewis and Clark, results from its construction as an elongated complex of overlapping cones aligned along a north-south axis. A wide apron of gently sloping lava fields surrounds the steep main cone and extends outward for 7 or 8 miles. Eighteen miles in diameter, the volcano's base covers an area of almost 250 square miles. With most of its bulk contained in its expansive lower flanks, Adams's total volume exceeds 50 cubic miles; at least half as much more eroded away during Pleistocene glaciations. In contrast to its gentle lower slopes, the main cone above an elevation of about 7,000 feet rises precipitously, with grades varying from 15 to 35 or even 50 degrees. Near-vertical cliffs are common on the eroded east side, where the Klickitat and Rusk glaciers have carved headwalls 2,000 feet high.

Many small tributaries of the Klickitat, Cispus, Lewis, and White Salmon Rivers drain radially from Mount Adams, fed by water percolating through the highly porous lava rubble composing the main cone. Many streams issue directly from glacier snouts, while most of the abundant springs on the mountain's lower flanks probably derive from the high annual precipitation, in the form of both rain and snow, on the volcano's upper cone.

During the maximum extent of the last Pleistocene glaciation, ice covered approximately 80 to 90 percent of Mount Adams. Today it covers only about 2.5 percent of the mountain's surface (about 6.2 square miles), most of it in the ten principal ice streams. Five of the largest glaciers, the Klickitat, Wilson, Lyman, Adams, and White Salmon, descend from the summit ice cap. Others, such as the Pinnacle, Lava, and Rusk, originate in cirques or broad trenches incised below the summit. The Adams glacier flows down a narrow channel on the steep northwest face in a series of spectacular icefalls, then spreads laterally in a large sheet to an elevation of about 7,000 feet.

On the east flank, the Klickitat glacier, fed by two ice streams plunging from the summit, has excavated a mile-wide cirque, the second largest of any active glacier in the Cascade Range. Only the cirque of the Carbon glacier on Rainier's north face is larger. Although the Klickitat now terminates at an altitude of about 6,000 feet, until recently it extended much farther downvalley. Beyond its present snout lies a succession of well-preserved

*Massive glaciers radiate from Mount Adams's broad summit ice cap. Mount
Hood, about 55 miles to the south, appears on the distant horizon (top left).*
—Austin Post photo, U.S. Geological Survey

moraines dating from the fourteenth to the twentieth century, remnants of
the glacier's alternating advances and retreats during various pulses of the
Little Ice Age.

After obtaining a permit from the Yakama Indian Nation, visitors can
explore the aptly named Ridge of Wonders on Adams's east side, a thousand feet above the floor of Hellroaring Canyon, where they can enjoy
stunning views of the Mazama and Klickitat glaciers. No maintained trail
leads to this rugged highland, but cross-country hikers are rewarded by an
intense experience of the mountain's rugged structure, with its steep-walled
cirques, massive icefalls, high cleavers—long, narrow ribs of lava rock dividing glacial trenches—and crumbling stacks of multicolored lava flows. The
frequent roar of avalanching snow, ice, and rock vividly demonstrates the
processes of erosion at work, tearing the mountain apart.

Geologic Setting and Eruptive History of Adams

Given the general neglect accorded this underrated peak, it is not surprising that it was one of the last of the Cascade volcanoes to attract scientific attention. Not until 1901, when local settler and mountaineer C. E. Rusk guided glaciologist Harry Reid on a circuit around Adams, was it systematically explored and its largest glaciers named. Another eighty years passed before the U.S. Geological Survey investigated Adams, including its possible usefulness as a geothermal resource. Fortunately, during the last two decades of the twentieth century, two Survey geologists, Wes Hildreth and Judy Fierstein, painstakingly mapped the volcano, unraveling its complex history, dating its deposits, and providing us with a comprehensive study of its growth and potential hazards.

Perhaps the most startling discovery about Adams is that, despite its battered and weather-beaten appearance, it is much younger than it looks. Notwithstanding the deep cirques etched on its east side, the main edifice above 7,000 feet formed in very late Pleistocene time, most of it probably between about 30,000 and 15,000 years ago. Although Holocene activity has been much less voluminous than the copious effusions of lava that immediately preceded it, Adams has erupted at least ten times during the last 15,000 years, both at the summit and from multiple vents dotting its broad flanks.

Hildreth and Fierstein's studies of Adams's volcanic history have revealed that this previously little-understood volcano is virtually the archetype of a subduction zone composite cone, typical of many others that line the Pacific Ring of Fire. Like Rainier, Shasta, and many similar circum-Pacific stratovolcanoes, Adams is phenomenally long-lived, with a highly irregular historical pattern of magma production. Its life span of 520,000 years is marked by relatively brief episodes of high eruption rates followed by much longer interludes of intermittent minor activity. During periods of intense eruptive activity, the volcano discharges enormous volumes of magma, emitting numerous lava flows in rapid succession and erecting a massive central cone. Long dormant periods then ensue, some lasting tens of thousands of years, typically punctuated only by sporadic eruptions of small volume. Although eruption rates slow down considerably during the long, relatively quiet phases, they rarely cease altogether. Small, infrequent eruptions, however, are not sufficient to keep pace with erosive forces working on the volcano. Pleistocene glaciations reduced two of Adams's earlier cones to eroded stumps, lowering them to altitudes of about 8,000 feet. After glaciers and other eroding agents have largely demolished the cone, Adams then begins a new cycle of vigorous magma production, rapidly erecting another large pile atop the dissected ruins of its predecessor. Hildreth and Fierstein found that this pattern has been repeated at least three times.

Mount Adams, despite its general anonymity, is the dominant topographical feature in Washington's southern Cascades. But it is only the central part of an extensive volcanic field that has been almost continuously active for nearly a million years. The largely andesitic stratovolcano is surrounded by a broad peripheral zone of basaltic volcanoes containing more than sixty recognized vents, including scores of cinder cones, lava fields, and overlapping shields. Encompassing both the main cone and the encircling peripheral vents, the Mount Adams volcanic field covers approximately 500 square miles. The older Simcoe Mountains volcanic field lies to the east, and the young Indian Heaven volcanic field to the west, midway between Adams and St. Helens. (An Indian Heaven vent produced a major effusion of basaltic lava about 9,000 years ago—the Big Lava Bed.) Adams itself sits midway in a north-south-trending volcanic zone, about 4 miles wide and 30 miles long, that contains at least fifty recognized eruption sites. During the last half million years since Mount Adams's inception, this volcanic corridor has produced a larger volume of magma than any other area in Washington.

Beginning about 520,000 years ago, the first Mount Adams—dubbed the Hellroaring volcano—built a cone at least as large as the present mountain. From its main vent located about 3 miles southeast of the present summit, the Hellroaring volcano erupted primarily andesite lavas, with minor quantities of dacite. Although erosion has removed much of this first-stage edifice, it has not yet uncovered its oldest lava flows. Flows exposed in the canyons of Hellroaring and Big Muddy Creeks, respectively, yield potassium-argon ages of 516,000 and 491,000 years (plus or minus about 10,000 years). The uppermost exposed lava flows, near the south bank of Hellroaring Creek, are dated at 511,000 years (plus or minus 9,000 years), indicating that the volcano grew rapidly, with one lava stream erupted on top of another in quick succession. Some lava flows, pouring down steep icy slopes of more than 35 degrees, disintegrated into hot avalanches, triggering block-and-ash flows. Only one pyroclastic flow of dacite pumice, which forms a layer 35 feet thick, has been found amid the predominant block-and-ash flow deposits. The uppermost Hellroaring lava flows dip westward underneath the present young central cone.

A second major pulse of high magma production took place about 450,000 years ago, constructing a second large pile of pyroxene andesite lava flows and forming a broad fan of thin flank flows west and south of the older Hellroaring vent. After an initially rapid cone-building episode, this middle-Pleistocene edifice underwent a much slower rate of intermittent growth during the next 130,000 years, sporadically erupting both andesite and dacite lavas that extend as far as 8 or 9 miles from the present summit.

A sudden surge in the eruption of peripheral basaltic magma occurred between about 120,000 and 100,000 years ago, emplacing an estimated 30 to 35 percent of the total volume of basalt in the Mount Adams volcanic field. Concentrated in the north-south corridor in which Adams stands, this effusion of basaltic magma built several shield volcanoes south of the main cone, including the Quigley Butte, King Mountain, and Meadow Butte shields. On Adams's north flank, basaltic magma formed the Potato Hill scoria cone, from which lava streamed 9 miles westward into the Cispus River canyon. Although Potato Hill, now blanketed in gray ash from the 1980 St. Helens eruptions, looks youthful, glaciation of its lava flows extending onto the Cispus River canyon floor demonstrates that it formed before the last Pleistocene ice advance.

During the same period that witnessed this upsurge in basaltic magma production in the peripheral volcanic field, Adams's main cone erupted voluminous flows of both andesite and dacite. On the north side, the copious andesite flows composing the Killen Creek lava fan, which extends north-northwest beyond Horseshoe Lake, are dated at about 120,000 years. On the southeast flank, an unusually large outpouring of andesite lava with a volume approximating a cubic mile—the Parrott Crossing flow—erupted from a vent near Bench Lake and spilled into the Klickitat River channel, filling its canyon for a distance of 15 miles. Another vent, at nearby Shadow Lake, erupted shortly thereafter, sending a lava stream about 5 miles to the southeast, into upper Bacon Creek.

Another vent active during this prodigious eruptive phase of about 120,000 years ago, also on the southeast side, produced the voluminous dacite flow underlying Bird Creek Meadows, the most silicic magma (68 percent silica) erupted in Adams's entire history. At about the same time, dacite magma spouting from a vent high on the southwest flank fed another lava flow that poured at least 16 miles down Cascade Creek and beyond. Two hundred feet thick, this dacite flow overwhelmed the channel of the White Salmon River, driving the stream from its former course and forcing it to excavate a new canyon more than half a mile to the east.

Following this bout of intense activity, Adams apparently rested for about 30,000 years, a lull during which no recognized deposits were emplaced. This long quiet interlude ended about 70,000 years ago when an infusion of basalt and basaltic andesite magma produced numerous flows from peripheral vents on Adams's outer flanks. Basalt magma first broke through low on the north-northeast side to form Glaciate Butte, with flows that poured many miles down the Klickitat River canyon. The most prominent edifice from this episode is the large spatter-and-scoria cone, about 450 feet high, of Little Mount Adams, perched high atop the Ridge of Wonders on the southeast side. From a distance, this strikingly symmetrical cone of basaltic andesite, with its capacious summit crater and steep slopes of red-dish scoria, seems freshly built. Its stack of fountain-fed lava flows, extending 4 miles down Hellroaring Creek, however, have been glacially eroded, and potassium-argon dating gives an age of about 63,000 years. Like that of Po-tato Hill, Little Mount Adams's cone was positioned high enough to escape scouring by the Pleistocene glaciers that occupied nearby valleys.

From a geologist's point of view, the most striking event during this post-lull eruptive period is the emergence of basaltic lava from Adam's main cone. The Riley Creek lava flows, emitted either from the central crater or from a vent high on the west side, represent the only basalt magma to have penetrated Adams's andesitic central plumbing during the stratovolcano's entire half-million-year-long history.

Another 10,000 to 15,000 years passed before andesitic eruptions re-sumed at the main cone. The first andesite magma to erupt during this phase formed two extensive lava-flow fans on the south and southeast flanks. One spread southward into the valley of the White Salmon River, while the other traveled down the west fork of the Klickitat River. The andesite lavas composing the Devils Garden shield may have been erupted a few thousand years later.

The third era of voluminous cone-building eruptions—that which erected most of the present mountain above an elevation of about 7,000 feet—began approximately 40,000 years ago and ended only 10,000 years ago. Hildreth and Fierstein suggest that most of the giant edifice was prob-ably constructed during an episode of high magma production—totaling 10 to 12 cubic miles—between about 30,000 and 15,000 years ago.

Because the present main cone developed during the last Pleistocene glaciation, most of Mount Adams's lava flows erupted under an extensive cover of glacial ice. Molten rock emerging from the central vent probably encountered an ice cap similar to, but significantly larger and thicker than, that now mantling the volcano's summit. Lava flows erupted at the sum-mit typically shattered as they met solid ice, creating a chaotic jumble of lava fragments that avalanched down the mountainside. As a result of this repeated interaction of hot magma and glacial ice, much of Adams's interior consists of andesite rubble, friable rock that has further weakened by pro-longed exposure to heat and gas emissions.

Where glaciers have cut deeply into the upper cone, particularly on the east and west sides, the volcano reveals a core of chemically altered breccia derived from shattered lava flows. Pervasive leaching by acidic hot water and steam converted much of the original rock into an unstable mixture of kaolinite clay, quartz, sulfur, and iron oxides. The oxidized minerals, deposits of yellow sulfur, and white, green, and red-stained gypsum, contrast vividly with the dark grays and blacks of Adams's unaltered summit rocks.

PLATE 1

Image 1. *Mono Lake and Mono Craters. This chain of bulbous lava flows, domes, and pyroclastic deposits has been repeatedly active during the last 5,000 years, most recently in the fourteenth century* AD. *Paoha Island in Mono Lake erupted frequently between about 1720 and 1850; it was still steaming in 1890.* —Phyllis Gray photo

Image 2. *Lassen Peak from Manzanita Lake. The dark tongue of 1915 lava appears near the west summit.* —Douglas Tustin photo

PLATE 2

Image 3. *Cinder Cone, Lassen Volcanic National Park, with a slaggy lava flow bordering Butte Lake in the foreground.* —Douglas Tustin photo

Image 4. *Painted Dunes, Lassen Volcanic National Park. Ash falling on Cinder Cone's still-hot lava flows oxidized to create pastel shades of pink, orange, and rust. The blocky lava surface in the background was formed after the ashfall phase of the eruption.* —Douglas Tustin photo

PLATE 3

Image 5. *Steaming hot spring, Bumpass Hell, Lassen Volcanic National Park. Years of hydrothermal action have changed formerly solid rock to friable claylike material in shades of white, orange, and yellow.* —Douglas Tustin photo

Image 6. *Mount Shasta at sunset.* —Phyllis Gray photo

PLATE 4

Image 7. *Mount Shasta from the northwest, with debris avalanche deposits in the foreground. About 340,000 years ago, the north flank of an ancestral Mount Shasta collapsed, forming the largest volcanic debris avalanche known. Many of the mounds and hummocks visible here are several hundred feet high.* —Phyllis Gray photo

Image 8. *Aerial view of Crater Lake. Five by six miles in diameter, the basin formed by ancient Mount Mazama's collapse now holds the deepest lake (1,949 feet) in the United States.* —William Scott photo, U.S. Geological Survey

PLATE 5

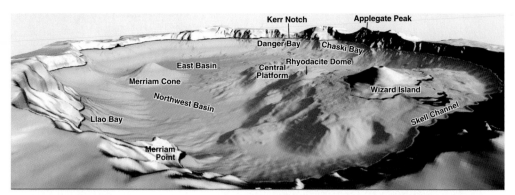

Image 9. *The floor of Crater Lake caldera. Shortly after Mount Mazama's collapse, further eruptions built several edifices inside the caldera, only one of which, Wizard Island, rises above the present lake surface.* —Courtesy of the U.S. Geological Survey

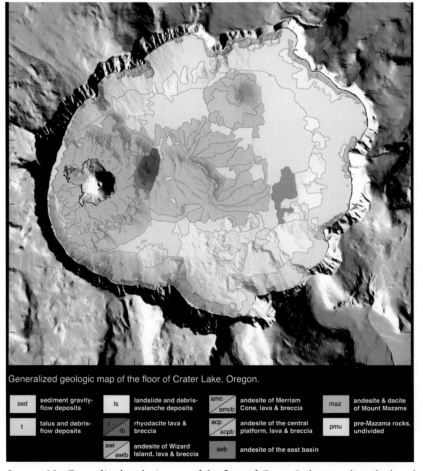

Image 10. *Generalized geologic map of the floor of Crater Lake, revealing the broad lava base of Wizard Island (left), the central platform with its rhyodacite dome (center), and Merriam Cone (top).* —Courtesy of the U.S. Geological Survey

PLATE 6

Image 11. *The Pumice Castle, Crater Lake. Partly welded because of its near-vent location, this colorfully oxidized pyroclastic deposit was exposed when Mount Mazama's former summit collapsed.* —Ronald G. Warfield photo

Image 12. *The Phantom Ship, Crater Lake. Its stony sails unfurled as if to catch furtive breezes sweeping across the lake, the Phantom Ship (which seems to vanish and reappear according to changing optical conditions) exposes the oldest rock in the caldera, a remnant of the Phantom cone, buried during Mount Mazama's growth and then exhumed when the volcano collapsed.* —Ronald G. Warfield photo

PLATE 7

Image 13. *The north face of South Sister viewed from Camp Lake. The youngest and most recently active of the Three Sisters, the volcano is geologically restless. Since 2001, ground deformation and sporadic earthquake swarms centered immediately west of the cone indicate that magma is currently rising toward the surface.* —David Wieprecht photo, U.S. Geological Survey, Cascades Volcano Observatory, Vancouver, Washington

PLATE 8

Image 14. *Mount Washington, central Oregon. Viewed from Big Lake, the deeply eroded volcano sports a mantle of late winter snow destined to vanish by early summer.* —David Wieprecht photo, U.S. Geological Survey, Cascades Volcano Observatory, Vancouver, Washington

Image 15. *Teardrop Pool, South Sister. Oregon's highest body of water, this seasonal pool forms from melting snow in the volcano's bowl-shaped crater.* —Douglas Tustin photo

PLATE 9

Image 16. *This ghostly stump testifies to Mount Hood's past violence. Probably killed in the late eighteenth century by a pyroclastic surge from Crater Rock, this and many similar snags lie atop the ridge high on Hood's southeast flank.* —Courtesy of Ellen Morris Bishop

Image 17. *Debris avalanche on Mount Adams. On August 31, 1997, a large volume of snow, ice, and hydrothermally altered rock cascaded from the cirque of Avalanche glacier (elevation about 12,000 feet) and streamed down Adams's southwest flank. Because they occur without warning, such avalanches present a hazard even at dormant volcanoes.* —Richard Iverson photo, U.S. Geological Survey, Cascades Volcano Observatory, Vancouver, Washington

PLATE 10

Image 18. *In his romantic painting of a night eruption at Mount St. Helens in the 1840s, Canadian artist Paul Kane correctly shows the active vent located considerably below the volcano's summit, probably at the site of the Goat Rocks dome.* —Reprinted by permission of the Royal Ontario Museum, Toronto, Canada

Image 19. *Mount St. Helens before 1980. This view of the glacier-mantled north side, with Spirit Lake in the foreground, shows the Goat Rocks dome (erupted in the 1840s) on the right.* —Jim Nieland photo, U.S. Forest Service, Mount St. Helens National Volcanic Monument, courtesy of the U. S. Geological Survey

PLATE 11

Image 20. *Mount St. Helens after the May 18, 1980, eruption had removed 1,300 feet from the summit and destroyed the entire north side. A plume of steam rises 3,000 feet above the crater rim on May 19, 1982.* —Lyn Topinka photo, U.S. Geological Survey, Cascades Volcano Observatory, Vancouver, Washington

Image 21. *Mount St. Helens ejects a column of ash 6 to 11 miles into the air. Following the May 18 Plinian outburst, St. Helens produced five more explosive eruptions during the summer and fall of 1980, including this July 22 event, which was visible in Seattle, 100 miles to the north. View is from the south.* —Michael P. Doukas photo, U.S. Geological Survey, Cascades Volcano Observatory, Vancouver, Washington

PLATE 12

Image 22. *Molten rock glows at the top of a new (2004) lava dome rising behind the snow-covered 1980–1986 lava dome in Mount St. Helens's 1.2-mile-wide crater. A small, ash-bearing steam plume rises from fractures in the new dome.* —Courtesy of the U.S. Geological Survey, Cascades Volcano Observatory, Vancouver, Washington

Image 23. *In this aerial view from the east looking into Mount St. Helens's enormous crater, a small steam plume ascends from the new lava dome that began growing between the south crater wall (left) and the snow-covered 1980–1986 dome (center) in October 2004.* —Ken McGee photo, U.S. Geological Survey, Cascades Volcano Observatory, Vancouver, Washington

PLATE 13

Image 24. *Waterfall near Paradise Valley, with Mount Rainier in the background.*
—Ronald G. Warfield photo

PLATE 14

Image 25. *Mount Rainier from the south. Its icy summit looming above Paradise Valley near the mile-high visitor center at Paradise, Mount Rainier regularly attracts up to two million tourists to view its unique combination of glacial and volcanic features.* —Ronald G. Warfield photo

Image 26. *Lenticular clouds over Mount Rainier. Viewed from the west, this cloud formation is reminiscent of an eruption plume.* —Ronald G. Warfield photo

PLATE 15

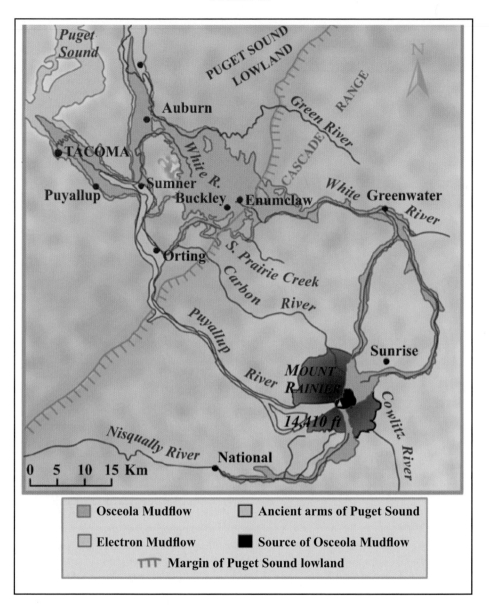

Image 27. *Map showing distribution of the Osceola and Electron Mudflows. Triggered when Rainier's former summit collapsed 5,600 years ago, the Osceola Mudflow devastated much of the eastern Puget lowland, including the sites of Tacoma and towns just south of Seattle. (The Paradise lahar, which traveled down Rainier's south flank, is shown as part of the Osceola event.) The Electron Mudflow, which swept down the Puyallup River valley and buried a forest where the town of Orting now stands, took place about AD 1500. Today about 150,000 people live atop Rainier's many Holocene mudflow deposits.*
—Adapted from Vallance and Scott, 1997; courtesy of James Vallance, U.S. Geological Survey

PLATE 16

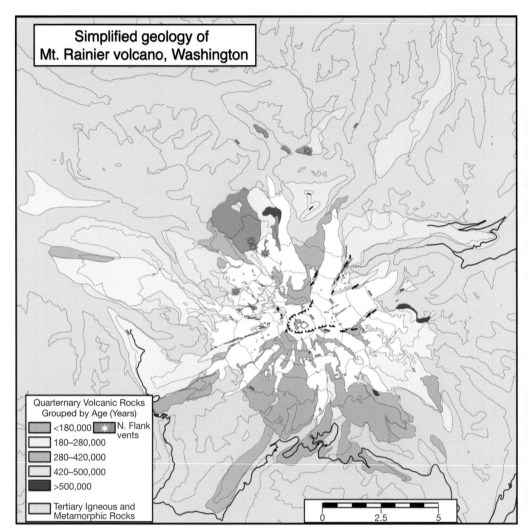

Image 28. *Simplified geology of Mount Rainier, showing the areal extent and approximate ages of lava flow sequences that built the volcanic cone. Although the highest sustained levels of magma output took place between about 500,000 and 420,000 years ago, and again between about 280,000 and 180,000 years ago, the volcano has also erupted numerous lava flows during the last 5,000 years.* —Thomas Sisson, U.S. Geological Survey

Lava flows making up the present cone issued from a number of separate vents, creating several overlapping edifices that give Adams several distinct summits. The long south slope, including a prominent buttress called Suksdorf Ridge, rises to a false summit known as Pikers Peak (elevation about 11,500 feet). It is the only part of the upper cone not mantled in glacier ice. From this broad shelf, a plain nearly half a mile across slopes gently up to the highest peak, a small lava and scoria cone standing about 800 feet above the southern false summit. Like the other summit andesite lavas, those composing this rather squat edifice show signs of contact with glacial ice and meltwater. The young cone has a snow-filled crater open along the west rim, as if part of the crater wall slid down Adams's steep west face. Cutting into the east base of the small cone, the summit ice cap has exposed thin glassy flows of dark gray to black andesite. A long-abandoned and rapidly disintegrating fire lookout cabin remains partly visible beneath the snowpack near the south rim.

Adams's icecap has also incised the west summit, where the Pinnacle, a steep lava outcrop, has been carved from summit deposits above and between the Adams and White Salmon glaciers. Another conspicuous erosional feature, the Castle, stands at the apex of Battlement Ridge, along the eastern margin of the broad summit area, immediately north of the Klickitat glacier.

SOME NOTABLE EVENTS IN THE MOUNT ADAMS REGION DURING THE LAST 15,000 YEARS

DATE OR APPROXIMATE AGE (YEARS)	EVENT
AD 1921	Debris avalanche in upper Salt Creek valley
500	Debris avalanche and lahar travel down Salt Creek and inundate part of Trout Lake lowland
1,000	Four tephra falls and perhaps small lava flows from two vents on upper cone
1,500	Lahar in upper Cascade Creek valley
5,000	Lava flows from at least four vents
6,000	Large debris avalanche and lahar inundate Trout Lake lowland, extending down White Salmon River at least to Husum; lava flow of West crater in area west of Indian Heaven volcanic field
10,000	Two lahars in lower Cascade Creek valley
15,000–10,000	Lava flows and tephra from vents near summit end period of cone building that took place during latest Pleistocene glacial maximum

Source: Scott et al, 1995

Holocene Activity

Adams's rate of magma production fell drastically after the main cone was completed about 15,000 to 10,000 years ago, but the volcano has remained sporadically active during Holocene time, producing lava flows, scoria-and-spatter cones, and thin layers of ash from at least ten different vents. The presence on Mount Adams of the distinctive ash layer from Mount Mazama (erupted 7,700 years ago), as well as several widespread ash layers from Mount St. Helens that have also been dated, help to determine the relative ages of Adams's Holocene eruptions.

As in previous eruptive periods, basaltic magma issued from peripheral vents low on Adams's flanks, while andesite erupted at vents higher on the central cone. After the main Pleistocene valley glaciers had withdrawn, a vent on the northeast side produced the Red Butte cinder cone and its associated Trappers Creek basaltic lava flows, which poured northeastward down the local drainages. Overlain by a thin soil and by St. Helens's tephra layer S (dated at 12,900 years), the Trappers Creek lava flows probably emplaced between about 15,000 and 14,000 years ago. The andesite lavas of Cunningham Creek, erupted from a short fissure on the southeast flank of the much older Goat Butte shield and also covered by layer S, are about the same age. Slightly younger are the series of thin basaltic lava flows from Smith Butte, located at an elevation of only 3,840 feet near Adams's south base, the lowest known Holocene eruptive vent.

Three mid-Holocene andesite lava flows overlie the Mazama ash but underlie tephra set Y of St. Helens, and are thus between about 7,700 and 3,800 years old. These include the A. G. Aiken lava bed, a rubbly lava stream a half mile across at its widest point, which emerged from a fissure at the southeast foot of South Butte (a prominent late Pleistocene cinder cone) and flowed downslope about 4.5 miles. Emerging from a vent now concealed by the Adams glacier and its recent moraines, another large blocky andesite extrusion, the Takh Takh Meadows flow, extends about 6 miles northwest and, with a volume of less than 0.1 of a cubic mile, represents Adams's largest Holocene eruption. Second in volume is the Muddy Fork flow, which issued from a fissure near the west side of Red Butte, divided into several lobes, and buried almost 5 square miles under blocky lava. Other Holocene flows, most in windswept locations unfavorable to ash deposition and hence difficult to date, include the High Camp lavas, short tongues of blocky to rubbly lava that issued from a vent near the base of Adams's North Cleaver.

Erupted from a high ridge only about 1.5 miles east of the summit, the Battlement Ridge andesite flows may represent the most recent eruption of Adams. Emerging at an elevation of about 8,200 feet, these consist of two thin tongues of glassy, scoriacious lava, reduced to rubble where they plunged off opposite sides of Battlement Ridge, disintegrating on its steep slopes. Because the southerly flow is sandwiched between recently deposited glacial tills, Hildreth and Fierstein estimated that it is probably no more than 1,000 years old. Another young lava flow, the smallest of the postglacial eruptive products, emerged from a vent at an altitude of about 8,350 feet on lower Suksdorf Ridge, only a short distance south of the summit. Forming a thin ribbon about 3,000 feet long, 320 feet wide, and 32 feet thick, the lava flowed directly down the crest of the ridge, banking against the uphill side of South Butte and deflecting its terminal lobe to the west.

Clues to the relative ages of the Holocene eruptive deposits of Mount Adams are found in a remarkable sequence of tephra layers deposited in an alpine meadow occupying a small shelf midway down the steep south wall of Hellroaring Creek. After Pleistocene glaciers finally retreated from this position, about 4 miles southeast of the volcano's summit, this boulder-strewn meadow has remained relatively undisturbed, accumulating layer after layer of ash fallout from Adams, St. Helens, and Mazama. The Mazama ash and the nine layers of St. Helens tephra exposed at this site all contain the mineral amphibole, which readily distinguishes them from the twenty-four layers of andesitic ash originating at Mount Adams. Unlike Mazama and St. Helens, Adams has never erupted large quantities of pumiceous tephra, but has produced thin layers of lithic ash, many derived from phreatic explosions triggered when hot magma encountered glacial ice high on the cone. Layer 14 in this meadow sequence, deposited about 5,500 years ago, is apparently composed of ash from shattered lava erupted at the small cone capping Adams's summit. Several other layers have been correlated with specific Holocene eruptions of lava on Adams's upper flanks; the most recent local ash-depositing events occurred roughly 2,350, 2,250, 1,750, and 1,000 years ago.

Major Hazards — Landslides and Debris Avalanches

High, steep, and rotten to its core, Mount Adams's glacier-burdened summit cone is a disaster waiting to happen. According to Hildreth and Fierstein, at least half a cubic mile of the volcano's interior consists of hydrothermally altered rock, into which encircling glaciers have cut deeply, further steepening its already unstable slopes. Given the cone's susceptibility to slope failure, it is not surprising that at least five or six times during Holocene time large masses of acid-weakened rock have collapsed, avalanching down the cone and, in some cases, transforming into mudflows that swept as far as 35 miles down valleys heading on the mountain. Small rockfalls and landslides are relatively common, but the wonder is that large avalanches and mudflows have not occurred with greater frequency.

As Adams's glaciers, like those at most other Cascade volcanoes, continue to thin and retreat, they remove support from the cirques and canyon walls bordering the glaciers, initiating rockfalls and landslides. On August 31, 1997, a sizable avalanche originated in the cirque of Avalanche glacier, which heads at an altitude of 12,000 feet on the volcano's upper southwest slope. (See image 17 on plate 9.) Although an estimated 90 percent of the avalanche's 6 million cubic yards of material consisted of snow and ice, it also included a substantial component of chemically decayed rock fragments ripped from the glacier's headwall. (A similar but smaller avalanche occurred from the same cirque in July 1983).

Less than two months after the August avalanche, another of almost equal volume originated high on Adams's east side. On October 20, 1997, a huge slab of hydrothermally altered rock suddenly detached from the south face of the Castle, the rocky knob at the top of Battlement Ridge, leaving a near-vertical triangle-shaped scar about 1,000 feet long on each side. Plunging

The dark mass of the September 8, 1997, avalanche, one of several during the late summer and fall of that year, contrasts with surrounding west-side snowfields on Mount Adams. Like its larger predecessor on August 31, it was probably triggered by rapid melting of an unusually heavy snowpack. —Richard Iverson photo, U.S. Geological Survey, Cascades Volcano Observatory

down the Klickitat glacier icefall, the avalanching rock—carrying blocks that weighed as much as 10,000 tons—scoured the glacier surface, incorporating large quantities of granular ice into the flowing debris. Continuing more than a mile beyond the Klickitat glacier terminus, the avalanche buried the upper reaches of Big Muddy Creek. In its 3-mile length, the avalanche traveled almost 6,000 vertical feet downslope from its origin on the Castle, coming to rest at an elevation of about 5,600 feet. The avalanche temporarily dammed Big Muddy Creek, causing a pond to form upstream, but the impounded water broke through the next day, restoring normal stream flow. On October 24, another mass of rock peeled away from the same scarp, forming a smaller avalanche that followed the same path as that of October 20.

Although the east and north sides of Mount Adams regularly experience large rockfalls, the largest avalanches have originated near the southwest summit area, in the cirques of the White Salmon and Avalanche glaciers. In 1921, about 5 million cubic yards of altered rock fell from the head of Avalanche glacier and traveled 4 miles down Salt Creek valley. By far the most voluminous avalanche, that which formed the devastating Trout Lake mudflow, occurred about 6,000 years ago, when a large section of the western rim of the summit plateau collapsed, isolating the Pinnacle as a prominent outlier and creating the broad shelf on which the White Salmon glacier subsequently formed. With a volume of approximately 90 million cubic yards, the avalanche contained enough water-saturated and clay-rich altered rock to transform into a mudflow that swept through the Trout Lake lowland and continued down the White Salmon River valley at least as far as Husum, more than 35 miles from its source. Leaving a deposit 3 to 65 feet thick, the mudflow permanently blocked the local drainage, forming Trout Lake. According to Hildreth, the deposits are well exposed in the banks of the White Salmon River, and lava blocks up to 16 feet in diameter protrude from fields and meadows in and near the present town of Trout Lake.

The most ominous aspect of Adam's severe avalanche and mudflow hazards is that they commonly occur without either earthquake or volcanic activity, triggered simply by gravitational collapse that takes place suddenly and without warning. Although small steam explosions may have generated the 1921 avalanche, known locally as the Great Slide, even these phenomena are not preceded by the kind of seismic or other pre-eruptive signals that normally allow people to prepare for a renewal of volcanic activity. The interior of Adams—degraded by relentless heat and chemical action that change formerly solid rock into slippery clay and continuously undermined by glacial cutting—will inevitably produce edifice collapses of cataclysmic proportions. Some may be much larger than that which created the Trout Lake mudflow.

Present Thermal Activity

Although the most recent eruptive deposits of Mount Adams are apparently 1,000 years old, native tribes remembered Pahto as one of three guardians of the Columbia that, along with Wy'east (Hood) and Loowit (St. Helens), once "smoked" continuously. The volcano has no record of historic eruptions, but its thermal activity, as tribal lore suggests, may have been more intense in the recent past. In 1924, Judge Fred W. Stadler discovered "a group of steam vents west of the summit and less than 1,000 feet below it and above White Salmon Glacier." More than a decade later, Kenneth Phillips, a researcher with the Mazamas mountaineering club, was unable to find Stadler's vents. He did find a single fumarole about a quarter mile north of the summit, in the center of a snowfield, with a maximum temperature of 100.5 degrees Fahrenheit. During exploration of the summit area for sulfur deposits in the 1930s, Claude Fowler, an Oregon geologist, discovered steam issuing from only one fumarole on the crater's south wall, but he found hydrogen sulfide leaking from numerous small crevices around the crater. Even today, many climbers notice a distinct odor of hydrogen sulfide gas near the summit, some of which, Hildreth suggests, may result from meltwater reacting with previously existing sulfides and sulfates formed beneath the ice cap. In a 1982 climb, the author noticed that, in spite of subfreezing temperatures and icy winds raking the peak, subsurface heat caused meltwater to flow beneath the ice along the southwestern crater rim. As Hildreth has pointed out, gas emission on Adams's summit is highly diffuse, originating at many shifting places, rather than issuing from well-defined vents like those at Crater Rock on Mount Hood.

Future Volcanic Hazards

Future eruptions at Mount Adams will probably repeat typical Holocene activity, with new vents most likely to open along the transition zone between the volcano's gently sloping outer flanks and steep main cone. Unless a large new infusion of magma causes Adams to return to the high rate of lava production that built its present main cone during the late Pleistocene, it is likely to stage only intermittent, low-volume effusions of andesite lava that will flow little more than 1 to 4 miles from their source. Although incandescent blocks cascading from advancing flow fronts can ignite forest fires, a repetition of Holocene effusive activity is not likely to threaten the human environment. Not only do most andesitic flows move too slowly to overtake the average hiker or backpacker, the area around Adams is too sparsely populated for an effusive eruption to affect many people. Lavas erupting from vents high on ridgetops, like the Battlement Ridge flows, can disintegrate on steep slopes, creating avalanches of hot rock that would certainly endanger climbers below, but such risky situations can be avoided by simply staying away from an active site.

Although many of Adams's lava streams were fed by fountains of molten rock jetting tens or hundreds of feet above the vent, causing a dangerous fall of airborne fragments downwind, such phenomena are likely to affect only a restricted area. Because Adams has almost never ejected large quantities of tephra or large pumiceous pyroclastic flows, geologists do not expect it to create a major ash-fall hazard to towns such as Goldendale or Yakima, where prevailing westerly winds would carry ash clouds. If summit eruptions occur, magma surging into the summit ice cap would probably shatter as it has in the past, generating columns of steam and ash that could rise thousands of feet above the peak. Although such ash clouds could interfere with air traffic, they would produce only thin layers of lithic tephra in populated areas to the east. The volcano has frequently produced block-and-ash flows derived from fragmented lava, which probably caused large mudflows comparable to some generated on Mount Rainier. Pleistocene valley glaciers, however, have removed virtually all such mudflow deposits, making it difficult to evaluate hazards associated with this phenomenon. Postglacial lava flows have been modest in size, and their blocky snouts commonly terminate on gentle slopes.

As described above, Adam's greatest threat to areas downvalley does not stem directly from eruptive activity but from sudden partial collapse of its hydrothermally weakened central cone. Another debris avalanche from the headwall of the White Salmon glacier equal to that which triggered the Trout Lake mudflow would not only overwhelm the town of Trout Lake, it would also inundate farms and settlements for many miles down the White Salmon River drainage, perhaps even impacting the Columbia River. Because such avalanches occur without the kind of warnings that precede a magmatic eruption and because they can travel at speeds up to 25 or 30 miles an hour, such mudflow-creating collapse events represent the single most significant danger posed by the volcano.

The Goat Rocks Volcano

Eighteen miles north of Mount Adams, along the serrated crest of the Washington Cascades, lies the eroded stump of a much older volcano. This large cluster of jagged ridges and sheer cliffs, named Goat Rocks after the bands of mountain goats that gambol about its precipices, offers a sobering view of what all the lofty Cascade volcanoes eventually will become following their extinction. Once a towering composite cone that may have rivaled Hood or Jefferson, the Goat Rocks volcano has been reduced to a glacier-ravaged remnant of its former stature.

Accessible only by foot via the Pacific Crest Trail or a few other alpine trails, the Goat Rocks Wilderness (82,680 acres) and the adjacent Goat Rocks Roadless Area (25,240 acres) lie in the Gifford Pinchot National Forest west of the Cascade Divide and in the Snoqualmie National Forest east of the crest. Elevations range from 2,930 feet along Upper Lake Creek to 8,184 feet at Gilbert Peak, now the highest point on the defunct Goat Rocks volcano.

The area's volcanic history is complex, involving a number of separate vents that erupted at different times over a long span of time. Volcanism began about 3.2 million years ago with an extraordinarily violent explosive eruption that deposited an enormous thickness of high silica rhyolite tuff, filling a caldera that is now exposed on the east flank of the (younger) Goat Rocks volcano. The ash flow layer, up to 2,100 feet thick, is visible beneath the ridge from Tieton Peak to Bear Creek Mountain. Following cessation of high-silica activity about 3 million years ago, effusions of andesite lava, along with some early basaltic flows, built the Goat Rocks edifice, which was active between about 2.5 million and 0.5 million years ago. During its remarkably long life span, this stratovolcano produced exceptionally voluminous lava flows that filled ancient valleys many miles from the erupting vent. Goat Rocks, in fact, has the distinction of emitting the world's largest known andesite lava flow—a massive stream that traveled 60 miles down the ancestral Tieton and Naches River channels approximately a million years ago.

Intense hydrothermal alteration of the volcano's interior, similar to that now taking place at Adams and Rainier, probably aided Pleistocene glaciers in dissecting the edifice, exposing the weakened rock of its core. Following a long period of erosion, new eruptions of hornblende andesite flowed over the volcano's denuded flanks. Gilbert Peak is capped by one of these later flows. A nearby vent at Old Snowy Mountain erupted similar streams of hornblende andesite that flowed westward into the glaciated Cispus River valley. These flows were in turn overridden by glaciers during the middle to late Pleistocene. According to USGS geologist Don Swanson, it is unclear whether these late andesites mark a rejuvenation of the Goat Rocks volcano or are the products of a different volcanic system.

Indian Heaven

Located about 20 miles southwest of Adams, the Indian Heaven volcanic field, about 20 miles in diameter, is a partly forested alignment of coalescing shield volcanoes, cinder cones, and associated lava flows. Active from mid-Pleistocene to early Holocene time, the field produced a total of about 25 cubic miles of magma. In mapping the area, geologist Paul Hammond identified forty-eight eruptive units, mostly from monogenetic cones, each of which were built during a single phase of activity. Unlike the large neighboring composite cones of Adams, Goat Rocks, Rainier, and St. Helens that remain intermittently active for hundreds of thousands of years, Indian Heaven volcanoes erupt for only brief intervals and then become extinct. When a fresh batch of magma next breaks the ground surface, it constructs a new shield or cinder cone. One particularly fluid basaltic flow poured eastward from Indian Heaven, covering the Trout Lake area, and then traveled several miles southward to within a few miles of the Columbia River. This voluminous flow is noted for its lava tube caves.

Some of the area's Pleistocene-age cones erupted beneath a thick sheet of ice. Móbergs, such as those at Crazy Hills, are cones that grew entirely under a glacier, their lavas forming characteristic pillow shapes as they encountered ice or meltwater. By contrast, Lone Butte is a tuya—a flat-topped, steep-sided cone erupted into a lake that formed when volcanic heat melted an overlying glacier. Although its lower section resembles a móberg, Lone Butte burst through the glacier surface so that its upper cone was built in the open air, forming pyroclastic surge deposits, lava flows, and air-fall tephra. Attaining a height of about 3,300 feet above its base, this isolated structure later had half its original bulk removed by continuing glaciation.

The most recent effusive eruption, that forming the Big Lava Bed flow, occurred about 9,000 years ago. This largely unvegetated basaltic stream, covering about 20 square miles, flowed generally southward down the Little White Salmon River drainage, filling it for a distance of 10 miles. Because the Indian Heaven volcanic field has been sporadically active for at least 700,000 years, it is likely to produce similarly copious lava flows in the future.

Farther to the west of Indian Heaven, in a volcanic corridor south of Mount St. Helens, West Crater also produced a significant Holocene eruption, perhaps only a few centuries after the Big Lava Bed was emplaced. With an elevation of only about 4,100 feet, the West Crater edifice consists of a large andesite dome that emerged on the floor of a glacial cirque carved in ancient Tertiary rock. About the same size as the 1980–1986 dome in St. Helens's crater, this andesite dome has a summit crater about 640 feet in diameter and 80 feet deep. A lava flow moving westward from West Crater overlapped the edge of a scoriacious andesite flow from the nearby Hackamore Creek cinder cone, which appears to have been simultaneously active. It also appears that a large phreatic explosion at Bare Mountain, blasting through old Tertiary rock to form a crater almost 1,300 feet wide and 880 feet deep, occurred at about the same time as the West Crater activity. Although the steam blast scattered fragments of old rock over a large area, no fresh magma was emitted.

Visiting Mount Adams

From Washington 14 along the Columbia's north bank, Washington 141 leads from White Salmon to the village of Trout Lake near Adams's south base. For a climb up the popular south-side route, drive from Trout Lake north to Forest Service Road 80/8040, marked as the Mount Adams Recreation Area Road, turning left off the surfaced highway in about 1.5 miles onto Forest Road 80, which becomes 8040 after a few miles. Follow the road 12.8 miles and then hike to Cold Springs, near timberline, the point of departure up Suksdorf Ridge to the summit. Although Adams's south ridge is not glaciated, the perennial snowfields make ice axes and crampons essential. From the north, Adams can be reached by Forest Service roads heading south from the town of Randle, which is on U.S. 12 about 50 miles east of Interstate 5.

Bird Creek Meadows, a particularly attractive alpine field on the southeast flank, is no longer open to vehicles, but well worth a hike when wildflowers are in bloom. Trails also lead from the Mirror Lake–Bench Lake road to Hellroaring Viewpoint. Another tentative path from Bench Lake along the Ridge of Wonders is not well defined or maintained. To find out which trails are open, inquire at the Forest Service ranger station in Trout Lake or Packwood. For permission to hike in the Yakama Indian Reservation on Adams's east side, call or write the Yakama Agency in Toppenish, Washington.

CHAPTER 17

Mount St. Helens

A LIVING FIRE MOUNTAIN

Now a global icon for geologic violence, before 1980 Mount St. Helens was generally regarded as just another snowy Cascade peak. Some awareness of its fiery past lingered in the public consciousness, but the almost ideally symmetrical cone of St. Helens was known mainly as a favorite subject of photographers, particularly when viewed from the old-growth conifer forests bordering Spirit Lake at its northern foot. (See image 19 on plate 10.) On May 18, 1980, however, this "Fujiyama of America" was suddenly changed beyond recognition—its summit, its entire north side, and most of its glacier cover utterly destroyed. Whereas geologic processes ordinarily take place with painful slowness, the transformation of St. Helens occurred within minutes, reducing its height from 9,677 feet to 8,363 feet as the largest known debris avalanche in recorded history removed about two-thirds of a cubic mile of rock from the mountain, triggering a laterally directed blast and a pyroclastic surge that devastated more than 230 square miles of timber and hurled a column of dark ash almost 100,000 feet into the stratosphere. Fifty-seven people were killed, as well about 7,000 deer and elk, and countless smaller animals. Its conical form obliterated, St. Helens was reduced to a horseshoe-shaped stump with a 1.2-mile-wide crater open to the north. (See image 20 on plate 11.)

After five more explosive outbursts during 1980—most of which sent ash clouds rocketing 50,000 feet above the mountaintop—Mount St. Helens then entered an effusive mode, oozing thick lobes of viscous lava onto the crater floor and erecting a new lava dome that, by 1986, reached a height of 876 feet. Except for occasional small steam explosions, the volcano remained silent until September 2004, when a series of earthquakes heralded the beginning of a new eruptive episode. In October, mild explosions ejected ash plumes 12,000 feet above sea level and opened a new vent between the 1980–1986 dome and the south crater wall, allowing fresh magma to begin constructing a second lava dome behind the first. Registering temperatures as high as 1,300 to 1,400 degrees Fahrenheit, incandescent tongues of dacite lava at the top of the dome radiated a ruddy glow frequently visible at night.

Quiet dome growth may continue intermittently for years or decades, but given St. Helens's deserved reputation as the most frequently explosive volcano in the forty-eight adjacent states, geologists will not be surprised if a new batch of gas-rich magma eventually reaches the surface, blasting the two domes to smithereens and igniting another Plinian eruption that may rival or exceed that of 1980.

The youngest of Washington's five principal stratovolcanoes, St. Helens has produced more than a hundred known layers of airborne ash since its inception between about 40,000 and 50,000 years ago. During the last

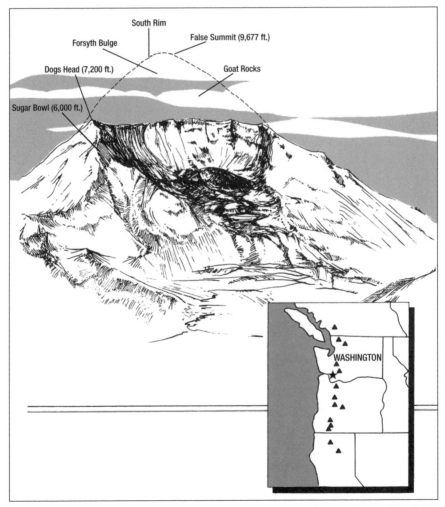

Post-1980 Mount St. Helens as viewed from the northeast, showing the profile of the former summit and the volcano's location in the Cascade Range

4,500 years, its eruption rate has apparently increased, averaging well over a cubic mile of juvenile material each millennium. A single layer of tephra, known as Yn, represents a cubic mile of pyroclastic material and extends hundreds of miles northeast into Canada. Forming a deposit of yellowish brown pumice up to 12 inches thick at Mount Rainier National Park, 50 miles to the north, Yn appears as far away as Banff National Park in Alberta. Another voluminous St. Helens tephra, layer Wn, also extends at least 300 miles into Canada. Ejected in AD 1479, this whitish gray pumice is more than 3 feet deep 6 miles northeast of the volcano's summit and forms a conspicuous stratum not far below the ground surface at Mount Rainier.

Three years later, St. Helens exploded again, depositing another broad lobe of pumice (layer We) hundreds of miles to the east. And in 1800 yet another Plinian outburst discharged clouds of dacite tephra that followed a path similar to that of the 1980 ash, blanketing much of eastern Washington, northern Idaho, and western Montana and bringing a plague of darkness that terrified many Native Americans who experienced it. Between 1831 and 1857, explorers, missionaries, and early settlers in Oregon Territory logged in more than a dozen additional eruptions, including the extrusion of a new lava dome—Goat Rocks—high on St. Helens's northwest side. That dome was destroyed on May 18, 1980.

Considering the number, volume, and widespread distribution of St. Helens's tephra falls, it is no wonder that native tribes in the Columbia region emphasized the peak's volatile nature. The Klickitat people called it (according to variant spellings) Loo-Wit Lat-kla, Louwala-Clough, or Tah-one-lat-clah, all meaning "fire mountain" or "smoking mountain." The native appellation is thus far more expressive of the volcano's tempestuous character than that which Vancouver gave it to commemorate yet another eighteenth-century British diplomat. Viewing the "high round snowy mountain" from his ship at the mouth of the Columbia on October 20, 1792, Vancouver named it for Alleyne Fitzherbert, George III's ambassador to Spain, whom the king had recently dubbed Lord St. Helens. Like the naval officers Peter Rainier and Samuel Hood, whom Vancouver similarly honored on his voyage down the Pacific Northwest Coast, this British courtier never saw the mountain that perpetuates his memory.

Although one of the smaller composite cones in the range, the pre-1980 St. Helens supported several active glaciers that included the Wishbone, Loowit, Leschi, Forsyth, Nelson, and Ape glaciers. These heavily crevassed ice streams, descending from the summit ice cap, shrouded most of the north and northeast face of the mountain. The Shoestring glacier, emerging from a gap in the crater rim, extended as a long narrow ribbon down the southeast flank. Unconnected to the summit ice fields, two small glaciers,

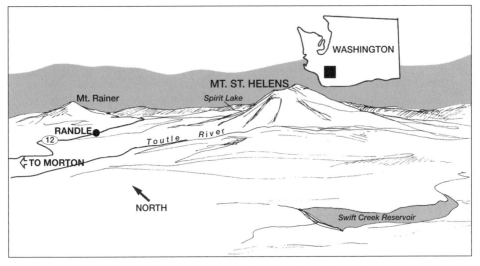

Relief map of the Mount St. Helens area from the southwest

the Toutle and the Talus, clung to the west slope, while two other small ice lobes, the Dyer and Swift glaciers, occupied shallow basins on the south side. After the 1980 eruption removed 70 percent of St. Helens's ice cover, only the beheaded lower portions of some northeast and east-side glaciers and the small glacial lobes on the south and west flanks remained in place. Most of these remnants have since vanished (see chapter 22).

The 1980 Reawakening

When St. Helens first stirred in March 1980, after a sleep of 123 years, its pristine ice mantle offered a vivid contrast to the dark ash that the initial eruptions deposited on its upper cone. After only a week of preliminary minor earthquakes (magnitudes of 2.0 to 4.0), at 12:36 PM on March 27, a column of ash-laden steam burst through the ice-filled summit crater, opening a new vent about 250 feet in diameter. As rising magma fractured crustal rock, generating additional swarms of earthquakes and causing groundwater within the porous cone to flash into steam, a series of explosions repeatedly ejected clouds of ash billowing 10,000 to 11,000 feet above the peak. Most of the ash was probably derived from pulverized old rock in the volcano's interior, but Richard Hoblitt of the U.S. Geological Survey recently found that some of these initial eruptions—previously regarded as entirely phreatic (steam-blast) in nature—also contained "a small proportion of juvenile (magmatic) material." Ash fall from these early phreatomagmagic explosions was largely confined to within three to a dozen miles of the peak, although variable winds wafted small quantities as far away as Bend, Oregon, 150 miles south; Tacoma, 70 miles north; and Spokane, almost 300 miles to the east.

As soon as spring snow flurries restored St. Helens's customary white cloak, fresh expulsions of ash, carried by shifting winds, blackened first one side of the mountain and then another, giving it an increasingly dark and sinister aspect. Some ash clouds rolling downslope produced static electricity, triggering lightning bolts up to 2 miles long. Powerful blasts on March 29 opened a second summit vent, from which an eerie blue flame, probably caused by volcanic gases, was seen to arch over the volcano's crest. On March 30, no fewer than ninety-three separate explosions were recorded, and by April 8 the two new vents inside the old summit crater had merged into one, which eventually expanded to a diameter of 1,700 feet and a depth of 850 feet.

Attracting scientists from the university community and the U.S. Geological Survey, as well as hoards of newspaper and television reporters, St. Helens soon became the most intensely studied composite cone in the world. Besides installing a network of seismographs to detect the shallow earthquakes focused beneath the north flank, 10,000 of which occurred between March 20 and mid-May, geologists also monitored the volcano by setting up devices to measure increased heat and gas emission, as well as evidence of ground deformation signaling the injection of new magma into the cone. Photographs taken shortly after the initial March 27 eruptions showed that a huge fracture system—16,000 feet long—had already begun to split the mountain, nearly bisecting the old summit crater. Another set of fractures, generally paralleling the major system along the crater's north rim, marked the boundary of a huge summit block that was rapidly shifting to the north.

Geologists did not realize the extent of St. Helens's deformation until the last week of April, when a USGS team found that a large section of the north face, approximately 1.5 miles in diameter, had been displaced at least 270 feet from its pre-1980 position. Even when phreatic eruptions temporarily ceased between late April and early May, this ominous swelling—soon known as "the bulge"—grew laterally at a steady rate of 5 to 6 feet a day. By mid-May (according to a USGS report published in 2000), it had expanded outward at least 450 feet, buckling and fracturing the Forsyth, Leschi, and Wishbone glaciers, their broken surfaces by then black with gritty ash. On April 30, geologists monitoring the volcano announced that the oversteepened north flank represented the greatest immediate danger, and that its failure might precipitate an eruption.

When the author flew around the visibly distorted summit of St. Helens on Sunday, May 11, phreatic activity had resumed, with intermittent explosions blowing ash thousands of feet into the air. After nearly two weeks of relative quiescence, the volcano seemed to be venting whatever pressure had built up within. A close look at the north flank, however, showed that the magma invading the volcano's interior had expanded the bulge to enormous proportions. If, as many geologists believed, the rising magma represented an incipient dome—a cryptodome—it was somehow blocked from erupting on the surface. Instead of being extruded on St. Helens's upper flank, as the Goat Rocks dome was during the 1840s, the 1980 cryptodome relentlessly pushed the bulge outward, simultaneously causing a large block of the north summit area to subside and heating the groundwater inside the volcano's porous cone to extreme temperatures.

At 8:32 Sunday morning, May 18, the forces building up inside the mountain found sudden and catastrophic release. The strongest earthquake to date, with a magnitude of 5.1 and centered directly beneath the north slope, is usually viewed as the mechanism that jolted St. Helens's already weakened edifice and precipitated the largest debris avalanche in historic time. Another interpretation, however, holds that the avalanche triggered the earthquake. As Richard Hoblitt explains, "the earthquake was produced by the initial slippage at the base of the landslide," adding that "a second large earthquake occurred about two minutes after the first."

Two geologists, Keith and Dorothy Stoffel, who were then flying almost directly over the mountain, saw "the whole north side of the summit crater begin to move instantaneously as one gigantic mass." For a few seconds the north summit "began to ripple and churn" in place, then peeled away from the main edifice and moved northward along a "deep-seated plane."

Breaking into three separate blocks of material, the summit and north side of St. Helens, carrying 0.67 cubic miles of rock, avalanched downslope at an estimated velocity of 155 to 180 miles an hour. The first landslide block swept across the west arm of Spirit Lake and slammed against Johnston Ridge, about 6 miles to the north. Momentum carried one lobe of this slide block over the 1,150-foot ridge and into the valley of Coldwater Creek, while the remainder was deposited in and around Spirit Lake and down the upper stretch of the North Fork Toutle River. Abruptly depressurized when the first slide block removed the outer north flank, the cryptodome exploded through the second landslide block, blasting away 27 percent of this block's mass, which thus did not become part of the main avalanche deposit. As the third landslide block slid downslope, it removed the south summit and much of the volcano's core, excavating the deep horseshoe-shaped crater that now occupies St. Helens's interior. Lubricated by steam, by groundwater contained in the porous volcanic rock, and by melting blocks of glacier ice, the second and third avalanche blocks, breaking into countless smaller fragments, traveled 15 miles westward down the North Fork Toutle River, filling the valley wall-to-wall with hummocky debris 150 to 600 feet thick.

As the first landslide block moved north, exposing the cryptodome and uncorking the hydrothermal system and gas-rich magma inside the cone, St. Helens began an eruption that was to continue uninterrupted for nine and a half hours. While a small plume of inky ash shot upward from the bisected summit crater, lighter-colored ash clouds burst through fractures

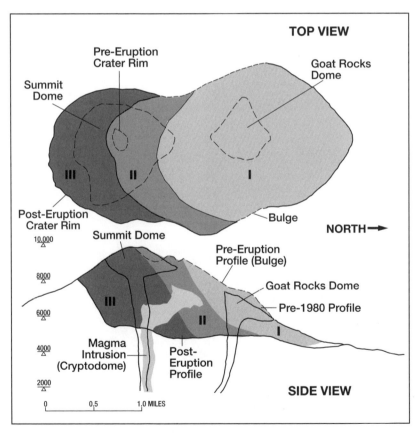

Diagram illustrating the body of magma that intruded St. Helens's cone prior to May 18, producing the bulge on the north flank. The three major landslide blocks (I, II, and III) shown here collapsed in quick succession to form the massive debris avalanche that swept across the west arm of Spirit Lake and poured 17 miles down the North Fork Toutle River valley. —Adapted from R. I. Tilling, 1990

Mount St. Helens one day before the eruption of May 18, 1980, viewed from Johnston Ridge to the northwest. —Harry Glicken photo, U. S. Geological Survey, Cascades Volcano Observatory, Vancouver, Washington

Mount St. Helens four months after the May 1980 eruption, viewed from Johnston Ridge. —Harry Glicken photo, U. S. Geological Survey, Cascades Volcano Observatory, Vancouver, Washington

in the disintegrating slide. Within twenty-one seconds of the eruption's onset, these turbulent ash clouds—a pyroclastic surge—overtook the slide, expanding in an arc of 180 degrees north of the volcano. Hugging the ground, the racing cloud accelerated from an initial speed of about 220 miles per hour to about 650 miles per hour. (According to some scientists, the steep moving front of the laterally directed ash cloud may have momentarily surpassed the speed of sound, 730 miles per hour.) In a hurricane of hot ash and rock fragments, the cloud rolled approximately 17 miles north of the crater, devastating a fan-shaped area 23 miles across from east to west. Racing across 230 square miles of densely forested mountainscape, the surge mowed down tens of thousands of trees, including Douglas firs 6 feet in diameter and 200 feet tall. Trees growing up to about 8 miles from the crater were uprooted, shredded, and carried away. In this zone of gray desolation, it looked as if the earth's surface had been swept clean by a giant sandblaster, the topsoil scoured down to bedrock. Farther from the crater, a zone of downed trees, stripped of their needles, limbs, and bark, were laid out like matchsticks. Along the margins of this blowdown area was a thin zone of standing trees, but even these were thoroughly seared and dead.

With temperatures of several hundred degrees Fahrenheit, the lateral blast and pyroclastic surge struck its victims with cyclonic force, killing most of the people caught in it within minutes. Several victims died of burns or abrasions from the "stone wind," but autopsies revealed that most died of asphyxiation caused by inhaling the pervasive ash. The few people who survived near the margins of the devastated area recounted unforgettable horrors of darkness, searing heat, and feelings of suffocation.

Studies of the deposits from the lateral blast, which are several feet thick near the volcano and only an inch deep at the edge of the blast zone, show that it contains angular fragments of old rock from St. Helens's cone as well as blocks and bombs of fresh lava, probably from the cryptodome. Of the approximately 0.046 cubic mile (250 million cubic yards) of material carried in the pyroclastic surge, almost two-thirds was fresh magma.

Photographs taken only a few minutes after the eruption's onset show an anvil-shaped ash plume, 45 miles in diameter, rising above St. Helens and the devastated area to the north. Some geologists believe that this giant mushroom cloud, the highest ash column of the entire eruption, resulted from a secondary explosion triggered when magma from the cryptodome plunged into the waters of Spirit Lake and the North Fork Toutle River, perhaps giving the laterally directed pyroclastic surge much of its lethal energy. The sound of this secondary detonation was reported as far away as Vancouver, Canada.

After the huge umbrella unfurling above the devastated area had reached its maximum extent and had begun to drift downwind, a large Plinian

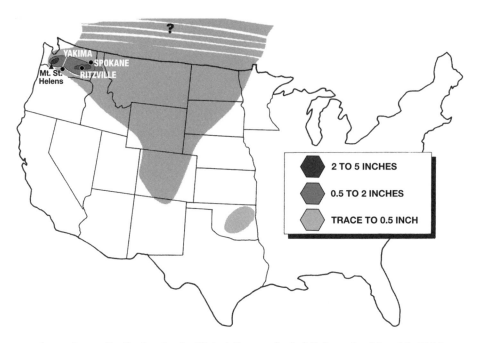

Approximate distribution in the United States of ash fall from the May 18, 1980, eruption of Mount St. Helens. Most areas beyond western Montana received only trace amounts. —Adapted from B. L. Foxworthy and M. Hill, *Volcanic Eruptions of 1980 at Mount St. Helens—The First 100 Days* (U.S. Geological Survey Professional Paper 1249 [1982])

column rose directly above the crater, quickly attaining an altitude of at least 12 miles. From 9:00 AM until near sunset, this vertical plume swept millions of tons of ash into the stratosphere, where strong winds blew it northeastward along a narrow band. Casting an eerie pall across the landscape over which it passed, the cloud deposited a layer of pumiceous tephra 10 inches thick 10 miles downwind and at least an inch thick at a distance of 60 miles. The plume began to sprinkle ash on the city of Yakima, 90 miles distant, at 10:10 AM. By 2:00 PM, the dark canopy hung over Spokane, almost 300 miles from the volcano, where a half inch of ash fell. At 10:15 PM, the cloud reached West Yellowstone, Montana, dusting the area with fine particles. On May 19, a trace of ash settled over Denver; later fine ash fell visibly in Minnesota and Oklahoma. Spreading across the United States in three days, the St. Helens ash circled the earth in fifteen days.

Although it first appeared that Yakima was shrouded under several inches of siltlike ash, reducing visibility to a few feet and seriously impeding traffic, the ash fall soon compacted to a much thinner layer. Facing an unprecedented cleanup problem, Yakima officials reported that 600,000 tons of ash that weighed 95 pounds per cubic foot covered 12 square miles of their city. Because of peculiar atmospheric conditions, the small town of Ritzville, Washington, received an unusually heavy burden of ash the consistency of talcum power. Near the northern edge of the cloud, Spokane was forced to close its airports while automatic street lighting switched on in mid-afternoon.

Pyroclastic Flows

For three hours the Plinian column soared vertically above St. Helens's crater. Shortly after noon, however, observers noted a marked change in the volcano's eruptive style as the ash plume became lighter in color and shifted to the north, away from the central vent. When the dense ash column collapsed at about 12:15 PM, it generated waves of incandescent pumice racing through the north-side breach in the crater toward Spirit Lake. Spreading over the earlier landslide deposits at speeds of 50 to 80 miles per hour, some of these pumiceous pyroclastic flows traveled 5 miles from the vent, building a complex fan that in places is 30 to 120 feet thick. These frothy light-gray pumice flows, described as "boiling over" from the crater, contrast sharply with the predominantly dark debris of the avalanche and mudflow deposits they partly cover.

Where the hot pumice encountered ice or water, steam explosions ripped through the pyroclastic material, tearing open secondary craters up to 65 feet in diameter and sending columns of ash-laden steam 6,500 feet into the air. Some of these phreatic craters were subsequently filled in by pyroclastic flows from later eruptions.

Continuing for more than four hours, the May 18 pyroclastic flows were typically fed by fountains of glowing tephra jetting from the crater. These fountain-derived pumice flows contained a significant quantity of andesite mixed with the predominant dacite, as St. Helens evidently tapped lower levels of its magma reservoir. At 4:30 PM, a sudden return to the Plinian mode carried the plume to an altitude of approximately 13 miles, its greatest height since the eruption's initial phase, when convecting ash from the lateral blast billowed above the devastated area. After 5:30 PM, the plume's vigor rapidly declined, although subdued activity extended into the morning of May 19.

Mudflows

As with most earlier eruptions of Mount St. Helens, large floods and mudflows accompanied the May 18 activity, affecting three of the four major drainage systems on the mountain. Early in the day, hot ash falling from

A Plinian eruption cloud soars miles above the truncated summit of Mount St. Helens, May 18, 1980. Falling ash blackens the sky to the east, while steam explosions (left of center) near Spirit Lake send white plumes thousands of feet into the air. Hot ash flows mantle most of the cone, partly covering blocky lava flows erupted during the Kalama episode. —U.S. Geological Survey

the initial eruption column melted snow and ice, triggering mudflows that streamed down the east and south flanks. Resembling liquid concrete as they poured down Smith Creek, Muddy River, and Pine Creek, the mudflows coalesced in the Lewis River valley, uprooting trees and destroying bridges at the mouth of Pine Creek and head of Swift Reservoir. Between about 9:00 AM and noon, the floods and mudflows dumped enough sediment and miscellaneous debris, including thousands of logs, into the reservoir to raise its level about 2.6 feet.

Larger mudflows raced down the South Fork Toutle River, which drains St. Helens's northwest slopes. An observer, trapped about 8:50 AM in the valley of the South Fork about 4.5 miles west of the mountain, watched "a huge mass of water, mud, and trees" crash past him, "snapping off trees."

Shortly after 10:00 AM, a wall of water and logs 12 feet high rushed by Weyerhauser Timber Company's Camp 12, having traveled 27 miles downriver in only 90 minutes. The Toutle River gauging station at Silver Lake, near the South Fork's confluence with the North Fork, recorded a flood stage of 23.5 feet, the highest ever observed there. By 1:00 PM the mudflow, carrying its burden of logs, a shattered railroad trestle, and other debris, had swept down the Toutle and entered the Cowlitz River.

By far the largest and most destructive mudflows were generated in the North Fork of the Toutle, which originates at the west end of Spirit Lake. By 9:00 AM on May 18, the upper North Fork held the former summit and north flank of Mount St. Helens, its channel clogged for a length of 15 miles by avalanche debris that lay 600 feet thick a mile below Spirit Lake and 150 feet thick at its western terminus. Landslide debris and freshly erupted material avalanching into Spirit Lake had repeatedly created enormous waves that splashed 600 feet up ridges to the north, sweeping over thousands of trees felled by the lateral blast and carrying them into the lake as displaced water flowed back to its source. Although the lake surface rose 200 feet

Deposits from the mightiest debris avalanche in historic time choke the North Fork Toutle River. Collapse of the entire north side of St. Helens on May 18, 1980, sent a debris flow up to 600 feet thick 17 miles down the valley. This view eastward toward St. Helens, taken June 30, 1980, shows part of the area devastated by the lateral blast, at the upper left. —U.S. Geological Survey

above its previous level, it still stood about 200 feet below the avalanche deposit blocking its western exit. Thoroughly saturated with groundwater, water from the North Fork, meltwater from snow and ice, and perhaps water draining from Spirit Lake, the avalanche mass was also subjected to incessant volcanic tremors. By early afternoon, continuous shaking caused part of the North Fork valley fill to liquefy and move downstream. At 2:30 PM, Weyerhauser's Camp Baker was obliterated by a deluge of flowing rock and mud, which picked up heavy trucks, logging equipment, and huge piles of stacked logs. The logs then served as battering rams, destroying many of the seven bridges swept away downstream. The Washington 504 bridge, which had survived the South Fork mudflow earlier in the day, succumbed to the onslaught about 6:00 PM. A nearby gauge showed that the North Fork mudflow rose about 30 feet higher than its South Fork predecessor.

Moving at speeds of up to 27 miles an hour (earlier mudflows originating high on the cone were clocked at 50 to 90 miles per hour), the mudflow traveled down the Toutle, emptying into the Cowlitz River, which carried the now-diluted flow with its burden of logs, shattered houses, and bridge wreckage 17 miles south to its confluence with the Columbia. Arriving at the Columbia shortly after midnight, runout from the mudflow dumped more than 45 million cubic yards of sediment into the Columbia's channel, reducing the river's depth from 38 feet to about 13 feet for a distance of 4 miles and stranding thirty-one vessels in upstream ports. Dredging reopened the Columbia to ocean-going freighters after about thirteen days, but it reportedly took three months to restore shipping traffic to normal. In the meantime, Columbia ports, including that of Portland, reportedly lost millions of dollars in revenue.

Overflowing its banks at Castle Rock, the sediment-burdened Cowlitz deposited mud as much as 10 feet thick on farms and grazing land. The fairgrounds on the opposite bank were buried under 3 to 5 feet of muck, while farm buildings a mile or two south of town were swamped with mud 15 feet thick. Although the Interstate 5 bridge survived the floods and mudflows, twenty-seven other bridges, as well as almost two hundred houses, were destroyed. By a modest estimate, economic losses from the eruption, including the 4 billion board-feet of timber toppled by the lateral blast (enough to build three hundred thousand two-bedroom houses) totaled at least a billion dollars.

Fortunately, only about 1 percent of the debris avalanche filling the North Fork Toutle River valley transformed into a mudflow. Had the entire avalanche fill been mobilized and poured down the Cowlitz into the Columbia, it would have triggered enormous waves sweeping tens of miles both upriver and downstream, devastating the port of Portland and many

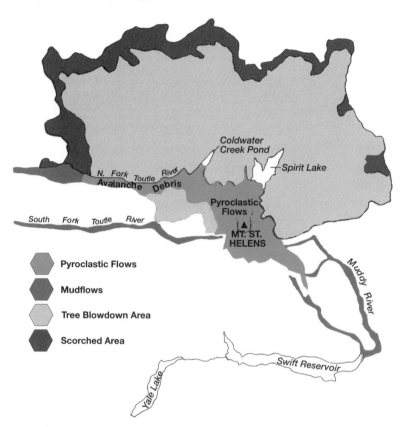

Map showing major features of the paroxysmal May 18, 1980, eruption of Mount St. Helens. The lightest gray area indicates effects of the pyroclastic surge (blowdown area of felled trees). Mudflows traveled down nearly every valley heading on the volcano. —Adapted from Lipman and Mullineaux, 1981

other communities along the Columbia. The loss of life and property would have been immeasurably greater.

The May 18 eruption released a staggering amount of energy—a force equivalent to 27,000 Hiroshima-size atomic bombs detonating sequentially over a span of nine and a half hours—but St. Helens still had a reserve of magmatic power. During the next five months, the volcano produced five additional explosive eruptions, each of which ejected ash clouds 35,000 to 50,000 feet above sea level and discharged pyroclastic flows through the wide breach in the crater's north rim. At 2:30 AM on May 25, during a sudden increase in seismicity, a second explosive burst sent lithic-rich ash spiraling 9 miles into the air, while incandescent pumice flows surged to

ERUPTIVE ACTIVITY AT MOUNT ST. HELENS, 1980–2005

DATE	EVENT
March 16, 1980	Series of small earthquakes begins
March 27, 1980	First phreatic explosions open new vent at summit; cracks bisect summit
May 18, 1980	5.1 earthquake accompanies catastrophic landslide on north flank; lateral blast; Plinian eruption; extensive ash fall, pyroclastic flows and lahars
May 25, 1980	Explosive eruption; pyroclastic flows; winds carry tephra to southwest
June 12, 1980	Explosive eruption; pyroclastic flows; dome growth over several days
July 22, 1980	Explosive eruption destroys incipient dome; pyroclastic flows
August 7, 1980	Explosive eruption; pyroclastic flows; dome growth
October 16–18, 1980	Explosive eruption; pyroclastic flows; viscous lava begins to form new dome
December 27, 1980	Effusion of lava enlarges dome
February 5, 1981	Lava emission enlarges dome
April 10, 1981	Growth of lava dome
June 18, 1981	Dome growth
September 6, 1981	Dome growth
October 30, 1981	Dome growth
March 19, 1982	Dome growth; small lahar
May 14, 1982	Dome growth
August 18, 1982	Dome growth
February 7, 1983–1984	Lava emission begins and continues for almost a year, elevating lava dome; lahars
March 29, 1984	Renewed dome growth
May 14, 1984	Small explosion at dome hurls rocks 1 mile over crater rim and triggers lahar down Toutle River
June 17, 1984	Dome growth
September 10, 1984	Dome growth
May 24, 1985	Dome growth
May 8, 1986	Dome growth; small lahar
October 21, 1986	Dome growth to present size (925 feet above 1980 crater floor)
1989–1991	Intermittent minor explosive eruptions at dome; small pyroclastic flows and lahars
1992–2004	A few minor phreatic events and rockfalls; intense fumarolic activity at dome
1998	Earthquake swarms indicate infusion of new magma deep beneath the volcano
2004–2005	Shallow earthquake swarms and steam explosions; extrusion of fresh magma in crater builds new lava dome

Source: Adapted from Brantley and Myers (2000); and P. T. Pringle and K. A. Cameron, "Eruption-Triggered Lahar on May 14, 1984," in *Hydrologic Consequences of Host-Rock/Snowpack Interactions at Mount St. Helens Volcano, Washington, 1982–84*, edited by T. C. Pierson (U.S. Geological Survey Professional Paper 1586 [1999])

the north. Caught by the erratic winds of a spring storm, fine ash swirled far to the south and west, where it damply coated large areas of western Washington and Oregon.

Two more explosive eruptions, also accompanied by pyroclastic flows, occurred on June 12, the second of which ejected an ash plume 10 miles high, dusting Portland with powdery grit. The small lava dome that rose on the crater floor after this event was blown away on July 22—with rock fragments hurled 4 miles from the vent—when a series of three spectacular cauliflower clouds rose 5 to 6 miles above the mountain. Although clear weather made the plumes visible from Seattle to the Willamette Valley, they dropped only a light sprinkling of ash over southwest Washington. (See image 21 on plate 11.)

Flying over the volcano's north flank on July 22, a USGS geologist enjoyed an unexpectedly close view of a pyroclastic flow's violent birth. Looking south into the crater, he saw "an ash fountain . . . ejected about 1,500 feet above the vent. As the projections of the fountain arched over and [fell to the ground near the vent], they gave rise to a pyroclastic flow and began to rapidly flow northward out of the amphitheater."

After similar outbursts on August 7 and October 16–18, which also destroyed rising domes, the volcano switched to a generally quieter mode of activity for the next six years, pouring out stubby tongues of dacite lava onto the crater floor. Although hundreds of small explosions accompanied this activity, most of the seventeen individual dome-building episodes were primarily effusive, emitting small lobes of viscous lava, 600 to 1,300 feet long and 65 to 130 feet thick, that piled up to form a steep mound that eventually measured 3,500 feet in diameter and 876 feet high. During an eruptive sequence that began in 1983 and lasted a full year, dome growth took place through infusions of fresh magma into the dome's interior, causing its east margin to swell out by 250 feet.

By late October 1986, when magma production temporarily stopped, the dome had a volume of approximately 97 million cubic yards of lava. In 1989 and 1991, small explosions hurled hot rocks 3 feet in diameter up to a half mile north of the dome and triggered small pyroclastic flows and mudflows, but eruptions of juvenile material did not resume until October 2004.

Conditions in the crater, which measures 1.2 miles wide and 1.8 miles long, changed significantly in the late 1980s as the crater floor cooled and a new glacier began to form behind the lava dome. Shaded by the south crater wall, which is 2,000 feet high and continuously sheds rock debris and snow avalanches onto the crater floor, the crescent-shaped glacier grew rapidly, wrapping its icy arms around the vigorously steaming dome. By 2004 the glacier had a volume of about 150 million cubic yards (of which about

30 percent consisted of rock fragments fallen from the crater walls) and a maximum thickness of about 700 feet.

According to a recent U.S. Geological Survey report, the new 2004 dome "began to grow centered roughly on the contact between the old lava dome and the glacier, in the process uplifting both ice and old dome rock." By early 2005, the growing dome had lifted the old crater floor by more than 900 feet above its previous level and the top of the new dome could be seen peeking above the summit of its predecessor. Surprisingly, little glacial ice melted during this phase of the eruption, probably because water-saturated rubble beneath the glacier forms an insulating layer between it and the emerging lava. Future explosions and/or dome collapse, however, may generate pyroclastic flows that can quickly melt large parts of the glacier and trigger lahars racing into Spirit Lake and the North Fork Toutle River.

Volcanic History of St. Helens

Since it began life at least 40,000 to 50,000 years ago, St. Helens has changed its shape and appearance many times, repeatedly shattering its cone with explosive violence and then constructing a new edifice atop the ruins of its predecessor. Given that it has scattered its eruptive products far and wide over the Pacific Northwest, it is not surprising that its cone contains a higher percentage of fragmental rock than any other composite volcano in the range. Unlike Adams, Rainier, or Baker, which are built primarily of andesite lava flows, St. Helens did not begin erupting a significant number of lava flows until its career was well advanced. Until sometime after 2,500 years ago, the volcano probably consisted mainly of an irregular cluster of dacite domes buttressed by voluminous aprons of pyroclastic debris that, along with countless mudflow deposits, formed thick valley fills extending many miles downslope from the central edifice. During its early stages of development, this ancestral volcano—old Mount St. Helens—may have resembled Chaos Crags, a collection of overlapping domes jutting above encircling ramparts of fragmental rock.

The "modern" St. Helens began when the volcano, abruptly changing its eruptive style, started to alternate its usual dacite ejecta with intermittent production of much less silicic magma, erupting andesite lava flows and even fluid streams of basalt. Near the end of the Castle Creek eruptive period (about 1,800 to 1,600 years ago), the volcano erupted its most extensive pahoehoe basalt flow—that containing the lava tube named Ape Cave at its southern foot. As Dwight Crandell of the USGS noted, only during the Castle Creek period did St. Helens metamorphose into a true stratovolcano, building a cone that was almost as high as it was before 1980.

In a comprehensive 1987 study of St. Helens's pyroclastic flow and mud-flow deposits, Crandell divided the volcano's eruptive history into four main stages—Ape Canyon, Cougar, Swift Creek, and Spirit Lake—each lasting several thousand years and separated by long dormant intervals. Crandell subdivided the current Spirit Lake stage, which began about 4,500 years ago,

ERUPTIVE STAGES OF MOUNT ST. HELENS

The Spirit Lake eruptive stage is divided into eruptive periods.

DATE OR APPROXIMATE AGE (YEARS)	ERUPTIVE PERIOD	TEPHRA LAYERS	OTHER PRODUCTS OF ERUPTION
AD 1980–2004	Modern	1980	1980 Lateral blast (pyroclastic surge); pyroclastic flows; lahars; dome growth in crater
AD 1800–1857	Goat Rocks	T	Floating Island lava flow; lahars; Goat Rocks dome; lithic ash
AD 1667–1750	Kalama	——	Continued growth of lava dome at summit; pyroclastic flows
AD 1479–1750	Kalama	W, X	Andesite lava flows; pyroclastic flows; summit dome; lahars
AD 800	Sugar Bowl	Unnamed	Lateral blast; pyroclastic flows; Sugar Bowl dome; east dome(?)
2,200–1,600	Castle Creek	B	Andesite and basalt lava flows (Cave Basalt); pyroclastic flows; lahars
3,000–2,500	Pine Creek	P	Minor tephra but voluminous pyroclastic flows; domes; some andesite flows; lahars
4,500–3,300	Smith Creek	Y	Large volumes of tephra; pyroclastic flows; domes; lahars
10,500–4,500	(Dormant interval of c. 6,000 years)		

Eruptive stages of Mount St. Helens prior to the Spirit Lake stage are not divided into individual eruptive periods.

APPROXIMATE AGE	ERUPTIVE STAGE	TEPHRA LAYERS	OTHER PRODUCTS OF ERUPTION
13,000–10,500	Swift Creek	J, S	Dacite domes; lithic and pumiceous pyroclastic flows; lahars
20,000(?)–18,000(?)	Cougar	K, M	Dacite domes; andesite lava flow; pyroclastic flows; lahars
50,000(?)–36,000(?)	Ape Canyon	C	Dome(?); pumiceous pyroclastic flows

Source: Adapted from R. P. Hoblitt et al., 1980; D. R. Crandell, 1987; and D. R. Mullineaux, 1996

into six shorter eruptive periods, each named for its characteristic deposits at a particular location: the Smith Creek, Pine Creek, Castle Creek, Sugar Bowl, Kalama, and Goat Rocks eruptive periods. In all four of its principal eruptive stages, St. Helens produced voluminous tephras, pyroclastic flows, domes, and mudflows. Until the last 2,500 years, lava flows, although not entirely absent, were rare.

Because material that erupted during the first two stages, the Ape Canyon and Cougar, was subjected to extensive erosion during the last Pleistocene glaciation, the volcano's oldest deposits are poorly preserved. Although researchers have tentatively identified ash layers in the loess of eastern Washington—dated between 100,000 and 50,000 years—as chemically similar to the Ape Canyon–age tephras, the earliest certain evidence of St. Helens's existence is thin layers of ash only 50,000 to 40,000 years old found near the volcano. In his 1996 report on St. Helens's tephra-fall deposits, Donal Mullineaux of the USGS suggests that this lithic ash—layer Cb—records the volcano's birth. This layer may derive from ash clouds accompanying the extrusion and partial collapse of St. Helens's first dacite dome. Further evidence indicating the early eruption of dacite domes is found in the bed of the Lewis River, where prismatically jointed dacite blocks are present. After its mildly explosive debut—followed by a dormant interval that may have lasted for several thousand years—St. Helens then revealed its true character as an enfant terrible, belching forth a huge quantity of tephra—layers Cs and Cy—that have been identified as far southeast as Nevada. The largest volume of tephra erupted during the Pleistocene, and perhaps the largest in the volcano's history, the C sequence was accompanied by large pyroclastic flows, surges, and mudflows. Rock debris pouring down the volcano's north flank probably clogged the Toutle River all the way to its confluence with the Cowlitz, damming the North Fork and perhaps impounding the first ancestral Spirit Lake.

After the tempestuous Ape Canyon stage ended about 36,000 years ago, the volcano seems to have rested for 15,000 years, although the presence of a few thin ash deposits suggests that some minor activity occurred. As at Mount Adams, phases of high magma production were probably interspersed with long spans of only minor activity, without the volcano ever entirely shutting down. When the Cougar stage began about 20,000 years ago, initial eruptions seem to have triggered a series of mudflows, followed by a partial collapse of the south flank, creating a voluminous debris avalanche composed of old rocks from the Ape Canyon period. An atypically large flow of andesite lava, probably issuing through a gap in the crater's south wall opened by the avalanche, traveled southward down the ancestral valley of Swift Creek. Up to 580 feet thick, this andesite flow is the largest of its kind in St. Helens's history. Because the area was largely immersed in glacial ice at this time, the flow's exceptional thickness may have resulted from its being emplaced next to a glacier (see the discussion of Rainier's glaciated lava flows in chapter 18). Explosive eruptions then generated tephra layers K and M, as well as large pumiceous pyroclastic flows down the south, southeast, and west sides of the cone. Pyroclastic flows traveling down the Lewis River valley filled it to depths of 370 feet, while mudflows pouring farther downstream filled channels with sediment more than 200 feet thick.

At the end of the Cougar stage, about 18,000 years ago, St. Helens probably stood at least 6,000 feet high, indicated by the highest outcrop of the large andesite lava flow. Although the intact north side was probably appreciably higher, forces of erosion were then at work lowering its elevation. The Cougar activity coincided with the expansion of Pleistocene glaciers to their final maximum, burying much of the range under ice thousands of feet thick, including the St. Helens area.

Ice-age glaciers were making their final retreat about 5,000 years later when St. Helens resumed activity, expelling prodigious volumes of pumiceous tephra, including the multiple parts of set S, the most copious tephra output since Ape Canyon time. This eruptive stage, named for deposits in Swift Creek, took place between about 13,000 and 10,500 radiocarbon years ago and included both pumiceous and lithic pyroclastic flows, the latter probably derived from a growing dome at or near the central vent. Additional explosive eruptions produced another sequence of tephras, J, which blanketed areas as far east as Montana. The last J ash, Jg, is one of the few that atypical winds carried west of the volcano.

For the next 6,000 years, the volcano was apparently quiescent, its longest unequivocal period of dormancy. (Earlier "dormant" intervals, in which deposits have been severely eroded, contain ambiguous traces of minor activity.) When St. Helens revived about 4,500 calendar years ago, introducing the current Spirit Lake stage, its first two eruptive periods, the Smith Creek and Pine Creek, largely duplicated earlier activity, producing large-volume dacite tephras, silicic domes, and pyroclastic flows.

Distinguished by its explosiveness, the Smith Creek period produced the largest quantity of tephra since the Ape Canyon stage, including that forming layer Yn, which was about thirteen times more voluminous than the 1980 tephra and which stretches in a narrow band northeast into Saskatchewan, Canada. Comparable in size to the AD 79 eruption of Vesuvius that entombed the Roman cities of Pompeii and Herculaneum, the Yn eruption ejected more than a cubic mile of magma (dense rock equivalent), which, when blown out as frothy vesicular rock, creates a significantly larger volume of air-fall pumice and ash. The Y-set contains at least a dozen tephra layers, including Ye (the second most voluminous in the set), which extends hundreds of miles to the east. Dome extrusion and collapse apparently punctuated the explosive eruptions, creating pyroclastic flows of nonvesicular rock fragments and mudflows that choked adjacent valleys and stream channels.

Occurring sporadically over a span of about 600 years, the Y tephras evidently had a severe impact on the affected region's human inhabitants. Although the degree of environmental damage to areas blanketed by Y pumice is not known, comparisons with similarly large eruptions at other volcanoes shows that a heavy fall of coarse lapilli typically defoliates trees, smothers vegetation, pollutes water sources, and depletes populations of animals and the human predators who depend on them. Recent studies by the U.S. Forest Service and other researchers indicate a hiatus in settlements throughout Washington's southwest Cascade Range between about 3,600 and 1,600 years ago (the former date probably the time of the Yn eruption). During approximately the same time span, there was a coincidental increase of native populations in the Columbia plateau to the east, a shift perhaps attributable to St. Helens's repeated ejections of voluminous tephra.

Whereas the Smith Creek activity is noted for explosiveness and tephra production, the Pine Creek eruptive period that followed (about 3,000 to 2,500 years ago) is characterized by a decrease in tephra and increase in both lithic and pumiceous pyroclastic flows, which are an order of magnitude larger than those of the previous period. During the Pine Creek period, the growth of new domes, along with a few andesite flows, probably filled a large crater at St. Helens's summit that had formed during expulsion of the Y tephras. (After the 1980 debris avalanche cored out St. Helen's interior, domes of probable Pine Creek age were exposed, their light color contrasting with the dark basalts that later capped them during the Castle Creek period.) As the rising domes shed massive avalanches of hot rock, they generated lithic pyroclastic flows, pyroclastic surges, and mudflows that swept down both the north and south sides of the mountain, creating a particularly massive deposit on the southeast flank between Muddy River on the east and Swift Creek on the west. The Lewis River valley was again swamped with debris; near its confluence with the Columbia, the Lewis channel was raised about 25 feet above its present level. Pine Creek deposits also filled the North Fork Toutle River bed with rock debris, raising the surface of the debris fan damming the west end of Spirit Lake. Mudflows also impacted the Cowlitz River, raising its bed at least 20 feet above its present elevation.

Even larger floods and mudflows occurred when lakes, impounded upstream by debris avalanches in the Toutle River drainage, suddenly broke through these natural barriers, inundating areas downvalley. So much sediment was swept down the Toutle about 2,500 years ago that it permanently blocked Outlet Creek, forming Silver Lake. As Patrick Pringle has observed, when geologists realized that similar catastrophic floods would occur if the 1980 debris avalanche dam at Spirit Lake were to fail, steps were quickly taken to stabilize the lake level. After constructing a pipeline to drain Spirit Lake in 1982, the Army Corps of Engineers then built a long tunnel to siphon off lake waters to South Coldwater Creek and the North Fork Toutle River.

At the close of the Pine Creek period, St. Helens was perhaps little more than 7,300 feet high, as suggested by the highest exposed rock of probable Pine Creek age, a dacite dome on the southwest flank. This scraggly aggregation of a few andesite flows and numerous dacitic domes mantled in fragmental debris, however, was soon largely buried beneath copious flows of andesite and basalt that, erupting primarily from a central vent, would gradually reshape the volcano into the classic conical form it had before 1980. During the Castle Creek eruptive period, which ended a 300-year dormant interval following the Pine Creek period, St. Helens introduced a major variation in its eruptive behavior: although dacite tephra (set B), pyroclastic flows, and possibly a dome (Dogs Head) were emitted during this time (about 2,200 to 1,600 years ago), it probably ejected less tephra than in any previous episode. Instead, as the "modern" volcano took shape, it apparently drew on deeper levels of low-silica magma, culminating in the eruption of pahoehoe basalt flows, some 8 to 9 miles long, that streamed down almost every side of the cone. On the north flank, basaltic flows traveled as far as the North Fork Toutle River, just west of Spirit Lake. Other thin flows poured over the Dogs Head dome, a prominent knob high on the northeast slope, but the most extensive basaltic lava stream, the Ape Cave flow (named for an exceptionally long lava tube cave in its interior), flowed down a shallow gully on the southwest flank, cascading into the Lewis River valley slightly west of the present site of Swift Dam. At the same time, another basaltic flow poured several miles down the Kalama River valley on the west side of the volcano. Fountains of highly fluid basalt may have fed some of these flows, as well as the layers of basaltic tephra produced during this phase. By the close of the Castle Creek period, St. Helens may have stood well over 9,000 feet high, only a few hundred feet below its pre-1980 maximum elevation.

During the next millennium, only one notable eruptive sequence occurred, that which formed the Sugar Bowl dome, a dacite mass about half a mile in diameter emplaced low on the north flank. Occurring about 1,200 years ago, this brief episode is notable because explosions during dome growth created laterally directed blasts similar to, but much smaller in scope than, that of 1980. Although angular rock fragments and a cloud of ash were hurled many miles northeast of the volcano, the blast area was only about 7 miles wide, affecting less than a third of the area devastated in 1980. According to Crandell, two blasts took place: The first, early in the process of dome extrusion, propelled ballistic shards of new rock that peppered ridges to the northeast. A second, larger blast, perhaps at the base of the dome, blew out older rock of Ape Canyon age. Both explosions generated pyroclastic flows derived from hot fragments rolling down hillsides on which they had landed. Fallout from accompanying ash clouds deposited thin layers of tephra downwind. Another dacite protrusion, the east dome, located low on St. Helens's east flank, may also have been emplaced at this time.

The Kalama Eruptive Period

Following a 700-year hiatus, St. Helens entered a major eruptive period—the Kalama—that continued intermittently for almost three centuries, completing the construction of its pre-1980 cone. Opening with a bang, the Kalama eruptions ejected the largest quantity of pumice since the Yn eruption. Tree-ring dating pinpoints the initial pumice fall (layer Wn), which had about six times the volume of the 1980 tephra, at AD 1479. It was followed only three years later by the smaller-volume tephra layer We (which was still 20 percent larger than that of 1980). Studies by David Yamaguchi, whose work analyzing the growth rings of the area's trees provides a chronological framework for St. Helens's recent history, demonstrated that these voluminous air-fall tephras severely damaged old-growth forests northeast of the volcano, killing thousands of conifers. As the dead trees decayed in their thick shroud of pumice, they left cylindrical holes in the deposit known as tree-wells, before 1980 an intriguing surface feature near Spirit Lake.

The violent explosions responsible for the W tephra set must have appreciably lowered the elevation of St. Helens, leaving a large crater at the summit. A dacite dome rising near the summit shortly after 1479 may have been the source of lithic pyroclastic flow deposits found on the southwest flank—deposits formed when the AD 1482 outburst destroyed the new dome. Both lithic and pumiceous pyroclastic flows raced several miles down the Kalama River valley on the southwest slope, triggering mudflows that left thick fills downstream.

As the Kalama period progressed, with short pulses of intense activity punctuating longer interludes of repose, St. Helens's magma became less silicic, producing andesite tephra set X, which consists of numerous beds of black and tan ash. Andesite lava flows then descended virtually every side of the cone, particularly on the southeast flank, where the thick blocky

Worm flows still form a conspicuous surface feature. During later phases of Kalama time, erupting magma reverted to a more silicic composition, filling the summit crater with a large dacite dome, its sporadic growth triggering avalanches of hot rock that formed lithic pyroclastic flows and mudflows on all flanks of the volcano. Perhaps generated by an explosion that blasted a V-shaped gap in the crater rim, an avalanche of angular blocks derived from the dome formed a jumbled debris fan on the southeast flank, into which the narrow Shoestring glacier later excavated its bed. Toward the close of the Kalama period, which ended between about AD 1667 and 1750, pumiceous pyroclastic flows repeatedly erupted at the summit, bathing the cone in hot ash.

Although streams later cut gullies and shallow trenches through some of the unconsolidated fragmental deposits mantling its steep slopes, the pre-1980 St. Helens, reshaped during the Kalama cone-building period, had fewer erosional scars than any other Pacific Northwest stratovolcano. The thick layers of light-gray (W) pumice lapilli covering its steep north flank—a bane to climbers who struggled for footholds in the loose, sliding material—also gave it the lowest timberline of any Cascade peak (about 4,400 feet).

The Goat Rocks Eruptions

The volcano was quiet for less than a century before it began a new cycle of activity, the Goat Rocks eruptive period (AD 1800–1857), which produced dacite tephra (layer T), a sizable andesite lava flow, a dacite dome (Goat Rocks), hot avalanches, mudflows, and numerous expulsions of lithic ash. Although it generated much less magma than the long-lived Kalama episode and did not appreciably modify the volcano's graceful contours, the Goat Rocks activity probably set the stage for the catastrophic collapse of St. Helens in 1980. Perhaps blocked by the recently emplaced summit dome, rising Goat Rocks magma was deflected to vents well below the summit, principally on the north or northwest sides. The Floating Island lava flow, a stream of blocky andesite lava about 3.5 miles long named for the discrete "islands" of conifers growing on its otherwise barren surface, probably issued from the same vent, high on the northwest flank, that was the source of the T tephra. As the lava flow traveled downslope, sporadic avalanches of older material from the volcano's upper flanks deposited patches of fragmental debris on its jagged crust, providing soil in which seedlings later took root. Whereas tree-ring dating indicates that the lava flow occurred within a few months of the 1800 tephra eruption, several decades passed before another vent, a short distance to the east, extruded the Goat Rocks dome. Eyewitness accounts indicate that major dome growth took place over several years in the 1840s, during which time other active vents were also reported on the upper southwest and northeast flanks. These subsidiary vents, probably located near the line of contact between the summit dome and the main cone, may have seriously weakened the upper edifice, extensively fracturing the rock, subjecting it to hydrothermal alteration, and thus contributing to its abrupt disintegration in 1980.

Although Vancouver (1792) arrived slightly too early to witness the explosive outburst that inaugurated this period, and Lewis and Clark (1805–1806) a few years too late, some Native Americans vividly remembered the 1800 tephra fall, transmitting oral reports of the event to Anglo-American

Deceptively peaceful less than a day before the catastrophic eruption of May 18, 1980, Mount St. Helens reveals the notorious bulge in its north flank (left-center). From left to right: Dogs Head dome; ash-blanketed Forsyth glacier; Goat Rocks dome and avalanche debris fan below; and the Floating Island lava flow, which cuts a swath over 3 miles long through the forest encircling the base of St. Helens. —U.S. Geological Survey

explorers and missionaries. One account, from the Nespelim tribe in north-eastern Washington, evokes a mysterious "dry snow" that disrupted the people's normal life pattern, causing many to substitute prayers and dancing for their usual food gathering and storing, a lapse that produced a severe famine the following winter, reportedly costing many lives. When explorer Charles Wilkes interviewed a Spokane tribal leader, Cornelius or "Big Head," in the 1840s, Cornelius told him that about fifty years earlier, "before [the native tribes] knew of white people, or had heard of them," a great eruption had occurred. When about ten years old, Cornelius was

> . . . suddenly awakened by his mother, who called out to him that the world was falling to pieces. He then heard a great noise of thunder overhead and all the people crying out in great terror. Something was falling very thick, which they at first took for snow, but on going out they found it to be dirt: it proved to be ashes, which fell to the depth of six inches and increased their fears, by causing them to suppose that the end of the world was actually at hand.

A geologist with Wilkes's expedition, James D. Dana, was probably referring to Cornelius's story in his 1849 report when he cited "an account . . . of ashes falling fifty years since." Two Presbyterian missionaries, Elkanah and Mary Walker, also heard tales of the ash fall from the Spokane. In his 1839 report to his mission board, the Reverend Walker summarized the tribal narratives:

> They say some forty or fifty years ago there was a great fall of ashes, the truth of which is very plain now to be seen in turning up the ground. They say that it was a very long night with heavy thunder. They feared the world would fall to pieces and their hearts were very small. The quantity which fell was about six inches.

Despite the exaggerated depth of the ash fall—it was probably about half the thickness claimed—the Spokane accounts anticipate the experience of several hundred thousand residents of eastern Washington, northern Idaho, and western Montana on May 18, 1980.

Dr. Meredith Gairdner, a physician for the Hudson's Bay Company at Fort Vancouver, provides the earliest direct eyewitness description of St. Helens in action. In March 1835, the twenty-six-year-old doctor from Edinburgh observed an eruption that so intrigued him that he resolved to climb the volcano, which in his day would have necessitated a major trek into a largely uncharted wilderness. Although poor health prevented him from making the ascent (he was to die of tuberculosis in Hawaii not long after), Gairdner sent an undated letter about the volcano to the *Edinburgh New Philosophical Journal,* published in January 1836:

> We have recently had an eruption of Mount Saint Helens, one of the
> snowy peaks of the Marine Chain of the north-west coast [the Cas-
> cade Range had not yet been officially christened], about 40 miles to
> the north of this place [Fort Vancouver]. There was no earthquake or
> preliminary noise here: the first thing which excited my notice was a
> dense haze for two or three days, accompanied with a fall of minute
> flocculi of ashes, which, on clearing off, disclosed the mountain des-
> titute of its cover of everlasting snow, and furrowed deeply by what
> through the glass appeared to be lava streams. I believe this is the first
> well ascertained proof of the existence of a volcano on the west coast
> of America, to the north of California on the mainland. At the same
> season of the year 1831, a much denser darkness occurred here, which
> doubtless arose from the same cause, although at that time no one
> thought of examining the appearance of the mountain.

Shortly after Gairdner wrote his account, American missionary Samuel
Parker arrived at Fort Vancouver. Although he noted that the volcano was
still active, "down to the present [sending] forth smoke and fine cinders to
a considerable distance," he did not actually see the main eruption. Parker's
secondhand version of the 1830s activity corresponds almost verbatim to
that of J. Quinn Thornton, a judge of the Oregon Supreme Court, who
claimed a "Dr. Gassner [a misspelling of "Gairdner"?], a distinguished naturalist of England," as well as "gentlemen connected with the Hudson Bay
Company," as his source. In the 1846 edition of his *Journal,* Parker wrote,

> There was in August 1831, an uncommonly dark day, which was
> thought to have been caused by an eruption of a volcano. The whole
> day was nearly as dark as night, except a slight red, lurid in appearance,
> which was perceptible until near night. Lighted candles were neces-
> sary during the day. The atmosphere was filled with ashes of wood,
> all having the appearance of having been produced by great fires, and
> yet none were known to have been in the whole region. The day was
> perfectly calm, without any wind. For a few days after, the fires out of
> doors were noticed to burn as though mixed with sulphur. There were
> no earthquakes. By observations which were made after the atmo-
> sphere became clear, it was thought the pure white perpetual snow of
> Mount St. Helens was discolored, presenting a brown appearance, and
> therefore it was concluded that there had been a slight eruption.

In a footnote, Parker added that he had "been creditably informed that
lava was ejected at that time from St. Helens." Because Dr. Gairdner's and
Parker's other informants viewed the activity from a considerable distance,
they probably mistook mudflows—or rock avalanching from a precursor

of the Goat Rocks dome or other vents on the northwest or southwest side—for lava flows.

The "Great Eruption" of 1842–1843

Because of southwest Washington's prevalent cloudiness and the paucity of literate observers in the area during the first half of the nineteenth century, many of St. Helens's eruptions probably went unrecorded. Considering how small the Oregon country's population was during this period, the wonder is that so many different people—ranging from fur trappers and explorers to missionaries and steamboat pilots, almost none of whom possessed a scientific education—were sufficiently impressed by the volcano to describe its eruptive behavior in letters, journals, memoirs, and, in the 1850s, even a few newspaper articles. For the fifteen years preceding 1857, witnesses logged in more than a dozen events—more than for any other historically active Cascade volcano—the most widely reported of which were spectacular expulsions of ash in November and December 1842.

In his meticulous study of St. Helens's tephra deposits, Donal Mullineaux of the USGS identified a thin ash layer southeast of the volcano that postdates the 1800 tephra and may be correlated to the 1842 ash plumes, which winds carried as far southeast as The Dalles in Oregon, about 60 miles distant. Another thin ash bed of about the same age occurs north of the volcano and probably represents another historic event. Careful study of trees killed or injured by a pyroclastic surge that swept down the northwest flank of St. Helens in the 1840s indicates that the Goat Rocks dome was then rising, accompanied by avalanches of hot rock and columns of lithic ash. Judging by accounts of eyewitnesses who saw the eruptions from different locations, vents on both the north and south sides of the cone may have been contemporaneously active.

According to Josiah L. Parrish, a Methodist missionary who observed the November 22 outburst from a distant vantage point "about ten miles below Salem" in the Willamette Valley, "no earthquake was felt, no noise was heard." Occurring on a clear fall day, the eruption was silent but awe inspiring: Parrish "saw vast columns of lurid smoke and fire shoot up; which spread out in a line parallel to the plane of the horizon, and presented the appearance of a vast table, supported by immense pillars of convolving flame and smoke." Fifty years later, in a letter published in *Steel Points,* William Gladstone Steel's short-lived mountaineering journal, Parrish added further details:

> Upon looking at the mountain we saw arising from its summit immense and beautiful scrolls of what seemed to be pure white steam,

which rose many degrees into the heavens. Then came a stratum just below those fine huge scrolls of steam, which was an indefinite shade of gray. Then down next the mountain's top the substance emitted was black as ink.

Parrish also described how the ash fall changed the volcano's appearance: "The next day after the eruption I was out on French Prairie where I had a good view of the mountain, and I noticed that she had changed her snowy dress of pure white for a somber black mantle, which she wore until the snows of the ensuing winter fell upon her." Like the phreatomagmatic eruptions that initiated the reawakening of St. Helens from late March to early May in 1980, the 1842 activity generated impressive ash clouds that darkened the peak's perennial snow cover.

Another missionary account, preserved in Frederick Plummer's 1893 compilation of Pacific Northwest volcanism, is that of the Reverend Gustavus Hines. Like Parrish, Hines emphasized the suddenness of the eruption cloud that, without warning, burst from St. Helens's snowy slopes:

> In the month of October [*sic*] 1842, St. Helens was discovered all at once to be covered with a dense cloud of smoke, which continued to enlarge and move off in dense masses to the eastward, and filling the heavens in that direction, presented an appearance like that occasioned by a tremendous conflagration viewed at a vast distance. When the first volume of smoke had cleared away it could be distinctly seen from different parts of the country that an eruption had taken place on the north side of St. Helens, a little below the summit, and from the smoke that continued to rise from the chasm or crater, it was pronounced to be a volcano in active operation. When the explosion took place the wind was north/northwest and on the same day and extending from thirty to fifty miles to the southeast there fell showers of ashes or dust, which covered the ground in some places so as to admit of its being gathered in quantities.

A few days later, winds again directed St. Helens's tephra plume to the southeast, showering the Methodist mission at The Dalles with powdery ash. On November 25, 1842, the Reverend Henry B. Brewer noted in his journal that "this morning was memorable for the shower of sand supposed to come from Mt. St. Helens or Hood." Brewer later added "The Dalles was covered with ashes, there was an odor of sulphur, no storm or noise, no fire to be seen, but lots of smoke, contrasting St. Helens' with other snow-covered peaks."

In his journal entry for November 13, 1843, Captain J. C. Frémont stated that "on the 23rd of the preceding November [according to Brewer, it was November 25, 1842], St. Helens had scattered its ashes, like a light fall of snow, over The Dalles of the Columbia, 50 miles distant. A specimen of these ashes was given to me by Mr. Brewer, one of the clergymen at The Dalles."

A second ash cloud wafted over The Dalles mission on November 30 to December 1, 1842, depositing another light ash fall that coincided with a visit from missionaries in the Willamette Valley. Writing about the event in his *Ten Years in Oregon,* Daniel Lee recalled that

> The evening [November 30, 1842] of our arrival there [at The Dalles] there was an eruption of Mount St. Helens; and the next morning [December 1] the ejected ashes were falling with a mist-like appearance, covering the leaves, fences, and stones, with a light, fine, gritty substance, in appearance like hoar frost, some specimens of which were collected.

In his 1854 memoir, *Sketches of Mission Life Among the Indians of Oregon,* Zachariah Atwell Mudge recounted the eruption's effect on The Dalles community:

> On a pleasant evening, in the month of November [30] 1843 [1842] . . . a dark, heavy cloud was seen rising in the direction of Mount Saint Helens. No special remark was excited by this fact; but, on going to the door the next morning, the missionaries were surprised to see the ground, the trees, the grass—everything—sprinkled with ashes. A dark cloud shrouded the sky. It seemed to rain; but the clouds were not dropping water. Something descended gently to the earth, in form like fine sand—in color, it appeared like ashes. Its odor was that of sulphur. The Indians said it had descended in larger quantities toward Mount St. Helens. Soon the mystery was solved: that mountain was broken forth in a splendid eruption, and the winds had wafted its ashes to the door of the missionaries.

Curious to see more of this phenomenon, The Dalles clergymen climbed a hill overlooking the Columbia River from which they commanded a sweeping panorama of the southern Washington Cascades. Unlike Adams, Rainier, and Hood, which remained in icy repose, St. Helens was smoldering fiercely: "Amid this group of lofty mountains, Helens threw out its dark cloud of smoke. Its fires seem smothered, but the issuing volumes of smoke and ashes contrasted impressively with the sparkling snow of the surrounding peaks."

St. Helens remained sporadically active throughout the winter of 1842–1843, repeatedly spewing plumes of ash visible for miles around. On December 13, 1842, another Methodist clergyman, John H. Frost, spotted "a column of smoke [ascending] from the N.W. side of Mt. St. Helens, toward the top. . . . It has been ascertained since that it was an actual volcanic eruption. I know not that it has as yet emitted anything but smoke. Have learned since that ashes have been thrown out in great abundance, even as far as The Dalles."

Earlier in December, a particularly vigorous ash column was observed from the Cowlitz Mission in what is now southwest Washington. Writing in December 1842 to his superiors in Quebec, Father J. B. Z. Bolduc reported seeing both smoke and flame:

> To the northeast and southeast are two mountains whose height I still do not know, but which are at least 4,000 [feet high—a 10,000-foot underestimate for Rainier!]. They are snowcovered, even in the greatest heat of summer. One of them—the one toward the southeast—is in the shape of a cone, and is opposite my dwelling. On the 5th of December, toward three o'clock in the afternoon, one of its sides opened and there was an eruption of smoke such that all our old voyageurs have never seen anything equal to it. These eruptions of smoke took place for several days at intervals not far apart, after which eruptions of flame began. They take place almost continuously, but with an intensity that varies greatly from time to time. I am led to believe that there are three craters at least, for I have observed several times three eruptions at once and at different places, although close to each other. Especially in the evening are these phenomena well observed, and they offer a magnificent sight to the spectator. There is at the foot of this mountain a little river whose waters empty into the Cowlitz. After the volcano manifested itself, almost all the fish that it used to feed died—which is attributed to the quantity of cinders with which the waters were affected.

Father Bolduc does not mention the November 22 outburst, perhaps because he did not arrive at his post until the thirtieth of that month. His reference to fish dying in the Toutle River, also noted by other observers, indicates that hot rock from the Goat Rocks vent probably triggered mudflows down the north/northwest flank.

Three years later, the Right Reverend Modeste Demers, also stationed at the Cowlitz Mission, wrote that St. Helens continued to be active and that "since the month of December 1842, the time when the mountain opened its sides from the drive of subterranean fires, the waters of this [the Toutle] river have carted cinders and scoria. After the first eruption the natives assured us that they had found dead fish."

In October 1843, Overton Johnson and William H. Winter stated in a journal later published as *Route Across the Rocky Mountains with a Description of Oregon and California* that St. Helens was then "burning": "Frequently the huge columns of black smoke may be seen, suddenly bursting from its crater, at the distance of thirty or forty miles. The crater is on the south side, below the summit." The following February 16 brought a particularly spectacular display. Peter H. Burnett, a lawyer who later became governor of California, observed it from a point near the confluence of the Willamette and Columbia Rivers: "Being a beautiful and clear day, the mountain burned magnificently. The dense masses of smoke rose up in one immense column, covering the whole crest of the mountain in clouds." After citing what seems to be a slightly altered version of Burnett's description, Plummer added that "in the evenings its fires lit up the mountainside in a flood of soft yet brilliant radiance." Burnett also indicated that lava—or, more likely, avalanches of hot rock fragments from the rising Goat Rocks dome—was then erupting:

> On the side of the mountain, near its top, is a large black object, amidst the pure white snow around it. This is supposed to be the mouth of a large cavern. From Indian accounts this mountain emitted a volume of burning lava about the time it first commenced burning [November 22, 1842]. An Indian came to Vancouver with his foot and leg badly burnt, who stated that he was on the side of the mountain hunting deer, and he came to a stream of something running down the mountain, and when he attempted to jump across it, he fell with one foot into it; and that was the way in which he got his foot and leg burned. This Indian came to the fort to get Doctor Barclay to administer some remedy to cure his foot.

The story of the Indian with the burned foot—which, along with the injuries Mount Lassen inflicted on Lance Graham, is one of the two pre-1980 casualties reportedly caused by an eruption on the U.S. mainland—eventually became part of early Pacific Northwest lore. It may, however, be apocryphal. Napoleon McGilvery, who claimed to have been in charge of the Fort Vancouver commissary at the time, disclaimed any knowledge of the incident. In a reminiscence published in 1899, McGilvery wrote:

> The mountain was not visible from Vancouver at any time. The eruption probably occurred on one day, and was not discovered by us until the next, when, upon going out early in the morning, gray white ashes were found to cover the ground as a light fall of snow. Both days were beautiful and clear. There was no traveling at that time away from the water course, except by Indians, and very little by them. It has been published that during this eruption an Indian was caught in the hot lava, was badly burned and taken to Vancouver, where he was treated by Dr. McLoughlin. I had charge of the commissary, so that such an incident could not have happened without my knowledge, and I never heard of it until recently.

In support of the original tale, it should be noted that Burnett's version states that the Indian was treated by Dr. Barclay, not the more famous Dr. McLoughlin, and that he is vague about the time of the incident.

Whatever the fate of Indians rash enough to approach this active fire mountain, St. Helens remained fitfully active throughout the 1840s. On May 30, 1844, the Reverend George Gary, then on a ship off the Oregon coast, had "a very distant view of a volcano in action, throwing up clouds of smoke." Although at first Gary was not sure if it was St. Helens or some other peak erupting, he wrote:

> On further inquiry, I have learned that this volcano [active crater] is in Mount Helen [sic] itself, and that either the snow is diminishing or the soot settling on the snow covering of the mountain presents the appearance of wasting snow. It is so cold near these snowy mountains and the snow is so deep I believe there has been no very thorough examination of them, and this volcano is as high up the mountain as that the temperature at its base is but little, if any, affected by it. The falling ashes or soot have been seen and gathered from boards or anything of a smooth surface, fifty miles from the crater.

Shortly after Christmas 1844, Burnett noted that St. Helens was still "a burning volcano." Bad weather probably obscured much of that winter's activity, but visibility was good enough on February 15, 1845, for Samuel B. Crockett to report that the volcano continued emitting "columns of smoke from its frozen top." Although less violent than the 1842 eruptions, those in the mid-1840s were noticeable enough to attract the attention of two itinerant artists, Henry J. Warre and Paul Kane. In the summer of 1845, Warre, a lieutenant in the British military, sketched the mountain from the Columbia River and later from a settlement on the Cowlitz River, in each case depicting a moderate ash cloud rising from the volcano's west or northwest flank. Kane, a Canadian, was on a long tour from Toronto to collect material for paintings. On March 26, 1847, from a point near the mouth of the Lewis River that commanded an unobstructed view of the peak, Kane made a preliminary drawing. As he noted in his journal, "There was not a cloud visible in the sky at the time I commenced my sketch, and not a breath of air was perceptible; suddenly a stream of white smoke shot up from the crater of the mountain and hovered a short time over its summit; it then settled down like a cap. This shape it retained for about an hour and a half, and then gradually disappeared." A watercolor apparently based on this sketch is in the Stark Museum of Art in Orange, Texas.

Four days later, after he had traveled north to the Cowlitz Farm of the Hudson's Bay Company near the present town of Toledo, Washington, Kane drew a second sketch, clearly depicting a plume of steam or light-colored ash rising from the Goat Rocks dome on the northwest flank. In contrast to the surrounding snowfields of St. Helens, the dome is depicted as gray bare rock. Harry Majors, a Pacific Northwest historian, argues persuasively

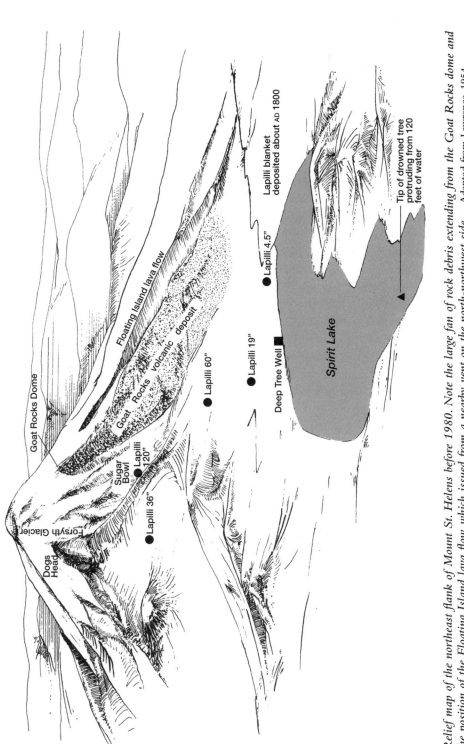

Relief map of the northeast flank of Mount St. Helens before 1980. Note the large fan of rock debris extending from the Goat Rocks dome and the position of the Floating Island lava flow, which issued from a nearby vent on the north-northwest side. —Adapted from Lawrence, 1954

that Kane's best known representation of the volcano, an oil painting showing a night eruption from the Lewis River, is a composite of his two earlier
sketches. It is a romantically dramatic work that shows a group of Indians
awed by the fire mountain, its ruddy glare reflected on their upturned faces
and on the river's still surface where their canoe is harbored. (See image 18
on plate 10.)

If it seems that Kane's painting exaggerates the mild activity he describes
in his journal, it is important to remember that he saw the mountain erupt
more than once—and that he delineates the erupting vent with great precision. On March 30, 1847, he had another "fine view of Mt. St. Helens' [sic]
throwing up a long column of dark smoke into the clear blue sky." In both
his two original sketches and his finished painting, Kane correctly shows
ash clouds emerging from an area of dark rock, the Goat Rocks dome,
about a third of the way down the west or northwest side, and not from
a summit crater as convention would dictate. The fiery jet rising from the
dome portrays incandescent rock reflecting on clouds of steam, while the
glowing material bordering both sides of Goat Rocks correctly indicates
the avalanches of hot rock fragments that cascaded downslope during dome
growth. As Crandell notes, the extrusion of Goat Rocks was accompanied
by avalanching debris that created pyroclastic flows, surges, and mudflows,
forming a large debris fan on the northwest flank.

Kane may have based his colorful nocturnal display partly on oral accounts of the 1842 outburst, when Parrish saw "vast columns of lurid smoke
and fire" and Father Bolduc "eruptions of flame," perhaps the ruddy glow
of hot rock from the elevating dome. In a letter dated April 1, 1848, Robert
Caulfield of Oregon City confirmed that St. Helens was still lighting up
night skies a full year after Kane had so portrayed it: "St. Helens which is still
a volcano and continuously covered with snow stands about 70 miles north
of this place. There has [sic] been two emptyings of this mountain since we
came here. The report we could hear distinctly and the reflections seen in
the sky at night." In an 1877 publication, geologist S. F. Emmons cited an
unnamed voyageur (French Canadian fur trapper) who claimed that "the
light from the burning volcano [in 1842] was so intense that one could see
to pick up a pin in the grass at midnight near his cabin, which is some 20
miles distant in a straight line [probably on the Toutle River]." Such references to light or flame are relatively common, but Caulfield is almost the
only eyewitness to mention hearing reports or explosions.

Viewing St. Helens from a ship at the Columbia's mouth, approximately
100 miles distant, Charles Stevens, a pioneer tailor who had brought his
wife and seven children over the Oregon Trail in 1852, wrote to his brother's family that the volcano was still emitting "smoke . . . that runs way up

above the clouds." At the bottom of his letter, dated April 10, 1853, Stevens included a rough sketch showing a plume rising from a vent below St. Helen's summit on the southwest side, explaining that "the little black spot near the top is a hole, where the fire and smoke comes out . . . the spots near the bottom looks like black lava." Stevens's views of St. Helens and Hood, with the broad Columbia in the foreground, he added, "are the grandest, the most beautiful sights, it appears to me, that a person can look on. The mountains are so high that no one can go half way to the top."

The Portland *Oregonian's* intrepid editor, Thomas J. Dryer, however, claimed to have made the first ascent of both peaks. In the September 3, 1853, issue of the *Oregonian*, Dryer published his account of climbing St. Helens via the south flank, insisting that its crater, as determined by his compass reading, was located on "the north-east side. The smoke was continually issuing from the mouth, giving unmistakable evidence that the fire was not extinguished." Five months later, Dryer followed up with a report in the *Oregonian* (February 25, 1854) that activity had increased:

> The crater of Mt. St. Helens has been unusually active for several days past. Those who have been in a position so as to obtain a view of the mountain, represent clouds of smoke and ashes constantly rising from it. The smoke appears to come up in puffs, which was the case at the time we visited in August last. There is now more smoke issuing from it than there was then, which indicates that the volcanic fires are rapidly increasing within the bowels of this majestic mountain.

Although Dryer was wrong about the ash "puffs" heralding more intense activity, this new pulse was strong enough to be noticed at various locations. In the *Oregon Weekly Times* of February 25, 1854, W. H. H. Halls, pilot of the *Whitcomb*, a Columbia River steamboat, confirmed that the volcano was producing "volumes of smoke . . . [that] were thrown out at intervals." Stevens also noted the activity in his diary, but added that he was not then in a position to see it.

Oddly enough, St. Helens's last recorded historic eruption before 1980 was not published in an Oregon journal, but in the *Republican*, a newspaper in Steilacoom, Washington. The issue of April 17, 1857, stated that "Mount St. Helens, or some other mount to the southward, is seen from the Nisqually plains in this country, to be in eruption. It has for the last few days been emitting huge volumes of dense smoke and fire, a grand and sublime spectacle." In perusing old newspaper reports, Harry Majors discovered brief references to minor activity in 1898, 1903, and 1921. Unlike the nineteenth-century accounts cited above, however, these events did not produce ash clouds visible at a distance and were probably short-lived thermal phenomena similar to the small phreatic bursts observed at various locations on Mount Rainier in the 1950s and 1960s.

The Position of the Crater

Although eyewitnesses agree almost unanimously that St. Helens's historic eruptions occurred at vents located well below the summit, with the majority placing the active crater(s) on the north or northwest side in the vicinity of Goat Rocks, two or three others, including careful observers like Josiah Parrish and Charles Stevens, refer to a vent on the south side. In describing the activity of November 1842, which he viewed from at least 100 miles to the southwest, Parrish stated that "the eruption was on the south side of the mountain, about two thirds of the distance from the bottom to the top," testimony corroborated by Stevens's 1853 sketch, which shows an ash plume issuing from an orifice high on the southwest flank. From his location northwest of the volcano, however, Father Bolduc wrote, "I am led to believe that there are three craters at least, for I have several times observed three eruptions at once at different places though close to each other." These closely spaced vents may have included those of the T tephra and the Floating Island lava flow, slightly west of Goat Rocks. Although Modeste Demers at the Cowlitz mission, Methodist missionary John Frost, geologist George Gibbs, and painters Henry Warre and Paul Kane offer both verbal and visual confirmation of the north/northwest crater, it seems probable that a southside vent was also active. Thomas Dryer didn't find it when he climbed the volcano's south flank in 1853, insisting that the "smoking" crater was on the northeast side, but later climbing parties detected thermal anomalies and even hot springs on the upper south or southwest side. In an 1860 ascent, climbers reported looking down the north side to a "yawning crater" that was then as cold as the snow around it. By contrast, the McBride party of 1874 or 1875 reported seeing "a crater from which a light steam with hot and sulphurous gases constantly issued," but, unfortunately, did not give the crater's location. Except for that plugged by Goat Rocks, all historically active vents were subsequently buried under debris sliding from the upper cone or obscured by snow and ice. Their hidden presence, however, partly encircling the upper cone from the northwest to the northeast, may have played a significant role in the north flank's 1980 collapse.

Future Hazards

Erratic, volatile, and violent, St. Helens has a larger eruptive repertory than any other Cascade volcano. During the three eruptive periods of the last 500 years—the Kalama, Goat Rocks, and modern periods—it has produced large volumes of tephra, almost innumerable pyroclastic flows, pyroclastic surges, lateral blasts, an edifice collapse, and extensive mudflows, as well as many lava flows and domes. Although future activity will include most or all of these phenomena, the radical changes that the 1980 eruptions made in the volcano's height and shape will strongly influence the areas affected. With its deep crater open to the north, most pyroclastic flows and mudflows will be directed toward Johnston Ridge, Spirit Lake, and the North Fork Toutle River.

Magma forming the new lava dome that began to grow in St. Helens's crater in 2004 had a low gas content, permitting it to exit quietly through a new vent behind the dome built between 1980 and 1986. (See images 22 and 23 on plate 12.) Similar gas-poor magma may erect additional domes in the crater, but eventually silicic magma with a high gas content will invade

A steam plume rises from the growing dome in St. Helens's crater in the early 1980s. —Lyn Topinka photo, U.S. Geological Survey

the volcano's conduit. As USGS geologists Edward Wolfe and Thomas Pierson noted in their assessment of future hazards of St. Helens, the solidified domes will effectively block the path of any future body of rising gas-rich magma. Because it will take tremendous pressure to remove this blockage, a future St. Helens eruption is likely to be extremely explosive and, as Wolfe and Pierson suggest, "as large or larger than the eruption of May 18, 1980." When a fresh batch of gas-charged dacite forces it way to the surface, the explosions will probably shatter the domes and hurl ballistic fragments of angular rock 2 or 3 miles to the north, possibly also generating a pyroclastic surge that may surmount neighboring ridgetops and propelling a Plinian ash column 12 to 20 miles into the stratosphere.

Prevailing winds will again carry the ash plume eastward, shrouding a broad swath of eastern Washington, northern Idaho, and western Montana in talclike powder. Bringing daytime darkness over perhaps 40,000 square miles, another extensive tephra fall from St. Helens will interfere with interstate transportation on a large scale, perhaps stalling motor vehicles on the highways and jetliners unlucky enough to fly into the ash cloud. If tephra discharge is as large as it was in AD 1479 when layer Wn erupted, it may trigger a regional disaster.

Rapid melting of the crater glacier, producing perhaps 100 million gallons of water laden with large quantities of rock debris fallen from the crater walls, will probably trigger a voluminous mudflow directed down the North Fork to the lower Toutle River and, via the Cowlitz, into the Columbia. The sediment retention structure (SRS) that the U.S. Army Corps of Engineers constructed in 1989 on the North Fork Toutle to keep large quantities of sediment from flushing down the river, eventually filling its bed and causing it to overflow its banks, may not protect populated areas downvalley. Expected to reach its full capacity of retaining sediment by 2005, the 184-foot-high dam, located just upstream of the Green River confluence, will then be insufficient to trap a large mudflow. To compound the mudflow hazards in the Toutle drainage is the presence of Castle Lake, impounded behind the 1980 debris avalanche. Holding about 30 million cubic yards of water, Castle Lake's debris dam is particularly susceptible to failure, not only by overtopping but also by collapse. A large mudflow from the crater, strengthened by an outbreak from Castle Lake, would inundate large areas bordering both the Toutle and the Cowlitz Rivers, discharging sufficiently large quantities of sediment into the Columbia to close its channel to shipping.

Mudflows triggered by melting snow on the south and southeast flanks of the volcano are not expected to be larger than those of 1980, which dumped 18 million cubic yards of debris into Swift Reservoir, raising its level only 2.8 feet. As in 1980, the reservoir operators, Pacific Power and Light, will likely again take the precaution of lowering the lake sufficiently to contain incoming mudflows.

No matter how destructive St. Helens's next eruptions may be, the volcano will eventually rebuild its truncated cone, probably through a Kalama-style extrusion of lava flows and domes. At some time in the future, perhaps before the end of the twenty-first century, residents of the Pacific Northwest will again behold a mountain of legendary beauty, reminiscent of the peak that captivated the sons of the Great Spirit, Wy'east (Hood) and Pahto (Adams), in the Bridge of the Gods tradition. In the words of Lewis and Clark, who marveled at the volcano's classic symmetry during their 1806 return trip up the Columbia, St. Helens will again become "the most noble looking object of its kind in nature."

Visiting Mount St. Helens

From Interstate 5, turn east at exit 49 onto Washington 504 near the town of Castle Rock. Follow 504 eastward for 5 miles to the Mount St. Helens National Volcanic Monument Visitor Center (operated by Washington State Parks and Recreation), which offers displays of the area's geology, movies, slide shows, and a view of Silver Lake and Mount St. Helens, 30 miles distant. About 38 miles farther on 504, which follows the Toutle River valley, is the Coldwater Ridge Visitor Center, a smaller facility with good views of the hummocky surface of the 1980 debris avalanche. Another 9 miles leads to the Johnston Ridge Observatory (about 52 miles from Castle Rock), located only 5 miles north of St. Helens's crater.

To reach the Windy Ridge viewpoint from the north, turn east from Interstate 5 at exit 68 and follow U.S. 12 for about 49 miles to the town of Randle, where you turn right (south) onto Washington 131. After crossing the Cispus River about 9 miles from Randle, Washington 131 becomes Forest Service Road 25. About 21 miles from Randle, at the junction of Forest Service Road 25 with Forest Service Road 99, turn right on 99 and proceed for another 17 or 18 miles to the Windy Ridge overlook and spectacular vistas of Spirit Lake and the devastated area.

CHAPTER 18

Mount Rainier

AMERICA'S MOST DANGEROUS VOLCANO

Looming over the Seattle-Tacoma metropolitan area, home to more than 2.5 million people, Mount Rainier (14,411 feet) is not only the highest and best-known landform in the Pacific Northwest, it is also the most dangerous volcano in America. Built high astride intersecting ridges and canyons of Washington's central Cascades, Rainier supports the largest single-peak glacier system in the forty-eight adjacent states—the source of several major rivers emptying into Puget Sound, the inland sea at its western foot. During the last 7,500 years, river valleys heading on the mountain—including the Puyallup, Nisqually, and White River drainages—have funneled dozens of large floods and mudflows into the Puget Sound lowland. Other lahars have traveled down the Cowlitz River valley, which drains Rainier's south flank, and poured into the Columbia River, thus bringing another half million residents of southwest Washington and northwest Oregon into the volcano's destructive orbit. The houses, schools, and businesses of at least 150,000 people are built directly atop these recent mudflow deposits. (See image 27 on plate 15.)

Although Mount Rainier became the nation's fifth national park in 1899, and draws more than two million visitors to its forested slopes every year, until recently its geologic history was not well known. During the 1950s and 1960s scientists with the U.S. Geological Survey, such as Dwight Crandell and Donal Mullineaux, studied its Holocene deposits and assessed the volcanic hazards they represent. But it was only in the 1990s, after Rainier was designated a "decade volcano" by the International Association of Volcanology and Chemistry of the Earth's Interior (IAVCEI), that geologists began a detailed mapping of the mountain, identifying and dating the kinds of eruptions it has produced during the full 500,000 years of its existence. The IAVCEI selected Rainier for special investigation—the only volcano on the U.S. mainland so chosen—not only because it has erupted during historic time and still emits enough heat and steam from its overlapping summit craters to keep the crater rims permanently free of snow and ice, but also because it is certain to erupt again, potentially threatening millions of people.

At the end of a dry summer, only glaciers and permanent ice fields remain on Mount Rainier: The Tahoma glacier cascades from the summit down the volcano's west face. Above the Puyallup glacier (center) is Sunset Amphitheater, a huge scar left by a debris avalanche that generated the Round Pass mudflow about 2,600 years ago. —Austin Post photo, U.S. Geological Survey

The complexity of Rainier's life story, with its dramatic interplay between the powers of volcanic fire and glacial ice, is evident in its present craggy, irregular shape. Lacking the conical symmetry that characterized St. Helens before 1980, Rainier is almost unrecognizable as the same mountain when seen from different directions. Viewed from the park visitor center at Paradise, a mile high on the south flank, Rainier has the profile of a broad ice-covered dome with long ribs of dark rock contrasting with the surrounding white snowfields. High on its east shoulder, the reddish brown lavas composing Gibraltar Rock give the mountain a bulky, elongated look. (See image 24 on plate 13 and image 25 on plate 14.) Farther east, Little Tahoma Peak (11,117 feet) points a jagged triangle toward the sky. Seen

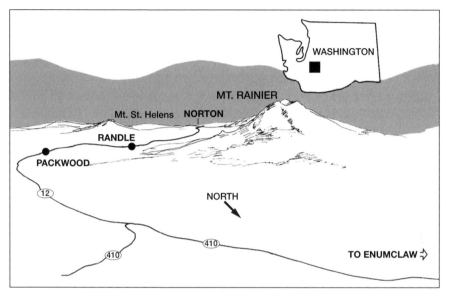

Relief map of the Mount Rainier area

from Olympia at the southern end of Puget Sound, Rainier more closely resembles a classic volcanic cone, albeit with irregular slopes and a wide truncated crest that boasts three separate peaks. From this southwestern vantage point, it fits geologist F. E. Matthes's comparison of the volcanic edifice to "an enormous tree stump with spreading base and broken top." (See image 26 on plate 14.)

From the north, Rainier most clearly shows the ravages of glacial erosion that has removed virtually every scrap of its original surface. The Carbon glacier has bitten deeply into the northwest flank of the cone, gouging out the largest natural amphitheater on any Cascade stratovolcano. Curtis Ridge on the east and Ptarmigan Ridge on the west partly enclose an enormous cirque with headwalls rising almost vertically 3,500 feet above the glacier's deck. The cirque's precipitous Willis Wall, heading the Carbon glacier, reveals scores of lava flows stacked up like pancakes, some more than 200,000 years old. Avalanches from the summit ice cap, 200 to 500 feet thick, frequently tumble down the Willis Wall to the glacier below, making ascents via this route particularly hazardous.

When viewed from the east, Mount Rainier reveals more of its geologic history than from any other perspective. The Sunrise Visitor Center on the grassy tableland of Yakima Park (elevation 6,400 feet) offers magnificent vistas of the Emmons glacier, which has the largest surface area of U.S. ice

streams south of Alaska. Descending 5 miles from the summit to the depths of
White River canyon 10,000 feet below, the lower section of the Emmons is
still mantled with rock debris that avalanched from the north side of Little Tahoma Peak in December 1963. Often mistaken for a secondary volcanic cone,
Little Tahoma is actually an erosional remnant of Rainier's once-continuous
eastern flank, now an irregular pyramid standing more than 2,500 feet above
the volcano's present surface, reminding us that Rainier has lost much of its
original mass to glacial cutting and other erosional processes.

Bordering the Emmons glacier on the north and separating it from the
Winthrop glacier, which also descends from the summit ice cap, is another
conspicuous erosional feature, a wedge-shaped protrusion known as Steamboat Prow (9,702 feet). Like Little Tahoma, Steamboat Prow is a remnant
of Rainier's former east flank, much of which was removed about 5,600
years ago during a catastrophic edifice collapse and debris avalanche similar
to that at Mount St. Helens in 1980. The east-side collapse generated an

*In this east-side view, Little Tahoma Peak rises above the Emmons glacier, with
wedge-shaped Steamboat Prow at the center right. The youthful summit cone stands
between Gibraltar Rock on the left and Russell Cliffs on the right.* —Austin Post
photo, U.S. Geological Survey

enormous lahar—the Osceola Mudflow—which traveled 65 miles down the White River valley to sweep over an area totaling 210 square miles, including 82 square miles of the Puget Sound lowland. Carrying away at least half a cubic mile of Rainier's former summit, the Osceola Mudflow incorporated an almost equal volume of additional debris as it spread down-valley and beyond the Cascade mountain front. Entering two different arms of Puget Sound (the Puyallup and Duwamish embayments), the Osceola also covered 60 square miles underwater, areas that are now dry land and densely populated. Approximately a cubic mile in total volume, the Osceola is one of the world's largest known mudflows and represents the single most cataclysmic event in Rainier's Holocene history.

Massive Russell Cliff, rising above the Winthrop glacier, marks the northern edge of the giant horseshoe-shaped basin formed when Rainier's former summit and east flank collapsed. Liberty Cap (14,112 feet), a sharp promontory along the narrow ridge that tops the Willis Wall, and Point Success (14,150 feet), a lava outcrop rising between the Tahoma and Kautz glaciers at the southwest corner of the broad summit area, represent the highest elevations of the post-Osceola crater rim.

Subsequent eruptions of lava and pyroclastic material have partly filled in the mile-wide Osceola collapse basin, erecting the present summit cone (14,411 feet), whose smooth, uneroded slopes contrast with the rugged contours of the rest of the mountain. Rainier erupted its youngest known lava flows, now concealed beneath the Emmons and Winthrop glaciers, about 2,200 to 2,600 years ago, when a series of lahars raced down the White, Nisqually, Puyallup, and Cowlitz River valleys. Additional summit eruptions occurred approximately 1,000 to 1,100 years ago, when mud-flows traveled as far as the site of Auburn, south of Seattle. About 500 years ago, renewed activity was probably responsible for triggering the Electron Mudflow, which buried the site of Orting and other parts of the Puyallup River valley. Although geologists have not yet identified an ash layer of this age, the occurrence of coeval lahars in the Nisqually Valley, Kautz Creek drainage, and both forks of the White River suggest some kind of volcano-wide disturbance at this time. The most recent magmatic activity, between about AD 1820 and 1854, apparently produced no significant lahars.

Although the present summit cone has long been recognized as the youngest part of Rainier's deeply eroded edifice, only recently did geologists map and date the many different lava sequences that compose other parts of the volcano. Such prominent erosional remnants as Gibraltar Rock, Little Tahoma Peak, Disappointment Cleaver, and Steamboat Prow turn out to be of widely differing ages; the lavas forming them erupted at different stages of Rainier's growth. Like Mount Adams, its bulky neighbor to the south, Rainier has undergone several discrete periods of cone building and cone erosion during its half-million-year history. As USGS geologist Tom Sisson points out, the volcano did not grow steadily or continuously until it reached a maximum height just before it was decapitated 5,600 years ago in the Osceola collapse. Instead, in two separate eruptive phases during the Pleistocene, Rainier had extended periods of high magma production, during which it emitted numerous lava flows in rapid succession and may have grown as large as or larger than it is today. After both of these phases of intense activity, the eruption rate then declined, allowing Pleistocene glaciers to eat into the cone and drastically lower its summit. (See image 28 on plate 16.)

For much of Rainier's history, thick sheets of ice immensely larger than the glaciers that mantle it today enveloped the volcano. During the penultimate Pleistocene glaciation, ice streams originating on Rainier extended scores of miles downvalley to merge with a tongue of the vast Cordilleran ice sheet that flowed south from Canada, smothering the Puget lowland. According to Crandell, in the most recent glacial advance, which ended about 10,000 to 12,000 years ago, a glacier 1,000 to 1,500 feet thick occupied each major valley adjoining the cone and extended 5 to 35 miles beyond the present park boundaries. As a result, even while Rainier was actively growing, it was simultaneously scoured by glaciers that burrowed deeply into the edifice, scraping away lava surfaces and leaving erosion-resistant cleavers—long free-standing ribs of lava rock—that functioned as dividers between ice streams. At the height of repeated glacial expansions, ice overrode even these projections.

When, after extensive dissection, the volcano entered a new phase of increased magma output, the cone either partially or completely reformed—only to suffer yet another period in which the forces of erosion again exceeded those of volcanic construction. Tom Sisson and David Lescinsky have shown that during glacial advances, Rainier's large lava flows typically moved along rocky divides between valley-filling glaciers. These ridge-capping lava flows are far better preserved than those that, between glaciations, poured onto valley floors, where subsequent glacier expansions largely obliterated them, an erosional process well documented at Mount Baker (see chapter 20). The Mount Rainier we see today is thus an assemblage of variously eroded lava flows and fragmental deposits of distinctly different ages, with rocks composing the upper north flank about 100,000 years older than those on the upper south side. Constructed during an earlier eruptive stage, the north flank, incised by the huge cirque heading the Carbon glacier, is correspondingly more eroded than most other parts of the volcano.

Portraying some of the tremendous changes that Mount Rainier has experienced during its long lifetime, the following section offers an imaginative

The Carbon glacier, largely covered with rock debris (center), bites deeply into Mount Rainier's north face and descends to the lowest altitude (about 3,200 feet) of any glacier in the forty-eight adjacent states. Winthrop glacier (left center) flows from the summit. Little Tahoma appears at the extreme left. The dark knobs at the right center are Echo and Observation Rocks, remnants of two ice-age peripheral vents. —Austin Post photo, U.S. Geological Survey

recreation of the volcano's birth a half million years ago and then surveys its complex evolution during later Pleistocene and Holocene time. The description of Rainier's early development draws on the work of Tom Sisson (who has recently mapped Rainier's eruptive products), Marvin Lanphere (who has dated the eruptive units), and Richard Fiske, Clifford Hopson, and Aaron Waters (who also examined its early history). The story of the last 10,000 years utilizes studies by Crandell, Mullineaux, Sisson, James Vallance, Kevin Scott, and other researchers with the USGS, as well as Pat Pringle of the Washington State Department of Natural Resources and Paul Zehfuss of the University of Washington. Vallance's recent analyses of thirty tephra layers and associated lahar deposits show that Rainier has had many more

Holocene eruptions than previously supposed. Freely interpreting these geologists' field research, we can embark on a journey back through time to
visit Mount Rainier from its inception in the remote past to the formation
of its last catastrophic lahar—the Electron Mudflow—about AD 1502.

Ancestral Mount Rainier

Like Mounts Hood, Adams, and Shasta, Rainier sits atop an older andesite
volcano. About 1.3 million years ago, a large ancestral cone formed on a rugged terrain composed of ancient Tertiary igneous and metamorphic rocks—
the Ohanapecosh, Stevens Ridge, Fifes Peak, and Tatoosh formations—on
which Rainier would later stand. The Tatoosh pluton, a large body of granitic magma that had intruded the crust tens of millions of years earlier,
had by this time already been uplifted several thousand feet and exposed
by glacial cutting. A classic roof pendant—a mass of older volcanic rock
that "roofs" or overlies a younger granitic intrusion—the Tatoosh Range,
glacier-carved into picturesque horns and crags, would form a barrier to
Rainier's southward-flowing lavas.

Although its dimensions are unknown, the ancestral volcano built a cone
large enough to affect the area's drainage patterns: The Carbon, White, Puyallup, and Mowich Rivers had already excavated canyons extending north,
northeast, and west to the Puget Sound basin. From twenty-first century
studies of the ancestral volcano's deposits in the Puget lowland—the Lily
Creek, Alderton, and Puyallup formations—we know that it repeatedly
produced extensive mudflows that traveled many tens of miles downvalley.
Rich in pumice fragments, these lahar deposits show that Rainier's ancestor
was frequently explosive, ejecting large quantities of pyroclastic material. It
also emitted lava flows, although only one flow remnant, at Panhandle Gap
near Rainier's east base, is clearly exposed today.

The Birth of Mount Rainier

If a time machine were to transport us to the site of Rainier's predecessor
just prior to the birth of modern Mount Rainier about 500,000 years ago,
we would find that Pleistocene glaciers have largely demolished the ancestral volcano, which lies smothered under ice thousands of feet thick. Vast
glaciers fill valleys wall-to-wall, extending far downvalley toward the Puget
lowland. Glacial scouring has increased the region's high relief, deepening
the canyons so that valley floors lie up to 4,000 feet below adjacent ridge
crests.

The first warning that a new volcano is about to appear comes in a
swarm of earthquakes centered on the ice-covered west flank of the ancestral

volcano. After a week of almost continuous temblors, a deep melt depression more than a half mile wide indents the ice surface. As the glacier deck fractures and subsides, we hear the sound of rushing water above the relentlessly howling wind. While incandescent magma oozes beneath the glacier, large meltwater streams snake through the porous ice, eroding long subglacial tunnels.

Only two days after its birth, Mount Rainier blasts its way through the ice. Vulcanian explosions hurl blocks of water-chilled lava thousands of feet into the air. Many land as far as 3 miles from the new vent. An eruption plume 20,000 feet high rains dark ash in a narrow band across the snowy mountainscape. Rapidly expelling a huge volume of magma, the new volcano quickly rises above the encircling ice. When glacial meltwater can no longer invade its vent, explosions sputter out and thick streams of blocky andesite lava pour quietly from the crater. Wherever glowing lava encounters ice or meltwater, columns of steam rise along flow margins. Heat radiating from these prodigious early lava flows soon enlarges the hole in the surrounding ice field to several miles in diameter, creating a catastrophic jokulhlaup—the first of many glacier outburst floods that Rainier will trigger during its long lifetime.

After flowing through subglacial caverns, the meltwater flood explodes though the glacier, carrying lava blocks and icebergs the size of houses, some weighing up to 1,000 tons, many miles downvalley. Like historic subglacial eruptions observed in Iceland, that of Mount Rainier wreaks havoc on the landscape. Rainier's early jokulhlaups discharge a peak of perhaps 50,000 to 60,000 cubic yards of meltwater per second, several times more than the twenty-first-century discharge of the Amazon, the world's largest river.

Pouring out one large lava flow after another, Rainier grows rapidly. Within a few millennia, it stands more than 10,000 feet above sea level. Because of its high elevation and its inception during a Pleistocene ice advance, Rainier's cone hosts glaciers almost from the beginning. During a temporary pause in magma production, expanding glaciers embrace the entire edifice, hollowing out cirques and deep trenches. Like that of its deeply dissected ancestor, Rainier's cone, so newly built, seems doomed to piecemeal destruction. Only thin wisps of vapor drifting lazily from the summit crater hint that the volcano merely dozes.

Glaciers Shape the Mountain

When Rainier suddenly awakens (about 496,000 years ago), the effects are cataclysmic. Explosions tear through the solidified plug in the volcano's conduit and propel fragments of old rock, mixed with fresh scoria and ash, thousands of feet into the air. When blocks of incandescent lava fall on ice

In its youth, Mount Rainier grew rapidly, disgorging voluminous flows of andesite and dacite lava. When large glaciers sheathed the volcano, flows were directed along high ridges dividing ice streams; between glaciations, flows poured onto valley floors, where subsequent glacial and stream cutting largely erased them.

sheathing the cone, the avalanching hot rock generates large pyroclastic flows that sweep down the volcano's flanks. Piling up in large aprons at the base of the cone, some of these block-and-ash flows construct the feature later known as Steamboat Prow, the large wedge on Rainier's east side. Abruptly changing from an explosive to an effusive mode, the volcano next emits an enormous andesite lava flow from a vent on the northeast side. About 1,200 feet thick and more than 6 miles long, the flow composing Burroughs Mountain approaches a cubic mile in volume.

Having witnessed Rainier's birth, phenomenally rapid growth to a height of well over 10,000 feet, and the emplacement of the Burroughs Mountain lava flow, we can now appreciate the key role glacial ice has played in shaping the volcano's present contours. The Burroughs Mountain flow is the oldest of at least twenty-three similarly massive lava flows that now form an array of long, steep-sided ridges radiating away from Rainier's main cone like the spokes on a wheel. Because these ridge-capping lava flows have exceptional thickness (up to 2,000 feet), length (extending as far as 15 miles from the summit), and volume (as much as 2 cubic miles), some mid-twentieth-century geologists concluded that they must have poured into deep canyons, where the lava accumulated to great depth. Following their emplacement, geologists believed, streams displaced by the canyon-filling flows subsequently cut along the flow margins, excavating new valleys on each side of the flow and leaving it as a free-standing ridge, a process known as reversal of topography. Although investigators in the 1960s recognized that these ridge-forming flows show numerous signs of ice contact—glassy columnar structures along their fronts and margins that indicate quick chilling by ice or meltwater—only recently did geologists realize that the flows did not form on valley floors. In the late 1990s, Tom Sisson and Marvin Lanphere of the USGS and David Lescinsky of the University of Western Ontario demonstrated that most of Rainier's largest lava flows occurred when Pleistocene glaciers not only overwhelmed valleys adjacent to the cone but also commonly overtopped neighboring ridges.

Because active glaciers are convex, bulging upward in the middle, lava flows issuing from Rainier's flank vents were deflected toward the glaciers' margins, where the advancing lava either melted channels alongside the glacier or flowed along bordering ridge crests where the ice was much thinner. Contemporary observations of lava flows encountering glaciers in Alaska, Iceland, and elsewhere show that a massive wall of ice makes an effective barrier and determines the flow's direction. Lava moving alongside a glacier quickly chills, forming a congealed crust, but as the eruption progresses and large volumes of magma continue to pour through the flow's interior, the flow inflates, the brittle shell at the flow's front ruptures, allowing tongues of molten rock to spill out, and the flow moves forward into a glacier-bordering channel it has melted out. (See "Inflating Lava and Lava Tube Caves" on page 116.)

After Rainier's most recent ice-age glaciers shriveled and retreated upvalley, flows that had traveled down meltwater channels alongside glaciers were left perched high on the valley walls. By contrast, those that had moved down rocky divides between glaciers remained as the steep-sided lava cliffs that now cap ridges radiating from the mountain. The intermittent presence of ice during the two periods of Rainier's most intense cone building—between about 500,000 and 420,000 years ago and again between about 280,000 and 180,000 years ago—actively shaped the volcano's present configuration, an eroded central cone flanked by hydralike arms, some 12 to 15 miles long, of ridge-capping lava flows. Not only did Pleistocene glaciers work unrelentingly to reduce the growing volcano in height and bulk, their presence also served to "deepen" glacial canyons as thick lava flows accumulated along the tops of canyon walls.

Although shrouded in glacial ice, during extended periods of high magma production Mount Rainier erected a cone that towered perhaps 16,000 feet above the Puget lowland.

Although 90 percent of Rainier's modern cone consists of lava flows, pyroclastic flows were also common throughout the volcano's history. Some occurred explosively as large volumes of ash and fragmental rock ejected out of the crater; others resulted from disintegrating lava flows as they plunged over high cliffs or skidded off steep icy slopes. Clouds of lithic ash kicked up by avalanching lava blocks repeatedly blanketed areas downwind. (Such processes also deposited many of the thirty lithic ash layers Rainier laid down during the last few thousand years.)

For the next 80,000 years following the Burroughs Mountain episode, Mount Rainier continued its prodigious magma output. Giant flows of this stage included those forming the Grand Park and Old Desolate–Marjorie Lake ridges on the north flank. Extending farther to the north than any other Rainier lava stream, the Grand Park flow was later severed from the mountain by glacial and stream erosion. The White River's west fork has cut a gorge almost perpendicular to the flow's north-northeast axis. Erosion has also isolated the Old Desolate flow from its source. To the west-northwest, other exceptionally large-volume flows traveled well beyond the present national park boundaries. Forming a broad lava apron on the west flank, these colossal flows built the conspicuous ridge between the North and

South Mowich glaciers, the long unnamed ridge between the South Mo-wich River and Rushingwater Creek, and the broad mass of the Colonnade that borders the North Puyallup River. As Sisson notes, all of these flows emitted during Rainier's first eruptive stage show evidence of interaction with ice. Like the Burroughs Mountain flow, they extended along topo-graphical highs between glacier-choked canyons.

Fluctuating Production of Magma

Time travelers visiting Rainier between about 400,000 and 280,000 years ago would observe a declining rate of magma production, although the volcano occasionally erupted a few lava flows with volumes rivaling those of its early youth. One of these large flows constructed Rampart Ridge, which extends for several miles down the southwest flank along the north side of the Nisqually River valley. Today's visitors driving through the park's south entrance toward the Paradise Visitor Center can easily observe this flow—a long, heavily forested ridge bordering the flowering meadows and hot springs at Longmire (2,761 feet), where the park headquarters is located. Other large flows underlie Cushman Crest and the ridge below Wilson gla-cier on the south side, the latter dated at about 370,000 years.

If we dropped by shortly before 280,000 years ago, near the close of Mount Rainier's second eruptive stage, with its generally small-volume eruptions separated by long dormant intervals, we could witness an ex-tremely rare event in the volcano's lifetime—a violently explosive outburst comparable to those that Mount St. Helens frequently produces. Ejecting a towering cloud of tephra-laden gas, Rainier rained pumiceous ash over a wide area to the northeast. Falling at least 6 to 7 feet thick on Sourdough Mountain, immediately north of the present Sunrise Visitor Center, the pumice deposit represents one of the two largest pyroclastic eruptions in the volcano's entire history. Almost all of Rainier's other pyroclastic depos-its consist of block-and-ash flows, commonly derived from shattered lava flows.

About 280,000 years ago, Rainier entered its third major phase with a significant upsurge in magma output. Again it produced exceptionally large lava flows on both the east and west flanks of the cone, including those that form Sunset Park, Klapatche Ridge, St. Andrews Park, Mount Ruth, Meany Crest, Cowlitz Park, and Whitman Crest. These voluminous flows were fed by numerous radial dikes, tabular sheets of magma that intruded the cone, subjecting the surrounding rock to intense hydrothermal alteration. Over long periods, hot water bearing acidic solutions converted formerly solid rock to soft, claylike substances. Most of this decomposed rock on the east flank was removed during the Osceola Mudflow. The largest remaining area of weakened rock, a yellowish orange mass, is exposed on Rainier's west face at Sunset Amphitheater. During Holocene time, several clay-rich avalanches of altered rock have originated in this vicinity, the latest only 500 years ago.

Hundreds of small to medium-sized lava flows, with thickness averaging from 15 to 60 feet, built much of Rainier's upper cone. These flows appear on the north and northwest portions of the edifice, forming the Mowich Face at the northwest summit and the stack of lavas rising to Liberty Cap. Some of the lava flows composing the upper cone thickened significantly as they moved downslope, forming aprons as much as 200 feet thick. During this cycle of frequent eruptions, Rainier's cone was again encased in glacial ice, and glaciers filling adjacent valleys again deflected larger lava flows along divides between the ice streams.

Aerial view of Mount Rainier's young summit cone and craters, the rims of which are kept largely snow free by heat and steam emission. The north summit, Liberty Cap, appears on the right, above Russell Cliff. Steamboat Prow appears at the bottom, dividing the lower Emmons and Winthrop glaciers. —Austin Post photo, U.S. Geological Survey

This phase of elevated magma production culminated about 194,000 years ago in a second major explosive eruption that ejected large volumes of tephra, including that forming a conspicuous band of light-colored pumice, 75 to 100 feet thick, now exposed high in the walls of Sunset Amphitheater, the large west-facing cirque in which the South Mowich and Puyallup glaciers now originate. This pumice fall is also preserved on the upper margins of Burroughs Mountain and on Goat Island Mountain, indicating that the upper surfaces of these lava ridges have not been glaciated for about 200,000 years. Another pumice exposure occurs along the road to the Sunrise Visitor Center, where a covering of rock talus protected it.

Rather than ending abruptly, Rainier's second extended pulse of cone building tapered off gradually. The pile of lava flows forming Little Tahoma Peak is undergirded by a large flow dated at about 195,000 years; flows exposed at midaltitudes are about 150,000 years old, and those near the top are 20,000 years younger. Tom Sisson suggests that the dikes cutting through this prominent stack of lava flows fed eruptions that built an oblong-shaped protrusion on Rainier's east flank, accounting for Little Tahoma's position to the east of the main cone. Although volcanism slowly declined between about 190,000 and 130,000 years ago, some eruptions produced copious amounts of lava: a vent on the north-northwest side erupted the massive flow composing Ptarmigan Ridge, while a vent slightly to the northeast emitted the flow underlying Curtis Ridge, a broad feature separating the Winthrop from the Carbon glaciers. At about the same time, a west-side vent produced the large lava stream forming Emerald Ridge, the eroded apex of which now divides the terminus of the Tahoma glacier into two distinct lobes.

Although Mount Rainier sporadically has continued to erupt cone-building lava flows during the last 120,000 years, the quantities of magma erupted have typically been less than they were during earlier stages of maximum lava output. An outstanding exception, however, is the voluminous eruption of about 90,000 years ago, a two-part event that closely resembled the Burroughs Mountain sequence. Initial explosive activity at the summit first ejected enough pyroclastic material to generate a voluminous block-and-ash flow that swept down the volcano's southwest flank, where it filled the upper reaches of Kautz Creek valley. Hot enough to weld, this pyroclastic flow deposit is still visible at Pearl Falls and below Mildred Point; the columnar features in Basalt Cliffs formed as this welded deposit cooled.

Switching to an effusive mode in the second part of the sequence, Rainier then disgorged a huge lava flow that streamed down the south flank into Stevens Canyon. Emerging from a vent high on the cone, this dacite flow poured down the crest of Mazama Ridge, bounded on both its east and west margins by walls of glacial ice that filled the adjacent valleys. When the lava

Mount Rainier from the east. From left to right the prominent features are Little Ta-homa Peak; Gibraltar Rock; the Emmons glacier; the inverted V of Steamboat Prow separating the Emmons from the Winthrop glacier; and Russell Cliff above the Win-throp glacier. The road (foreground) leads to Yakima Park and Sunrise Visitor Center.
—Courtesy of the Washington State Department of Commerce and Economic Development

front banked against the Tatoosh Range at Rainier's south foot, the flow was diverted to the east and traveled along the edge of the ancestral Paradise glacier, which then occupied Stevens Canyon. Temporarily dammed when it encountered a tributary glacier filling the valley of Union Creek, the flow thickened considerably, rising high enough on the south wall of Stevens Canyon to form a conspicuous terrace called the Bench, which now stands 500 feet above the present canyon floor.

Melting its way through the Union Creek ice dam, the dacite stream continued to flow downslope along the margin of the ancestral Paradise glacier until it reached a second ice dam formed by another tributary glacier, that filling the Maple Creek valley, where it again ponded to form a second lava bench. (The lava flow slowed to a temporary halt wherever the ice was thickest, at points where tributary ice streams added their mass to the Paradise glacier.) After burning through the Maple Creek ice barrier, the flow continued to advance by melting a channel on the lower canyon floor alongside the glacier's southern edge. Unmistakable signs of the Mazama Ridge–Stevens Canyon flow's contact with the long-vanished glacier are abundant along the clifflike northern side of the flow, where glassy columns, roughly perpendicular to the flow's near-vertical edge, betray a rapid chilling when the solidifying lava crust pressed against glacial ice. Much of this voluminous flow, from its terraces perched high on valley walls to its lower reaches on the valley floor, is clearly displayed along the road through Stevens Canyon.

North- and South-Flank Eruptions

On the north flank of the mountain, eruptions of fluid basaltic andesite about 100,000 years ago built two peripheral cones, the dissected remains of which form Echo Rock and Observation Rock, at the head of Spray Park. These north-side vents flooded the valleys and depressions at Rainier's northern foot to maximum depths of 500 feet, but Old Desolate, the lava ridge erupted 400,000 years earlier, blocked their lavas on the northeast. At least two Pleistocene glacial advances occurred after these north-side lavas were emplaced, incising a large cirque into the flow deposits and severing several of them from their source vent. The head of the Carbon glacier has since cut through the Echo Rock flows and deeply into the older Rainier lava beneath them, leaving isolated benches of basaltic andesite clinging to the sides of Old Desolate.

Most of the lava flows dated between about 40,000 years ago and the Osceola collapse (5,600 years ago) occur on the volcano's upper south side, suggesting that these late Pleistocene lavas may have filled a south-facing collapse depression that formed about 40,000 years ago. Volume estimates for the south flank lavas indicate an average rate of magma extrusion for this period at about 0.1 cubic mile per 1,000 years. A few individual flows, however, were sizable—including the large ridge-capping flow that terminates at Ricksecker Point, overlooking the confluence of the Nisqually and Paradise Rivers. Erupted early in the penultimate Pleistocene glacial advance, when Rainier was again sheathed in ice and a glacier descending the Cowlitz Valley eventually reached 65 miles beyond the volcano's summit, the Ricksecker flow, like most of its predecessors, was confined by walls of ice. Good exposures showing lava-ice contact occur at Narada Falls, which spills spectacularly over lava cliffs a short distance below the Paradise Visitor Center. Overlying the Ricksecker flow is one of similar age that floors the Muir snowfield and extends from above Panorama Point to Camp Muir, at an altitude of 10,000 feet. High-elevation younger flows on the upper south side include those underlying Camp Muir, Point Success, Success Cleaver, and Gibraltar Rock, as well as the flows composing Tahoma Cleaver on the southwest flank. Some 20,000- to 30,000-year-old flows are partially visible beneath the terminuses of south-side glaciers, such as the flow forming a bench west of Cushman Crest on the way to Comet Falls. The age of younger small flows, now mostly concealed beneath ice and snow, is unknown. Any lava flows erupted during the latest Pleistocene and early Holocene that traveled to the northeast were probably swept away in the Osceola collapse 5,600 years ago, although remnants may be hidden under the Emmons and Winthrop glaciers.

The Holocene

Mount Rainier emerged from the most recent Pleistocene glaciation battered but unbowed. Ice had scraped away its original constructional surface, planing away the sides and rubbly surfaces of even its youngest lava flows, but the volcano's summit still rose to an altitude of more than 15,000 feet. On the east flank, Little Tahoma Peak and Steamboat Prow were then significantly larger features than at present, broader in their north-south diameters and extending much higher up the mountain. Between these prominent remnants, a series of rocky cleavers protruded through the surface of the ancestral Emmons glacier, some of which consisted of eroded

Repeated glaciations reduced Mount Rainier's cone to an irregular mass of steep cliffs, cirques, and ridges. Seen from the east, as they may have appeared about 10,000 to 12,000 years ago, are the incipient Little Tahoma, Steamboat Prow, and Russell Cliff.

dikes (similar to the Puyallup Cleaver on the west flank), whereas others represented the upper parts of ancient lava flows that connected with the ridge-capping flows radiating from the eastern base of the cone.

Rainier's earliest known Holocene activity was mildly explosive, depositing a thin, poorly preserved layer of reddish brown tephra (layer R) that extends in a broad arc east of the summit. It was the violent outburst of a volcano 275 miles to the south, however, that laid down the most widespread Holocene tephra at the site of Mount Rainier National Park. Southwesterly winds of 7,700 years ago wafted the Plinian ash plume from Mount Mazama's caldera-forming eruption in southern Oregon over the entire Pacific Northwest and well beyond the Canadian boundary. Two inches thick in the park, this tephra (layer O) is easily recognized by its distinctive yellowish orange color and fine, flourlike substance. The two other most voluminous tephras found in Rainier's vicinity (layers Yn and Wn) came from a closer Cascade neighbor—Mount St. Helens.

HOLOCENE ERUPTIVE PERIODS AT MOUNT RAINIER

DATE OR APPROXIMATE AGE (YEARS)	ERUPTIVE PERIOD	TEPHRA LAYERS AND/OR PYROCLASTIC FLOWS	LARGE LAHARS
AD 1820–1854	Historic	X pumice	——
AD 1500	——	——	Electron
1,100–1,000	——	Two nameless pyroclastic flows	White River; Deadman Flat; nameless
2,600–1,600	Summerland	Layer C (bombs, pumice); twelve layers of lithic ash; block-and-ash flow	Round Pass; South Puyallup; National; multiple nameless
4,400–2,600	Apparently dormant		
5,600–4,400	Osceola	Layers B, H, F, S; two pyroclastic flows; White River	Osceola; Paradise; Buck Creek (multiple)
6,800–5,600	Dormant(?)		
7,500–6,800	Cowlitz Park	Layers N, D, L, A	Multiple nameless
9,800	——	Layer R	Nameless (poor preservation)

Source: Adapted from D. R. Mullineaux, "Pumice and Other Pyroclastic Deposits in Mount Rainier National Park, Washington" (*U.S. Geological Survey Bulletin* 1326, 1974); Crandell (1971); and J. W. Vallance et al., "Late Holocene Eruptions at Mount Rainier, Washington" (*Eos, Transactions, American Geophysical Union* 82, no. 47, fall meeting supplement, abstract V42C-1043, 2001)

In addition to pioneering studies by Crandell, who identified most of Rainier's Holocene lahars, and Mullineaux, who mapped its comparatively rare deposits of pumiceous tephra, much of our knowledge about the volcano's behavior during the last 10,000 years comes from recent fieldwork by James Vallance and his associates, Sue Donoghue and Jack McGeehin, as well as from the work of Patrick Pringle and Paul Zehfuss on lahars and buried forests. In examining more than thirty thin layers of lithic tephra, Vallance and his colleagues discovered that the volcano has been much more active during Holocene time than previously recognized. Temporally clustered in eruptive periods or episodes, these tephra layers typically contain lithic fragments, with many also containing glass shards and pumice particles that indicate their magmatic origin. Derived from ash billowing off pyroclastic flows, from small explosions during lava extrusion, and from discrete explosive events, these ash deposits are important despite their small volume.

WHAT DID RAINIER LOOK LIKE
BEFORE THE OSCEOLA COLLAPSE?

Although Rainier's pre-Osceola summit stood hundreds of feet higher than California's Mount Whitney (14,495 feet), now the loftiest peak in the forty-eight adjacent states, the volcano was distinctly asymmetrical. Because different parts of the edifice formed during discrete eruptive stages—the north flank is much older than the south—it is not possible simply to project upward the angle of dip of lava flows on all sides of the cone to their presumed source in a summit crater. As James Vallance has noted, the late Pleistocene extrusions of lava flows composing the south side did not erect a cone large enough for the lavas to spill northward over Liberty Cap and the Willis Wall, suggesting that the volcano's former summit rose no more than about 500 to 1,500 feet above its present elevation.

The high clay content in both the Osceola and Paradise mudflows of 5,600 years ago, as well as in an earlier lahar that traveled down Rainier's south flank during the Cowlitz eruptive episode, shows that Rainier's former summit had an active thermal system that produced large quantities of altered rock. When volcanically heated water and acidic gases in solution percolated through the summit lavas over a long period, the once-solid rock transformed to a soft, crumbly substance susceptible to failure and collapse. The Osceola event removed most of the altered material on Rainier's east flank, but large volumes of clayey, unstable rock remain on the volcano's west face, particularly in the vicinity of Sunset Amphitheater, where several subsequent lahars, including the Round Pass mudflow, originated. Geologists expect this area to produce more large-scale avalanches and mudflows in the future.

As Vallance observes, many of the tephras are associated with major lahars that swept tens of miles from the mountain, devastating valley floors now occupied by thousands of people. Vallance's recent research offers a fresh perspective on Rainier's Holocene behavior.

The Cowlitz Park Period

If we visited the mountain about two centuries after the Mazama ash fall, we would find that Mount Rainier also staged intermittent explosive eruptions, albeit on a more modest scale. By carefully timing our arrival during the Cowlitz Park eruptive period (between about 7,500 and 6,800 years ago), we could witness Rainier repeatedly eject ash plumes thousands of feet above its icy summit, triggering pyroclastic flows, numerous lahars, and at least one south-slope avalanche of hydrothermally altered rock that buried the site of Reflection Lakes near Mazama Ridge. During this moderately explosive sequence, the volcano erupted both pumiceous and lithic tephra, producing layers A, L, and D, as well as several smaller ash falls. The final pumiceous tephra (layer N) of the Cowlitz Park period, erupted about 6,800 years ago, was deposited between thin layers of lithic ash, probably derived from ash clouds rising above block-and-ash flows. This episode also generated sizable lahars that poured many tens of miles downvalley.

The Osceola Period: The Destruction of Rainier's Summit

Rainier's next eruptive period—the Osceola—was unquestionably the most cataclysmic since the end of the ice age (10,000 years ago), radically altering the volcano's shape and devastating large areas far from the mountain. Geologists, including Crandell, Mullineaux, Vallance, and Pringle, have carefully analyzed deposits from this period, enabling us to visualize the sequence of events that led, perhaps in a matter of hours or minutes, to the destruction of the volcano's summit and northeast side.

Following a long dormant interval, about 5,600 years ago magma again rose into the volcano's central conduit, causing the edifice to swell and generating phreatic explosions in the summit crater. Clouds of ash mushroomed above the peak, showering it with rock fragments torn from the volcano's throat. As magma-induced deformation increased and earthquakes repeatedly shook the cone, Rainier's summit, riddled with weak, hydrothermally decayed and water-saturated rock, suddenly began to crumble and slide to the northeast in a series of debris avalanches that cut progressively deeper into the cone. The first landslide block, composed of both solid and altered rock veneering the east flank, crashed into the upper White River valley, filling it with hummocky debris containing huge blocks of andesite lava.

After the collapse of Mount Rainier's former summit about 5,600 years ago, which triggered the Osceola Mudflow, a huge, horseshoe-shaped crater similar to that formed at Mount St. Helens in 1980 occupied the northeast flank.

(This avalanche component was previously thought to be a slightly older lahar, the Greenwater mudflow, but is now recognized as the initial part of the Osceola Mudflow.) A more fluid wave of extensively altered rock from Rainier's interior instantly followed. At the same time, a laterally directed blast from the crater spewed ash and angular rock fragments to the east, peppering adjacent ridgetops with ballistic projectiles. Lying more than 6 feet thick atop Goat Mountain a few miles east of the crater, this deposit of shattered rock (layer S) is also found on the ridge between Dege Peak and Sunrise, where it overlies layer D and the Mazama ash.

Hundreds of feet thick, the avalanche had already transformed into a mudflow by the time it swept over Steamboat Prow, momentarily submerging the structure. One massive wave rolled down the ancestral Emmons glacier, carrying away the entire flank between the Prow and Disappointment Cleaver before flooding the White River valley; another arm, removing the flank between the Prow and Russell Cliff, sped northward over the Winthrop glacier and down the west fork of the White River. Converging beyond the base of the mountain, the mudflow temporarily rode up to 500 feet high on canyon walls before exiting the Cascade Range front to spread out over the Puget lowland and into Puget Sound. As the mudflow traveled downslope, it rapidly increased in volume, incorporating glacial till, stream gravel, and other debris, as well as countless thousands of uprooted trees. After burying the future town sites of Buckley, Enumclaw, and Osceola under a broad expanse of rock and sediment, the Osceola Mudflow followed the valley of South Prairie Creek southwestward to join the Puyallup River valley at Orting, through which it flowed into an arm of Puget Sound (the Puyallup embayment), inundating the sites of Sumner, Puyallup, and Tacoma. The mudflow also continued northwestward to the Green River drainage, entering another arm of the Sound (the Duwamish embayment) near the site of Auburn. Within hours, rocks that had previously stood more than 15,000 feet above sea level lay under the waters of Puget Sound.

Over time, runoff from the mudflow deposits, which had transformed the lowland's previously uneven terrain into a wide, level plain, filled in several miles of both the Puyallup and Duwamish inlets. This sediment built the valley floors on which Auburn, Kent, Puyallup, and much of Tacoma now stand. Cores from wells dug at various locations near these towns reveal that sediment from the Osceola covers at least 60 square miles of former waterways of Puget Sound, although the runoff deposits occur far below the present ground surface.

As the Osceola Mudflow streamed to the northeast, summit rock avalanching down Rainier's south slope created the Paradise lahar. Sweeping across Paradise Park, this lahar temporarily surged as high as 800 feet on the walls of the Paradise River valley. After burying the site of Longmire, where it was still several hundred feet thick, the lahar traveled downvalley at least as far as the present hamlet of National, 12 miles farther to the west. Originating in partly altered rock that formerly stood between and above Point Success and Gibraltar Rock, the Paradise lahar probably removed considerable material from around Gibraltar Rock, aiding the work of glaciers that had already cut deeply into both sides of this prominent outlier.

While the Osceola Mudflow was still moving, explosive activity at Rainier's now-truncated summit laid down a sequence of three tephra deposits (layer F) that offers clues about the nature of the eruption. The first layer, F1, consists of lithic ash and clay minerals, with only minor amounts of fresh pumice. Phreatic blasts propelled the F1 ejecta almost horizontally, depositing it in a narrow lobe to the northeast following the same axis as the mudflow. The second tephra, Fm, is composed largely of juvenile pumice and lithic ash, laid down in a broad arc east and southeast of the volcano. The third tephra, Fu, represents a return to phreatic explosions and, like the first, has an abundance of clay minerals and old rock, as well as some pumice. Apparently, the initial outburst blew out primarily old rock from Rainier's suddenly exposed core, then progressed to an eruption of juvenile magma, and finally returned to a mixture of both steam-blast and magmatic activity.

To Native Americans camped near the site of Enumclaw, their position 25 miles northwest of Mount Rainier—which was 45 miles via the twisting

A heavily glaciated young summit cone now occupies the large collapse basin created by the Osceola Mudflow 5,600 years ago. Remnants of the post-Osceola crater rim include Point Success (left) and Liberty Cap (top center). —Austin Post photo, U.S. Geological Survey

White River valley—must have seemed secure. From a high terrace about 150 feet above the valley floor, they could see a gigantic eruption plume rising above the mountainous horizon, but winds carried the ash eastward, leaving skies above them deceptively clear.

But when their lookouts first noticed what was advancing toward them, they must have dropped their stone implements in terror. Rushing across the lowland toward their camp was a wall of rock, mud, and trees that was more than 200 feet high. The Indians ran toward a neighboring ridge, but the Osceola Mudflow bore down on them at speeds of 25 to 40 miles an hour, overwhelming them and their settlement. Charcoal from their camp-fires would later help twentieth-century anthropologists date the projectile points and other stone tools buried at the site.

After the Osceola disaster, Mount Rainier assumed a completely different appearance. Drastically reduced in height, the volcano's summit now housed a vast semicircular amphitheater, about 1.1 miles in diameter. Open to the northeast, this horseshoe-shaped depression probably extended to about the 12,000-foot level. The western part of the summit stood considerably higher, however, with a generally intact crater rim extending northward from Point Success (14,150 feet) toward Mowich Face on the northwest, a feature that the Round Pass mudflow would remove about 3,000 years later.

Shortly after the summit collapse, renewed explosive activity ejected small quantities of tephra (layers H and B), which may have accompanied effusions of lava that began to fill in the east-facing summit depression. Eruptions continued intermittently for about the next 1,200 years, when the Osceola period ended.

The Summerland Eruptive Period

One of Rainier's most intense Holocene eruptive periods—the Summerland —began about 2,600 years ago with another major collapse of the volcanic edifice, generating the Round Pass mudflow. Originating in the hydrothermally altered mass of unstable rock that forms the headwalls of Sunset Amphitheater, the Round Pass mudflow—the second largest in Rainier's Holocene history—rushed down the volcano's western face in a wave 1,000 feet high. While one branch of the mudflow overtopped the divide between the South Puyallup River valley and Tahoma Creek, traveling a few miles downstream, the main part of the mudflow poured a much longer distance down the Puyallup River drainage. The Round Pass mudflow, like many others that followed it from the same source area of weak, altered rock, extensively deepened the cirque at Sunset Amphitheater, into which the heads of the South Mowich and Puyallup glaciers continue to gnaw relentlessly. The avalanches triggering this mudflow also probably removed the western rim of the post-Osceola summit crater, opening a breach through which the icefalls of the Tahoma glacier now descend.

Numerous mid- to late Holocene lava flows and pyroclastic flows built the symmetrical summit cone that now rises between Gibraltar Rock (left) and Russell Cliffs (right). The most recent block-and-ash flows probably erupted about 1,000 to 1,100 years ago.

It is uncertain if an earthquake, the rise of magma into the cone, or the simple pull of gravity on water-saturated, rotten rock that had been undermined by glacial cutting triggered the Round Pass mudflow, but a magmatic eruption depositing lithic ash occurred at about the same time or shortly afterward. By about 2,400 to 2,500 years ago, eruptions of lava and pyroclastics had built the growing summit cone high enough for its ejecta to surmount the breached western rim of the post-Osceola crater, sending a massive block-and-ash flow into the upper valley of the South Puyallup River, about 7.5 miles west of the summit. Containing numerous bread-crust bombs, as well as angular chunks of fresh lava, this pyroclastic flow was extremely hot—well over 600 degrees Fahrenheit—even after it came to rest, and it generated a lahar that swept many miles downstream. Pringle and Vallance found that runout from this pyroclastic flow assemblage underlies Orting and continues downvalley at least as far as the Puyallup fairgrounds, which are located above a thick deposit of volcanic sand from Mount Rainier. Good exposures of the bomb-bearing block-and-ash flow occur on the (frequently closed) West Side Road near the bridge across the South Puyallup River.

Rainier's explosive activity during the Summerland period culminated in an outburst that hurled an ash column perhaps 50,000 feet into the air and ejected the volcano's most voluminous Holocene pumice fall. Blanketing the ground east of the summit near Yakima Park and on Burroughs Mountain, this widespread tephra (layer C), 5 to 6 inches thick, contains a mixture of fresh andesite and dacite pumice. Besides abundant pumice bombs several inches in diameter, layer C also contains numerous rock fragments torn from the volcano's conduit. Hot tephra raining on ice fields generated lahars that flowed down the south, southeast, and west flanks of the volcano. About 2,200 years ago, an exceptionally large mudflow of this origin—the National—inundated the Nisqually River valley to depths of 30 to 120 feet and traveled all the way to Puget Sound. During the Summerland period, blocky lava flows also traveled down Rainier's east flanks. Recently dated at about 2,200 years, they represent the volcano's latest effusive eruptions. Moderate explosive bursts that produced much smaller tephra falls and lahars continued sporadically until about 1,600 years ago.

Between about AD 900 and 1000, renewed activity generated another series of voluminous lahars, probably caused when explosions threw out hot fragmental material that cascaded down Rainier's south and east flanks, rapidly melting large quantities of snow and ice. A pyroclastic surge accompanying these block-and-ash flows swept 7 miles down the White River valley, leaving a telltale layer of lithic ash. Floods carrying debris from these pyroclastic flows and surges quickly picked up additional loose material from valley floors, creating torrents of rock and mud that swamped both forks of the White River, as well as the Nisqually River valley. These lahars deposited a thick fill that raised canyon floors 60 to 90 feet above their present levels. This eruptive episode included multiple mudflows that occurred over an extended time span, at least one or more in each fork of the White River. Ash from a lateral blast or pyroclastic surge overlies the lahar assemblage.

Some of the mudflows in this episode traveled more than 65 miles into the Puget Sound basin, covering the lower Duwamish, White, and Puyallup River valleys in muck up to 30 feet deep. Filling the Duwamish valley wall-to-wall, the mudflows, which contain numerous pumice fragments, inundated the site of Auburn and Kent, entombing a forest. Subsequent runoff and erosion of these lahar deposits transported large quantities of sand to bury tidal flats in what are now Seattle suburbs near the Boeing aircraft company. These reworked sands extend as far north as the Port of Seattle Terminal 107, about 2 miles from Elliot Bay, the inlet along which downtown Seattle is built.

Although geologists have found no tephra layers from the next episode of Rainier's volcanic unrest—which Pringle's tree-ring dating pinpoints at AD 1502–1503—numerous lahars of this age poured down the northeast, south, and west flanks of the cone, which is a strong indication that the volcano was then active. Vallance found distinctive glassy fragments of lava rock, identified as magmatic in origin, that are entrained in a lahar in the White River drainage. The major event during this time was the Electron Mudflow, which, like the Round Pass lahar, began as an exceptionally large avalanche of clay-rich, hydrothermally altered rock on the upper west flank of the volcano. Unlike the earlier west-side lahar, the Electron was exceptionally fluid and left only a thin deposit in its upper reaches. Moving downslope in a wave hundreds of feet high, the Electron Mudflow streamed down the Puyallup River valley and into the Puget lowland at least as far as the site of Sumner. Following part of the same pathway as the earlier Osceola, it overwhelmed some of the same town sites, including Electron and Orting. In the late twentieth century, developers bulldozing ground for a new housing subdivision near Orting uncovered large stumps from a forest entombed by the mudflow.

Following the destruction of its former summit about 3600 BC, Rainier's average rate of magma extrusion—mostly in the form of lava flows that built the new summit cone—has averaged about a tenth of a cubic mile per thousand years. This rate approximately equals its average output during the previous 35,000 years. But, as Vallance notes, Rainier's eruptive output has been irregular: most lava flows erupted only during the Osceola and Summerland periods. Although late Holocene eruptions have largely filled in the enormous depression left by the Osceola Mudflow, the volcano's

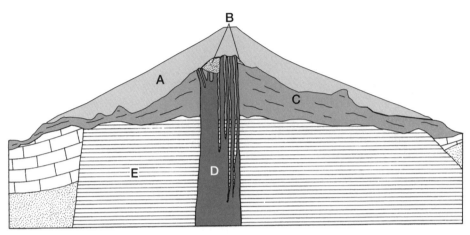

Cross-section of Mount Rainier. (A) Maximum height and volume (probably attained during Pleistocene eruptive stages of high magma output). (B) Holocene summit cone. (C) Lava flows composing the present cone. (D) Lava conduits. (E) Granodiorite basement rocks. —Adapted from R. S. Fiske, C. A. Hopson, and A. C. Waters, *Geology of Mount Rainier National Park, Washington* (U.S. Geological Survey Professional Paper 1365 [1963])

recent lava emission does not keep pace with the countless tons of material removed daily from its cone by rockfalls, landslides, glacial scouring, stream cutting, and other erosional processes.

Reports of Historic Eruptions

Historic time in the Pacific Northwest goes back little more than 150 years. Almost until the American Civil War, non-native inhabitants of western Washington included only a handful of missionaries, settlers, and employees of the Hudson's Bay Company. Olympia, Tacoma, and Seattle did not really take root until the 1850s. Despite the scanty population—and the relentlessly cloudy weather that keeps Rainier hidden from view for weeks or months at a time—observers between 1820 and 1894 reported no fewer than sixteen eruptions.

The earliest historic activity supposedly occurred about 1820. Years afterward, an aged Indian named John Hiaton claimed that he had seen fire, heard noise, and felt an earthquake emanating from Rainier. He added that in the past his forebears had witnessed many eruptive events. Interestingly, Patrick Pringle has pinpointed the death of a Douglas fir, killed and partly buried by a rockfall from Mount Wow, to about AD 1821, noting that the large avalanche is typical of those triggered by earthquakes.

A second reference to Rainier's activity appears in the 1841 bulletin of Belgian seismologist Alexis Perrey, who listed "violent eruptions of Mt. Raynier [*sic*], Oregon" for that year. Although Perrey also reported eruptions in 1842 and November 23, 1843, his sources are unknown. Captain John Frémont noted in his journal on November 13, 1843, "At this time two of the great snowy cones, Mount Reignier [*sic*] and St. Helens, were in action." Father De Smet, an early missionary who observed several eruptions of St. Helens, also alluded to "signs of activity" at Rainier in 1846. In his 1914 book on Rainier, F. E. Matthes states that "actual records exist of slight eruptions in 1843, 1854, 1858, and 1870." Unfortunately, neither De Smet nor Matthes provides any concrete details about the alleged activity. Because both Baker and St. Helens had authenticated eruptions in 1843, it is possible that some observers confused Rainier with one of the other two volcanoes.

Because mid-nineteenth-century accounts of Rainier's activity are so vague, many twentieth-century geologists discounted them altogether. In 1967, however, Donal Mullineaux discovered a previously unrecognized deposit of fresh, light-brown pumice (layer X) on young glacial moraines formed between about 1820 and 1854, offering proof that the volcano had indeed been active between those dates.

Indirect confirmation of historic activity comes from the testimony of a Yakama Indian named Saluskin. According to his story (told when he was an old man), in June 1855 he had guided two "King George men," then a common term for Anglo-Americans, to the east flank of Rainier. After their safe return from the summit, they informed Saluskin, who had waited at base camp, that there was "ice all over top, lake in center and smoke or steam coming out all around like sweat-house." Although many mountaineering historians discount this tale of an 1855 ascent (fifteen years before the first official climb), it has an aura of plausibility, primarily because the unnamed climbers could have described the thermal anomalies in Rainier's crater only by reaching the summit.

Approximately 1,300 feet in diameter, the eastern crater now contains snow and ice equivalent to one billion gallons of water, sufficient to form a small lake. If heat emission in the 1850s had melted the crater's snowpack and created a body of standing water, the "eruption" of 1854 may have resulted from water seeping through crevices to subsurface hot rock, triggering a steam blast. If the ejection of layer X pumice had occurred not long before, thermal activity then may have been considerably more intense than it is today.

When Hazard Stevens and Philemon Van Trump made the first authenticated climb of Rainier in August 1870, they saw quantities of steam issuing from fumaroles in both craters, but no sign of a crater lake. Heat and steam emission had evidently decreased to the relatively mild but constant state it still maintains. Assaulted by fierce winds, Stevens and Van Trump took refuge in the firn caves (passageways melted in the crater ice fill) of the west crater, where they spent a miserable night nauseated by the odor of hydrogen sulfide and alternately scalded by steam jets or frozen by icy gusts.

The 1870 party saw no evidence of recent volcanic activity, casting doubt on an eruption reported that year. A strong earthquake the following September, however, reportedly caused a large rockfall from Liberty Cap, sending an estimated 80 acres of rock thundering downslope and perhaps kicking up a dust cloud that was mistaken for an ash plume.

Frederick Plummer, a scientist who compiled a list of reported eruptions in the Pacific Northwest for the *Tacoma Daily Ledger* in 1893 (revised in 1898 for Edward Holden's *Catalogue of Earthquakes*), cited activity that supposedly began on October 18, 1873, and lasted for a week. An Olympia newspaper, the *Washington Standard* (which may have been Plummer's source) also mentioned the event, stating that on October 25, 1873, "clouds of smoke were seen pouring from the highest peak of Mount Rainier. The smoke was seen until nearly dark when clouds shut down upon the mountain hiding it from view." The following November 29 the same paper noted, "Smoke has been ascending from the highest peak of Mount Rainier, within the past few days."

Len Longmire, a pioneer settler, recalled seeing "a series of brown, billowy clouds" issuing from the crater in 1879 and again in 1882. Plummer also recorded that "on June 16, 1884, at about 7 p.m., jets of steam were seen shooting upward from the summit of Mount Tacoma [Rainier] to a considerable height. This phenomena [*sic*] was repeated at short intervals until darkness cut off the view. There was no fire, and no earth tremors were reported."

The last nineteenth-century eruption sighting was highly publicized by two influential newspapers, the Seattle *Post-Intelligencer* and the *Tacoma Daily Ledger*, in November and December 1894. Although the news articles are much more detailed than earlier eruption accounts, and although the 1894 event is now commonly cited even in modern scientific publications, it is highly doubtful that Rainier was then active. Plummer, who was working in Tacoma at the time, compared the sensational news stories, with their feverish "eye-witness" reports of steam and ash spouting from Rainier's crest, with his own careful observation of the mountain, concluding that not nature but the journalistic imagination was at work. In a preface to his 1898 compilation of volcanic activity on the Pacific Coast, Plummer wrote with bracing skepticism:

> There can be no doubt that many eruptions were reported which
> might be contradicted if examination were possible. For example, the

reports of the eruption and change in the summit of Mount Tacoma [Rainier] from November 21 to December 25, 1894, filled many columns of press dispatches, and possibly were intended for that purpose. December 25 was the most perfect day for observation, and, with my 6½-inch refractor, the crater-peak and its surroundings were carefully examined, and no change could be seen. No eruption was noted, other than the usual emission of steam, which varies with the barometer.

Geologic Restlessness

Although Rainier has not erupted fresh magma since the early to mid-nineteenth century, neither has it remained entirely at rest. Not only do areas of hot rock and fumaroles partly encircle the rims of both summit craters, keeping them largely ice free throughout the year, steam is occasionally seen issuing from the outer flanks. During the 1960s climbers reported hearing loud reports and seeing columns of vapor rise from crevices in the rock. In 1961, a small steam explosion occurred near Gibraltar Rock, ejecting a steam plume 200 feet into the air and scattering debris over the surface of Cowlitz glacier. This vent remained active over the summer, although with diminishing energy. In March 1965, skiers saw clouds of steam spouting from a ridge above the Kautz glacier and apparently triggering a rockfall. Three years later, steam clouds also were seen billowing from cliffs above the South Tahoma glacier. At about the same time, small floods and mudflows repeatedly descended the Tahoma Creek valley, possibly caused by increased heat emission beneath the glacier.

A decade of unusual geologic restlessness culminated in 1969 when an apparent heat source beneath the Emmons glacier, between elevations of about 10,000 to 13,000 feet, broke the glacier surface into a network of potholes and crevasses. In some places, the ice cracked widely enough to expose the glacier's rocky bed. Although ominous, this thermal phenomenon was short-lived; by the following summer new fallen snow had filled in most of the Emmons glacier's heat-generated crevasses and collapse pits. Even so, such thermal anomalies, unrelated to weather conditions, are exactly the kind of warning geologists expect to herald future eruptions.

Volcanic activity, however, apparently played no role in initiating the largest avalanche to occur on Rainier in historic time. About noon on December 14, 1963, forest rangers about 12 miles northeast of the mountain heard a "very loud, sharp boom in the direction of Mount Rainier." After clouds and falling snow cleared enough for the rangers to observe the east flank, they saw a freshly deposited mass of rock debris covering the lower Emmons glacier.

When geologists later investigated the scene, they found that approximately 14 million cubic yards of shattered lava rock had fallen from the north face of Little Tahoma Peak. Plummeting 1,700 feet onto the glacier's surface, the avalanche struck with tremendous force. Because of its large volume and the steepness of its landing site, the avalanche shot across the glacier at speeds up to 100 miles per hour. When it reached the glacier's snout, the mass soared into space, passing over the top of a 6-foot-high stream-gauging station, which was left untouched as millions of tons of rock hurtled overhead. Where the upper White River valley curves or is constricted, the flowing mass of rock fragments and trapped air surged up the canyon walls as high as 300 feet. Finally coming to rest a scant half mile from the White River Campground, the avalanche extended 4 miles from its source on Little Tahoma, a drop in altitude of 6,200 feet. Covering 2 square miles of the Emmons glacier and upper White River valley, the avalanche contained many lava blocks of remarkable size, one measuring 60 by 130 by 160 feet and weighing 50,000 tons!

Research in the early 2000s indicates that the Little Tahoma rockfall probably occurred a few days earlier than originally supposed. By comparing seismogram readings taken at Longmire for December 1963 with those that registered large avalanches from Russell Cliff in 1974 and 1989, Robert Norris of the USGS has concluded that the 1963 event took place on December 6.

Fire under Ice: The Summit Firn Caves

Weary climbers who reach the 14,411-foot Columbia Crest, the highest point on Rainier, seldom have either the time or the desire to explore one of Rainier's most interesting features—a 1.5-mile-long maze of twisting corridors, interspersed with a few high-ceilinged caverns, melted under the firn ice that almost fills the volcano's twin summit craters. In North America, apparently only Rainier, Baker, and Wrangell in Alaska have the sustained equilibrium between snowfall and heat emission that creates the special conditions in which a system of interlinked caves can occur. (The fumaroles around Crater Rock on Mount Hood have also melted out individual caves in the surrounding ice, but they do not form an interconnecting system comparable to that in Rainier's craters.)

Snow fills the east crater to an estimated depth of 360 feet, but currents of warm air generated by heat and steam emission in the crater have melted out a series of passageways with a cumulative length of at least a mile. These summit caves—typically linear spaces between the inner crater walls and the overlying ice—are extremely steep and littered with blocks of andesite, pumice fragments, and mud. When Eugene Kiver, a geologist at Eastern Washington University, first surveyed and mapped the caves in the early 1970s, the lowest point to which investigators could descend was about 540 feet below the highest point on the crater rim, or 340 feet below the crater snowpack. At this depth the crater walls, sloping inward at an angle of 32 degrees, touch the ice ceiling, preventing further exploration.

Only about 1,000 feet in diameter, Rainier's smaller western crater has a shorter cave system. But it contains a pool of meltwater which, when first surveyed in 1972, measured about 120 by 40 feet across. This crater lake is 18 feet deep and stands 14,000 feet above sea level, shielded from view under an arching canopy of ice. When an international team headed by François Le Guern of France studied the caves in 1997–1998, they found that fumaroles "in the cave lake" were producing sulfur crystals at temperatures of 187 degrees Fahrenheit. In the summer of 2002, Le Guern and his associates found that although fumarolic emissions remained constant, increased climatic warming had radically affected the summit caves, causing ice roofs to collapse and making many caves impassable (see chapter 22).

Rainier's Volcanic Hazards

Mount Rainier represents a greater threat to more people than any other volcano in the United States, including Alaska and Hawaii. Hawaii's currently active volcanoes, Mauna Loa and Kilauea, erupt much more frequently than Rainier, but their typically slow-moving basaltic lava flows, which can burn and/or bury entire villages or housing developments on the Big Island, do not usually endanger human lives. Some highly explosive Alaskan volcanoes, such as Pavlov, Augustine, or Shishaldin, also erupt more often, but in general are too geographically isolated to have a serious effect on Anchorage, where about half of Alaska's citizens live, or even on smaller communities. By contrast, Rainier—covered with 34 square miles of perennial snow and ice and bearing extensive areas of unstable, hydrothermally altered rock on its steep west face—is poised to threaten the property and disrupt the lives of perhaps three million people living in eastern Puget Sound and along the lower Columbia River.

Whereas geologists do not expect Rainier's future lava flows or pyroclastic flows to travel beyond national park boundaries, the secondary effects of these eruptive products—floods and lahars generated by melting snow and ice—will sweep like churning masses of wet concrete scores of miles down valleys heading on the volcano. By far the most dangerous volcanic hazard on any U.S. fire mountain, Rainier's lahars will have a devastating effect on the areas involved, including many economically important commercial centers from Tacoma to south Seattle. A 1998 USGS report states that a lahar the size of the 500-year-old Electron Mudflow—pitching 300 million cubic yards of rock and mud down the Puyallup valley—"could destroy all or parts of Orting, Sumner, Puyallup, Fife, the Port of Tacoma,

Auburn." Because much of this terrain has been stripped of its old-growth forest, removing obstacles that slowed down or restricted the areal extent of lahars in the past, geologists estimate that future mudflows like the Electron will spread farther and faster, overwhelming an area about 40 percent larger than that buried five centuries ago.

As expanding developments relentlessly creep upvalley from Puget Sound into the Cascade foothills, the 150,000 people who now live directly atop Rainier's recent mudflow deposits will soon be joined by tens of thousands more. If residents of these ever-growing communities suddenly face evacuation from the path of oncoming lahars, the prospect of jammed highways and frantic attempts to reach high ground staggers the imagination.

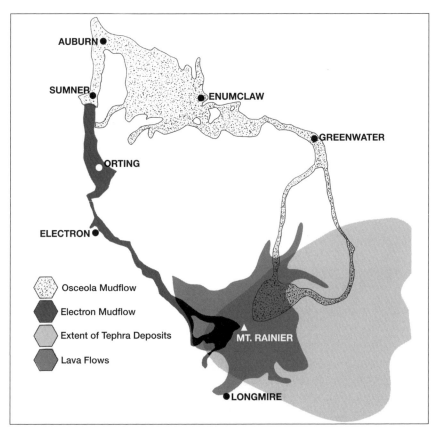

Map of the lava flows, mudflows, and tephra deposits from Mount Rainier. The Osceola Mudflow, triggered when Rainier's former summit collapsed, buried 210 square miles, including the sites of numerous towns presently in the Puget lowland. Collapse of hydro-thermally altered rock on the volcano's west face generated the Electron Mudflow, which also inundated areas now densely populated. —Adapted from Crandell, 1973

As Crandell pointed out in his early evaluations of Rainier's hazards, careful long-term planning for the region's future growth is a necessity. Foresight is particularly needed for the location and construction of dams, reservoirs, and essential utilities. The USGS study notes that Alder Lake, on the Nisqually River—with its electrical power facilities owned by the City of Tacoma Department of Public Utilities—will be unable to contain or stop an Electron-size mudflow: such a lahar "entering the reservoir could either cause failure of the dam or could catastrophically displace a significant volume of the water in storage." If filled with rainwater when an eruption occurs, Mud Mountain reservoir in the lower White River valley is also at risk.

When future eruptions at Rainier's young summit cone again trigger block-and-ash flows down the Emmons and Winthrop glaciers, as occurred about 1,100 years ago, the subsequent lahars will again overwhelm both forks of the White River, filling it to depths of 60 to 90 feet, and will possibly inundate Auburn, 60 miles distant. As Paul Zehfuss points out, although the Mud Mountain reservoir, with a total storage capacity of about 157 million cubic yards, stands in the way of future White River mudflows, it "equals only about half the volume" of lahars that USGS researchers believe will occur at intervals of between 500 and 1,000 years. Partial melting of the Nisqually glacier will produce similarly destructive mudflows downvalley and—if large enough to overtop Alder Dam—perhaps all the way to Puget Sound. As in most previous eruptions, lahars will probably descend at least two or more separate drainage systems simultaneously, endangering different locations at once and perhaps stretching local emergency services beyond their capacity to respond effectively.

Visiting Rainier

Attracting more than two million visitors annually, Mount Rainier National Park offers a unique combination of volcanic and glacial features. Both seasoned climbers and casual day hikers can enjoy its spectacular scenery, ranging from old-growth conifer forests to flowering alpine meadows to vast expanses of rock and ice.

Accessible from almost every direction by good paved roads, the park has two major visitor centers, at Paradise on the south side and at Sunrise on the east. The more developed Paradise location, reached by a steep road from Longmire (Washington 706), provides overnight accommodations at the historic Paradise Inn, as well as restaurants, restrooms, an observation tower, informational displays, a climbing school, and various tourist facilities. A gentle stroll from the visitor center on a short segment (1.2 miles roundtrip) of the Skyline Trail leads to the Nisqually Glacier Vista, an overlook offering memorable views of this 3-mile-long river of ice, the most thoroughly studied glacier in America. The Skyline trailhead is located at the parking lot near the ranger station at Paradise.

For a stunning overview of the Cascade Range south of Rainier, including the jagged Tatoosh peaks and the snowy cones of Goat Rocks, Adams, St. Helens, and Hood, hike 2.5 miles north up the Panorama Point Trail from the Paradise Visitor Center to a meadow at almost 7,000 feet. Early morning and after five in the evening, when summer haze is at a minimum, are the best times.

Sunrise Visitor Center (6,400 feet) at Yakima Park on the less-visited east side has no hotel, but it offers magnificent views of Emmons glacier, still littered with the 1963 rockfall from Little Tahoma Peak, and the symmetrical young summit cone rising between Gibraltar Rock on the south and Russell Cliff on the north. From Paradise or Longmire, continue on Washington 706 to Stevens Canyon Road, with its spectacular lava flow bluffs and waterfalls, and around Rainier's southern base to Washington 123. Take 123 north and at Cayuse Pass continue on Washington 410; turn left onto the White River Road at the sign for the White River entrance station and follow the signs to Sunrise (about 7 miles beyond the junction for the White River campground). If driving to Sunrise from the north, take Washington 410 south; about 4.5 miles after crossing the park boundary turn right on the White River Road and follow the signs to Sunrise.

Climbing Rainier, in any season, requires experienced guides and proper equipment, including suitable clothing, mountain boots, crampons, ice axes, ropes, head lanterns, sun goggles, overnight supplies, and other indispensables. Rainier stands so high that it creates its own highly changeable weather; sudden storms may rage around the summit while valleys below bask in sunlight.

CHAPTER 19

Glacier Peak

WHITE GODDESS OF THE NORTH CASCADES

In Greek mythology, Mount Olympus was home to the twelve major Hellenic gods. If each of the dozen Olympian deities were to choose an individual dwelling place on one of the Cascade mountains, Artemis (the Roman Diana) would undoubtedly select Glacier Peak. Hidden in the most inaccessible part of the range, lonely Glacier Peak offers a congenial environment for this virgin goddess of wildlife and the hunt. Here the privacy-loving Artemis could roam with her beloved wild creatures in almost complete isolation.

Tucked away in the heart of the rugged North Cascades, Glacier Peak (10,541 feet) is perhaps the least known Cascade stratovolcano. Although located only 70 miles northeast of Seattle, its position deep in the range—which has its highest average elevations and greatest width in this segment—makes it almost invisible. If glimpsed from a high point in northwestern Washington, it is merely a summit among other peaks of the range's jagged crest.

Glacier Peak nonetheless poses a significant geologic threat to communities in western Washington. Like Mount St. Helens, Glacier Peak is highly explosive, erupting at least two of the largest and most widespread tephra falls of any Cascade volcano since the end of the most recent ice age. Besides blanketing vast areas of the Pacific Northwest and southern Canada in layers of dacite ash, it has repeatedly produced extensive pyroclastic flows and lahars. Some lahars traveled into the lower Skagit River valley, inundating lowlands now occupied by the towns of Mount Vernon, Burlington, La Conner, and Sedro Woolley. Prehistoric eruptions have even dispatched mudflows down the north fork of the Stillaguamish River, burying the sites of Darrington and Arlington. Although Glacier Peak's largest Plinian outburst occurred about 13,000 calendar years ago, it has continued to erupt intermittently throughout Holocene time, producing additional tephra, lava domes, pyroclastic flows, and numerous lahars. A small ash eruption occurred as recently as the eighteenth century, and in the 1850s Indians informed naturalist George Gibbs that this ice-shrouded peak north of Mount Rainier "once smoked."

The third-most heavily glaciated composite cone in the range, Glacier Peak—85 miles north of Mount Rainier—surmounts a sea of sharp ridges and twisting valleys in the rugged North Cascades. One of the Pacific Northwest's most violently explosive volcanoes, it repeatedly produced pyroclastic flows and mudflows during the last 15,000 years. —Austin Post photo, U.S. Geological Survey

Glacier Peak, named for the many glaciers visible from its summit, and the surrounding mountains seem to be in the midst of a contemporary ice age. Today's North Cascade ice cover is impressive, but it is much smaller than the enormous ice sheets that smothered this end of the range during the Pleistocene. The Cordilleran lobe of the continental ice sheet advancing southward from Canada repeatedly overrode the North Cascades, burying all but the highest peaks and ridges under ice thousands of feet thick. Recurrent glacial advances so thoroughly scoured the region that most early Pleistocene and older volcanic deposits were entirely removed. Existing small glaciers still whittle the high-relief terrain into steep divides and sharp horns.

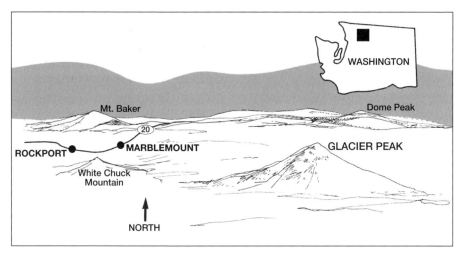

Relief map of the Glacier Peak area

Composed of ancient metamorphic and other nonvolcanic rock (glaciers erased its previous veneer of volcanic material), the North Cascades today have only two concentrations of volcanism: Glacier Peak and the Mount Baker volcanic field near the Canadian boundary. Neither volcano is included in North Cascades National Park, but Glacier Peak presides over a federally designated wilderness bearing its name—a region where dark evergreen forests carpet valley floors and walls, thinning upward into austere highlands of glacier-scoured rock and perennial ice fields. Glacier Peak is perched atop Lime Ridge (8,000 feet) just west of the Cascade divide. The Suiattle River drains it on the north and east, flowing, via the Sauk, to the Skagit River and then to northern Puget Sound. Draining the west flank, the White Chuck River also flows into the Sauk. Backpackers and climbers usually approach the mountain from the west up the White Chuck route. From the east they can hike from the western end of Lake Chelan, a deep fjordlike body of water that extends from the eastern Cascades deep into the interior.

Glacier Peak's Eruptive History

Glacier Peak is distinguished by its catastrophic ejections of pumiceous tephra, which form distinctive layers over tens of thousands of square miles. But the cone was built primarily of quiet effusions of dacite lava. The earliest flows, unusually fluid for dacites, issued from a vent on the east flank of

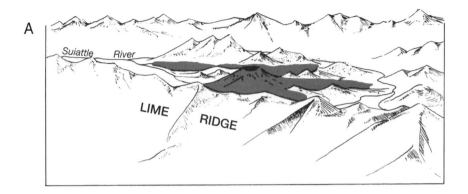

A

Suiattle   River

LIME   RIDGE

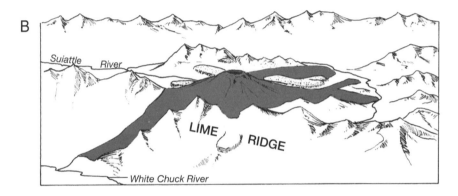

B

Suiattle   River

LIME   RIDGE

White Chuck River

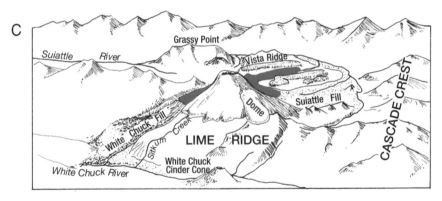

C

Grassy Point

Suiattle   River

Vista Ridge

Suiattle Fill

CASCADE CREST

White Chuck Fill

Dome

Sitkum Creek

LIME RIDGE

White Chuck Cinder Cone

White Chuck River

The growth of Glacier Peak volcano. (A) In Pleistocene time, the earliest Glacier Peak lavas erupted east of Lime Ridge and flowed along ridgetops between valleys tributary to the Suiattle River. (B) As the volcano grew, its lava flows overtopped Lime Ridge and poured westward along divides between tributary valleys of the White Chuck River. Younger flows descended valleys of the ancestral Vista Creek and Kennedy Creek. (C) Dome growth and collapse initiated pyroclastic flows and mudflows that created large fans of fragmental debris in both the White Chuck and Suiattle drainages. Lahars traveled many tens of miles down valleys, some extending to Puget Sound. —Adapted from Tabor and Crowder, 1969; and Begét, 1982

Lime Ridge, a spur off the Cascade crest trending northwest. Because the high barrier of Lime Ridge blocked their westward expansion, these initial lava flows traveled eastward along divides between valleys tributary to the Suiattle River. Not until after the volcano had grown to a height of at least 2,000 feet above its base could Glacier Peak's flows spill over the ridgetop and down its western slope to the ancestral White Chuck River.

Like other Cascade volcanoes during the Pleistocene, Glacier Peak erupted lava streams that flowed down divides between valley-filling glaciers. After the last ice-age glaciers withdrew, these flows extending from the mountain remained, capping ridges or stranded high on valley walls. Some flows survive as only isolated remnants, their original connection to the cone severed by ice and stream erosion. Apparently erupted after glaciers had receded, a few flows occupy valley floors at the volcano's east foot, such as those that descended the ancestral Vista, Chocolate, and Dusty Creek valleys. As at Mount Rainier, glaciers have probably shrouded Glacier Peak for most of its existence, removing much of its original surface and carving numerous cleavers, or lava ribs, standing hundreds of feet above surrounding ice fields.

The Great Eruptions

About 13,000 years ago, after ice-age glaciers had retreated far upvalley, Glacier Peak staged a series of violent eruptions that affected the Pacific Northwest landscape for many miles in all directions. This sequence of multiple paroxysms—ejecting at least nine distinct layers of pumiceous tephra and numerous pyroclastic flows and surges—may have begun with a partial collapse of the volcanic cone. James Begét, who has studied the volcano's history in detail, found a large mudflow containing a high proportion of hydrothermally altered rock underlying the pyroclastic deposits. This clay-rich mudflow, perhaps triggered by hydrothermally altered material avalanching from the volcano's summit, streamed down the west slope to Kennedy Creek, and thence to White Chuck valley, down which it flowed at least 18 miles.

During this eruptive episode, Begét estimates, Glacier Peak may have ejected as much as 2.5 cubic miles of pyroclastic material, approximately half of which was blown into the air and transported by winds at least 620 miles to the east. Extending in a broad band across eastern Washington, northeastern Oregon, the Idaho panhandle, western Montana, and parts of southern Canada, Glacier Peak's ash fall covers a larger territory than that from any other Cascade volcano during Holocene time—except for ash from Mount Mazama (Crater Lake) 7,700 years ago.

Map showing the area covered by Glacier Peak ash about 15,000 years ago

Shifting winds carried one of the two largest tephra plumes south along the Cascade Range. Together, the nine tephra falls form a distinctive and widespread layer that scientists can use as a time marker, helping them to determine the relative ages of other geologic deposits or archaeologic artifacts.

In the North Cascades, the Glacier Peak tephra consists mainly of yellowish or light-gray pumice bombs and lapilli, as thick as 12 feet at a distance of 12 miles downwind from the volcano. Near Chelan in the east Cascades, the tephra is a foot thick. In western Montana, hundreds of miles from its source, the ash still lies an inch thick.

Perhaps only a short time before the explosive pumice eruptions, Glacier Peak extruded viscous lava high on its cone, producing domes that shattered and collapsed, sending avalanches of incandescent rock fragments down both its east and west flanks. At least ten pyroclastic flows and mudflows poured down the west side into the White Chuck and Sauk valleys, where they accumulated up to 350 feet deep. Topping the sequence is a thick pyroclastic flow, the White Chuck tuff, which was still hot enough to weld in some places 10 miles from its source. As Begét notes, a collapsing ash column probably formed the White Chuck tuff during one of the volcano's two largest tephra eruptions.

Later pulses of this eruptive episode sent a renewed wave of pyroclastic flows and mudflows pouring into stream valleys west of the peak. Some of these deposits consist of reworked pumice derived from earlier eruptions, but others were composed of freshly erupted pumice. Large floods and mudflows again traveled down the White Chuck, Sauk, and Skagit valleys all the way to Puget Sound. Overwhelmed with so much debris, the rivers were forced to cut new channels.

Some rivers buried by the eruptions changed their courses. Before the eruptions, it appears that the Sauk and perhaps the Suiattle Rivers flowed west through the Stillaguamish valley. After the Stillaguamish was choked with pyroclastic debris that extended more than 60 downstream miles to near Arlington, where it lies 7 feet thick, the Sauk and Suiattle Rivers abandoned their original routes to flow north into the Skagit River, as they do today.

By the end of this eruptive period, which may have spanned several centuries, Glacier Peak ash blanketed not only the North Cascade landscape, but also a broad fan-shaped area extending for hundreds of miles northeast, east, and south. Gray drifts of pumiceous ash shrouded glaciers, mountaintops, and canyons, as well as the great Columbia River plateau and the Snake River plain beyond. Huge aprons of debris sloped outward from the cone, glutting both the Stillaguamish and Skagit drainages and probably extending tens of miles downstream to the shores of northern Puget Sound.

A dormant interval—perhaps as long as 6,000 to 7,000 years—followed. Streams eroded new canyons into the pyroclastic and mudflow deposits that had filled their old valleys. The new V-shaped ravines would later be partly refilled by the ejecta of fresh eruptions, which would form new debris terraces on recently excavated valley floors.

When Glacier Peak reawakened about 5,900 years ago, another partial collapse of the volcanic edifice triggered a mudflow of hydrothermally altered rock debris now exposed in the White Chuck River above Kennedy Hot Springs. This mudflow may correlate with a similar deposit in Baekos Creek on the southwest side of the mountain, and with a small layer of altered rock fragments east of the volcano. After initial phreatic explosions, fresh magma extruded to form new lava domes, which typically disintegrated into block-and-ash flows that raced into adjacent valleys. Dozens of pyroclastic flows, including pumice flows, swept downslope to bury large forests under debris aprons extending tens of miles downvalley. Floods and mudflows, this time confined to Skagit River valley, again reached Puget Sound.

View of Glacier Peak and the Cool glacier (center). The ice-encased upper cone consists primarily of domes and attendant pyroclastic material, which probably filled in a large crater left by the volcano's early Holocene explosive eruptions. —Austin Post photo, U.S. Geological Survey

Dusty Creek, which issues from the Dusty glacier on the volcano's west flank and flows into the Suiattle River, received large quantities of pyroclastic effluvia, as did Chocolate Creek just to the south. Hundreds of pyroclastic flows with an aggregate thickness of more than 1,000 feet fill Dusty Creek's gorge with about a cubic mile of debris. Ash that probably billowed above the pyroclastic flows mantled the Dusty Creek fill as well as adjacent ridges. The presence of buried soils, lake sediments, and peat layers interbedded with layers of volcanic rock indicate that debris flows several times dammed the White Chuck River. Water impounded behind these dams temporarily formed a succession of lakes.

Much of the area near Darrington is underlain by deposits of this mid-Holocene eruptive period. Flood sediment laid down at about the same time extends as far as Minkler Lake, 70 miles downstream from Glacier Peak.

After resting for a few millennia, Glacier Peak revived about 1,800 years ago, again extruding a series of lava domes high on the cone. Although the volume of material ejected was much smaller than in the previous episode, it sufficed to bury valley floors many miles from the volcano. Collapsing domes repeatedly shed block-and-ash flows down both the east and west flanks, partly filling gullies cut into older volcanic deposits. Floods and mud-flows transported debris more than 60 miles to the Skagit River delta, emp-tying into Puget Sound. Some time later, another large mudflow traveled at least 19 miles west of the cone, perhaps triggered by steam explosions that dislodged portions of the former summit.

Renewed dome growth and collapse about 1,000 years ago produced yet another series of pyroclastic flows and lahars, some of which accumulated to thicknesses of 350 feet in adjacent valleys. Some time before 300 years ago, a series of large floods and lahars inundated canyons near the volcano, carrying material 20 to 30 miles downvalley.

A widespread layer of fine gray ash covers much of the north and east slopes of Glacier Peak as much as a foot deep near the mouth of Dusty Creek. Seven inches thick on Gamma Ridge, the ash is in turn overlain by scattered lapilli up to 4 inches in diameter. These ash layers and pumice fragments lie atop recent glacial moraines that support trees slightly more than 300 years old. The presence of this young tephra shows that the latest eruptions occurred only two or three centuries ago, the last perhaps in the early 1700s.

Glacier Peak's summit area is formed mainly of eroded lava domes, most of which probably contributed to the abundant pyroclastic flow deposits surrounding the cone. Disappointment Peak—a "false summit"—is a large, prominent dome protruding through ice fields south of the true summit. Only rough outlines of the summit crater remain, breached at both the east and west walls, from which, respectively, issue the Chocolate and Scimitar glaciers. The crater's north rim is highly oxidized, some of its rock stained a blotchy yellow, a result of long-term hydrothermal alteration. Although no fumaroles remain active at the summit, the presence of three hot springs on the flanks—Gamma, Kennedy, and Sulphur hot springs—suggest that hot rock exists at relatively shallow depths.

Future Hazards

Because Glacier Peak's eruptive episodes are typically separated by several hundred to a few thousand years, a U.S. Geological Survey evaluation of the volcano's potential hazards, published in 2000, concludes that the prob-ability of its reawakening in any given year is "roughly one in a thousand," adding that it is "unlikely that we will see an eruption within our lifetimes." Besides the irregularity of its eruptive schedule, the uncertainty factor about Glacier Peak's future behavior is compounded by the great variety of its eruptive repertory and by the large variations in the size and scale of its Holocene activity. Unlike many other Cascade volcanoes, Glacier Peak exhibits a wide range of behaviors, from violent explosive outbursts that eject large volumes of pumiceous tephra to the quiet extrusion of viscous lava that builds domes high on the cone. Even quiet eruptions involving dome growth, however, commonly produce voluminous pyroclastic flows that race into adjacent valleys.

Both its Plinian and Peléan activity melt glacial ice and generate highly mobile mudflows that can travel 60 miles or more downvalley, extending into lowlands where tens of thousands of people now live. The USGS study points out that large-volume lahars—which can destroy highways, bridges, houses, and other structures in their paths—are likely to occur most often in the White Chuck and upper Suiattle River valleys. Although they happen less frequently, lahars entering the Sauk and Skagit River valleys pose a greater hazard because they will affect larger population centers.

When Glacier Peak next erupts, it is more likely to have small eruptions than large ones. Because winds blow eastward 80 percent of the time, minor tephra eruptions similar to those of the last 200 to 300 years will probably not affect most settled areas. But if the volcano continues its habit of extruding viscous magma at or near the summit, erecting steep domes that shed hot pyroclastic flows down the east and west flanks, resultant lahars could travel many miles downvalley. If pyroclastic flows melt large quantities of ice, floods and lahars may extend into populated areas.

Capable of producing violently explosive eruptions as large as those of Mount St. Helens, Glacier Peak could cover a huge area from Washington to Montana with pumiceous ash, creating a regional disaster. A reversal of typical wind patterns could carry an ash plume over Puget Sound, reducing visibility to near zero, halting traffic on all roads and highways, endangering aircraft, depositing ash several inches deep on rooftops and streets in numerous towns and cities, and radically disrupting the regional economy. An outburst comparable to the largest of 13,000 years ago—five times larger than that of Mount St. Helens in 1980—would not only affect areas many tens of miles downwind, but would also trigger mudflows large enough to inundate downvalley settlements in the Puget lowland.

Intrusion of magma into Glacier Peak's eroded and chemically weakened upper cone could cause as much as a tenth of the volcano's edifice to collapse, initiating what the USGS hypothesizes as the "largest credible lahar," a churning clay-rich mixture of altered rock and meltwater that, in mere hours, would reach the Skagit River delta. It would overwhelm and destroy most human-made structures on a large portion of the Skagit and Sauk River flood plains. Although such calamitous events have been rare during the last 13,000 years, several have occurred. Solitary and unnoticed as it usually is, Glacier Peak cannot safely be ignored.

Visiting Glacier Peak

Secluded in the Glacier Peak Wilderness, the volcano is accessible via steep hiking trails many miles long. To reach a popular western route, take Washington 530 east from Interstate 5 to Darrington. Take the Mountain Loop Highway south from Darrington about 9 miles, to a bridge across the Sauk River and then up the White Chuck Road (Forest Road 23) east for 10.5 miles to the White Chuck trailhead. From there it is 5 miles on foot to the Kennedy hot springs at Glacier Peak's west foot. Those planning an ascent should consult climbing guides by such mountaineers as Jeff Smoot.

CHAPTER 20

Mount Baker

FIRE UNDER ICE

An ice-clad sentinel standing about 15 miles south of the Canadian boundary, Mount Baker (10,781 feet) is an international landmark, on clear days visible from northern Puget Sound to the cities of Vancouver and Victoria in British Columbia. When the weather is both clear and cold, local residents frequently spot a fleecy plume of steam rising from Sherman crater, the bowl-shaped vent located about 1,200 feet lower than and half a mile south of Baker's summit. Next to that of Mount St. Helens, Baker's crater is the most thermally active in the Cascade Range, vigorously spewing carbon dioxide and hydrogen sulfide gases from dozens of fumarole clusters, disseminating a "rotten egg" odor often perceptible many miles downslope. A second cluster of sulfurous steam vents, the Dorr fumaroles, is located on Baker's north side at an elevation of about 7,800 feet.

In March 1975, exactly five years before St. Helens began the series of phreatic explosions that culminated in the cataclysm of May 18, 1980, Mount Baker suddenly increased its heat and steam emission, ejecting minor quantities of ash that thinly veneered the Boulder glacier on its east flank. Most of the ash came from a large new fumarole at the base of Lahar Lookout, a crumbling mass of chemically decayed rock that borders a 500-foot-deep gap in the Sherman crater's east rim. By April, a lake—warm and distinctly acidic—had developed inside a 130-foot-deep pit melted in the crater ice-fill. On July 11, the lake was high enough to drain through the crater wall's eastern cleft and flow through the porous ice of the Boulder glacier. By August, the intensified heat flow had caused a spectacular breakup of the glacier descending from Grant Peak (Baker's highest point) southward into the crater. Two years later, a large section of the glacier collapsed, producing an avalanche of snow and ice that buried half of the crater floor.

As Baker increased its release of hydrogen sulfide gas from 2,800 pounds per hour in March 1975 to about 21,000 pounds per hour the next July, scientists from the U.S. Geological Survey and the University of Washington began close monitoring of the volcano, installing seismic sensors to register earth tremors that would signal the rise of magma into the cone and visiting the crater to detect changes in temperature and gas emission. Fearing

Baker's relatively smooth cone contrasts with the Black Buttes, eroded remnants of an older Pleistocene volcano. Ice sheets moving south from Canada repeatedly scoured the Mount Baker volcanic field. Today's glaciers occupy only the head of the deep ice-carved canyon visible in the center of the photo. —Austin Post photo, U.S. Geological Survey

that earthquakes or steam explosions would cause areas of unstable, hydrothermally altered rock in the eastern part of Sherman crater to collapse and generate lahars that could flow into Baker Lake at the volcano's eastern foot, the U.S. Forest Service closed the area, placing many popular boat launches, campsites, and hiking trails off limits to the public. Signs announcing the official closure explained that potential lahars "could enter the lake with great force, sending a wave of water along the lakeshore and into the campground areas." Authorities also took the precaution of lowering Baker Lake to a level that could accommodate a lahar similar to that which occurred during an eruption in 1843, in order to avert a possible overtopping of Baker Dam and the consequent flooding of the downstream Skagit River valley.

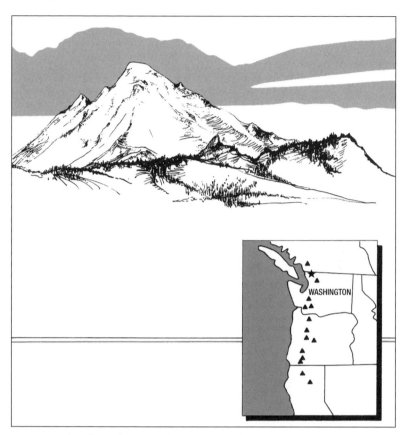

Mount Baker from the east. Sherman crater lies between the main summit (Grant Peak) and Sherman Peak on the far left.

After fluctuating in intensity for the next two years, Baker's heat flow gradually declined, but continues into the twenty-first century at a higher rate than it had before 1975. Scientists believe that monitoring the volcano is still advisable, although the absence of earthquakes indicates that a magmatic eruption is not imminent. Sudden steam blasts, however, apparently unaccompanied by the presence of fresh magma, have frequently occurred in Baker's recent past and remain a cause of genuine concern. During the mid-nineteenth century, Baker, along with St. Helens, was the most frequently active volcano in the Pacific Northwest. In 1843, steam explosions blew out a large quantity of old rock from Sherman crater, "covering the whole country with ashes," clogging nearby rivers with debris, and allegedly causing massive fish kills. Phreatic explosions, some propelling ash clouds thousands of feet into the air, continued sporadically until about

1880, sparking considerable interest throughout northwest Washington and southwest Canada.

Because of its documented historic eruptions and present high rate of thermal activity, Mount Baker is considered an active volcano. Like Rainier, its much larger and taller neighbor 130 miles to the south, Baker's principal threat is to settlements built on the floors of lahar-ridden valleys that head on the volcano, including those in the lower Skagit River valley, such as Mount Vernon, Burlington, and Sedro Woolley. (Subject to a double whammy, these sites are also threatened by lahars from Glacier Peak, which also drains into the Skagit River.) Several other towns on various branches of the Nooksack River, which drain Baker's northern and southwestern slopes, are also at high risk, including Glacier, Maple Falls, Deming, Sumas, Everson, and Lynden. Fortunately, the region's largest city, Bellingham, though located about 30 miles directly west of the volcano, does not occupy a lahar-prone lowland. Particularly troubling for those who do live in Baker's

Resembling "an ice floe on a frying pan," the Sherman crater ice pack disintegrates as fumaroles with temperatures approaching 270 degrees Fahrenheit release columns of hot gas and deposit thick layers of sulfur on the crater floor. —Courtesy of Fred Munich

hazard zones, however, is the fact that a large proportion of its Holocene lahars have occurred when the volcano was quiet. Whereas typical precursors of an impending eruption—earthquake swarms, cone deformation, and accelerated gas output—can alert people to potential danger, destructive lahars triggered by the sudden collapse of hydrothermally altered rock high on the mountain can occur without any warning.

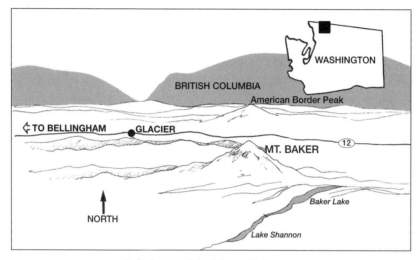

Relief map of the Mount Baker area

Names of the Volcano

Although contemporary accounts indicate that the 1843 event was Baker's largest historic outburst, the volcano may have been mildly active even earlier, when a Spanish expedition was exploring Bellingham Bay in June 1792. According to a ship's log published anonymously in 1802, the crews of the vessels *Sutil* and *Mexicana* recognized in "the ominous rumbling and flashes of fire to the east that continued day and night signs of a volcanic eruption." Most geologists, however, incline to think that the Spanish officers probably mistook an unusually intense thunder and lightning storm for an eruption. Captain George Vancouver, who sailed through the Strait of Juan de Fuca only weeks earlier, did not record any activity on Baker, but did give the peak its present name. While their ship was anchored near the site of Dungeness, Washington, Vancouver's third lieutenant sighted "a very high, conspicuous, craggy mountain . . . towering above the clouds; as low down as it was visible, it was covered with snow; and south of it was a long ridge of very rugged snowy mountains, much less elevated, which seemed to stretch to a considerable distance." On April 30, 1792, Vancouver named this lofty peak after junior officer Joseph Baker, who had first observed it. Two years earlier, the Spanish explorer Manuel Quimper had seen Baker and christened it La Gran Montana del Carmelo, probably commemorating the feast day of the Carmelite order, although the name's evocation of a white-robed figure standing guard over a virgin wilderness is also apt.

According to some historians, the Lummi tribe called Baker Kulshan Koma (often printed as Komo Kulshan), which has been variously translated as "white, shining, steep mountain," or "shot at the point," referring to a legend in which the Great Spirit allegedly wounded the peak, causing it to burn and smoke. This allusion to Baker's wounding is suggestive, for Sherman crater, lying between the main summit of Grant Peak and the lower prominence of Sherman Peak to the south, blasted open in postglacial time, radically altering the mountain's profile. To prehistoric observers, the new vent—enlarged to its present size by the 1843 outburst—must have resembled a supernaturally afflicted gash that "bled fire."

As Harry Majors states in his book on Baker's early history and historic eruptions, other Native American names emphasized the mountain's perennial snow cover: the Nooksack tribe called it Quck-sman-ik (signifying "white rock"), while the Koma people, who lived on the Skagit River, called it Tukullum ("white stone"). Again, the native terms are appropriate: In a 1971 inventory, glaciologist Austin Post catalogued no fewer than thirty-two glaciers on or near Mount Baker. With Mount Rainier excepted, Baker's slim cone supports more glacial ice than all the other Cascade volcanoes combined. In fact, wrapped in an almost seamless mantle of coalescing glaciers and permanent ice fields it is proportionately even more heavily glaciated than Rainier. Exposed to the fierce winter storms that gust through the Strait of Juan de Fuca, Baker receives extremely heavy precipitation, currently holding the North American record for annual snowfall—1,140 inches in 1998–1999.

The Mount Baker Volcanic Field

Although Mount Baker appears to stand as a solitary cone, geologists have recently discovered that it is merely the youngest in a cluster of volcanoes that represents a virtually continuous record of volcanism spanning at least 1.3 million years. In the late 1990s and early 2000s, Wes Hildreth and his colleagues at the U.S. Geological Survey completed a detailed mapping and dating of eruptive deposits in the Mount Baker volcanic field. According to this study, the Baker volcanic field's long eruptive history can be divided into five main stages: early Pleistocene activity that culminated in a huge explosive eruption, forming the Kulshan caldera (located at Baker's northeast foot); a

Mount Baker owes its shapely contours to its comparative youth: much of the visible cone formed near the end of the most recent Pleistocene glacial advance. This view shows the glacier-sheathed north face of Grant Peak (center), with the tip of Sherman Peak to the left and the crags of Black Buttes on the right. —Austin Post photo, U.S. Geological Survey

sequence of postcaldera rhyodacite lava flows; a series of later andesite flows in or near the caldera; the construction of the mid–Pleistocene Black Buttes stratovolcano; and the late Pleistocene building of Mount Baker's composite cone.

Evidence for early to mid–Pleistocene eruptive events is scanty because glaciers have deeply scoured the Baker region, removing most of the material erupted during the first, second, and third stages. During the last 1.8 million years, a lobe of the Cordilleran ice sheet repeatedly moved south from Canada into the Puget lowland, overriding the North Cascades and stripping away layers of rock thousands of feet thick. So intense was the erosion that, in most cases, only scraps of once-towering volcanic edifices and some isolated fragments of their adjacent lava flows remain. In some areas, an array of dikes penetrates old bedrock, but the lava flows, domes, and cones they once fed have largely vanished.

The Kulshan caldera, one of only three known Pleistocene or Holocene calderas in the Cascade Range, collapsed about 1.15 million years ago and subsequently underwent such extensive glacial dissection that its existence was not recognized until the Hildreth team's recent investigations. Of the two other calderas, the older, which produced the widespread Rockland tephra about 600,000 years ago and is now almost entirely buried by later silicic lava flows, is located at the Lassen volcanic center (see chapter 6); the much younger caldera is that holding Crater Lake (see chapter 10). In size and volume of ejecta, the Kulshan outburst was similar to that at Crater Lake. Like the eruption that beheaded Mount Mazama, the Kulshan event must have involved large pyroclastic flows and a voluminous tephra fall, which probably extended over most of the Pacific Northwest and southern Canada. However, except for ash deposits filling the caldera interior to a depth of at least 3,500 to 4,000 feet (erosion has not yet exposed the base of the caldera fill), glaciers have removed all traces of this fragmental material from the Baker vicinity.

Although the Cordilleran ice sheet did a spectacularly thorough job in erasing air-fall and pyroclastic flow deposits that formerly surrounded the caldera, Hildreth has correlated the Kulshan ejecta with a foot-thick layer of rhyodacite ash found about 125 miles to the south—the Lake Tapps tephra. Preserved in the Puget lowland at several points east of Tacoma and near the village of Hoodsport to the west, presumably just beyond the ice sheet's margins, the Lake Tapps tephra chemically matches the pumiceous fill in the Kulshan caldera. Showing signs that it was deposited wet, the Kulshan tephra may have been erupted through an overlying glacier or a lake melted in the ice then covering the volcano. If so, the rapid chilling of the ejecta explains why much of the ash filling the caldera was not welded.

For about 160,000 years after the Kulshan collapse, the volcano inter-mittently extruded a series of rhyodacite lava flows and domes atop the caldera ash-fill. Later switching to less silicic magma, the Kulshan vents then erupted a sequence of andesite lava flows. Glaciers have cut through and removed most of the postcaldera lavas, but two particularly prominent andesite remnants survive, Ptarmigan Ridge and the picturesque mesalike Table Mountain, both of which contain flows erupted about 300,000 years ago. Renewed advances of the massive Cordilleran ice sheet surmounting ridge crests as high as 6,000 feet—added to the vigorous scouring of thick valley glaciers and those mantling the large volcanic cones at higher alti-tudes—obliterated all of the constructional landforms, commonly leaving only disconnected scraps behind.

Much more remains of Mount Baker's immediate predecessor, the Black Buttes stratovolcano, which built a large andesite cone between about

500,000 and 290,000 years ago, its growth overlapping the waning activity of the Kulshan volcano a few miles to the northeast. (Hildreth found that the region's focus of volcanism has shifted steadily southwestward during the last several million years.) Formerly about twice the size of the present Mount Baker, the extensively dissected Black Buttes edifice is partly visible on Baker's west flank, where the dark lavas of jagged Lincoln Peak and Colfax Peak (9,335 feet) stand out in bleak contrast against the smooth snowfields of the younger cone. The Deming glacier has eaten into the hydrothermally altered core of Black Buttes, exiting through a deep trench to the southwest.

Besides the prominent crags jutting from Baker's southwest flank, the Black Buttes andesite lavas are also exposed to the northwest on Heliotrope Ridge, which forms the north wall of Thunder glacier cirque. To the south, a thick pile of Black Buttes lavas appears at Meadow Point, while the contact between underlying bedrock and Black Buttes andesite flows (elevation 4,400 feet) is exposed at the terminus of the Deming glacier. The younger andesite lavas of Mount Baker have largely buried whatever remains of the eastern part of the Black Buttes edifice. As with the Kulshan volcano, contemporaneous peripheral vents around Black Buttes also erupted voluminous lava flows, including the stack of at least fourteen flows at Bastille Ridge, which forms the divide between Roosevelt glacier and Smith Basin on Baker's north flank. Most of these peripheral vents and their products were scraped away when the Cordilleran ice lobes again moved south from British Columbia.

Mount Baker Volcano

Mount Baker's high-standing cone owes its shapely contours to its relative youth. Although a few early andesite lava flows near its base are older than 100,000 years—such as the two sets of flows exposed at Boulder Ridge, which divides Park and Boulder Creeks—Hildreth found that most of the edifice formed during the last 40,000 years, with much of the upper part of the cone less than 15,000 to 20,000 years old. Like Rainier, Baker is composed of hundreds of individual andesite flows, with only a minor component of pyroclastic material. The upper part of Grant Peak, however, is draped with fragmental debris, part of which derives from the last summit eruptions about 12,000 years ago, which produced voluminous block-and-ash flows that extend outward from rubbly lava flows. Today, the summit crater—which Hildreth has dubbed the Carmelo crater, evoking the Spanish explorer Quimper's name for the mountain—is completely filled with ice. Photographs taken in late summer during years of low snowfall, however, show a clearly defined circular rim bordering the 1,400-foot-wide crater. On its north edge, the Carmelo crater rim has been breached by the Roosevelt glacier, which has cut a steep headwall into Baker's north flank.

Because of its almost unbroken glacial sheath, there are only a few windows in Baker's ice cover to reveal the volcano's structure. On the partially eroded east flank, the seven principal cleavers rising above adjacent glacier surfaces reveal only a few superimposed lava flows, about four to eight each. Thinner on the upper cleavers, the flows tend to thicken downslope, some attaining a thickness of 60 to 100 feet. High on the northeast slope, a finlike eminence called the Cockscomb consists of breccia at the top but farther downslope splits into two separate cleavers, each made up of about five thin lava flows that also thicken near the base of the cone.

Not far below the Roman Wall, a conspicuous scarp on the upper southwest flank, a cleaver informally known as Pumice Ridge is composed of about four slaggy flows, blanketed in scoriaceous rubble. On the west flank, a cleaver called the Roman Nose exposes a stack of about twenty-five individual lava flows, while the Coleman glacier's headwall displays strata containing twenty to twenty-five superimposed lava flows through openings in the ice. Perhaps the most impressive glimpse into Baker's internal structure, however, is found in a 1,500-foot-high stack of lava in the east wall of the Deming glacier cirque, where about twenty andesite flows, ranging in thickness from about 30 to almost 200 feet, are visible. Other flows appear beneath the snouts of several glaciers, including the Coleman and the Roosevelt.

Many of the larger lava flows that fan out around Mount Baker's base probably once extended far beyond the main cone. As at Mount Rainier, voluminous flows erupted during Pleistocene time must have traveled several miles along ridgetops that divided valley-filling glaciers. At least some of Baker's later flows, however, filled adjacent valleys wall-to-wall, indicating emplacement after the last maximum glacial advance. Isolated remnants of a formerly extensive intracanyon andesite flow now cling to the sides of Glacier Creek gorge on Baker's northwest side. Like Rainier's Mazama Ridge–Stevens Canyon flow, this Glacier Creek andesite was thick enough to pond, forming benches high on both canyon walls. Although it is much younger than the Rainier lava stream—latest Pleistocene or early Holocene—90 percent of the Glacier Creek flow has disappeared, ground to dust by neoglacial advances and carried away in meltwater streams. Some Glacier Creek flow remnants occur at the present creek level, whereas its farthest downstream remains are located on canyon sides more than 400 feet above the creek, suggesting not only the flow's large volume, but also the remarkable swiftness with which it eroded, even though the last Pleistocene glaciers had already withdrawn from valley floors.

Thermally active Sherman crater occupies the saddle between Sherman Peak (left) and Grant Peak (right). A small debris flow from a deep notch in the crater's east rim creates a dark streak on the Boulder glacier's surface (left center). —Austin Post photo, U.S. Geological Survey

Hildreth found that the Glacier Creek lava flow belongs to a sequence of similar andesite flows that can be traced upslope to the topmost flow exposed on the Roman Wall, a short distance below Baker's summit. A sample of this lava gave a potassium-argon age of 14,000 years, plus or minus 9,000 years, almost identical to the age of the nearly erased Glacier Creek andesite.

The few surviving remnants of the Glacier Creek intracanyon flow suggest that glaciers have also eradicated many other of Baker's similarly voluminous canyon-filling or ridge-capping flows. An accumulation of six to ten andesite flows recently uncovered by the retreating snouts of the Roosevelt and Coleman glaciers now ends abruptly in glacially scoured terraces, but, as Hildreth observes, these flows also probably once extended several miles down Glacier Creek gorge. At the bottom of this andesite pile, the lowermost flow, about 200 feet thick, has a potassium-argon age of about 24,000 years, while the flow of the same thickness at the top of the stack is about

10,000 years younger. Other youthful flows—latest Pleistocene or early Holocene—such as those exposed at Crag View and between the Deming and Easton glaciers, crop out on the south flank. Because of the similarity of ages determined for the extensive lava flow remnants in different stream valleys and gorges on the south slopes, Hildreth concludes that a major period of cone building began between about 30,000 and 40,000 years ago and continued almost until the final recession of Pleistocene glaciers. The particularly intense glacial and stream erosion of the shaded northeast flank totally removed any late-Pleistocene flows that traveled down that side of the mountain into the gorges of Bar, Rainbow, or Park Creeks.

A major eruptive episode about 12,000 years ago, perhaps the last from the Carmelo summit crater, discharged a voluminous series of pyroclastic flows, pyroclastic surges, lava flows, and lahars that accumulated in thicknesses of up to 1,400 feet on the southeast flank of the cone. Although deposits from this event are apparently also present in the Sandy Creek valley, they are best exposed in the Boulder Creek valley, where they are identified

The sudden increase in heat flow and gas emission that began in March 1975 caused rapid melting of the Sherman crater ice fill, exposing vigorous new steam vents on the crater floor. —Courtesy of Fred Munich

as the Boulder Creek assemblage. Whereas glaciers removed virtually all pyroclastic material erupted during the Pleistocene, these deposits along Boulder Creek (recently ice free at the time of this eruptive episode) are relatively well preserved, extending in a broad fan across the Baker River valley, now partly submerged in Baker Lake. Because the proportion of lava flows to fragmental material increases upvalley, the Boulder Creek deposits probably originated when some of the lava flows that had erupted over glacial ice high on the cone disintegrated, producing numerous block-and-ash flows intermixed with mudflows.

Baker's Holocene Activity

Although Mount Baker had several phreatic explosions and ejections of lithic ash as late as the mid-nineteenth century, it seems to have produced only two unequivocally magmatic eruptions during the last 10,000 years. The first occurred at a peripheral vent at the volcano's southern toe about 9,800 years ago, building the Schreibers Meadow cinder cone. After ejecting both andesitic and basaltic scoria that deposited ash many miles to the northeast, and building a fragmental cone less than 250 feet high, the volcano poured out several lava flows, with clinkery or blocky surfaces, that traveled as far as 7 miles southeastward down Sulphur Creek, damming the stream and entering the Baker River. A basaltic remnant of the longest flow is preserved on the eastern shore of Baker Lake, suggesting that if it was not stripped away by the Baker River, some of the lava is concealed underwater. Sulphur Creek and Rocky Creek now pursue new courses marginal to the lava flows.

The most recent magmatic eruption, about 6,500 years ago, seems to have coincided with the opening of Sherman crater, when violent explosions blew out large quantities of hydrothermally decayed rock, expelling a white to yellowish orange lithic tephra. Immediately afterward, the volcano erupted fresh magma, ejecting a widespread layer of coarse black ash. On Table Mountain, 6 or 7 miles northeast of the peak, the sand-sized ash lies up to 18 inches thick; at a distance of 20 miles it is still several inches thick. Deposited in rapid succession, the two tephra layers, lithic and juvenile, white and black, form a striking contrast.

The earliest event in this two-part eruption also produced Baker's largest known avalanches and lahars. (If larger events occurred during Pleistocene time, glaciers have since removed all evidence of them.) When a large section of hydrothermally altered rock near the Roman Wall on the volcano's upper southwest flank collapsed, the avalanching rock transformed into a lahar that poured down the middle fork of the Nooksack River in a wave 325 feet high. After traveling 30 miles from its source, this mudflow was

A steam plume rises from Sherman crater, one of the most thermally active vents in the Cascade Range. The Black Buttes appear on the left. —Robert Kimmel photo, U.S. Geological Survey

still 25 feet thick and probably reached all the way to Bellingham Bay. A second large avalanche, initiated by phreatic explosions in Sherman crater, originated just east of the Roman Wall and moved along the same path as the first for at least 20 miles, overflowing into tributaries of Baker River. Leaving a veneer of mud and rocks on the divide between the Easton and Deming glaciers, one arm of the mudflow swept over Schreibers Meadow and about 7.5 miles down Sulphur Creek valley.

Since its last magmatic eruption 6,500 years ago, Baker has produced numerous smaller avalanches and/or lahars that were apparently unrelated to volcanic activity. Most were triggered by collapses of chemically decayed rock in the vicinity of Sherman crater and poured down valleys on the east and west flanks, including a lahar that traveled at least 5 miles down the middle fork of the Nooksack River and one that moved 9 miles down Park Creek, the latter between about 500 to 600 years ago.

Baker's Historic Eruptions

Although many nineteenth-century accounts of Baker's eruptive activity, including brief items in frontier newspapers, are secondhand and unreliable, the volcano did produce a series of phreatic explosions between 1843 and 1880 that left recognizable tephra and lahar deposits.

Two derivative reports refer to activity around 1820. Edmund T. Coleman, an English mountaineer who made the first ascent of Baker in 1868, wrote that on an earlier attempt in 1866, he interviewed "an old Indian" who recalled that when he was a boy, the mountain "burst out with a terrible fire and great smoke" and that "all the fish in the [Skagit] river were poisoned." Frederick Plummer seems to refer to the same event in his 1893 article "Western Volcanoes" in the *Tacoma Daily Ledger*, citing the report of John Hiaton, who claimed to have witnessed "fire from Mount Baker" about 1820.

In reviewing early descriptions of Baker's eruptive behavior, it is important to remember that some assertions, such as claims that all the fish in the Skagit River died, are probably rhetorical exaggerations. Geologists are also skeptical of eye-witness testimony about seeing "fire" or "flames" issuing from Sherman crater. Because the nineteenth-century phreatic explosions ejected no fresh magma, it is likely that observers mistook lightning flashes generated by static electricity—extremely common in eruption clouds—for incandescent material. Nor was the ejected tephra hot enough to ignite forest fires, although lightning strikes associated with the eruptions may have set some trees ablaze.

SOME MAJOR HOLOCENE EVENTS AT MOUNT BAKER

DATE OR APPROXIMATE AGE (YEARS)	EVENT
AD 1975–1976	Sudden increase in heat and steam emission in Sherman Crater; minor ash
AD 1958–	Series of at least six small avalanches down Boulder glacier
AD 1843–1880	Phreatic explosions eject hydrothermally altered rock, enlarging Sherman crater and generating lahars into Baker Lake; intermittent expulsions of steam and lithic ash
500–600	Clay-rich lahar travels 9 miles down Park Creek
?	Lahar travels 5 miles down Middle Fork Nooksack River
6,500	Two-part eruption discharges large volume of hydrothermally altered rock followed by magmatic ejection of black andesite tephra; major clayey lahars travel down Middle Fork Nooksack River and down Sulphur Creek
?	Clayey lahar moves 9 miles down Park Creek
?	Clayey lahar travels down Sulphur Creek to near Schreibers Meadow cinder cone
9,800	Eruption of Sulphur Creek basalt at Schreibers Meadow; lava flows extend to east side of Baker Lake
12,000	Eruption of lava flows, eleven block-and-ash flows, pyroclastic surges, and at least sixteen lahars form voluminous deposit in Boulder Creek

In his pioneering reconnaissance of the Pacific Coast's physical geography, geologist George Gibbs, who visited the area in the 1850s, preserved a typical secondhand report. Stating that Baker was then an active volcano, Gibbs wrote that he had learned from "officers of the Hudson Bay Company, and also Indians, that the eruption of 1843 was the first known. It broke out simultaneously with St. Helens' and covered the whole country with ashes." Gibbs added that Native American informants told him that the Skagit River "was obstructed in its course, and all the fish died." Repeating the claim that the eruption had ignited forest fires "for miles round," Gibbs concluded that the salmon kill resulted from "the quantity of cinders and ashes brought down by the Hokullum [Baker River]." Since Baker's reawakening in 1843, he noted, "smoke is frequently seen issuing from the mountain."

Composed of hydrothermally altered old rock blown from Sherman crater, the 1843 tephra forms a distinctive layer around the crater rim and is found at scattered locations east and northeast of the volcano. According to a USGS report by Jack Hyde and Dwight Crandell, this young tephra consists of "gray to white silt, sand, and rock fragments as much as [4 inches] in diameter" that is typically exposed on or near the ground surface, where it lies "at the grass roots or at the base of forest duff." On Boulder Ridge to the east, it ranges from a thickness of about 4 inches 3 miles from the crater to an inch or less at a distance of 6 miles. A roadcut 6 miles northeast of the summit exposes a layer of angular fragments from about an inch to 4 inches thick. Geologists found no evidence that this tephra was ever hot enough to start fires.

A short time after the tephra eruptions, two separate collapses of Sherman crater's east wall generated two moderate-sized lahars. According to a USGS study published in 2000, the first and larger mudflow poured down the east flank into Baker Lake, "raising its level at least ten feet." Some prospectors or miners who traversed Baker's eastern foot several years later described to George Gibbs the devastation wrought by the mudflows, which created "a level plain two or three miles wide, of black volcanic rock and sand, upon which were vast piles of half-burned timber [perhaps charred by lightning strikes before being entrained in a mudflow], apparently swept down, by a current of, as they supposed, lava, but more probably water." The miners, who observed "smoke ascending" from the upper east side "about two thirds the distance above the snow line" (probably steam vents at the newly enlarged cleft in Sherman crater's east rim), also claimed to have seen lava flows dotted with patches of "sulphur" on their surfaces. As with other untrained observers, the miners apparently confused lahar deposits containing chemically altered rock for lava flows.

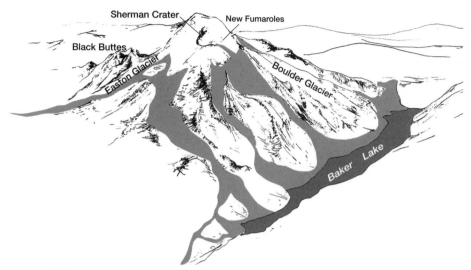

Relief map of the Mount Baker area, showing zones potentially endangered by future eruptions. Ash falls have blanketed the area east of the volcano during Holocene time, most recently in AD 1843. Debris avalanches and mudflows repeatedly inundated valley floors east and south of Baker. Two lahars reached Baker Lake during the nineteenth-century activity. —Adapted from Hyde and Crandell, 1978

During the next two decades, numerous reports were published of Baker's continuing activity, which probably consisted mainly of intense steaming punctuated by occasional small phreatic explosions. In his adventure narrative, *The Canoe and the Saddle,* Theodore Winthrop stated that a General Todd of Victoria, British Columbia, informed him that Baker was active in 1852, "sending up flame [probably lightning flashes] and smoke for several days." In his 1893 report, Plummer wrote that "in January, 1853, persons living down Sound could distinctly see a long black streak on the southwest slopes of Mount Baker which was variously estimated from 1,000 to 2,000 feet in width," adding that the streak emerged from Sherman crater's west rim. Although Plummer assumed that the "black streak" that remained free of snow for several months was a lava flow, it was probably another landslide or lahar deposit resulting from the collapse of decayed rock on the west wall of the crater. In an 1855 notation, Gibbs confirmed that during the winter of 1853–1854 Baker "had been in action, throwing out light clouds of smoke."

The most valuable eyewitness account of Baker's post-1843 activity is that of George Davidson, a geographer-surveyor who saw the volcano erupting on several occasions between 1854 and 1870. In an 1885 issue of the journal *Science*, Davidson published his detailed observations:

> In 1854 I was one day observing at the trigonometrical station on Obstruction Island in the Rosario Strait, Washington Sound [in the San Juan Islands, directly west of the volcano]: I had finished the measure for horizontal direction of the summit of Mount Baker, and was commencing a series of measures of the vertical angles for elevation, when I found the whole summit of the mountain suddenly obscured by vast rolling masses of dense smoke, which in a few minutes reached an estimated height of two thousand feet above the mountain, and soon enveloped the higher parts. Baker was distant thirty-nine geographical miles from my station. . . . The weather was fine, and we hoped to see a brilliant display at night; but unfortunately the sky clouded, and we could not see the light at night, nor the mountain the next day; when the weather cleared, the eruption had ceased; and instead of the white mountain mass, we discovered the snow covering it was apparently melted away for two or three thousand feet below the two heads. Of course the snow may not have been melted, but only covered with ashes and scoriae; and we had not the means of deciding the question at that distance.

Davidson's second explanation is correct: as was the case in similar expulsions of lithic ash from Hood and St. Helens in the 1840s and 1850s, falling tephra darkened Baker's snowfields.

Davidson also correctly notes that the active crater "was not on the summit [Grant Peak], or on the secondary peak to the south-eastward [Sherman Peak], but on the flank of the higher peak, and opening toward the south or southwest [Sherman Crater occupies the saddle between the two peaks]. In subsequent years we occasionally saw small volumes of smoke issuing from this crater."

Four years later, observers were treated to a night display that bad weather had denied Davidson in 1854. Friends in Victoria later informed the scientist that "night clouds over Mount Baker were brilliantly illuminated by the light [lightning?] from an eruption." In November 1859, the Olympia *Pioneer and Democrat* published the account of a territory legislator, John Tennant of Whatcom County, who had a similar report: "Two large and bright jects [jets] of flame were seen, having the appearance as if issuing from separate fissures or openings." Noting that the pyrotechnics were "not accompanied by that quantity of dark smoke usually attendant upon occurrences of this kind," the news article added that such eruptions "are very unusual."

In Port Townsend, James G. Swan, for many years an agent to the Makah tribe, jotted in his diary that shortly after 7:30 PM on December 3, 1859, he "saw bright flashes as of lightning with report like heavy cannon—judged it to be thunder but afterwards found it to proceed from Mount Baker which is in a state of eruption." (A thunderstorm probably coincided with a minor ash eruption.) The next day Swan observed "a great cloud of smoke and steam from Mount Baker," which issued "a dense cloud of smoke all day." A year later, the Olympia *Pioneer and Democrat* (December 28, 1860), reprinting an article from the Port Townsend *Register*, announced that the volcano was then particularly active: A clear, calm day gave local settlers a "magnificent view of the snow clad giant from whose summit ascended a column of smoke which, by aid of a telescope, presents the appearance of a steamboat blowing off surplus steam." The article emphasized that the steam cloud "was more distinctly visible than we have ever seen it before."

In July 1863, Victoria's *Daily British Colonist* reported that Baker was again erupting, with its "flames plainly seen from Beacon Hill." Like the "flames" sighted in 1858 and 1859, Baker's nocturnal flares undoubtedly had the same origin as those observed at Lassen Peak in the winter of 1914—flashes of lightning caused by static electricity rather than the glow from molten rock. Although none of Baker's historic eruptions emitted fresh magma, ordinary ash clouds commonly produce lightning.

Sporadic activity during the 1860s was intense enough, however, to in-spire wildly exaggerated tales about the supposed collapse of Baker's sum-mit. In 1865, a writer in *The American Journal of Science* quoted a story from the *Oregonian* (April 18, 1865) claiming that the volcano "is rapidly sinking in. It is asserted that the mountain has fallen 1,000 or 1,500 feet, and that its summit, which was formerly a sharp point, is now much flattened. This peak has been for some time in a state of active eruption. Dense clouds of smoke have of late issued from it. Correspondents of the California papers speak of the same phenomenon, one of whom asserts that the emission of steam is immense, and that 1200 feet of the summit has fallen in."

Davidson's sober observations in *Science* offer a corrective to this jour-nalistic excess. He took pains to make an accurate drawing of the volcano's profile, "the more particularly because rumors had found their way into the newspapers, asserting that the summit of Mount Baker had fallen in. On the contrary, I was perfectly satisfied, from my years of familiarity with its fea-tures [since 1852], that no such catastrophe had taken place between 1852 and 1870; nor was I able to detect any changes in 1877, when I was daily in sight of Baker for some time."

Edmund Coleman confirms Davidson's conclusions. On September 1, 1868, the *Oregonian* carried an interview with members of Coleman's climbing party, which affirmed that Baker's two peaks remained intact. In a mountain-eering article published in *Harpers* the following year, Coleman described the "summit plateau" of flat-topped Grant Peak as "about a quarter of a mile in diameter . . . [where] the white surface of the snow [is] unrelieved by a single rock." One of the climbers, David Ogilvey, tentatively explored Sherman crater, affirming that "the existence of the volcano is established beyond a doubt, the crater being about 300 [yards] wide, and at least 600 feet deep, from which puffs of sulphurous vapor are being emitted. The crater lies between two high peaks of the mountain, where the summits form a plateau [col or saddle?] quite bare and free from snow." At the east side of Sherman crater, Coleman said, "300 feet of the lip had been torn away where successive layers of lava [avalanches and lahars] had flowed out and cooled." He also commented that "no traces of fire were visible by daylight but smoke was plainly observed. Fire must be slumbering beneath as there is no snow on the lava."

In a separate interview for the Port Townsend *Weekly Message*, Thomas Stratton, who participated in the 1868 ascent, stated that the climbers "had a full view of the burning crater, which at intervals would emit a nauseous, sulphury smoke. . . . The smoke was of a vapory appearance and did not extend far above the top of the crater." Looking into the deep vent, Stratton found it "an awful sight. Down, down—all dark and sulphury, with green, black, red and yellow sides. . . . The lava and scora [scoria] escape at the east side of the crater, which is lower by several hundreds of feet than the west. The course of the lava [avalanches or lahars] down the mountain was free from snow or glacier." As in 1975–1976, Baker's heat emission had melted much of the crater's ice fill, exposing brilliantly colored strata of chemically altered rock.

Only two years after Coleman's initial climb, George Davidson witnessed another minor eruptive pulse. At a distance of 60 miles from the peak, he "beheld great volumes of smoke projected from the crater to an estimated height of eight hundred feet above the higher peak." A decade later, Baker apparently produced its last significant activity. After tersely stating on April 30, 1880, that Baker was "smoking," *The Washington Standard* of Olympia published a fuller account the following September 17: According to a "Capt. Smith of the steamer *Josephine*," who had sailed up the Skagit River on September 7, 1880, he had seen "flames streaming up from the summit and large volumes of smoke ascending skyward." By the time of his return trip, the activity had noticeably subsided. The December 14, 1880, issue of the *Oregonian* ran an account by an unnamed Whatcom County correspondent whose dog had awakened him at 3:00 AM on the previous November 27 to the sight of "Mount Baker lighted up in a grand style, the whole top of the mountain as plainly to be seen [as] by the sunlight, and fire shot up far above the mountain top. There did not seem to be much smoke, but shooting far into the heavens could be seen bright flashes and huge red sparks. The latter must have been lava." (As noted above, geologists discount the reports of incandescence.) Baker has steamed visibly many times since, but 1880 evidently marked the end of its nineteenth-century cycle of minor phreatic eruptions.

Thermal activity was still at a high level in the early twentieth century. When mountaineer C. E. Rusk climbed the east side route in 1903, his party "saw huge volumes of smoke rolling from between two peaks." Looking down into the interior of Sherman crater was "the most thrillingly weird spectacle" the climber had ever seen. In his *Tales of a Western Mountaineer*, Rusk described the crater fumaroles:

> In the bowl-like depression immediately between the two peaks [Grant and Sherman] was a great orifice in the snow. It was perhaps fifty feet across, although the western side was partly blocked with snow so that the opening had somewhat the shape of a half moon. At a distance of possibly two hundred feet a semicircular crevasse swept halfway around it. From the unknown depths of this abyss the black smoke rolled. It drifted away, shifting with the wind, until it was finally dissipated in the rarefied air. The wild, unearthly loneliness of the scene impressed us profoundly, for its counterpart perhaps does not exist on earth.

Rusk added that a photograph taken about 1900 shows the crater "in practically the same condition" as when he visited it in 1903. But by August 1906 thermal activity had apparently declined, for later climbers told Rusk there was then "no sign either of orifice in the snow or smoke." Heat flow and hydrogen sulfide gas emission from Sherman crater have fluctuated widely since, reaching a maximum in 1975–1976.

The Cave System in Sherman Crater

In August 1974, seven months before Baker abruptly pumped up its heat output, Eugene Kiver of Eastern Washington University led the first party (including the author) to explore and survey the cave system in Sherman crater. Like the summit caves on Mount Rainier, those on Baker formed by the circulation of fumarole-warmed air, which melted a series of passageways and ice-roofed chambers between the crater walls and the overlying crater ice fill. Unlike the Rainier caves, most of which tend to parallel the curve of the inner crater rim, Baker's main passageway in 1974 seemed to extend directly across the crater floor, under ice at least 150 feet thick. Descending into the dark cave system through an opening in firn ice along the northwest rim of the crater, our group—with flashlight beams penetrating only a few feet through the steamy atmosphere—followed a tunnel-like

passage toward the east that eventually connected with the large ice perfo-
ration near the wide notch in the east wall of the crater. Unfortunately, the
stench of hydrogen sulfide was so overpowering—even though we were
wearing gas masks—and the cave floor was so deep in mud near its terminus that we could not exit from the east end. Although we observed several
small pools of standing water, there was no hint of a lake. When Kiver made
his second exploration of Sherman crater the next year, he found that the
passage from the western rim then ended in a warm, acidic lake occupying
a steep-sided pit that Baker's increased heat flow had melted in the crater
snowpack.

Although a post-1976 gradual reduction in heat emission has allowed
ice to refill the central meltwater pit, the many fumaroles in Sherman crater remain active enough to maintain a modified cave system. Beginning
in the late 1990s, François Le Guern has led several annual expeditions to
map Baker's caves. In 2002, Le Guern found that a heavy snowpack blocked
the usual cave entrances along the crater's western edge. Entering at other
points was impossible because of the high concentration of carbon dioxide
then permeating the caves.

Hazards of Future Activity at Mount Baker

As at Mount Rainier, Baker's chief hazard—that most likely to affect populated areas many miles downvalley from the volcano—consists of debris
avalanches and lahars. Like those at Rainier, Baker's lahars are of two general
types. Cohesive mudflows, which contain 3 to 5 percent clay and are relatively "sticky," are generated by avalanches of hydrothermally altered rock
high on the cone. Although they are sometimes triggered by eruptions,
many at Baker have occurred without any eruptive activity. A 1995 USGS
report on the volcano's potential hazards estimates that the largest con-
ceivable lahar of this kind may have a volume up to 0.6 cubic mile, larger
than any known mudflow in the last 14,000 years. A recurrence of the
debris avalanches from the Roman Wall and other nearby areas of chemically decayed rock that took place 6,500 years ago, which transformed into
mudflows extending down the Nooksack River into Bellingham Bay, could
be disastrous for the towns of Deming, Everson, and Lynden. Altered rock
avalanching from Sherman Peak or the unstable east walls of Sherman crater
could pour down Boulder Creek and/or Sulphur Creek into Baker Lake,
generating waves that might overtop Upper Baker Dam. If the weakened
west wall of Sherman crater, already the source of earlier lahars, were to
collapse, the resulting mudflows could pour into Lake Shannon, perhaps
causing dam failure and floods that would sweep down the channel of the

Skagit River, inundating settlements on or near its flood plain, including the towns of Sedro Woolley, Burlington, and Mount Vernon.

The phreatic bursts of 1843—probably Baker's most significant historic activity—ejected quantities of chemically weakened rock, which showered down over areas several miles to the east and northeast of the volcano. Subsequently, avalanches of altered rock from Sherman crater formed lahars that raced down Boulder Creek into Baker Lake, raising its level by 10 feet or more. Similar but smaller avalanches have occurred since; in 1891 about 20 million cubic yards of rock peeled away from the south flank, causing a lahar that traveled 6 miles downslope, covering a square mile. Since 1958, at least six small lahars have streamed from the east side of Sherman crater down Boulder glacier, although all were of small volume (less than 650,000 cubic yards) and none reached a length of 2 miles. The extensive areas of white or yellowish orange rock—slippery, crumbly, and water-saturated—encircling Sherman crater, however, will eventually collapse, creating voluminous lahars that will travel many miles from their source to affect communities south and west of the volcano.

Although all historic activity centered at Sherman crater, it is possible that future eruptions similar to those of about 12,000 years ago may occur at Baker's summit, an eventuality that would impact all sides of the volcano. Future lava flows and pyroclastic flows are not expected to extend more than 6 miles from their source, although their secondary effects—floods and lahars—will inflict damage at much greater distances. The eruption of block-and-ash flows derived from lava streams that shatter when pitching over glacial headwalls or skidding off steep icy slopes (common throughout Baker's eruptive history) will rapidly melt snow and ice, generating sandy (noncohesive) lahars that could travel down every valley heading on the cone, including both forks of the Nooksack River, Baker and Shannon Lakes, and the Skagit River.

Unlike Glacier Peak or St. Helens, Baker rarely produces large quantities of tephra—the largest preserved deposit, the black andesite ash of 6,500 years ago, was about 10 percent the quantity that St. Helens erupted on May 18, 1980. Although prevailing southwesterly winds will direct tephra falls into largely unpopulated areas, it is possible that atypical winds could deposit an inch or two of ash over Bellingham and other communities located 30 miles or more west of the peak.

Mount Baker's next eruptions will perhaps resemble those of the mid-nineteenth century, blowing out old decayed rock from Sherman crater, scattering ash to the northeast, and pitching lahars down Boulder Creek into Baker Lake, perhaps inundating it with enough debris to overtop its dam or cause dam failure that would release a catastrophic flood through

Shannon Lake and down the Skagit River. It is also possible that Baker will produce a genuine magmatic eruption equal to some of its late Pleistocene events. In that case, Kulshan Koma may live up to the reputation it had among indigenous people as a supernaturally wounded peak that bleeds "fire."

Visiting Mount Baker

By automobile, the best unobstructed views of Mount Baker are found on Glacier Creek Road. From Interstate 5 in Bellingham, take exit 255 onto Washington 542 (watch for the Mount Baker exit sign). Drive about a half mile beyond the Glacier Ranger Station and turn south onto Glacier Creek Road (3904). Drive 8 miles over easy switchbacks to a turnaround view-point (elevation about 4,000 feet). The view eastward to Mount Baker takes in the Black Buttes as well as the Roosevelt and Coleman glaciers.

A 6-mile round-trip hike brings tremendous views of Baker's north side. About 100 yards after turning onto Glacier Creek Road, turn left onto Deadhorse Road (3907). At 12 miles is a parking area and the trailhead. The trail ascends fairly steeply to a large meadow. Continue on the trail for another three-fourths of a mile around the right side of a knoll that partly blocks the view of Baker. Once around it, walk up the easy slope of the knoll to a superb view from the top.

Views of Baker's south side are available from the Shuksan Creek Road (No. 394). From the town of Concrete on Washington 20, drive Baker Lake Road to about 3 miles beyond Baker Lake Resort. Turn left onto Shuksan Creek Road (No. 394) and follow it to its end with views of Baker's snowy cone all the way.

The Boulder Ridge Trail (No. 605), a round-trip hike of 8 strenuous miles, affords the best view of the Boulder glacier, directly below Sherman crater, and a good vantage point for glimpsing Baker's intermittent steam plumes. From Sedro Woolley, drive 14.5 miles east on Washington 20, turn left on the Grandy Lake Road (also signed for Baker Lake), following it for 12 miles, at which point it becomes Forest Service Road 11. Immediately after the road crosses Boulder Creek, about 16 miles from Washington 20, turn left onto Forest Service Road 1130, and 1.5 miles later turn left again onto Forest Service Road 1131. Continue for 2 miles to the Boulder Ridge trailhead, where the road ends.

CHAPTER 21

Mount Garibaldi

THE VOLCANO THAT OVERLAPPED A GLACIER

A few miles north of the Canadian border, the mighty Fraser River has carved a broad valley separating the American Cascade Range from its northern extension into the Coast Mountains of southwest British Columbia. This segment of the Cascade volcanoes, the Garibaldi volcanic belt, extends northwest from Watts Point on Howe Sound to Silverthrone Mountain and Franklin glacier. Containing at least eighteen volcanic clusters, this chain produced the only ice-age composite cone known to have formed partly atop an active glacier. Raised by volcanic fire on top of flowing ice, Mount Garibaldi (8,787 feet) stands about 40 miles north of Vancouver, western Canada's largest city, as the central feature of Garibaldi Provincial Park.

The largest composite cone in the southern part of the Garibaldi belt, Mount Garibaldi rises majestically above the head of Howe Sound. It is, along with Glacier Peak, one of only two Cascade stratovolcanoes composed entirely of dacite. (Lassen Peak, also dacite, is a plug dome.) With only a few lava flows veneering part of the edifice, Mount Garibaldi consists largely of eroded lava domes and spires, surrounded by voluminous pyroclastic flow deposits.

Garibaldi's twin-peaked cone formed in three discrete eruptive stages, with a long dormant interval between the first two. In the first phase of activity, during mid-Pleistocene time, an ancestral volcano erected a broad composite cone of dacite flows and breccia. Remnants of this dissected edifice now form the upper 800 feet of Brohm Ridge and the lower north and east flanks of the mountain. A series of coalescing dacite domes were then extruded at Columnar Peak on the southeast flank and possibly on the northern edge of the edifice at Glacier Pikes. Potassium-argon dates show that the ancestral cone formed about 250,000 years ago.

After the old Garibaldi fell silent, recurrent glaciations thoroughly scoured the area, and the Cheekye River excavated a deep valley into the west flanks of the dacite pile. The valley later filled with glacial ice derived at least in part from a glacier in the Cheakamus Valley.

While glaciers still filled the Cheekye basin, but after the ice had already attained its maximum extent and had begun to recede, the modern volcano built much of its visible cone. Surrounded by a branch of the Cordilleran

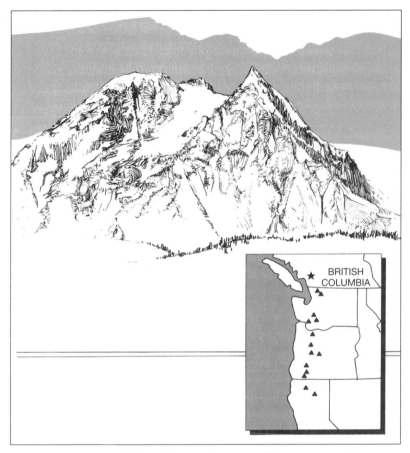

Mount Garibaldi in the Cascade Range (Coast Mountains)
of southern British Columbia

ice sheet thousands of feet thick, Garibaldi discharged much of its ejecta directly onto the surface of a glacier filling the Squamish River valley at its southwestern foot. Garibaldi's eruptive style was Peléan, characterized by the extrusion of stiff, viscous dacite that formed massive lava domes and spires centered at Atwell Peak. As growing domes shed incandescent rock fragments, forming large block-and-ash flows, extensive aprons of breccia accumulated around a solid core. Apparently laid down in rapid succession, these pyroclastic flows spread out to build a broad fragmental cone with a volume of about 1.5 cubic miles. Garibaldi's original slopes were exceptionally gentle for a stratovolcano, averaging only 12 to 15 degrees. Subsequent erosion, however, has made its flanks notably steeper and more precipitous.

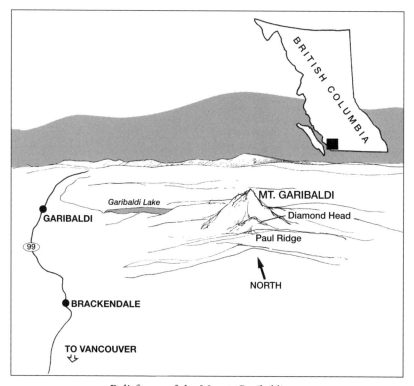

Relief map of the Mount Garibaldi area

Where the growing cone rested on the encircling ice or on ridges only slightly above the general ice level, the pyroclastic flow deposits extend at least 3 miles away from their source. Where the cone banked against higher ground, the volcano's flanks are correspondingly shorter and more abrupt. On the west, and to a lesser degree the south, Garibaldi significantly overlapped a lobe of the Cordilleran ice sheet. Melting of glacial ice by hot pyroclastic flows caused water to pond against the southern arm of Brohm Ridge. Ash flows deposited underwater in this meltwater lake created the volcanic sandstones atop Brohm Ridge, nearly 2,000 feet above the present floor of the Cheekye drainage basin.

After the main Peléan eruptions had ceased, the surrounding ice surface rose to an elevation of 5,500 feet. Whether this resurgence was merely a return to the pre-eruption levels after the thawing effect of the pyroclastic flows had ended or whether it resulted from general climatic cooling is unknown. Shortly afterward, the ice sheet finally receded, with disastrous effects on Garibaldi. As the glacier supporting it dwindled, Garibaldi's west flank began to collapse in a series of landslides and mudflows.

Where the layer of ice between the pyroclastic flow deposits and bedrock was thin, melting of the ice caused only minor breaks in the cone's surface. The conspicuous scarp at Cheekye Ridge is probably an example of this process. However, where the volcano overlay ice hundreds or thousands of feet thick, as in the Cheekye basin, radical disruption of the edifice occurred. As the underlying ice melted, Garibaldi's broken and oversteepened west flank disintegrated into rockslides and avalanches that carried nearly half the original cone into the Squamish Valley.

A large quantity of debris derived from Garibaldi's disintegrating cone fills much of the Squamish Valley, an extensive depression at the head of Howe Sound. Approximately 10 square miles of the valley floor are underlain by an average thickness of about 300 feet of dacite blocks and rubble that formerly composed the volcano's west flank. Not all this material, approximately 0.6 cubic mile, poured into the Squamish Valley at once. Several fans of debris now form terraces upvalley toward the ruined cone, recording a series of slides or avalanches that occurred as the glacier wasted.

After most, or all, of the ice sheet had thawed, Garibaldi again became active. Changing its eruptive mode, the volcano quietly emitted streams of liquid dacite from a crater north of the Atwell Peak plug dome. Some of the dacitic lava flowed down the north and northeast flanks of the mountain. But one lava flow poured several thousand feet westward over the landslide scar on Garibaldi's west face. This late flow traveled down a slope of 30 to 35 degrees, a grade far steeper that the 12- to 15-degree angle of Garibaldi's original slopes. Partial destruction of this flow by the subsequent slumping of the pyroclastic deposits on which it lies shows that the flow erupted only a short time after the ice beneath the west flank disappeared.

Opal cone, on Garibaldi's southeast flank, produced the area's most recent postglacial eruption, emitting the Ring Creek lava flow. Unusually long for a dacite flow, the Ring Creek lava traveled more than 10 miles downslope.

Two prominent dacite domes of different ages underlie Garibaldi's twin peaks. The pyramidal Atwell spire, from which many of the cone-building pyroclastic flows derived, forms the lower southern peak. The Dalton dome, associated with the last dacite lava flows, forms the slightly higher northern summit. With a volume of about 0.15 cubic mile, the most recent lava flows cover the north and part of the west flanks with a thin veneer of solid rock. Slightly more than half, about 0.8 of a cubic mile, of the original Peléan deposits remains in place; an almost equal volume of Garibaldi's edifice now lies in the Squamish Valley.

The Garibaldi Lake Volcanic Field

Although the highest, Mount Garibaldi is only one of many diverse volcanic edifices in the area. The Table, a conspicuous flat-topped pile of silicic andesite rising about 1,000 feet above its base, stands 3.5 miles to the north. From a distance it resembles a mesa like those in the southwestern United States. From other directions, it evokes the famous Devil's Tower in Wyoming. Up close it appears as a stack of horizontally layered lava flows spread out one atop the other like slices of burnt toast on a plate.

The Table is a tuya, formed by the repeated flooding of lava into a roughly cylindrical pit melted through the Cordilleran ice sheet during its waning stages. The thin lava flows partly plastering its steep sides like frosting on a cake probably originated when molten rock trickled down into the gap thawed between the andesite pile and the encircling walls of glacial ice. Because the edifice is relatively uneroded—with no glacial deposits on its summit—the Table most likely formed in early Holocene time when the last continental ice sheet was already in rapid retreat.

Another intriguing volcanic feature, the Black Tusk—a massive spire of dark lava resembling a walrus tusk—is much older than the Table. According to geologist Nathan Green, the deeply eroded Black Tusk is the most striking part of a volcanic complex built during two distinct eruptive phases. Beginning well over a million years ago, the first stage erected a large andesite edifice that now forms cliffs to the northwest and south of the Tusk. After glaciation extensively dissected this ancestral cone, a second eruptive stage produced a sequence of andesite lava flows that chilled against walls of the surrounding ice. A final eruptive pulse extruded a large dome, which subsequent glaciation carved into the present summit spire. Scouring action of the continental ice sheet also excavated a deep U-shaped canyon on the east flank of this second-stage cone, a valley that was afterward filled by lava flows from Cinder Cone, a much younger volcano located about 1.5 miles east of the Black Tusk. About 500 feet high, this asymmetrical pyroclastic cone is nestled between two arms of the Helmet glacier.

Immediately north of Garibaldi, a vent at Clinker Peak erupted two large lava flows when the continental ice sheet was already withdrawing. Pouring into the valley of Rubble Creek, the northernmost flow encountered a wall of ice blocking its path and causing the lava to pond to a depth of 800 feet. After the glacier receded, the steep, clifflike northern edge of the flow—known as "the Barrier"—partly crumbled, producing a series of rockfalls and avalanches, the latest in 1855–1856. The continuing danger of landslides along Rubble Creek prompted the provincial government in 1981 to declare the unstable area "too hazardous for human habitation." The nearby village of Garibaldi had to be abandoned.

The Northern Coast Range Volcanoes

North of Garibaldi and the Garibaldi Lake volcanoes form several other volcanic clusters. The largest composite cone in the Garibaldi belt's middle section is Mount Cayley, a glacially dissected mass of dacite and rhyodacite lava. Formed during two extended stages of activity, the earliest of which began in Pliocene time about four million years ago, Cayley retains little of its original form. Early eruptions of dacite lava flows, interbedded with pyroclastic material, culminated in the extrusion of a massive plug dome, which underlies its present summit spire. A secondary summit, the jagged Vulcan's Thumb on the south flank, consists of welded breccia erupted during Cayley's second stage of growth. Intense glacial scouring erased most of the older edifice before activity resumed at several peripheral vents. This late phase included emission of a large dacite lava flow into the valley of Shovelnose Creek and the extrusion of two small domes.

Mount Garibaldi (8,787 feet) is the only major Pleistocene composite cone in North America known to have been built partly atop an active glacier, part of the huge Cordilleran ice sheet that smothered most of Canada. When the underlying glacier melted, approximately half of the original Garibaldi edifice collapsed.
—Catherine Hickson photo, Geological Survey of Canada

The sheer cliffs and precipitous ice-sharpened spires of Cayley's glaciated summit area are highly unstable. According to Jack Souther of the Geological Survey of Canada, the southwest slope spawns "repeated rockfalls, avalanches, and periodic debris flows which frequently damage roads and bridges in the Squamish valley." Even while quiescent, Mount Caley's incessant shedding of rock makes it a hazard to anyone traveling in its vicinity.

The northernmost stratovolcano in the Garibaldi belt—and by far the most recently active—Mount Meager is part of an eroded volcanic complex west of Meager Creek and the Lillooet River. Formed during at least four different eruptive cycles that spanned the last two million years, the Meager volcanic complex erupted a variety of lava types, from basalt and andesite to dacite and rhyolite. The most abundant rocks are andesitic flows and breccias emplaced between one million and a half million years ago. All of these lavas are so severely eroded that in many cases all that remains are erosion-resistant lava plugs filling the volcanoes' conduits or dikes that fed the now-vanished flows. Many andesite flows issued from vents at the Devastator, a high-standing volcanic neck that produces numerous rockfalls. Isolated remnants of the glacier-stripped andesite flows underlie the crags at Pylon Peak. Although Mount Meager is the youngest of four overlapping composite cones that erupted from eight distinct vents, its denuded edifice bears little resemblance to the volcano's original form.

About 2,400 years ago, a vent on the northeast shoulder of Plinth Peak, a feature north of Mount Meager's main summit, produced Canada's most recent large explosive eruption. Beginning with a Plinian outburst about the same size as that of St. Helens in 1980, the volcano ejected a voluminous dacite tephra, the Bridge River ash. Extending hundreds of miles eastward across British Columbia and into Alberta, the ash fall formed layers up to 70 feet thick on some ridgetops near its source on Plinth Peak. Blocks of dacite pumice up to 188 feet in diameter catapulted hundreds of yards from the crater.

Perhaps caused by partial collapse of the Plinian ash column, the eruption's second phase initiated several pyroclastic flows. Because the active vent was located in an amphitheater-like basin surrounded by high cliffs, the pyroclastic flows were directed to the northeast, where they raced 4 miles downslope into the narrow confines of the Lillooet River valley. In the next eruptive stage, viscous magma forming a series of domes or thick lava flows broke apart on the steep slope. The resultant block-and-ash flows, hot enough to weld, filled the valley and dammed the Lillooet River. Although the river, swift and energetic, soon cut through the first debris dam, successive waves of pyroclastic material again choked the valley, building a more stable dam. Overlying the air-fall pumice, these pyroclastic flows and the welded block-and-ash flow deposits have an aggregate thickness of about 475 feet.

Following the explosive events, a large dacite lava flow spilled from the vent and pitched over cliffs on Mount Meager's precipitous north flank. Part of the flow disintegrated, forming an unusual deposit of welded lava fragments adjacent to the flow. Hot rock cascading downslope from recurrent collapses of the thick lava stream also contributed to the dam blocking the Lillooet River, creating a lake upstream that was eventually almost 200 feet deep. When impounded waters overtopped the dam, a powerful flood transported boulders the size of houses downriver for several miles. The Lillooet River has since incised a gorge about 35 feet wide and 100 feet deep in the welded valley-fill. Today commercial miners quarry the abundant pumice deposits on Mount Meager's northeast flank, the only such enterprise in Canada.

The presence of two clusters of hot springs in the Mount Meager complex indicates that a magmatic heat source still exists below the surface. If the volcano produces another explosive eruption similar to that of about 2,400 years ago, it could have a devastating effect on nearby logging and mining operations as well as a fishery in the Lillooet River, which hosts a significant salmon run. The town of Pemberton, about 30 miles downstream from the mountain, is likely to suffer considerable damage from a heavy ash fall, as well as from floods and mudflows. The ash plume from another Plinian eruption is likely to disrupt both air and vehicular traffic from southern British Columbia to Alberta.

Visiting Garibaldi

Drive Provincial Highway 99 northward from Vancouver, British Columbia, past the town of Squamish. The turnoff to Diamond Head in Garibaldi Provincial Park is posted along the east side of the highway between Squamish and Brackendale. Drive to Diamond Head base camp and hike the jeep trail 6 miles to Diamond Head Lodge. There is no automobile travel from base camp to the lodge. From Diamond Head to the Gargoyles, grotesquely sculptured crags, the distance is about 2 more miles. The elevation gain from the parking lot to the Gargoyles is 2,000 feet. From the base of the Gargoyles the view of Garibaldi's south side is unobstructed.

CHAPTER 22

Glacial Ice and Volcanic Fire

NOW AND IN THE FUTURE

For almost two million years, the Cascade volcanoes have had an intimate relationship with the shimmering streams of ice that repeatedly formed on their slopes, an association of volcanic fire and glacial ice that will continue indefinitely into the future. During Pleistocene time, the almost ubiquitous presence of valley-filling glaciers heading on the large stratovolcanoes significantly determined their shape, not only sculpturing their cones but also directing the paths of their lava flows, typically along adjacent ridgetops to form long arms of steep-sided lava cliffs radiating from the main cone.

Glaciers also selectively determined the kinds of material that have survived from ice-age eruptions. Stripping away many of the volcanoes' pyroclastic deposits, Pleistocene glaciers typically spared only the most erosion-resistant parts of the great composite cones, redesigning their original constructional forms. In many cases, massive glaciers hundreds to thousands of feet thick virtually demolished older volcanic edifices, leaving only scraps of once-towering cones behind. Although considerably reduced in size today, approximately 1,000 glaciers still cling to the highest Cascade peaks from Mount Shasta to the Garibaldi volcanic belt in British Columbia, their persistence contributing to both the region's economy and its volcanic hazards.

Glaciers in Flux

Whether viewed at a distance reflecting the pink glow of a setting sun or experienced directly by hikers and mountaineers who scale their icefalls or negotiate their yawning crevasses, glaciers are not only a familiar feature of the Cascade landscape but also an important economic resource. In addition to their aesthetic and recreational appeal that draws myriads of tourists, glaciers serve as frozen reservoirs of fresh water, accumulating snow in winter and releasing water when it is most needed in summer. Even during drought years, when the seasonal snowpack is low, meltwater issuing from glaciers keeps major rivers in the Pacific Northwest flowing all year round.

A crucial resource, glaciers provide water for industry, agricultural irrigation, and domestic use, as well as for powering hydroelectric facilities that supply electricity to several western states.

Because the behavior of glaciers affects the daily lives of a large segment of the Pacific Coast population, as well as the natural environments of plants, animals, and fish, current glacial trends and probable future changes have important consequences for a wide region. Extremely sensitive to variations in climate, the glaciers' expansion or retreat is typically the harbinger of long-term changes in regional weather patterns. Since humans first settled in the Western Hemisphere, the most dramatic and rapid climatic change affecting North American glaciers took place between about 15,000 and 10,000 years ago, when vast continental ice sheets melted away and valley-filling alpine glaciers withdrew upslope to nest in high-altitude cirques. In this sudden global warming, temperatures at northern latitudes were probably somewhat higher than they are today, and many mountain glaciers may have disappeared altogether. Most of the glaciers now mantling Cascade volcanoes such as Baker, Rainier, Hood, Shasta, or the Three Sisters are not shrunken remnants of Pleistocene glaciers, but are descendants of ice streams formed during recent Holocene neoglaciations, when global temperatures again cooled and alpine glaciers expanded, creeping considerably farther downvalley than they do now. The Little Ice Age, which brought a prolonged chill to Europe and North America between about AD 1350 and 1850, witnessed a significant growth of ice cover in many different areas, from the Cascades and Rockies to Greenland and the Swiss Alps.

The gradual recession of northern-latitude glaciers that began after 1850 escalated notably after about 1920, with glaciers beating an increasingly rapid retreat. Although there have been brief periods—a few years or decades—when some glaciers expanded, the last part of the twentieth century witnessed a particularly striking worldwide shrinkage of alpine glaciers that continues into the present.

Glaciers of Rainier

At Mount Rainier, where glaciers have been studied more extensively and for a longer period than elsewhere, perennial ice mantled approximately 40 square miles of the cone in 1913, but by 1950 the areal extent of Rainier's twenty-five named glaciers had shrunk to 37 square miles. Today, ice covers about 34 square miles.

Recent fluctuations of Rainier's ice streams offer a representative example of glaciers' irregular responses to shifts in snow levels and mean annual temperatures. Although the general trend is recession, individual glaciers, depending on their size, altitude, location on the mountain, and amount of precipitation and sunlight they receive, showed diverse responses to changing weather patterns. Generally speaking, large glaciers on the south and west slopes, where they are subject to more solar radiation, are retreating faster than those on the shaded north and east sides. Although snowfall is heaviest on the south flank, the less-well-nourished glaciers on the north or northeast flanks show much less wasting, probably because their favored northern position shields them from sunlight.

Heading at the Willis Wall, the huge glacial cirque incised in Mount Rainier's north face, the Carbon glacier is in the shadow of high canyon walls for almost its entire length. It is not only the longest (5.7 miles), thickest (700 feet), and most voluminous (0.2 cubic miles) ice stream in the forty-eight contiguous states, it also descends to the lowest elevation of any U.S. glacier south of Alaska (about 3,200 feet). Advancing about 425 feet between 1965 and 1973, it has fluctuated only a little since. Because it has retreated much less than most other Cascade glaciers from its Little Ice Age

The Emmons and the Winthrop glaciers stream from Mount Rainier's summit cone, divided in their lower reaches by Steamboat Prow, the tip of which appears at the bottom of the photo. —Austin Post, U.S. Geological Survey

maximum, the Carbon glacier snout stands only about half a mile from its terminal moraine. The Douglas fir, alder, and other trees and shrubs crowding near its terminus testify to its long-term stability.

The Emmons glacier, which covers 4.3 square miles on Rainier's east flank and has the largest surface area of any glacier in the lower forty-eight states, receded upvalley nearly a mile between 1913 and the early 1960s, but since then the Emmons has advanced steadily, occasionally pausing, but never retreating. After the massive rockfall from Little Tahoma Peak in 1963 covered its lower extent under rubble from 50 to 200 feet thick, effectively insulating the ice and retarding ablation, the rate of growth markedly accelerated, advancing 601 feet between 1967 and 1973. By 1992, the terminus had advanced a total of about 1,800 feet from its 1970 position, while the glacier gained 350 feet in thickness. In the early twenty-first century, its advance seems to have slowed appreciably.

Large rockfalls from Russell Cliff, the latest in 1989, have partly buried the surface of the Winthrop glacier on Rainier's northeast slope, but the effects here have been less well studied. The insulating qualities of the rock cover may have acted to stabilize the Winthrop's terminus.

Nisqually glacier, which sweeps from the summit ice cap down Rainier's south flank and skirts the Paradise Visitor Center, often fluctuates in both size and thickness, perhaps because its southern exposure makes it particularly sensitive to climatic changes. Studied continuously over a longer period than any other glacier in the United States, the Nisqually has been annually monitored since 1918, when it was undergoing steady recession. After thirty-four years of unbroken retreats, it had melted back a half mile from its 1918 position, leaving a residue of dirty, stagnant ice masking its terminus. Beginning in 1953, however, the revitalized glacier overrode the stagnant ice and pushed forward until 1969. Between 1969 and 1974, the Nisqually again lost ground, retreating 197 feet, but then—responding to heavier snowfalls in the 1970s—reversed direction and moved downvalley about 560 feet between 1974 and 1980. During this episode of expansion, the Nisqually traveled at remarkable speed for a glacier: in May 1979 it was clocked at a dizzying 29 inches per day! Perhaps because of drier and warmer weather between 1977 and 1997, the Nisqually is again in retreat.

In 1947, a major flood swallowed the lower portion of the Kautz glacier, a smaller ice body on Rainier's south flank. Heavy October rains apparently added to the quantity of water already stored in the glacier, resulting in sudden collapse of its lower extremity and the catastrophic release of a large volume of water, triggering the area's largest glacier outburst flood and debris flow in historic time. Torrents of rock and mud raced 5.5 miles down Kautz Creek and into the Nisqually Valley, burying the main park road under debris 28 feet thick and killing hundreds of trees, many of which now stand as ghostly snags along the present highway. Approximately 50 million cubic yards of rock and sediment, including boulders 13 feet in diameter, were transported in the mudflow. By 1966, the Kautz began to regain some of its volume lost almost twenty years earlier, advancing 438 feet by 1980, although smaller debris flows have also moved along Kautz Creek in 1961, 1985, and 1986.

In August 2001, rapid melting of the lower Kautz glacier that undermined adjacent deposits of loose glacial sediments produced another series of small mudflows that traveled down Van Trump Creek to its confluence with the Nisqually River. Comparable in size to numerous others that have occurred in the valleys of South Tahoma, Kautz, Nisqually, and Winthrop glaciers in recent decades, these debris flows are typical products of glacial wasting. As Rainier's ice cover continues to melt, such jokulhlaups, sudden outbursts of water from a glacier, will become increasingly common; because they take place on many different parts of the mountain with little or no warning, jokulhlaups present a genuine hazard to park visitors.

South Tahoma glacier, on Rainier's southwest flank, was making slight advances until the summer of 1967, when a flood burst from it at about the 7,400-foot level. Although the terminus was virtually severed from the upper part of the glacier, the South Tahoma front continued to advance, pushing ahead about 600 feet from 1967 to 1969. Between 1969 and 1974, the advance slowed noticeably to 250 feet, and to only 50 feet during the next two years. Meanwhile, the lower 3,000 feet of the glacier, which the jokulhlaups had detached from its zone of snow accumulation, began to stagnate and shrivel.

Like many other receding glaciers, the South Tahoma continues to produce outburst floods and resultant debris flows—at least twenty-three since 1967—carving out a gorge 130 feet deep into sediment and stagnant ice below its terminus. Because bouldery debris flows have buried the Westside Road on several occasions since 1988, the National Park Service has repeatedly closed this route to vehicular traffic about 2.5 miles from the junction with the Nisqually-Longmire Road.

Flowing from the summit ice cap in a magnificent icefall down the volcano's western face, the Tahoma glacier then divides into two ice lobes that descend into different valleys. The lobe feeding Tahoma Creek advanced about 350 feet between 1967 and 1977, building a moraine from which it had retreated about 147 feet by 1980. In the following decade, the Tahoma not only thinned considerably—its surface lowering by about 40 feet or more—but also receded along its margins. Water impounded within the deteriorating lobes or behind dams of stagnant ice will probably supply numerous jokulhlaups in the future.

Perhaps the most disturbing change that increasing mean temperatures at high elevations have brought to Mount Rainier's ice cover has occurred in the volcano's twin summit craters. Since 1870, when climbers first discovered it, the summit firn cave system has been maintained by a near-perfect balance between heat flow from the crater steam vents and the annual replenishment of the crater ice-fill from snowfall. Volcanically heated air circulating through the long passageways and high-roofed chambers beneath the ice canopy keeps the caves open, while their location in perpetual cold more than 14,000 feet above sea level keeps the cave walls and roofs stable. In an ongoing study of the summit caves that began in the late 1990s, François Le Guern sampled volcanic gases issuing from Rainier's fumaroles and mapped the caves in both craters; in the unusually warm summer of 2002, however, he found that radical changes were taking place: Part of the roof of the eastern crater entrance—the "Airplane Cave"—had collapsed directly over the fumaroles from which Le Guern's team ordinarily collects gas samples. The "Rabbit Hole," a passage giving access to the ice-roofed lake in the western crater, not only was flooded with sand, but the danger of falling ice made the route impassable. Le Guern observed no changes in the craters' heat or gas emission, but the summit snow cover had diminished by many feet and the surface was pocked with "sun cups," or "penitents," sharp blades of ice up to 3 feet tall, a phenomenon that occurs, Le Guern noted, "when snow and ice melt under [a] tropical climate."

If this deterioration continues, one of Rainier's rarest features (comparable cave systems are known to exist only in Baker's Sherman Crater and Alaska's Mount Wrangell) may soon vanish, lost to global warming.

Glaciers of St. Helens

The loss of Mount St. Helens's glaciers—70 percent of the volcano's glacier cover—did not stem from gradual climatic change but occurred almost instantaneously when the 1980 eruptions destroyed the volcano's former summit and north side, removing an estimated 3.5 billion cubic feet of ice, including most of the Forsyth, Leschi, Loowit, and Wishbone glaciers. Only a narrow tongue of the lower Forsyth glacier remained, while the Nelson, Ape, and Shoestring glaciers were beheaded when St. Helens's former summit was removed, exposing cross-sections of the ice streams along the crater's east rim. The hot pyroclastic flows that scoured the glaciers' surfaces further reduced them, melting layers of snow and ice tens of feet thick and triggering numerous mudflows. Because the vanished summit no longer provided areas of snow accumulation, in the 1980s St. Helens's glaciers rapidly shrank. By 2000, the Forsyth, Shoestring, Dryer, and Nelson glaciers had disappeared altogether, while the Toutle, Talus, Swift, and Ape glaciers continued to shrink.

Although devastating to St. Helens's previously existing glaciers, the 1980 eruptions also created a unique environment for the growth of an entirely new glacier inside the volcano's mile-wide crater. Until the mid-1990s, the crater floor remained too warm for permanent ice fields to develop, but beginning in 1996 USGS geologists identified a new glacier forming between the 2,000-foot-high southern wall of the crater and the actively steaming lava dome. Forming a half circle wrapped around the south, east, and west sides of the 1980–1986 dome, the informally named Crescent glacier by 2004 had a maximum thickness of 700 feet and a volume of about 170 million cubic yards, about a third of which consisted of rockfall debris from the crater walls. Following an upsurge in earthquake activity and a series of moderate explosions that blew ash 11,000 feet into the air, opening a new vent between the old dome and the encircling glacier, in October 2004 St. Helens began oozing fresh magma to erect a second dome. As the new dome rose and expanded, the Crescent glacier was uplifted more than 1,000 feet above its previous level, tilting and severely fracturing the surrounding ice. Because a thick layer of rubble apparently insulated the ice from the growing lava dome, little melting occurred during this initial phase. The glacier's prospects for long-term survival, however, are bleak: when St. Helens produces more vigorous explosions or sends large quantities of hot rock avalanching from the new dome, the Crescent glacier—after mobilizing lahars into Spirit Lake and the North Fork Toutle River—will join the vanished Forsyth, Shoestring, and Dryer glaciers in oblivion.

Glaciers of Mount Baker and the North Cascades

Bearing an even heavier burden of ice for its size than Rainier, Mount Baker stands closer to the sea than any other large Cascade stratovolcano, and receives the full brunt of winter storms blowing in from the Pacific. Positioned in a maritime environment, warmer and wetter in winter and cooler in summer than in most other parts of the North Cascades, Baker's glaciers experienced a phenomenal thirty-year advance between about 1948 and 1978. According to a 1993 report by Joel Harper, each of the six glaciers he studied—the Coleman, Boulder, Deming, Easton, Rainbow, and Roosevelt—showed notably similar fluctuations during three sequential periods: All continued a rapid retreat that had begun before 1940 and extended into the late 1940s and early 1950s. They then began an advance that lasted until the late 1970s or early 1980s, after which they started another retreat that continued into the 1990s. The three-decade-long advance of Baker's glaciers, in which some ice streams lengthened as much as half a mile, contrasts strikingly with the behavior of most other North Cascade glaciers during the same period, which either stagnated or underwent consistent wasting.

Harper suggests that Baker's glaciers grew at the same time that inland glaciers dwindled not only because of the volcano's maritime location and high level of precipitation, but also because it is significantly higher than glacier-bearing mountains farther east in the range. Baker's glaciers, most of which descend from its 10,781-foot summit, have a large percentage of their total area above 7,000 feet, while other North Cascade glaciers have much lower elevations and a correspondingly drier and warmer environment. Because Baker's glaciers show a remarkable sensitivity to variations in annual precipitation and mean temperatures, it will be interesting to observe the future effects of the 1998–1999 winter storms, during which 95 feet of snow fell on the mountain.

Wrapped in an almost unbroken sheath of ice, Mount Baker sustains more glaciers than any other Cascade volcano except Mount Rainier. —Austin Post photo, U.S. Geological Survey

Since 1945, the Cascade Range has experienced several winters of abnormally high snowfall, interspersed with years of lower precipitation. In the 1960s and 1970s, the average snowpack in the North Cascades was about 50 percent greater than it had been in the 1920s and 1930s. Winters from 1969 into the early 1970s set new records. A warming, drying trend that began in 1977, however, brought near-drought conditions, which persisted into the late 1990s.

To discover the effects of this trend on the region's ice cover, geologist Frank Granshaw undertook a study of glaciers in the North Cascades National Park Complex, which contains 25 percent of all glaciers in the forty-eight adjacent states. Granshaw found that between 1958, when the last previous glacial inventory had been made, and 1998, the number of glaciers in the park had dropped from 321 to 316. Not only had five small glaciers entirely disappeared during the forty-year period, but 80 percent of the remaining glaciers had declined in mass. Studies of the South Cascade glacier, which is located southwest of the park, show that it has lost 40 percent of its mass, withdrawing two-thirds of a mile upvalley between 1928 and 2000. As at many other shrinking glaciers, most notably in central Oregon, a new lake has formed in front of the receding terminus. If the record 1998–1999 snowfalls prove to be an anomaly in the overall warming trend, and mean annual temperatures continue to rise at their present rate, Granshaw suggests that all North Cascade glaciers may be gone within a few centuries.

Glaciers of Oregon

With nine principal glaciers, Mount Hood sustains 12.3 billion cubic feet of ice, more than any other Oregon volcano, but only slightly more than half that mantling the bulkier Mount Adams on the north side of the Columbia River. Hood's largest and best-studied glacier—the Eliot, entrenched on the northeast flank—is also the thickest ice stream, measured 361 feet in a 1981 survey. After reaching its greatest Little Ice Age extent about AD 1740, when it built steep lateral and terminal moraines that now rise about 130 to 300 feet above the present ice surface, the Eliot glacier began a decline that apparently accelerated in the later decades of the twentieth century. Studying the glacier between 1984 and 1989, Scott Lundstrom, now of the U.S. Geological Survey, discovered that the Eliot thinned an average of approximately 13 feet during that five-year period. Lundstrom also found that the thinning was not spatially uniform: there was less at the debris-covered terminus, where the ice is shielded from solar heat, than at the debris-free upper part of the glacier. Noting that the 1984–1989 mean thinning rate represented "an annual loss of about one per cent of the [Eliot's] 1980 volume," Lundstrom concluded that the glacier is presently losing mass at three times the pre-1980 rate, as indicated by its relation to the adjoining lateral moraines.

The Three Sisters cluster of volcanoes currently sustains seventeen named glaciers, with the three highest peaks—North, Middle, and South Sisters—bearing about 5.7 billion cubic feet of ice. Tree-ring dating of moraines in the central Oregon Cascades shows that many glaciers here did not reach their Little Ice Age maximum extent until the 1850s and 1860s, significantly later than those on Mount Hood and other more northerly mountains. The Sisters' glaciers also lingered longer at their neoglacial terminal moraines than did ice streams in other parts of the range. Although they had thinned considerably during the later nineteenth century, photographs taken in 1910 show that most of the Sisters' glaciers had not yet begun the rapid shrinkage that took place during the next several decades. Central Oregon's largest glacier—the Collier, which originates on Middle Sister's northwest shoulder—is also the best studied, and exhibits a behavior pattern that also characterizes the area's other glaciers. Although the Collier retreated rapidly after 1910, by about 1950 it began to regain some of its lost mass. But while glaciers at Rainier and Baker, responding to a cooler, wetter climate, generally advanced during the next two or three decades, the Collier merely stabilized, building small lateral and terminal moraines during the 1960s and 1970s. After the early 1980s, almost all central Oregon glaciers again shrank and withdrew upvalley.

Although exact measurements are unavailable, casual observation of the Three Sisters' glaciers in the early twenty-first century indicates that they continue to dwindle, uncovering ground that had been buried under ice for centuries. As Jim O'Connor and his colleagues at the U.S. Geological Survey have found, the glaciers' recession has created a phenomenon that poses a new geologic hazard—the formation of glacial lakes impounded by abandoned moraines. When glaciers withdraw upvalley, they leave in their wake the steep lateral and terminal moraines that bordered their former margins. Meltwater from the receding glacier typically accumulates many tens of feet deep behind these moraines, some of which are hundreds of feet high and composed of unstable, loosely consolidated glacial till. During the last century, such moraine-dammed lakes have formed in glaciated mountain ranges all over the world, from the Peruvian Andes to the Himalayas of Nepal. Although more than a dozen lakes have formed elsewhere in the Cascades—Adams and Glacier Peak have two, Baker, Goat Rocks, and Jefferson have one each, and ten others exist in the nonvolcanic North Cascades—the Three Sisters area has, as the USGS observes, "the highest concentration of past and present Neoglacial moraine-dammed lakes in the conterminous United States."

The best-documented rise—and fall—of a moraine-bounded glacial lake is that of Collier glacier, which Ruth Hopson Keen studied and photographed for more than 40 years for the Mazama mountaineering club of Portland. In 1931, the Collier's terminus still abutted Collier cone, a cinder cone at the northwest base of North Sister. Three years later, the glacier had drastically receded, and a large meltwater lake formed, contained by the Collier's lateral and terminal moraines. Overflow from the lake spilled through a low point in the moraine, via a stream called the White Branch. During a hot dry July in 1942, the rising level of meltwater suddenly burst through the White Branch notch, carving a gorge many feet deep in the moraine and releasing about 1.5 million cubic yards of water that quickly transformed into a debris flow, distributing boulders and sediment for several miles downslope. A similar but much smaller outbreak occurred between 1954 and 1956.

The area's earliest recorded outburst flood from the rupturing of a glacial moraine occurred in August 1933, when a large volume of water and ice poured from Eugene glacier, a relatively small body of ice on the north flank of South Sister. Eventually carrying sediment into the McKenzie River, the flood was responsible for temporarily polluting the city of Eugene's water supply. A few years later, a small lake that formed between the Eugene glacier's terminus and its end moraine discharged another flood downslope. In 1966, the outbreak of water from a lake fed by the East Bend glacier on Broken Top, located east of South Sister, traveled down Crater Creek and Soda Creek, depositing a broad fan of debris over the meadows near Sparks Lake.

The latest in this series of glacial lake floods occurred about 1970, when a moraine dam below the snout of Diller glacier, on Middle Sister's east flank, was breached, releasing approximately a million cubic yards of water into the Squaw Creek drainage. Completely draining the lake, which had been 75 to 80 feet deep, the flood transformed into a debris flow that buried part of the north fork of Squaw Creek under boulders and gravel 14 feet thick.

Today, several moraine-bounded lakes remain, the largest occupying a basin below South Sister's Prouty glacier and containing perhaps 3 million cubic feet of water. Chambers Lakes also contain sizable quantities of glacial meltwater, as does the lake at the terminus of Thayer glacier on North Sister's east flank. Both the Thayer and the East Bend glaciers on Broken Top are actively calving—shedding blocks of glacial ice—into the lakes they border. As the region's mean annual temperatures continue to rise, accelerating melting, the rupturing of moraine dams and outburst glacial floods will continue to occur, potentially endangering backcountry visitors in the Three Sisters Wilderness.

Glaciers of Mount Shasta

Standing 40 miles south of the Oregon-California border, Mount Shasta (14,162 feet) is the southernmost Cascade volcano to support glaciers, with more than 4.7 billion cubic feet of ice. It is also the only mountain in California that presently stands above the permanent snow line, the altitude above which the snow cover survives summer melting. According to an estimate made in 2001, the vertical distance that Shasta's summit rises above the snow line is only about 1,000 feet on the south face and about 3,000 feet on the north, making its glacier system particularly susceptible to fluctuations in climate. During the twentieth century, Shasta's glaciers, including California's largest—the Hotlum—have repeatedly advanced or retreated in response to comparatively slight changes in annual temperature and precipitation.

When Clarence King first inventoried Shasta's glaciers for the U.S. Geological Survey in 1870, he officially recognized only five ice streams, named here in diminishing order of size: the Hotlum, Whitney, Bolam, Wintun, and Konwakiton. Some recent researchers, such as Philip T. Rhodes, however, have identified at least four or five others. In a 1987 report for *California Geology*, Rhodes lists the Stuhl (Mud Creek) glacier (honoring Edward Stuhl, a local naturalist); the Chicago glacier, once connected to the Hotlum glacier but now self-contained; the Upper Wintun glacier; the Watkins (Clear Creek) glacier, embedded in a perennial snowpack on the east flank; and the Olberman, a glacieret on the sunny south side, which seems to show signs of life only after seasons of exceptionally heavy snowfall, such as that of 1981–1983. According to Rhodes, all of these informally named glaciers reveal one or more characteristics of flowing ice, including bergschrunds and crevasses.

Shasta's glaciers were probably dwindling when King first explored them, but about 1900 they responded to seasons of increased snowfall by expanding, a modest growth that continued until 1916. From 1917 to 1936, however, the glaciers suffered from drought conditions; Rhodes estimates that during this 20-year-long dry period the volume of glacial ice diminished by half. By 1934, the Wintun, on Shasta's east slope, had shriveled and stagnated. Slightly increased precipitation (about half an inch per year) in the later 1930s—along with an average temperature decrease of 1 degree Fahrenheit—permitted the glaciers to regain some of their lost mass, with the Whitney advancing about 1,500 feet between 1944 and 1972. Even the moribund Wintun revived, expanding to a length of about 3,500 feet. Following increased snowfall in the early 1980s, the glaciers showed another spurt of growth, with a large ice wave progressing down the Whitney ice stream.

In 2002, when Slawek Tulaczyk and Ian Howat of the University of California, Santa Cruz, began a systematic study of Shasta's glaciers, they made some surprising discoveries: Unlike other Cascade glaciers to the north or those in the Sierra to the south, the Shasta ice streams are still growing! According to Tulaczyk and Howat, between 1951 and 2002, the Hotlum and Wintun "approximately doubled in area," while the Bolam grew by 50 percent and the Whitney and Konwakiton by about one third. This unexpected ice resurgence apparently results from slightly warmer winter temperatures that favor increased precipitation. Although Shasta stands in the rain shadow of the Klamath Mountains, its summit is high enough to capture storms moving in from the Pacific. As warm moist air rises up the volcano's slopes, it releases snow in what Tulaczyk calls the "snow-gun effect," similar to a process now occurring on some of Norway's glaciers, where advancing ice is also countering the global trend.

The present warming trend will probably continue until it reaches the point at which it will negate the increase in precipitation, causing Shasta's glaciers to recede like those in other parts of the range. According to the Intergovernmental Panel on Climate Change, temperatures could be 2.5 to 10.4 degrees Fahrenheit warmer in 100 years, a change that can spell disaster for glaciers and for the human, animal, and plant populations that depend upon them for resources ranging from drinking water to hydroelectric power. As the glaciers thin and recede, outburst floods in summer and fall will become more common, potentially endangering people who venture into our western mountains to seek recreation for both body and spirit.

Expanding Population and Increasing Volcanic Hazards

Because they erupt less often than many volcanoes in Indonesia, Japan, Alaska, Central America, or other parts of the circum-Pacific Ring of Fire, our western volcanoes tend to impart a false sense of security, fostering the mistaken impression that they are no more than a scenic backdrop to people's daily lives. Producing an average of about two eruptions per century—in contrast to the two or three eruptions occurring every year in Alaska—the Cascade and Mono Lake volcanoes are too easily ignored by government officials and the general public. But the comparative infrequency of their eruptions must be balanced against the probable consequences—and absolute certainty—of future activity, particularly when Rainier, Hood, or Shasta erupt again on the same scale they have during the last 2,000 years.

Potential loss of life and property from future volcanic eruptions on the Pacific Coast continues to increase as residential and commercial developments proliferate in lowlands adjacent to volcanoes in the Pacific Northwest and northern California. Pressure from a rapidly growing population in the eastern Puget Sound region, for example, has already stimulated the building of multitudinous new structures in the Cascade foothills, as construction projects expand up lahar-prone valleys heading on Baker, Glacier Peak, and Rainier. In addition, thousands of summer homes and scores of lumber camps, hydroelectric facilities, ski resorts, and dams already located in or near volcanic hazard zones annually draw a large and mixed population of summer residents, loggers, forest workers, tourists, hikers, campers, and skiers to exploit the mountains' economic or recreational resources. Despite the devastating mudflows that swept down the Toutle River from Mount St. Helens in 1980, destroying bridges, highways, logging camps, and two hundred houses, most people living or working near the Cascade or Mono Lake volcanoes do not yet seem to realize that similar—but vastly larger—events could strike their own communities.

Anticipating Volcanic Hazards

In facing potential dangers from nearby volcanoes, residents should have a clear idea of what kinds of hazards they face and what steps they can take to minimize their vulnerability. Some dangers can safely be ruled out. Although a few television or newspaper journalists have implied that Seattle, Tacoma, or Portland eventually might suffer the same fate as Pompeii, this claim is misleading. The Roman city of Pompeii stood only 6 miles from the summit of Mount Vesuvius, and, being downwind during the AD 79 eruption, was buried under a heavy tephra fall, followed by a series of massive pyroclastic flows that completed its destruction. Because no major city in the Pacific Northwest is as close to an explosive volcano as Pompeii and Herculaneum were to Vesuvius, they will not be entombed in ash. (Towns sitting at the base of Mount Shasta are an exception.)

Because prevailing westerly winds from the Pacific would direct ash clouds to the east, away from the most densely populated areas—as was the case with the Plinian ash plume of St. Helens on May 18, 1980—cities like Seattle and Portland are not likely to receive significant tephra falls. However, a large explosive eruption may take place when winds reverse their usual direction, as happened on three occasions in 1980: St. Helens's outbursts on May 25, June 12, and October 16 showered fine ash over Portland and other towns in western Oregon and Washington. At the beginning of the Holocene, atypical winds carried one of Glacier Peak's most voluminous ash clouds hundreds of miles to the south.

Even relatively light ash falls can seriously disrupt traffic flow and communication systems over a broad area. As a USGS study points out, "Clouds of fine ash block sunlight, diminish or eliminate visibility, and thus stop motor-vehicle travel. Ash can cause or exacerbate pulmonary problems in people and animals. Even thin tephra accumulation may ruin crops . . . contaminate surface water, plug storm-sewer and even sanitary-sewer systems, and obstruct highways and irrigation canals." In addition, wet tephra can "short out power lines" and, because of its abrasive qualities, sharply increase wear on machinery.

The greater the quantity of tephra that falls, the longer it takes a community to recover from its disruptive effects. Residents of areas blanketed by St. Helens's 1980 ash falls found that while a layer less than 0.25 inch creates a major inconvenience, a thickness greater than about 0.67 inch causes an economic disaster, as happened at the town of Ritzville, Washington. Within two weeks, however, even communities struggling under ash 3 inches deep returned to normal functioning.

Although few in number, western communities subject to pyroclastic flows and surges face an even graver menace. Built on the lower slopes of Mount Shasta, which, next to St. Helens, is the most frequently active Cascade stratovolcano, the towns of Weed and Mount Shasta sit atop extensive pyroclastic flow deposits. When Shasta reawakens, their future is highly uncertain (see chapter 23). Because of their high temperatures (typically several hundred degrees or more) and high velocity (up to 225 miles per hour), pyroclastic flows are the most lethal of volcanic phenomena, flattening and burning everything in their path. Although pyroclastic flows are generally confined to topographical depressions and rarely travel more than 6 to 8 miles beyond their source, accompanying pyroclastic surges can sweep over high ridgetops and devastate larger areas. A pyroclastic surge's terrifying power to destroy was vividly illustrated at Mont Pelée in 1902, when searing ash clouds raced through nearby St. Pierre, leveling the city and incinerating or asphyxiating its 30,000 inhabitants. In 1982, similar pyroclastic flows and surges killed 2,000 people near El Chichon volcano in Mexico.

For residents of the Pacific Northwest, however, the most far-reaching and potentially destructive volcanic hazard is the near-certain prospect of voluminous mudflows originating at Baker, Glacier Peak, Rainier, St. Helens, or Hood, all of which have been active during historic time. During the last few thousand years, scores of lahars have traveled up to 65 miles downvalley from these peaks, burying the present sites of numerous towns and cities along the eastern shore of Puget Sound and along tributaries of the Columbia River. Whether triggered by the sudden collapse of hydrothermally altered rock high on a volcanic cone, or by the eruption of hot magma on summit ice fields, future lahars much larger than those produced at St. Helens in 1980 are inevitable. Filling valleys wall-to-wall in waves hundreds of feet high, lahars—like a churning mass of liquid concrete—grow larger as they move downslope, picking up additional rock debris from valley floors and incorporating felled trees, bridges, houses, cars, trucks, and other objects as they advance. Except for air-fall tephra, lahars extend farther from their source than any other volcanic phenomena, and are even more destructive. If of sufficiently large volume, like many from Mount Rainier, they can overflow reservoirs, overtop dams, and eradicate highways and entire towns. Even years after their emplacement, runout and sedimentation from lahar deposits can disrupt large areas.

As one geologist observed, lahars triggered by the spontaneous collapse of a chemically decayed volcanic edifice are analogous to the sudden collapse of a rotten, termite-infested house. Fortunately for people living in their paths, however, most lahars are generated by volcanic eruptions, which are usually preceded by small-scale precursory activity that can alert authorities to the danger. Swarms of small earthquakes centered under the volcano, increased heat flow or steam emission, and swelling of the volcanic cone are all signs of an impending eruption, warning the area's residents to move out of the hazard zone. Even before the major eruption occurs, rising magma may cause extensive deformation of the volcano—similar to the notorious "bulge" at St. Helens in 1980—causing a landslide of unstable rock than can transform into a catastrophic mudflow. The town of Orting, Washington, has installed a warning signal to alert residents of an oncoming lahar from Mount Rainier, giving residents perhaps 45 minutes to an hour to evacuate. When a lahar is on its way, people are advised to drive—or run—to high ground immediately. Climbing a few hundred feet above valley floors may mean the difference between life and death.

Because small events are more likely than large ones, most future eruptions will be of small or moderate size, like the majority of those witnessed in the nineteenth century. During the last 2,500 years, however, numerous large eruptions have occurred at several volcanoes, including Rainier, St. Helens, Hood, Newberry, Medicine Lake, and Shasta. A repetition of this activity could affect millions of people and create enormous economic losses.

A volcano might also erupt on a much larger scale than it has in the recent geologic past, producing a cataclysmic outburst like that of Mount Mazama 7,700 years ago. Because such volcanic catastrophes occur so infrequently, geologists do not recommend planning for such an abnormal event. Public officials, however, must be prepared to cope with the consequences of moderate eruptions similar to those at Mount Rainier between about 2,600 and 1,100 years ago. A repeat of Rainier's recent activity, when numerous lahars poured into several river valleys emptying into Puget Sound, would be sufficient to cause widespread devastation and seriously disrupt the economy of the Pacific Northwest.

A Preview of Volcanic Hazards

To evaluate potential hazards at a particular volcano, it helps to know as much as possible about its past behavior. Fortunately, geologists have recently gathered important information about the life histories of several volcanoes most likely to threaten inhabited areas, providing us with a clearer idea of their typical activity and eruptive frequency. Although geologists generally assume that a volcano's future conduct will conform to that of its recent past, it is always possible that it will change its eruptive style in new and unexpected ways—as did St. Helens with its north-side collapse and lateral blast in 1980.

THE MONO LAKE–LONG VALLEY REGION. Next to St. Helens, the U.S. Geological Survey considers this area the most likely source of the next volcanic eruption in the forty-eight adjacent states. Repeated earthquake swarms and ground deformation in the 1980s and 1990s indicate that magma has already been intruded at shallow depths in Long Valley; carbon dioxide gas escaping from magma emplaced under Mammoth Mountain has killed hundreds of trees on the volcano's slopes. If a dike (a tabular sheet of magma) reaches the surface, it could produce a long chain of vents erupting almost simultaneously at the Mono and/or Inyo Craters. If it follows recent eruptive patterns, the activity would probably occur in three stages: (1) steam-blast explosions ejecting towering columns of ash that will blanket large areas many miles downwind; (2) ejections of moderate volumes of rhyolitic pumice, some in the form of pyroclastic flows; and (3) after the magma has degassed, the comparatively quiet effusion of pasty rhyolite that will build steep-sided lava domes, filling the eruptive vents. Renewed activity may also occur at one or more of the island volcanoes in Mono Lake. If eruptions take place close to resort communities such as Mammoth Lakes, property losses may be high.

LASSEN PEAK–CHAOS CRAGS. Almost any part of Lassen Volcanic National Park or Hat Creek valley to the north could witness future eruptions. Activity in the Lassen volcanic center, however, has been extremely episodic, with long dormant intervals intervening between eruptive events. After the Lassen plug dome was emplaced about 27,000 years ago, about 26,000 years passed before the Chaos Crags cluster of dacite domes was erupted. Cinder Cone, a basaltic-andesite tephra pile with its accompanying blocky lava flows, formed only about 350 years ago at the northeastern corner of the park. After a year of minor phreatic eruptions beginning in May 1914, Lassen Peak produced a short lava flow, pyroclastic flows and surges, mudflows, and a moderate quantity of juvenile tephra in May 1915, after which declining phreatic explosions continued until 1917. Future activity will probably produce additional silicic domes and pyroclastic flows in the western part of the park and basaltic-andesite cinder cones or small shield volcanoes in the eastern portion. Elevation of the Chaos Crags domes was accompanied by explosive eruptions and pyroclastic flows, some of which traveled about 13 miles down adjacent valleys, a repetition of which could threaten resorts and campgrounds in the vicinity. Rockfalls unaccompanied by volcanic activity, such as those that formed Chaos Jumbles about 300 years ago, also present a continuing hazard. Eruptions occurring during winter and spring, when the region bears a heavy snowpack, could generate mudflows down the Manzanita Creek, Lost Creek, and/or Hat Creek valleys.

MOUNT SHASTA. Second only to St. Helens in the large number of its Holocene eruptions, Shasta represents a major geologic hazard to nearby communities. Although large tephra eruptions are uncommon at Shasta, lithic ash falls from ash clouds associated with pyroclastic flows derived from collapsing domes mantle the volcano's east flanks to a depth of a foot or more. Activity has centered at the Hotlum cone for the last 9,000 years, but new vents could open anywhere on the edifice. Extrusions and collapse of domes erupted high on Shasta's west flank could send hot pyroclastic flows or surges sweeping over the towns of Weed and Mount Shasta, while mudflows could inundate the communities of McCloud and Dunsmuir, burying major transportation routes, including Interstate 5, U.S. 97, and California 89. Rapid melting of Shasta's winter snow cover could initiate flooding of the upper Sacramento River, possibly impacting Shasta Lake and Dam.

MEDICINE LAKE. With seventeen Holocene eruptions, the Medicine Lake volcano is one of the most frequently active in the Cascade Range, erupting extensive basalt flows on the shield's outer flanks and highly silicic lava in or near the summit caldera. Like those at most long-lived volcanoes, Medicine Lake's eruptions tend to occur in clusters, with a few centuries of intense intermittent activity followed by long dormant intervals. The most recent eruptive episodes built Little Glass Mountain about 1,000 years ago and Glass Mountain about 800 years ago. Future flank eruptions will produce basaltic or basaltic andesite cinder cones and associated lava flows; rhyolitic magma erupted at near-summit vents may produce moderate volumes of tephra, followed by the extrusion of thick viscous lava similar to that forming Glass Mountain. Because it has produced only one large-scale pyroclastic event, which formed the Antelope Well tuff about 180,000 years ago, the Medicine Lake volcano is not expected to stage a violently explosive eruption.

MOUNT McLOUGHLIN. Apparently quiet since late Pleistocene time, this small volcano is not likely to erupt in the near future. If it does revive,

McLoughlin is likely to produce effusive eruptions of andesite from vents on its flanks, although small-scale pyroclastic eruptions at the glacier-exposed central conduit are possible. Except for winter and spring, when it is snow covered, McLoughlin poses little danger from flood or mudflows.

MOUNT MAZAMA (CRATER LAKE). Since Mazama's collapse about 7,700 years ago, all activity has been confined to the caldera, where numerous andesite or dacite flows built a central lava platform and the edifices forming Wizard Island and Merriam cone. Except for the extrusion of a small dacite dome underwater about 5,000 years ago, Mazama has been dormant since its early postcaldera activity. Future eruptions will probably occur inside the western part of the caldera, producing lava flows and cinder cones of andesite or dacite. Although explosive outbursts may generate large waves in Crater Lake and hurl ballistic projectiles over the caldera rim, geologists do not expect the caldera walls to rupture.

MOUNT THIELSEN REGION. Mount Thielsen, Union Peak, Diamond Peak, Mount Washington, and Three-Fingered Jack are extinct.

NEWBERRY VOLCANO. This enormous shield-shaped composite cone erupts a wide variety of lava types, emitting copious streams of fluid basalt on its broad flanks and viscous masses of silicic rhyolite in its summit caldera. Although late Pleistocene basaltic lava flows traveled many tens of miles to the north, covering the sites of Bend and Redmond, future flank eruptions are likely to be more restricted, resembling those that occurred on the northwest rift zone about 7,000 years ago, when a dozen separate lava flows erupted from different vents along a fissure. Lava Butte, only 10 miles south of Bend, marks the northern terminus of this rift eruption. The latest activity took place in the caldera about 1,300 years ago, beginning with an explosive ejection of tephra (the Newberry pumice, which extends hundreds of miles eastward into Idaho) and culminating in extrusion of the Big Obsidian flow east of Paulina Lake.

MOUNT BACHELOR. This volcano may be either dormant or extinct. Marking the northern end of a chain of late Pleistocene shield volcanoes, Bachelor was formed after the last ice-age maximum. If it is dormant rather than extinct, its future eruptions will probably emit sluggish streams of blocky lava from flank vents. Activity in winter or late spring could produce enough meltwater to trigger mudflows endangering nearby ski resorts and blocking the Cascade Lakes Highway. Lava or mudflow damming of local streams could impound new lakes, which could overflow to cause downstream flooding.

BROKEN TOP. This deeply eroded volcano is probably extinct.

SOUTH SISTER. Most recently active of the Three Sisters, about 2,000 years ago it produced flank eruptions of pumiceous tephra and viscous lava flows that dammed Fall Creek to form the Green Lakes. In addition to the 2,000-year-old Rock Mesa and Devils Hill chain of rhyodacite domes on its southeast slope, South Sister erupted more voluminous silicic lava flows and domes along its flanks during late Pleistocene time. If the ground deformation first detected in the early 2000s continues, it may be the harbinger of similar silicic eruptions; light falls of ash may affect Bend, Sisters, or other communities to the north or east.

MIDDLE SISTER. Recent dating of the lava flows composing its upper cone indicates that it was repeatedly active during late Pleistocene time, although glaciers have cut deeply into its east face. Future eruptions of andesite, dacite, or even more viscous magma are possible.

NORTH SISTER. This volcano is extinct, although more cinder cones, similar to Collier cone, may form along its north base.

BELKNAP SHIELD. This young shield produced many voluminous flows of basaltic andesite during multiple eruptive episodes between about 3,000 and 1,500 years ago and will probably erupt again, perhaps ejecting tephra from vents near the summit and lava flows along its flanks. It is not considered a threat to settled areas.

MOUNT JEFFERSON. Although it has not erupted during Holocene time, Jefferson is a long-lived stratovolcano that may be dormant rather than extinct. Voluminous eruptions of tephra, like those it produced in the late Pleistocene, could adversely affect broad areas north and east of the volcano, including U.S. 97 and U.S. 26, as well as the towns of Redmond and Madras and the Warm Springs Reservation.

MOUNT HOOD. After a dormant interval lasting more than 10,000 years, Hood revived about 1,500 years ago, intermittently erupting domes and large pyroclastic flows that built a large debris fan on the south slope where Timberline Lodge and its associated ski developments now stand. Pyroclastic surges have repeatedly swept down the south flank, some as far as Government Camp, while massive lahars have repeatedly traveled down the White, Zigzag, and Sandy River drainages, many as far as the Columbia. Extruded only about 200 years ago, Crater Rock hosts numerous active steam vents. When Hood revives, it will probably extrude new lava domes at or near Crater Rock. Dome collapse will generate pyroclastic flows and surges that may endanger the Timberline resort area and the town of Government Camp. Lahars may impact the White and Sandy River drainages for many tens of miles downvalley.

MOUNT ADAMS. Most of Adams's huge cone above the 7,000-foot level formed between about 30,000 and 15,000 years ago. During Holocene time, Adams has produced smaller volumes of magma, erupting at least seven lava flows and minor quantities of tephra. Collapses of hydrothermally altered rock high on its west face could create mudflows threatening farms and small settlements, including Trout Lake.

MOUNT ST. HELENS. The most consistently explosive volcano in the forty-eight adjacent states, St. Helens has repeatedly ejected large volumes of tephra that blanketed tens of thousands of square miles, as well as innumerable pyroclastic flows and surges. Because the 1980 event removed its former summit and north flank, leaving its wide crater open to the north, future eruptions, including lava flows and pyroclastic flows, will be directed toward the Spirit Lake area, while mudflows will pour down the North Fork Toutle River. Failure of the debris plug damming the North Fork could create catastrophic flooding downstream, impacting the Cowlitz River and perhaps closing the Columbia to shipping. Although the new dome-building eruptions that began in 2004 have not melted the crater glacier (as of this writing, February 2005), the rise of gas-rich magma into the conduit could trigger violent explosions, perhaps shattering the dome and hurling ballistic projectiles 2 to 3 miles over the crater rim. Melting of the crater glacier will also precipitate lahars. Sustained moderate eruptions, including lava flows and new domes, will eventually rebuild the cone.

MOUNT RAINIER. Because huge lahars from this heavily glaciated giant have repeatedly inundated large areas of eastern Puget Sound that are now densely populated, Rainier—which has erupted at least twenty times in the last 9,700 years—is the most potentially dangerous volcano in the United States. Large mudflows, triggered by the collapse of hydrothermally altered rock on the upper west flank, have also occurred when the volcano was quiet and may occur again without warning. Like other Holocene eruptive episodes that spanned many decades or centuries, Rainier's next eruptions—probably emitting lava flows and pyroclastic flows and surges from the summit craters—may continue sporadically for a long period, generating numerous destructive lahars down the White, Nisqually, and Puyallup (and perhaps the Cowlitz) drainages. As in the recent geologic past, lahars and floods may impact towns from Orting and Sumner to Tacoma and southern Seattle.

GLACIER PEAK. In addition to generating numerous lahars, this comparatively obscure volcano sequestered deep in the North Cascades has also erupted large volumes of tephra, as well as domes and pyroclastic flows. Despite its remote location and relatively small stature, Glacier Peak has affected large areas both downwind and downvalley, including the sites of towns located in the Skagit River valley. Its irregular pattern of eruptive events suggests that it is not likely to erupt again soon, but both large explosive outbursts and the extrusion of lava domes and pyroclastic flows are possible.

MOUNT BAKER. Unlike Glacier Peak and St. Helens, Baker has typically erupted only small-to-moderate quantities of tephra during the last 10,000 years. Although its Holocene eruptions have been infrequent, with long dormant intervals separating eruptive events, it is a relatively young volcano and may stage eruptions comparable to those of 12,000 years ago, when lava flows and numerous pyroclastic flows traveled down its slopes, particularly on the east side. More likely, intermittent phreatic eruptions at Sherman crater will eject minor quantities of tephra and trigger lahars from hydrothermally altered rock on the crater walls. Because Baker's upper cone contains extensive areas of chemically altered rock, large-volume debris avalanches and mudflows on the east, south, and west flanks of the volcano may occur even without magmatic activity. In addition to Baker Lake and Baker River on the east side, the valleys of the Nooksack and Skagit Rivers, including the towns of Burlington, Sedro Woolley, and Mount Vernon, are particularly at risk from large-scale lahars.

THE GARIBALDI VOLCANIC BELT. Although Garibaldi has been quiet since early Holocene time, it may erupt again, extruding lava domes that collapse to form pyroclastic flows and generating mudflows that will sweep down adjacent stream valleys. Lava flows are not likely to travel more than 3 or 4 miles from their source. The most recently active volcano in the Garibaldi belt, Mount Meager, produced a violent explosive eruption about 2,400 years ago, discharging large volumes of tephra, pyroclastic flows, and lava flows. A similar eruption today would imperil several small communities downstream from the volcano, as well as disrupt traffic and communications over a wide area. Encompassing a wide range of volcanic landforms, the Garibaldi volcanic belt could produce new vents at many different locations between Howe Sound and Bridge River.

Preparing for the Next Eruption

What can people do to protect themselves and their families from such a powerful geologic force as a volcanic eruption? Carolyn Driedger at the Cascades Volcano Observatory in Vancouver, Washington, suggests taking three concise steps:

1. **Learn.** Find out whether you live in an area that has been previously subjected to large mudflows or other volcanic phenomena. Learn as much

as you can about how the volcano in your neighborhood has behaved in the past and what geologists expect it to do in the future.

2. **Inquire.** Ask public officials in your town or state about how to respond in a geologic emergency. Ask whether escape routes have been established, and know what they are in case it becomes necessary to evacuate.

3. **Plan.** Work out an emergency plan with your family so that if a nearby volcano erupts everyone has a clear idea of what to do—such as leaving lahar-prone valley floors for high ground, out of the reach of impending floods or debris flows. Although volcanic eruptions may seem remote from one's ordinary experience, they are inevitable—and how you and your community respond to them may make the difference between life and death.

CHAPTER 23

When Mount
Shasta Erupts

The following fictional account describes what might happen were Mount Shasta to become the second Cascade volcano to erupt during the twenty-first century. Based on the volcano's known behavior during the recent geologic past—in Holocene time Shasta is second only to St. Helens in the frequency of its eruptions—the narrative presents the kinds of dangerous activity we can expect when the sleeping giant awakes. When the inevitable occurs, the survival of people living in threatened areas will depend not only on the nature and size of the eruptions, but also on the social, political, and scientific response to the volcanic crisis, particularly on how wisely and effectively government officials act to protect the endangered population.

The glaciated stratovolcano that dominates the horizon throughout most of northern California is beginning to stir. On September 2, climbers report having seen "wisps of steam" issuing from the crater of Shastina, the large secondary cone on Shasta's northwest flank. Forest Service rangers who investigate the story can find no new steam vents, but note a strong sulfurous odor, indicating the emission of hydrogen sulfide gas. The next day a team from the U.S. Geological Survey's Cascades Volcano Observatory in Vancouver, Washington, arrives to install an array of seismometers around the volcano, as well as instruments to detect swelling or deformation of the cone. A USGS helicopter, with a forward looking infrared (FLIR) device mounted beneath the helicopter's nose, makes reconnaissance flights over the volcano, taking thermal images that might reveal new hot spots. According to a USGS press release, Shasta last erupted during the late eighteenth century, when it produced hot pyroclastic flows and mudflows that inundated the site of McCloud, the historic lumber town now at the mountain's southern foot.

In a report dated September 6, the USGS states that it detected no increase in heat flow on Shastina or at the summit of Hotlum cone. Because all known eruptive activity has centered at the Hotlum vent for the last 9,000 years, geologists expect most future eruptions to occur there, although the spokesperson cautioned that a new vent could open anywhere on the mountain.

On September 7, a sharp earthquake jolts the towns of Dunsmuir, McCloud, Weed, and Mount Shasta City. Seismologists place the focus of the shock about a mile west of Shasta's crest, at a depth of approximately 12 miles. Registering a magnitude of 4.0 on the Richter scale, the tremor is felt as far away as Yreka.

A second earthquake, scoring 4.7 on the Richter scale, rolls through parts of Siskiyou County the night of September 7. The next morning two lighter shocks, at subsurface depths of between 9 and 10 miles, are recorded at the seismometers recently installed in Weed. A more severe jolt follows the next day, causing a mild alarm from Yreka to Redding, the region's largest city. Centered at a depth of only 7 miles, this quake registers a magnitude of 5.1. Geologists report that the increasing shallowness of the earthquake foci may indicate that magma is rising toward the surface.

During the next forty-eight hours, USGS seismographs record at least 320 earthquakes, only a dozen of which are strong enough to be felt. A second USGS FLIR flight discovers two large hot spots on Shastina, both along the summit crater's western rim. The larger is close to the narrow gash that heads Diller Canyon.

With more than a dozen global positioning systems (GPS) now installed on and around Mount Shasta, the USGS crew monitoring the volcano is able to measure any deformation accompanying the swarm of earthquakes that began a week earlier. Operating from helicopters, the team has also installed gas monitoring equipment and two portable telemeters stations—also known as "Spyders"—on Shastina's crater rim. The Spyders are able to measure and transmit electronically any changes in the distance between their position and a fixed location not affected by tumescence, enabling scientists to detect deformations caused by injection of magma into the cone.

By the evening of September 10, residents of Weed, Mount Shasta City, Dunsmuir, and McCloud experience an almost constant rattling of windows and dishes in cupboards. Timbers in old farmhouses creek eerily as the earth shifts beneath them. After consulting with representatives from the USGS, the California State Board of Emergency Preparedness alerts the local police and Forest Service to a possible mass evacuation. The governor of California has already placed the state police on alert and has requested help from the National Guard should the speedy removal of several thousand people become necessary.

Angry delegations from local businesses, as well as public relations agents for timber and railroad companies that own land around the mountain, immediately protest these announcements. Reminding the governor and state legislators of the loss of business resulting from "unnecessary" and "premature" actions, commercial interests point to what they call the "fiasco of 1980," when volcanic earthquakes in the Mammoth Lakes area prompted similar warnings of a volcanic hazard, only to have no activity take place. Decades later, despite repeated earthquake swarms at the Mammoth resorts, these spokespersons insist, no eruption has occurred. Local motel, restaurant, and shop owners also point out that stemming the profitable influx of tourists eager to see an active volcano will rob mountain communities of significant income potential and further depress an already stagnant local economy. California's governor and the speaker of the assembly promise "not to act hastily."

After a brief lull, another swarm of earthquakes, now focused a scant 2 miles beneath the volcano's west flank, strikes the Mount Shasta region shortly before dawn on September 12. By noon, the seismographs are recording almost continuous shocks. At 12:35 PM a column of dark ash suddenly bursts from the top of Shastina, rising about 12,000 feet skyward. A low rumbling, reminiscent of distant thunder, accompanies the ash cloud, which swells and unfurls like a great black umbrella. Fortunately, prevailing winds direct the plume toward the sparsely inhabited country east of the volcano, where fine ash begins to dust the Medicine Lake area, 35 miles distant.

A Forest Service airplane radios that Mount Shasta's snowfields are blackened by the ash fall. Rock fragments littering the Bolam, Hotlum, and Whitney glacier surfaces seem to have been ejected cold, for they have not melted pits in the underlying ice. Most of the material thrown out thus far, a USGS geologist explains, is probably derived from steam explosions blasting through the plug of solidified lava that blocked Shastina's central conduit.

Small to moderate phreatic eruptions occur sporadically for more than a week, while the swarms of small earthquakes centered beneath the peak increase in number. Although these phreatic bursts disable several of the GPS stations, others near Shastina's crater continue to function, providing evidence that the summit area is rising and swelling outward at the rate of 3 to 4 feet a day. Because of hazards from laterally directed explosions, rockfalls, and avalanches, the general public is barred from the mountain's vicinity. Citizens of Weed, McCloud, Dunsmuir, and Mount Shasta City as well as ranchers and summer residents near the volcano's base are warned that they may have to leave immediately if the eruptions grow more violent. The Yakohovians and Seekers of Light, two of the many local religious cults, formally protest this restriction, which they claim infringes upon their constitutional freedom. The prohibition against climbing the mountain will interfere with the international festival of mystics and psychics that they had planned to celebrate on Shasta's heights at the fall equinox.

Columnists in the San Francisco Chronicle complain that the volcano is the biggest disappointment since the Comet Kohoutek failed to show in the 1970s. A federal agency issues an official press release pointing out that since the most recent ice age, Shasta has produced only one large explosive eruption, depositing the Red Banks pumice about 9,700 years ago. "Considering the laws of probability," one government geologist observes, "smaller events rather than larger ones are to be expected."

Shortly before the dinner hour on September 19, local conjecture about Shasta's intentions ends with a roar heard for a hundred miles in every direction. As a column of charcoal gray ash soars 50,000 feet above Shastina, lava blocks large enough to be seen from miles away are tossed high into the air and crash downslope. The whole mountain trembles with these detonations, triggering avalanches of freshly erupted material and dislodging old rock formations.

Local officials, including deputies from the county sheriff's office, immediately organize a previously adopted evacuation plan for Mount Shasta City and Weed. Guided by California state troopers, long auto caravans head north on Interstate 5 toward Yreka, ultimately transporting almost 10,000 people out of the immediate danger zone.

By sunset the eruption has reached its height. A ruddy glare shows fitfully amid the turbulent ash plume billowing above Shastina's crest. High-altitude northerly winds now bear the ash plume over the head of the Sacramento Valley, raining powdery ash at Shasta Dam, 45 miles south of the volcano. Radio and TV stations in Redding, 9 miles farther south, report that fine ash has begun to drift through the upper Sacramento Valley, compounding the usual smoky haze of this agricultural region.

Roused from his bed in Sacramento, the governor of California issues a state-of-emergency proclamation. The canopy of ash extending over Shasta Lake, a reservoir holding an estimated 3.8 million acre-feet of water, has alarmed Forest Service and U.S. Geological Survey officials, who have been up all night evaluating measures to ensure the safety of people living in the affected area. In spite of protests from owners of large ranches downvalley from Shasta Dam, the governor orders the dam sluices opened to permit a large flow down the Sacramento River. Because of hot tephra falling on Shasta's snowfields, authorities fear that meltwater will generate destructive lahars. If an exceptionally large mudflow were to reach Shasta Lake, it could displace millions of acre-feet of water over the dam crest and flood the upper Sacramento Valley.

At midnight the explosive eruption of frothy pumice continues unabated, but the winds above the mountain have virtually ceased. Instead of being directed to the south-southeast as before, the huge mushroom cloud now hangs suspended in stagnant air above Shasta. Ash and walnut-sized pumice fragments are now showering down over the entire mountain and adjacent terrain.

State authorities have barricaded U.S. 97 at Dorris, a tiny hamlet just south of the California-Oregon border. They have also closed Interstate 5, the Pacific Coast's main transportation corridor, between Yreka in the north and Redding in the south. With the curtain of ash reducing visibility to near zero, traffic is slowed to a crawl, transporting the last evacuees. The fate of people remaining in isolated farms and summer homes is unknown, but radio bulletins urge those trapped by the choking ash fall to remain indoors.

Hours after sunrise on September 20, northern California is a land in twilight. It is almost noon before the titanic cauliflower cloud begins to diminish. Although it will take days for all the ash to settle—every movement outdoors stirs up billowing clouds of fine grit—the slowly clearing air reveals a thick blanket of beige to orange pumiceous tephra. Preliminary estimates indicate that the pumice layer is nearly a foot thick over Mount Shasta City and Weed, with progressively thinner layers extending over Dunsmuir and McCloud.

As Shastina's ash plume declines in height, aerial surveys reveal that numerous pyroclastic flows have swept down the volcano's flanks. Several, 3 to 5 miles in length, descended Diller Canyon to the outskirts of Weed. One of the largest poured through a newly formed breach in the northeast rim of Shastina's crater and across Whitney glacier, the thick ice stream occupying the saddle between Shastina and the main cone. Meltwater from glacial ice, mixed with pyroclastic material, initiated a turbulent mudflow that poured down Whitney Creek, burying a long segment of U.S. 97, as well as a major railroad line, at Shasta's northern foot.

Almost miraculously, no lives were lost during the explosive activity, but property damage is estimated in tens of millions of dollars. Roofs throughout McCloud, Weed, and Mount Shasta City collapsed under the weight of accumulated ash. On the mountain's flanks, thousands of trees were totally defoliated. With an early autumn night closing over the ash-shrouded landscape, a lurid glare radiates ominously from Shastina's summit, while intermittent explosions spray glowing projectiles over the cone.

Thousands of tourists and sensation seekers flocking to witness the spectacle have impeded the evacuation. Closure of all roads between Redding and the Oregon boundary continues, but drivers of SUVs and owners of off-road vehicles continue to circumvent the barricades. Fine ash sucked up into their engines soon stalls most roadblock runners, however, forcing them to abandon their vehicles and walk.

By September 24, the eruption appears to be over and displaced residents in Dunsmuir, Weed, McCloud, and Mount Shasta clamor to return to their homes. Scientists, however, are reluctant to advise civil authorities that the volcano is again safe; seismographs have begun to record earthquakes different in nature from the sharp jolts and harmonic tremors that preceded and accompanied the explosive outburst. When USGS helicopters deploy new GPS stations to replace those destroyed by the eruption, the instruments indicate that the swelling of Shastina's summit continues unabated, with the crater floor bulging upward about 4 feet per day. When pressed by TV reporters to interpret the significance of the seismic signals, a University of California seismologist says it is too soon to decipher Shasta's message and that scientists can only wait and see what will happen next.

Because Shastina is now only mildly steaming, most state and federal officials agree that those who so wish are free to return home and begin digging their homes and possessions out of the ash and mud. However, a bearded young seismologist from a private university, now working on contract to a state agency, emphasizes to a local TV newswoman that the current earthquake swarms, though producing events of much lower magnitude than those that heralded the pumice eruption, are steadily increasing in frequency.

"An alarmist," declares Mr. James Fitz-Brown, president of the Mount Shasta Summer Development Association. "We understand the concern which the recent little blow-off can inspire," Fitz-Brown adds, "but we have been assured by several world-famous scientists that whatever pressure had built up inside Mount Shasta is now relieved. We who have lived and worked near this wonderful mountain know that it is fundamentally a recreational attraction, not a menace. We don't need nervous nellies who needlessly worry people or keep them away from their jobs and homes." A resort owner emphasizes that the financial loss to the tourist industry was already great and that it is "vital" to the region's economic welfare to reassure the public that the volcano is no longer a threat.

As the debate to reopen the Shasta area continues, aerial surveys of the peak show that a large dark mass has risen into Shastina's crater, almost filling the western half of the vent. One prominent resort developer from southern California argues that this proves the volcano's throat is now plugged, ending the volcanic threat. Some geologists are skeptical: predawn flights on September 25 indicate that heat emission has increased significantly. The new lava dome growing at Shastina's western summit bristles with spires and spines, which split and crumble rapidly, undermined by small steam explosions.

For the next five days Shastina smolders quietly, occasionally discharging puffs of steam darkened with ash and sending small avalanches of incandescent lava blocks from the elevating dome down its steep flanks. Spyders transmit the disquieting news that deformation of Shastina's upper cone has accelerated to 5 or 6 feet a day. Refugees from the earlier eruption are eager to return to their homes and businesses, but the U.S. Geological Survey scientists, remembering the lethal suddenness with which St. Helens exploded in 1980, are reluctant to sound an all-clear.

Some petroleum geologists, brought in by real estate brokers headquartered in Los Angeles, speak acidly of scientific "hypercaution" and announce that it is as safe to reoccupy Weed, McCloud, Mount Shasta, and other nearby communities as it is to live in Miami, Galveston, or other cities that have survived hurricane disasters. The annual probability of a killer storm or a second major eruption is equally low.

Two presidentially appointed scientists confer with federal geologists, concluding that "The government cannot in conscience continue to disrupt people's lives or interfere with their free movement unless there is a clear and immediate danger to life, which we believe to be highly unlikely at this particular volcano." When asked about the young geologist who had warned that "we are living in the eye of a hurricane, a moment of calm between two catastrophes," the official explained that the young man had been reassigned to studying 700,000-year-old ash flow deposits in the Nevada desert.

Welcoming the opportunity to lift a politically unpopular closure, the California governor announces that people may return to their homes around Mount Shasta. Residents have already gone back to Dunsmuir on the assurance that too little snow remains on the southwest side of the cone to form a mudflow large enough to reach town.

Another conference of USGS administrators with a contingent of field geologists leads to a significantly different view. The concerned scientists urge that federal and state authorities allow people who work in the area to enter the danger zone only during daylight hours. Roadblocks are maintained at all major access routes, but hundreds of people continue to use the many logging roads.

Near midnight, September 29, a USGS group in the fire lookout west of the volcano reports that Shastina's growing lava dome now extends over the head of Diller Canyon and that large slabs of the dome's west side are peeling off, exposing its incandescent interior. While the network of seismographs positioned around Shasta are saturated with an endless succession of tremors, small avalanches of glowing rock cascade down Diller Canyon.

At exactly 6:21 on the morning of September 30, a violent explosion shatters the massive dome filling Shastina's crater, triggering an immense avalanche of seething gas and molten blocks of lava that sweeps down the volcano's west face. Spreading laterally far beyond the limits of the py-

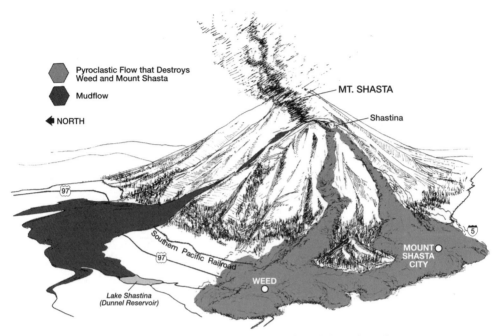

Map showing the areas affected by Mount Shasta's hypothetical eruption

roclastic flow, a deadly pyroclastic surge races westward toward Interstate 5. In moments, the towns of Weed and Mount Shasta are engulfed and totally consumed. With temperatures approaching 2,000 degrees Fahrenheit, the pyroclastic surge causes iron roofs, steel frame buildings, and glass windows to melt into unrecognizable heaps. Most wooden structures simply vaporize, along with their human contents. Smoke from the burning forest and towns mingles with the clouds of ash settling from the turbulent surge.

From their vantage point several miles west of Shasta, USGS geologists have a panoramic view of the catastrophe. The grotesquely convoluted ash cloud roiling above the pyroclastic flow and surge, rent by lightning flashes, resembles the mushroom of an atomic blast. Adding to the surrealistic scene is the near silence with which the deadly ash clouds travel outward—they sound strangely like wind rushing through a forest.

Because only a small percentage of the inhabitants of Weed and Mount Shasta City had elected to return to their homes while the volcano was still active, the death toll is considerably less than it might have been. The pyroclastic surge claims about 280 victims, some of whom die instantaneously, their bodies vaporized or incinerated; the majority are asphyxiated in the clouds of gas and ash. Least fortunate are people caught on the fringes of the lethal ash cloud. A few, badly burned, manage to walk or crawl from the devastated area only to perish a few hours or days later.

During the next two months, as a steep lava dome continues to grow and crumble in Shastina's crater, five more pyroclastic flows race down Shastina's west flank, at least two of which are as large as the first. To the small towns in their path, however, the subsequent eruptions matter little: not a wall or other human-made structure remains standing after the September 30 holocaust.

When the first heavy winter snowfall blankets the Siskiyou and southern Cascade mountains in early December, Mount Shasta is not transformed into the dazzling white tower it ordinarily becomes at this time of year. Devoid of its customary ermine mantle, Shastina turns a seared and blackened face to the devastated area below. Aided by federal emergency funds, state road crews using snow plows and other heavy equipment rapidly clear the pyroclastic deposits from Interstate 5, but the signs for Weed and Mount Shasta are not replaced: the towns no longer exist.

This hypothetical description of Mount Shasta's display of volcanic power reminds us that the Cascade volcanoes—too often regarded as mere scenic backdrops to recreational pursuits—can wreak havoc on the human environment. Because they erupt infrequently in terms of a single human lifetime, many people living near them tend to ignore the volcanoes' deadly potential. We can do little to protect property already located in areas susceptible to heavy ash falls, pyroclastic flows, or massive lahars. But, by developing long-range plans in advance to cope with future volcanic crises, we can avoid the confusion, political irresolution, and short-sighted influence of commercial interests that lead to unnecessary loss of life.

No one knows when or where the next western fire mountain will erupt—it could be Rainier, Baker, Hood, or the volcanoes near Mono Lake. What we can confidently expect, however, is that the next large-scale eruption will affect populated areas many miles downvalley from the volcano, destroying property worth hundreds of millions of dollars and—unless evacuation plans are in place and carried out efficiently—claiming an incalculable number of lives.

Glossary

aa. Hawaiian word used to describe a lava flow with a surface broken into angular, jagged fragments.

ablation. The process by which a glacier loses mass, typically through the melting of ice and snow, evaporation, and/or erosion.

active volcano. A volcano that is currently erupting or, based on its recent history, is expected to erupt. The distinction between active and dormant is not sharply defined.

agglutinate. A volcanic deposit formed by the accumulation of flattened and welded rock fragments, typically derived from showers of molten particles ejected in magma fountains. The liquid fragments may accumulate to form a stream of lava.

andesite. A lava of intermediate composition (between basalt and rhyolite), usually fine grained and light gray or brown. With a silica content ranging from about 54 to 62 percent, andesite is the predominant lava type in most Cascade stratovolcanoes.

angle of repose. The maximum slope or angle, ranging from about 34 to 37 degrees, at which loose, unconsolidated material remains stable.

Ar. Abbreviation for the element argon.

arete. A sharp ridge that separates adjacent glacially carved valleys.

ash. Fine particles of pulverized rock blown from a volcano. Measuring less than about 0.1 inch in diameter ash may be either solid or molten when first erupted. By far the most common variety is vitric ash, glassy particles formed by gas bubbles bursting through liquid magma. Lithic ash is formed of older rock blown apart during a phreatic or nonmagmatic eruption, while in crystal ash each grain is composed of a single crystal or groups of crystals with only traces of glass adhering to them. Many volcanic ash deposits contain mixtures of all three kinds in various proportions.

ash cloud. A turbulent cloud of ash particles that is generated by a pyroclastic flow and rises above it. It can also refer to an eruption column or ash plume.

ashfall. A rain of ash from an eruption cloud.

ash flow. A ground-hugging cloud of hot volcanic ash and gases that typically travels great distances at high speeds from an erupting vent. Large-volume ash flow deposits, emplaced while still hot, commonly solidify to form ignimbrites. See also **pyroclastic flow**.

basalt. A dark, fine-grained lava rich in iron and magnesium and relatively poor in silica (less than 54 percent). The most common of earth's volcanic rocks, basaltic lavas compose all the ocean floors and many continental formations as well. Typically very fluid because of their high temperatures and low silica content, basaltic lavas can flow great distances from their source, forming broad lava plains such as the Columbia River plateau. Shield volcanoes are typically formed almost exclusively of basalt.

Basin and Range. A geologic province of the western United States in which the earth's crust stretched, breaking into a pattern of alternating mountain ranges and valleys that trend generally to the north. Ongoing crustal extension in northern California and Oregon abuts against the Cascade Range.

bergschrund. A crevasse at the back of a glacier between the glacier and its rock headwall, formed by partial melting and movement of the glacier.

block. An angular fragment of lava rock measuring a minimum of 2.5 inches to several tens of feet in diameter.

block-and-ash flow. A variety of pyroclastic flow consisting of lava blocks in a matrix of fine ash that avalanche downslope during an eruption. They are commonly triggered by the collapse of a lava dome while it is still hot or the disintegration of lava flows erupted on steep, icy slopes.

blocky lava. A lava flow with a surface characterized by a jumble of large angular blocks.

bomb. A lump of plastic or molten lava thrown out during an explosive eruption. Bombs range in size from 2.5 inches to many feet in diameter. Because of their plastic condition when first ejected, bombs are commonly modified in shape during their flight through the air and/or by their impact on the ground. As the outer crust cools and solidifies, continued expansion of the bomb's interior by gas pressure sometimes causes crinkling and cracking, which may form a surface resembling the crust of freshly baked bread.

bread-crust bomb. *See* **bomb**.

breccia. Rock deposits composed of many distinct fragments, typically sharp and/or angular, embedded in a matrix of fine material. Breccias are sometimes formed when shattered lava fragments are carried in a block-and-ash flow, in mudflows, or by the avalanching of rock from a growing lava dome.

caldera. A large basin-shaped volcanic depression at least a mile in diameter. Calderas are usually formed during violent and voluminous explosive eruptions that drain magma from the underlying magma chamber, causing the roof to collapse and the volcanic edifice above it to subside.

cinder cone. A generally small volcanic cone built entirely of tephra (cinders), typically by mildly explosive Strombolian eruptions that eject semimolten or plastic lava fragments at a central vent and lava flows from vents near its base. Most cinder cones are monogenetic, built during a single eruptive episode.

cinders. Vesicular rock fragments ejected during explosive eruptions.

circum-Pacific belt. A narrow zone around the margin of the Pacific Ocean basin where most of the world's composite cones are located and where most earthquakes occur.

cirque. An amphitheater-like basin or depression in alpine regions, formed by glacial ice that carves a steep, semicircular headwall.

cleaver. A long, thin rib of erosion-resistant rock standing above the general surface of a volcanic edifice, typically formed by glacial cutting.

clinkery. Consisting of rough, jagged lava fragments.

composite cone. Another term for a stratovolcano, a large volcanic edifice constructed of both lava flows and pyroclastic material. Most of the world's great continental volcanoes, including Fuji, Vesuvius, Etna, Rainier, Shasta, and St. Helens, are composite cones.

conduit. The internal feeding pipe of a volcano, through which magma passes in a volcanic cone on its way to the surface.

convection (convection currents). Movements of material caused by differences in density and temperature, typically the result of heating.

convergent plate boundary. A zone of intersection of two plates of the lithosphere that are moving toward each other.

core. The central region of the earth, thought to be composed largely of iron and nickel, with a solid inner core surrounded by molten material.

crater. The bowl- or funnel-shaped hollow at or near the top of a volcano, through which volcanic gas, lava, and or pyroclastic material are ejected. The term derives from the Greek word for "wine-mixing bowl."

crust. The brittle outer layer of rock that forms a thin skin on the earth's surface.

dacite. A (usually) light-colored lava with a high silica content, 64 percent or more. Gas-rich dacite magmas are commonly highly explosive, producing pumice and other pyroclastic ejecta, while gas-poor dacites typically form thick, viscous tongues of lava. When particularly stiff and pasty, dacite lavas may form steep-sided domes.

debris avalanche. A rapidly moving landslide on a volcano, typically composed of a turbulent, sliding mass of hydrothermally altered rock.

debris flow. A chaotic mixture of rock debris and water that rapidly moves downslope, also called a **lahar** or **mudflow**.

deposit. An accumulation of rock material at rest, formed by a geologic process such as a volcanic eruption.

detonation. An explosion made by a combination of gases or by the abrupt release of gases from a volcanic vent.

dike. A relatively thin sheetlike body of igneous rock that cuts through, in a generally vertical direction, older rock formations. Dikes form when narrow tabular magma sheets intrude a volcanic cone or other structure, filling a fracture that intersects previously existing strata.

dip. The angle or direction at which a stratum or any tabular plane is inclined from the horizontal.

dome. A mounded extrusion of lava that, when erupted, was too viscous to flow far laterally and instead piled up over the erupting vent to form a mushroom-shaped cap. When the lava mass is an uplifted, consolidated lava conduit filling, the resultant extrusion is called a plug dome.

dormant volcano. A volcano that is presently quiet but is expected to erupt again.

earthquake (volcanic). A shaking of the ground caused by the fracturing and displacement of rock underground as magma rises toward the surface. Most volcanic tremors are relatively small and their effects largely restricted to the immediate vicinity of the volcano.

effusive eruption. A relatively quiet outpouring of lava flows, with little or no explosive activity.

epicenter. The point on the earth's surface directly above the focus of an earthquake.

eruption. The geologic process by which solid, liquid, and gaseous material is ejected onto the earth's surface by volcanic activity. Eruptions vary in style from the quiet outflow of molten rock (effusive type) to the violent expulsion of pyroclastic material (explosive type).

eruption cloud. A column of gases, ash, and larger rock fragments rising from a volcanic vent. If it is of sufficient volume and velocity, the gaseous column may reach 30 miles or more into the stratosphere, where high winds may carry it hundreds of miles from its source.

explosive eruption. Any eruption in which the release of dissolved gasses tears the magma into fragments and ejects them into the air.

extinct volcano. A volcano that will not erupt again.

extrusion. The eruption of igneous rock onto the surface of the earth; also, the volcanic rock formed by this process.

extrusive rock. Igneous rock that forms at the earth's surface, also called volcanic rock.

fault. A crack or fracture in the earth's crust along which there has been differential movement. It may represent the juncture between two adjoining crustal blocks or plates into which the earth's lithosphere is broken. Movement along a fault can cause earthquakes, or, in the process of mountain building (orogeny), can release underlying magma and permit it to rise to the surface, creating a volcanic eruption.

firn. A compact mass of granular ice made of old snow that has been recrystallized.

fissure eruption. A volcanic eruption that occurs along a narrow fissure or line of closely spaced fractures in the earth's crust.

flood basalt. The high-volume fissure eruptions of basaltic lava that cover extremely large areas, such as the Columbia plateau basalts.

focus. The point within the earth at which an earthquake originates.

fountain. A gas-charged spray of fluid magma jetting into the air above a fissure or other volcanic vent.

fulgurite. A glassy material formed when lightning fuses sand or rock.

fumarole. A vent or opening through which issues steam or other volcanic gases, such as carbon dioxide or hydrogen sulfide.

fumarolic activity. Gas emission that may be accompanied by an increase in temperature of the gases issuing from a vent.

fume. A gaseous volcanic cloud not containing tephra.

geothermal energy. Energy derived from the earth's internal heat.

geothermal gradient. Rate of temperature increase associated with increasing depth beneath the earth's surface, normally about 25 degrees Celsius per kilometer (124 degrees Fahrenheit per mile).

geothermal power. Power derived from harnessing and exploiting the heat energy of the earth, as by tapping the heat from a hot spring, geyser, or volcano.

glacial lobe. A large tongue of ice projecting outward from the margin of a continental ice sheet, such as the Puget lobe that covered the Puget lowland during Pleistocene glacial advances.

glacial maximum. The time or position of the greatest advance of a glacier, or of the maximum extent of glaciers during recurrent Pleistocene ice advances.

glacial outburst flood. The sudden release of water stored in a glacier or glacier-dammed lake that can cause severe flooding.

glacial till. An unstratified deposit of rock fragments, sand, and silt formed by a glacier.

glacier. A large, dense mass of ice, formed on land by the compaction and recrystallization of snow, which moves downslope because of its weight and gravity. Active glaciers are effective eroding agents and have played an important role in sculpturing the present shape of the Cascade Range.

graben. A segment of crustal rock that has sunk along bounding faults; from the German word for "grave."

granite. A coarse-grained igneous rock composed of quartz and feldspar. In chemical composition, it is equivalent to rhyolite.

granodiorite. A granular igneous rock intermediate between granite and quartz diorite. Massive intrusions of granodiorite occur adjacent to Mount Rainier, Mount Baker, and other parts of the Cascades.

Hawaiian eruption. Effusive eruption of basaltic lava typical of shield volcanoes in Hawaii. Although usually nonexplosive, Hawaiian eruptions commonly produce lava fountaining, formation of lava lakes in summit vents, and, during the second stage of the eruption, production of voluminous quantities of fluid lava that issue from lengthy fissures along the volcano's flanks.

Holocene. The 10,000- to 12,000-year span of time that has elapsed since the end of Pleistocene time; the division of geologic time in which we now live.

hornblende. A (usually) dark-colored mineral commonly found in igneous and metamorphic rocks.

hot spot. A persistent heat source in the upper mantle of the earth unrelated to plate boundaries. Isolated hot spots generating magma underlie the Hawaiian Islands and the Yellowstone region.

hydromagmatic. Eruption involving interaction of water and magma, commonly triggering steam explosions.

hydrothermal alteration. The action of acidic hot water and other fluids percolating through rock and chemically altering it to claylike substances susceptible to collapse.

icefall. A chaotic jumble of ice blocks and crevasses formed when a glacier flows over a cliff or other steep, uneven declivity.

ice wave. A wave of thickened ice that moves downglacier, typically at a speed higher than that of thinner ice.

igneous rock. Rock derived from the solidification of magma. Igneous rocks that congeal beneath the earth's surface are called plutonic, while those formed on the surface are volcanic.

ignimbrite. A highly silicic volcanic rock formed by the eruption of large-volume ash flows. Dense clouds of incandescent rock fragments erupted at extremely high temperatures settle and congeal so that individual particles are fused together. See also **tuff.**

inactive volcano. A volcano that is dormant (it is not expected to erupt soon) but not extinct (it is expected to erupt again).

inflation. (1) The swelling or tumescence of a volcanic cone caused by injection of magma or other volcanic fluids. (2) The process by which lava-tube-fed flows of molten rock swell and thicken.

intrusion. An igneous rock formation created when subterranean magma invades a body of surrounding rocks and then solidifies.

intrusive rock. An igneous rock body formed underground when magma is injected into an older body of rock.

jokulhlaup. An Icelandic term denoting a sudden outburst of water that a glacier releases. The water may exit from cavities in the glacier, subglacial lakes, or glacier-dammed lakes in tributary valleys.

Juan de Fuca plate. A relatively small segment of the Pacific Ocean plate that is presently being subducted beneath the margin of the North American plate. The Juan de Fuca slab extends from northern California northward to southwestern British Columbia.

juvenile material. Volcanic rocks formed from magma during an eruption.

lahar. A mudflow originating on a volcano; a volcanic debris flow composed of rock fragments and water that travels downslope into topographical lows.

lapilli. Round to angular rock fragments measuring 0.1 to 2.5 inches in diameter that are erupted explosively in either a solid or molten state; from the Latin word for "little stones."

lateral blast. Term used to describe a horizontally directed explosion, such as that at Mount St. Helens on May 18, 1980. See also **pyroclastic surge**.

lateral moraine. A long ridge of rock fragments that accumulate along the side margins of an active glacier.

lava. Magma erupted on the earth's surface. The term most commonly applies to streams of molten rock flowing from a volcanic vent, but also refers to solidified volcanic rock.

lava dome. A mushroom-shaped mound of lava formed by the extrusion of highly viscous magma.

lava fountain. See **fountain**.

lava lake. A large pool of molten rock in a crater or other volcanic depression. The term also refers to a lake of solidified lava.

lava tube. A cave or tunnel formed inside an active lava flow. Tubes can form in several ways, commonly when lava spatter roofs (arches and solidifies) over a surface of molten rock, or when the outer crust of the lava stream cools and solidifies but the molten interior continues to flow and drains away, leaving behind a long hollow tube.

lithic. Composed of solid fragments of previously formed rock.

lithic ash. Volcanic ash derived from the explosive pulverizing of previously existing rock.

lithic pyroclastic flow. A pyroclastic flow containing mainly rock derived from previously erupted material. See also **block-and-ash flow**.

lithosphere. The rigid outer shell of the earth, including the rocky crust and the solid upper portion of the mantle.

Little Ice Age. The period of climatic cooling between about AD 1350 and 1850, when alpine glaciers typically advanced downvalley.

mafic rock. Rock that contains a relatively low percentage of silica and a relatively high content of ferromagnesian minerals, such as magnesium, iron, and calcium.

magma. Gas-rich molten rock confined beneath the earth's surface; erupted on the surface, it is called **lava**.

magma chamber. Underground pocket or reservoir of magma, from which volcanoes draw the molten material they erupt.

magnetic pole. A region where the strength of the earth's magnetic field is greatest and where the magnetic lines of force apparently enter or leave the earth.

magnetic reversal. A change in the polarity of the earth's magnetic field. The last magnetic reversal occurred about 770,000 years ago.

magnitude. The amount of energy released during an earthquake or volcanic eruption.

mantle. That portion of the earth's interior lying between the molten outer core and the rigid outer crust. A zone of hot plastic rock extending about 1,800 miles beneath the surface, it is the region in which magma is generated.

medial moraine. The linear accumulation of dark rocky debris in the center of a glacier, formed when alpine glaciers bearing lateral moraines combine. They appear as dark streaks near the middle of the glacier's surface.

midoceanic ridge. An enormous submarine mountain range that extends around the globe.

monogenetic volcano. A volcano that erupts only once.

moraine. A typically linear ridge of loose rock fragments and silt deposited by a glacier.

mudflow. A water-saturated mass of rock debris that travels downslope as a liquid under the pull of gravity. A major potential hazard at many Cascade volcanoes, mudflows (lahars) typically originate in two ways: by the sudden collapse of areas of hydrothermally altered rock high on the volcanic cone or by melting snow and ice during an eruption. Both types commonly travel tens of miles down valleys beyond the volcano.

neck. See **plug**.

nuée ardente. French term for a "glowing cloud" of hot gas and volcanic ash that typically rises above and extends beyond the margins of a pyroclastic flow. See also **pyroclastic surge**.

obsidian. A dense, black, glassy volcanic rock largely devoid of bubbles or mineral crystals. It is formed from highly silicic magma, typically by the collapse of frothy, pumiceous rhyolite. Prominent domes or flows of obsidian occur at the Newberry and Medicine Lake volcanoes.

oceanic crust. The relatively thin slabs of basaltic crust forming the ocean floors.

pahoehoe. Hawaiian word for lava with a smooth, ropy, or billowy crust. Always composed of basalt, pahoehoe flows commonly contain lava tubes.

paroxysm. A violently explosive eruption of great magnitude.

Peléan eruption. Explosive eruption producing pyroclastic flows and surges, commonly associated with dome growth and collapse. Named for the 1902 eruption of Mont Pelée, a volcano on the Carribean island of Martinique that killed 30,000 people, this type of activity is typical of Glacier Peak, Lassen Peak–Chaos Crags, and Mounts Shasta, St. Helens, and Hood.

phreatic eruption. A violent steam explosion that produces little or no new lava, typically ejecting solid fragments of pre-existing rock from the volcanic edifice. Triggered by the conversion of groundwater into steam by an underground heat source, small phreatic eruptions characterize the opening stage of many volcanic episodes, including those at Lassen Peak in 1914 and St. Helens in 1980.

pillow lava. A lava flow emplaced underwater that is characterized by interconnected sacklike formations.

plastic. Capable of being molded or bent under stress.

plate. A large mobile slab of rock composing part of the earth's surface.

plate tectonics. The geologic theory that the earth's rigid outer shell is broken up into about sixteen large slabs or plates that are in constant motion, their margins separating from, colliding with, or sliding past each other. Concentrations of seismic and volcanic activity occur at plate boundaries.

Pleistocene. The division of geologic time immediately preceding the Holocene and lasting from about 1.8 million to 10,000 or 12,000 years ago. It is characterized by the development of large continental ice sheets throughout the Northern Hemisphere and by the formation of ice caps and valley glaciers in mountain ranges, including the Cascades, Rockies, and Sierra Nevada.

Plinian eruption. A violently explosive eruption that produces an unusually high ash plume carrying tephra far into the stratosphere, commonly with associated pyroclastic flows; it also refers to a paroxysmal outburst. Named after Pliny the Younger who described the catastrophic eruption of Mount Vesuvius, Italy, in AD 79.

Pliocene. The division of geologic time immediately preceding the Pleistocene and lasting from about 5.3 million to about 1.8 million years ago. Uplift of the modern Cascade Range began during this time.

plug. Solidified lava filling the conduit of a volcano. Commonly more resistant to erosion than the rock composing the surrounding cone, a plug may remain standing as a solitary "neck" after the rest of the original volcano has been eroded away.

plug dome. See **dome**.

plume. (1) The vertical cloud of hot gas and fragmental rock ejected into the air during an explosive eruption. (2) The subterranean column of magma rising from deep within the mantle to produce hot-spot volcanoes such as those in Hawaii, Iceland, or Yellowstone.

plutonic rock. See **igneous rock**.

pumice. A highly porous volcanic rock formed of glassy magmatic froth blown from a vent. Usually light colored, pumice is so full of tiny bubbles that it typically is buoyant.

pyroclastic flow. A turbulent avalanche of incandescent rock fragments and hot gas that travels downslope like a heavy fluid; it may be composed either of frothy pumice or of dense lithic (nonporous) rock debris, such as the hot fragments from a collapsing lava dome.

pyroclastic rock. Volcanic rock erupted in fragments.

pyroclastic surge. A highly mobile cloud of hot gas and ash, less dense than a ground-hugging pyroclastic flow that it typically accompanies. Surges are capable of surmounting topographical barriers and spreading laterally over large areas.

pyroxene. A common mineral group (metasilicate), chiefly of calcium and magnesium, usually occurring in short, thick prismatic crystals or in massive forms, and typically found in igneous rocks.

quartz. An important rock-forming mineral composed of silicon and oxygen.

Quaternary. The youngest geologic period (encompassing Pleistocene and Holocene time), which began about 1.8 million years ago and includes the present time.

radiocarbon dating. The calculation of the age of geologic deposits by any of the methods based on nuclear decay of natural radioactive elements in carbonaceous material, such as charcoal or wood from trees or other plants found in layers of volcanic ash.

radiocarbon years. The age of a geologic deposit or formation given, by convention, in years before 1950, as calculated by the proportion of the carbon 14 isotope to normal carbon atoms in formerly living material, such as trees, associated with the deposit.

relief. The vertical distance between the highest peaks or ridges and the lowest topographical depressions.

rhyolite. A typically light-colored lava rock with a high silica content (72 percent or more). Rich in sodium and potassium, it is thick and pasty when erupted. Because gases dissolved in rhyolitic magma cannot escape easily, it can be extremely explosive.

Richter scale. A numerical scale used to measure the size (magnitude) of an earthquake at its source.

ridge (oceanic). A large submarine mountain range formed by volcanic eruptions along fissures on the ocean floor, the best known of which is the Mid-Atlantic Ridge.

rift zone. A linear spreading center along plate boundaries where crustal plates are separating and moving apart. Magma is erupted along active rifts, creating new crust.

Ring of Fire. The seismically and volcanically active margin of the Pacific Ocean basin. This circum-Pacific zone contains about 70 percent of the world's active land volcanoes.

scarp. An abbreviation for escarpment. A long line of cliffs produced by movement along an earthquake fault or by erosion.

scoria. Glassy fragments of dark-colored volcanic rock, less porous than pumice, commonly produced by jets of semiliquid magma shot into the air.

sea-floor-spreading. See **spreading center**.

seismograph. A seismometer with an apparatus that makes a permanent record of earthquakes, including those too weak to be perceptible to most people.

seismometer. An instrument used to detect the seismic waves initiated by an earthquake.

serac. A sharp ridge or angular block of ice standing above the surface of a crevassed glacier.

shield volcano. A broad, gently sloping volcanic edifice built almost exclusively of thin lava flows. Named for their supposed resemblance to an Icelandic warrior's shield laid down flat with the curved side upward, shield volcanoes typically form by the quiet effusion of fluid basaltic lava.

silica. The chemical combination of silicon and oxygen (SiO_2), which is a primary constituent of volcanic rocks.

silicic lava. Lava rich in silica (over 62–64 percent) and having a relatively low melting point (about 1,500 degrees Fahrenheit). Silicic magma typically emerges as a stiff, viscous mass and does not flow long distances, commonly piling up over the erupting vent to form a steep-sided lava dome.

spatter. Liquid or plastic fragments of lava blown from a vent.

spreading center. The crest of a midoceanic ridge where rising magma pushes the seafloor in opposite directions; a divergent boundary at which two plates move apart.

stratovolcano. See **composite cone**.

stratum (pl. strata). A bed or layer of rock deposits; rocks displaying layering or bedding are described as having stratification.

striations. The straight scratches or grooves incised on a rock surface by a moving glacier.

Strombolian eruption. Rhythmic, mildly explosive eruptions of incandescent pyroclastic material that commonly build cinder cones. Strombolian activity may also include emission of lava flows, which are usually short and thin. Named for the Stromboli volcano, an island off the southwest coast of Italy, such eruptions may continue with little variation for years or decades.

subduction. A process of plate convergence by which the seafloor sinks beneath the margin of a continent or island arc.

subduction zone. The elongate region of convergence of two tectonic plates, one of which slides beneath the other, such as the Cascadia subduction zone, where part of the Pacific plate is sinking beneath the Pacific Northwest coast of North America.

tarn. A small mountain lake that occupies a cirque or other depression carved by a glacier.

tectonic. Referring to movement or deformation of part of the earth's crust, such as the uplift that results in mountain building (orogeny).

tephra. Pyroclastic material that is thrown into the air above a volcano. Tephra can range in size from fine dust and ash to lava blocks tens of feet in diameter. The term, first used by Aristotle, is the Greek word for "ash."

terminal moraine. A steep, ridgelike accumulation of rock debris eroded by a glacier and deposited at its terminus, marking its farthest advance.

terminus. The snout or lower edge of a glacier.

terrace. A long, narrow, nearly flat surface that forms a bench along canyon walls. Large mudflows from Cascade volcanoes typically form these steplike terraces along valley sides, where they represent a lahar's maximum depth as it moved in a wave downvalley.

terrane. A large block of the earth's crust, bounded by faults, the components of which share a generally similar geologic origin and history.

Tertiary. The geologic period covering the span of time between about 65 million and 1.8 million years ago, encompassing Paleocene, Eocene, Oligocene, Miocene, and Pliocene time.

till. Unstratified (unlayered) rock debris eroded and deposited by a glacier, typically consisting of unconsolidated gravel, sand, boulders, silt, and mud.

tree-ring dating. A method of dating events by counting and comparing the annual growth rings on representative trees, both dead and growing, in a particular area.

trimline. A line of demarcation, commonly seen on canyon walls, that marks the boundary between an upper undisturbed area and a lower part that has been scoured by debris avalanches, mudflows, or glaciers. In valleys from which glaciers have recently withdrawn, valley sides below the trimline may be barren or only thinly vegetated, whereas those above it may be densely forested. Plant growth on valley walls below or above the trimline typically shows visible differences in age, color, and density.

tuff. Fine-grained rock composed mostly of volcanic ash. Welded tuff is a rock formed from pyroclastic material hot enough to fuse or weld together when emplaced.

valley glacier. An alpine glacier that heads on a cirque and extends into, and is confined by, a valley.

vent. An opening, typically cylindrical in form, in the earth's surface through which volcanic material is ejected.

vesicular. Referring to pores or tiny cavities in a volcanic rock, formed by the development of gas bubbles in the liquid magma. Some pumice is vesicular enough to resemble a sponge.

viscosity. A liquid's resistance to flow. In magma, viscosity is largely determined by temperature, gas content, and the chemical composition of the molten material, particularly its silica content.

vitric. Referring to volcanic material consisting mainly of glassy matter, such as vitric ash, which is at least 75 percent glass.

volcanic arc. A curved line of volcanoes paralleling a subduction zone.

volcanic rock. See **igneous rock**.

Vulcan. The Roman god of fire and the forge, believed in classical times to have established his workshop beneath an island in the Mediterranean called Vulcano, after which volcanoes are named. His Greek counterpart is Hephaestus.

Vulcanian eruption. The violent ejection of towering cauliflower-like clouds of dark ash and angular rock fragments. This kind of eruption commonly expels large quantities of old rock and little fresh magma.

welded tuff. See **tuff**.

zone of ablation. That portion of a glacier in which ice is lost, typically the lower part in which melting exceeds snow accumulation.

zone of accumulation. That portion of a glacier that maintains a perennial snow cover, typically the upper portion in which snow accumulation exceeds melting.

Selected Bibliography

GENERAL

Ambrose, S. H. "Late Pleistocene Human Population Bottlenecks, Volcanic Winter, and Differentiation of Modern Humans." *Journal of Human Evolution* 34 (June 1998).

Bardintzeff, J.-M., and A. R. McBirney. *Volcanology.* 2nd ed. Boston: Jones & Bartlett Publishers, 2000.

Blong, R. J. *Volcanic Hazards: A Sourcebook on the Effects of Eruptions.* Orlando, Fla.: Academic Press, 1984.

Bullard, F. M. *Volcanoes of the Earth.* 2nd ed. Austin: University of Texas Press, 1984.

Decker, R., and B. Decker. *Volcanoes.* 3rd ed. New York: W. H. Freeman & Co., 1998.

———. *Volcanoes in America's National Parks.* New York: W. W. Norton & Co., 2001.

Ewart, J. W., M. Guffanti, and T. L. Murray. *An Assessment of Volcanic Threat and Monitoring Capabilities in the United States: Framework for a National Volcano Early Warning System.* U.S. Geological Survey Open-File Report 2005–1164 (2005).

Fisher, R. V., G. Heiken, and J. B. Hulen. *Volcanoes: Crucibles of Change.* Princeton, N.J.: Princeton University Press, 1997.

Folsom, M. M. "Volcanic Eruptions: The Pioneers' Attitude on the Pacific Coast from 1800 to 1875." *The Ore Bin* 32 (1970).

Harris, S. L. "Cascade Volcanoes: Historic Eruptions and Their Implications for the Future." *Columbia: The Magazine of Northwest History* 4, no. 4 (1991).

———. "The *Other* Cascade Volcanoes: Historic Eruptions at Mount St. Helens' Sister Peaks." In *Mount St. Helens: Five Years Later,* edited by S. A. C. Keller. Cheney: Eastern Washington University Press, 1985.

Johnston, D. A., and J. M. Donnelly-Nolan. *Guides to Some Volcanic Terranes in Washington, Idaho, Oregon, and Northern California.* U.S. Geological Survey Circular 838 (1981).

McBirney, A. R. "Volcanic Evolution of the Cascade Range." *Annual Reviews of Earth and Planetary Sciences* 6 (1978).

Myers, B., S. P. Brantley, P. Stoffer, and J. W. Hendley II. *What Are Volcano Hazards?* U.S. Geological Survey Fact Sheet 002-97 (1998).

Newhall, C., J. W. Hendley II, and P. H. Stauffer. *Benefits of Volcano Monitoring Far Outweigh Costs—The Case of Mount Pinatubo.* U.S. Geological Survey Fact Sheet 115-97 (1997).

Plummer, F. G. "Reported Volcanic Eruptions in Alaska, Puget Sound, etc., 1690 to 1896." In *A Catalogue of Earthquakes on the Pacific Coast, 1769 to 1897,* edited by E. S. Holden. Smithsonian Miscellaneous Collection, no. 1087 (1898).

———. "Western Volcanoes: Chances That Western Washington May See Disastrous Eruptions." *Tacoma Daily Ledger,* February 28, 1893.

Sheets, P. D., and D. K. Grayson. *Volcanic Activity and Human Ecology.* New York: Academic Press, 1979.

Sherrod, D. R., and J. G. Smith. "Quaternary Extrusion Rates of the Cascade Range, Northwestern United States and Southwestern British Columbia." *Journal of Geophysical Research* 95 (1990).

Sieh, K., and S. LeVay. *The Earth in Turmoil: Earthquakes, Volcanoes, and Their Impact on Humankind.* New York: W. H. Freeman & Co., 1998.

Sigurdsson, H. *Melting the Earth: The History of Ideas on Volcanic Eruptions.* New York: Oxford University Press, 1999.

————, ed. *Encyclopedia of Volcanoes.* New York: Academic Press, 2000.

Simkin, T., and L. Siebert. *Volcanoes of the World: A Regional Directory, Gazetteer, and Chronology of Volcanism During the Last 10,000 Years.* 2nd ed. Published in association with the Smithsonian Institution, Global Volcanism Program. Tucson, Ariz.: Geoscience Press, 1994.

Smoot, J. *Climbing the Cascade Volcanoes.* Helena, Mont.: Falcon Press, 1993.

Tabor, R. W., and R. A. Haugerud. *Geology of the North Cascades: A Mountain Mosaic.* Seattle: The Mountaineers, 1999.

Thomas, J. *Oregon High: A Climbing Guide to Nine Cascade Volcanoes.* Portland, Oreg.: Keep Climbing Press, 1991.

U.S. Geological Survey Web site, http://vulcan.wr.usgs.gov

Wood, C. A., and J. Kienle, eds. *Volcanoes of North America: United States and Canada.* New York: Cambridge University Press, 1990.

GLACIERS

Brugman, M. M., and A. Post. *Effects of Volcanism on the Glaciers of Mount St. Helens.* U.S. Geological Survey Circular 850 D (1981).

Chorlton, W. *Ice Ages.* Alexandria, Va.: Time-Life Books, 1983.

Crandell, D. R. "Glacial History of Western Washington and Oregon." In *Quaternary of the United States,* edited by H. E. Wright and D. G. Frey. Princeton, N.J.: Princeton University Press, 1965.

Crandell, D. R., and R. D. Miller. *Quaternary Stratigraphy and Extent of Glaciation in the Mount Rainier Region, Washington.* U.S. Geological Survey Professional Paper 847 (1974).

Davis, P. T. "Holocene Glacier Fluctuations in the American Cordillera." *Quaternary Science Reviews* 7 (1988).

Driedger, C. L. *Glaciers on Mount Rainier.* U.S. Geological Survey Open-File Report 92-474 (1992).

————. *A Visitor's Guide to Mount Rainier Glaciers.* Longmire, Wash.: Pacific Northwest National Parks and Forests Association, 1986.

Driedger, C. L., and P. M. Kennard. *Ice Volumes on Cascade Volcanoes: Mount Rainier, Mount Hood, Three Sisters, and Mount Shasta.* U.S. Geological Survey Professional Paper 1365 (1986).

Granshaw, F. D. "Glacier Change in the North Cascades National Park Complex, Washington State, USA, 1958 to 1998." Master's thesis, Portland State University, Portland, Oreg., 2002.

Grove, J. M. *The Little Ice Age.* London: Methuen, 1988. Reprint, New York: Routledge, 1990.

Guyton, B. *Glaciers of California.* California Natural History Guides 59. Berkeley: University of California Press, 1998.

Heine, J. T. "Glacier Advances Near Mount Rainier at the Last Glacial/Interglacial Transition." *Washington Geology* 28, nos. 1–2 (2000).

Pelto, M. S. "Current Behavior of Glaciers in the North Cascades and Effect on Regional Water Supplies." *Washington Geology* 21, no. 2 (1993).

Post, A., and E. R. LaChapelle. *Glacier Ice.* Seattle: University of Washington Press, 1971.

Post, A., D. Richardson, W. Tangborn, and F. Rosselot. *Inventory of Glaciers in the North Cascades, Washington.* U.S. Geological Survey Professional Paper 705-A (1971).

Richmond, G. M., and D. S. Fullerton. "Introduction to Quaternary Glaciations in the United States of America." *Quaternary Science Reviews* 5 (1985).

Riedel, J. L., A. Fountain, and R. Krimmel. "Glacier Monitoring Program Progress Report." North Cascades National Park Service Complex, 2002. http://www.nps.gov/noca/massbalance.htm (accessed March 2005).

Walder, J., and C. Driedger. *Volcano Fact Sheet: Glacier-generated Debris Flows at Mount Rainier.* U.S. Geological Survey Open-File Report 93-124 (1993).

MONO LAKE–LONG VALLEY

Bailey, R. A. *Geologic Map of Long Valley Caldera, Mono-Inyo Craters Volcanic Chain, and Vicinity, Mono County, California.* U.S. Geological Survey Miscellaneous Investigations Map I-1933 (1989).

Farrar, C. D., M. L. Sorey, W. C. Evans, et al. "Forest-Killing Diffuse CO_2 Emission at Mammoth Mountain as a Sign of Magmatic Unrest, *Nature* 376 (1995).

Hill, D. P. "Science, Geologic Hazards, and the Public in a Large, Restless Caldera." *Seismological Research Letters* 69, no. 5 (September-October 1998).

Hill, D. P., R. A. Bailey, C. D. Miller, J. W. Hendley II, and P. H. Stauffer. *Future Eruptions in California's Long Valley Area—What's Likely?* U.S. Geological Survey Fact Sheet 073-97 (1998).

Hill, D. P., R. A. Bailey, and A. S. Ryall. "Active Tectonic and Magmatic Processes Beneath Long Valley Caldera, Eastern California: An Overview." *Journal of Geophysical Research* 90 (1985).

Hill, D. P., R. A. Bailey, M. L. Sorey, J. W. Hendley II, and P. H. Stauffer. *Living with a Restless Caldera—Long Valley, California.* U.S. Geological Survey Fact Sheet 108-96, version 2.1 (2000).

Hill, D. P., D. Dzurisin, W. L. Ellsworth, et al. "Response Plan for Volcano Hazards in the Long Valley Caldera and Mono Craters Region, California." *U.S. Geological Survey Bulletin* 2185 (2002).

Miller, C. D. "Holocene Eruptions at the Inyo Volcanic Chain, California—Implications for Possible Eruptions in the Long Valley Caldera." *Geology* 13 (1985).

Miller, C. D., D. R. Mullineaux, D. R. Crandell, and R. A. Bailey. *Potential Hazards from Future Volcanic Eruptions in the Long Valley-Mono Lake Area, East-Central California and Southwest Nevada—A Preliminary Assessment.* U.S. Geological Survey Circular 877 (1982).

Russell, I. C. *Quaternary History of Mono Valley, California.* Reprinted from the Eighth Annual Report of the United States Geological Survey, 1889. Lee Vining, Calif.: Artemisia Press, 1984.

Sieh, K., and M. Bursik. "Most Recent Eruption of the Mono Craters, Eastern Central California." *Journal of Geophysical Research* 91 (1986).

Sorey, M. L., C. D. Farrar, W. C. Evans, et al. *Invisible CO_2 Gas Killing Trees at Mammoth Mountain, California.* U.S. Geological Survey Fact Sheet 177-96 (1996).

Stine, S. "Late Holocene Lake Level Fluctuations and Island Volcanism at Mono Lake, California." In *Geologic Guide to Aspen Valley, Mono Lake, Mono Craters and Inyo Craters*, Field Trip Guide for the Friends of the Pleistocene Pacific Cell, October 12–14, 1984.

LASSEN PEAK

Christiansen, R. L., M. A. Clynne, and L. J. P. Muffler. *Geologic Map of the Area of Lassen Peak, Chaos Crags, and Upper Hat Creek, California.* U.S. Geological Survey Map I-2723 (2002).

Clynne, M. A., D. E. Champion, D. A. Trimble, J. W. Hendley II, and P. H. Stauffer. *How Old Is "Cinder Cone"? Solving a Mystery in Lassen Volcanic Park, California.* U.S. Geological Survey Fact Sheet 023-00 (2000).

Clynne, M. A., R. L. Christiansen, C. D. Miller, P. H. Stauffer, and J. W. Hendley II. *Volcano Hazards of the Lassen Volcanic National Park Area, California.* U.S. Geological Survey Fact Sheet 022-00 (2000).

Clynne, M. A., R. L. Christiansen, T. J. Felger, P. H. Stauffer, and J. W. Hendley II. *Eruptions of Lassen Peak, California, 1914 to 1917.* U.S. Geological Survey Fact Sheet 173-98 (1998).

Crandell, D. R., D. R. Mullineaux, R. S. Sigafoos, and R. Meyer. "Chaos Crags Eruptions and Rockfall-avalanches, Lassen Volcanic National Park, California." *U.S. Geological Survey Journal of Research* 2, no. 1 (1974).

Day, A. L., and E. T. Allen. *The Volcanic Activity and Hot Springs of Lassen Peak.* Carnegie Institution of Washington, publication no. 360, Washington DC, 1925.

Diller, J. S. "The Latest Volcanic Eruptions in Northern California." *American Journal of Science 33,* 3rd ser. (1887).

———. "A Late Volcanic Eruption in Northern California and Its Peculiar Lava." *U.S. Geological Survey Bulletin* 79 (1891).

Harkness, H. W. "A Recent Volcano in Plumas Country." *California Academy of Sciences Proceedings* 5 (1873–1874).

Kane, P. "Pleistocene Glaciation—Lassen Volcanic National Park." *California Geology* 35 (1982).

Loomis, B. F. *Pictorial History of the Lassen Volcano.* Reprint, Mineral, Calif.: Lassen Loomis Museum Association, 1926.

Schaffer, J. P. *Lassen Volcanic National Park and Vicinity.* 2nd ed. Berkeley: Wilderness Press, 1986.

Turrin, B. D., R. L. Christiansen, M. A. Clynne, et al. "Age of Lassen Peak, California, and Implications for the Ages of Late Pleistocene Glaciations in the Southern Cascade Range." *Geological Society of America Bulletin* 110 (1998).

Willendrup, A. W. *The Lassen Park Eruptions and Their Lingering Legacy.* Association for Northern California Records and Research, occasional publication no. 8 (1983).

Williams, H. *Geology of the Lassen Volcanic National Park, California*. University of California publication, Department of Geological Sciences Bulletin 21, no. 8 (1932).

MOUNT SHASTA

Crandell, D. R. "Gigantic Debris Avalanche of Pleistocene Age from Ancestral Mount Shasta Volcano, California, and Debris-Avalanche Hazard Zonation." *U.S. Geological Survey Bulletin* 1861 (1989).

Crandell, D. R., C. D. Miller, H. X. Glicken, R. L. Christiansen, and C. G. Newhall. "Catastrophic Debris Avalanche from Ancestral Mount Shasta Volcano, California." *Geology* 12 (1984).

Diller, J. S. "Mount Shasta: A Typical Volcano." *National Geographic Society Monograph* 1, no. 8 (1895).

Finch, R. H. "Activity of a California Volcano in 1786." *The Volcano Letter,* no. 308 (1930).

Miller, C. D. "Potential Hazards from Future Eruptions in the Vicinity of Mount Shasta Volcano, Northern California." *U.S. Geological Survey Bulletin* 1503 (1980).

Rhodes, P. T. Historic Glacier Fluctuations at Mount Shasta, Siskiyou County." *California Geology* 40 (1987).

Walton, B., ed. *Mount Shasta: Home of the Ancients*. Mokelumne Hill, Calif.: Health Research, 1985.

Williams, H. "Mount Shasta, A Cascade Volcano." *Journal of Geology* 40, no. 5 (1932).

Zanger, M. *Mt. Shasta: History, Legend and Lore*. Berkeley: Celestial Arts, 1992.

MEDICINE LAKE VOLCANO

Anderson, C. A. *Volcanoes of the Medicine Lake Highland, California*. University of California publication, Department of Geological Sciences Bulletin 25 (1941).

Chitwood, L. A. "Inflated Basaltic Lava—Examples of Processes and Landforms from Central and Southeast Oregon." *Oregon Geology* 56, no. 1 (1994).

Donnelly-Nolan, J. M. *Geologic Map of Medicine Lake Volcano*. U.S. Geological Survey Map (in press).

Donnelly-Nolan, J. M., and D. E. Champion. *Geologic Map of Lava Beds National Monument, Northern California*. U.S. Geological Survey Map I-804 (1987).

Donnelly-Nolan, J. M., D. E. Champion, C. D. Miller, T. L. Grove, and D. Trimble. "Post-11,000-Year Volcanism at Medicine Lake Volcano, Cascade Range, Northern California." *Journal of Geophysical Research* 95 (1990).

Donnelly-Nolan, J. M., and K. M. Nolan. "Catastrophic Flooding and Eruption of Ash Flow Tuff at Medicine Lake Volcano, California." *Geology* 14 (1986).

Grove, T. L., J. M. Donnelly-Nolan, and T. Housh. "Magmatic Processes That Generated the Rhyolite of Glass Mountain, Medicine Lake Volcano, N. California." *Contributions to Mineralogy and Petrology* 127 (1997).

Heiken, G. "Plinian-Type Eruptions in the Medicine Lake Highland California, and the Nature of the Underlying Magma." *Journal of Volcanology and Geothermal Research* 4 (1978).

Nathenson, M. "Probabilities of Volcanic Eruptions and Application to the Recent History of Medicine Lake Volcano." In *A Unified Approach toward Probabilistic Risk Assessment for Earthquakes, Floods, Landslides, and Volcanoes* (proceedings of a multidisciplinary workshop held in Golden Colorado, November 1999), edited by A.V. Vecchia. U.S. Geological Survey Open-File Report 01-324 (2001).

Walter, S., and D. Dzurisin. "The September Earthquake Swarm at Medicine Lake Volcano, Northern California" (abstract). *Eos, Transactions, American Geophysical Union* (1989).

Waters, A. C. "Captain Jack's Stronghold: The Geologic Events That Created a Natural Fortress, Siskiyou County." *California Geology,* September-October 1992.

Waters, A. C., J. M. Donnelly-Nolan, and B. W. Rogers. "Selected Caves and Lava-Tube Systems in and near Lava Beds National Monument, California." *U.S. Geological Survey Bulletin* 1673 (1990).

MOUNT MCLOUGHLIN

Maynard, L. G. "Geology of Mount McLoughlin." Master's thesis, University of Oregon, Eugene, 1974.

Montague, M. J. "The Little Glacier That Couldn't." *Mazama* 40 (1973).

Phillips, K. "Farewell to Sholes Glacier." *Mazama* 21, no. 12 (1939).

Smith, J. G. *Geologic Map of the Sky Lakes Roadless Area and Mountain Lakes Wilderness, Jackson and Klamath Counties, Oregon.* U.S. Geological Survey Miscellaneous Field Studies Map MF 1507A (1983).

CRATER LAKE

Atwood, W. W., Jr. "The Glacial History of an Extinct Volcano, Crater Lake National Park." *Journal of Geology* 43 (1935).

Bacon, C. R. "Eruptive History of Mount Mazama and Crater Lake Caldera, Cascade Range, U.S.A." *Journal of Volcanology and Geothermal Research* 18 (1983).

Bacon, C. R., and M. A. Lanphere. "Geologic Setting of Crater Lake, Oregon." In *Crater Lake: An Ecosystems Study,* edited by E. T. Drake, et al. American Association for the Advancement of Science, Pacific Division, San Francisco, 1990.

Bacon, C. R., L. G. Mastin, K. M. Scott, M. Nathenson. *Volcano and Earthquake Hazards in the Crater Lake Region, Oregon.* U.S. Geological Survey Open-File Report OFR-97-487 (1997).

Decker, R., and B. Decker. *Road Guide to Crater Lake National Park.* Mariposa, Calif.: Double Decker Press, 1995.

Deur, D. "A Most Sacred Place: The Significance of Crater Lake Among the Indians of Southern Oregon." *Oregon Historical Quarterly* 103, no. 1 (2002).

Harmon, R. *Crater Lake National Park: A History.* Corvallis: Oregon State University Press, 2002.

Harris, S. L. "Geomythology: The Battle of Llao and Skell." In *Agents of Chaos: Earthquakes, Volcanoes, and Other Natural Disasters.* Missoula, Mont.: Mountain Press, 1990.

Lidstrom, J. W. "A New Model for the Formation of Crater Lake Caldera, Oregon." PhD dissertation, Oregon State University, Corvallis, 1971.

Nathenson, M., C. R. Bacon, and J. V. Gardner. "Models for the Filling of Crater Lake, Oregon" (abstract). *Eos, Transactions, American Geophysical Union* 82, no. 47, fall meeting supplement (2001).

Warfield, R. G., L. Smith, and L. Juillerat. *Crater Lake: The Story Behind the Scenery.* Rev. ed. Las Vegas, Nev.: KC Publications, 2001.

Weiselberg, E. "He All But Made the Mountains: William Gladstone Steel, Mountain Climbing, and the Establishment of Crater Lake National Park." *Oregon Historical Quarterly* 103, no. 1 (2002).

Williams, H. "The Geology of Crater Lake National Park, Oregon." Carnegie Institution of Washington, publication no. 540, Washington DC, 1942.

Young, S. R. "Physical Volcanology of Holocene Airfall Deposits from Mt. Mazama, Crater Lake, Oregon." PhD dissertation, University of Lancaster, UK, 1990.

Zdanowicz, C. M., G. A. Zielinski, and M. S. Germani. "Mount Mazama Eruption: Calendrical Age Verified and Atmospheric Impact Assessed." *Geology* 27, no. 7 (1999).

MOUNT THIELSEN

Davie, E. J. "The Geology and Petrology of Three Fingered Jack, A High Cascade Volcano in Central Oregon." Master's thesis, University of Oregon, Eugene, 1980.

Nafziger, R. H. "Oregon's Southernmost Glacier: A Three Year Report." *Mazama* 53, no. 13 (1971).

Sherrod, D. R. "Thielsen, Oregon." In *Volcanoes of North America: United States and Canada,* edited by C. A. Wood and J. Kienle. New York: Cambridge University Press, 1990.

Williams, H. *Mount Thielsen: A Dissected Cascade Volcano.* University of California publications, Department of Geological Sciences Bulletin 23 (1933).

NEWBERRY VOLCANO

Champion, D. E., J. M. Donnelly-Nolan, and M. A. Lanphere. "Mapping Newberry Volcano's Extensive North Flank Basalts" (abstract). Geological Society of America Cordilleran Section meeting, 2002.

Connolly, T. J., ed. *Newberry Crater: A Ten-Thousand-Year Record of Human Occupation and Environmental Change in the Basin-Plateau Borderlands.* University of Utah Anthropological Papers no. 121. Salt Lake City: The University of Utah Press, 1999.

Donnelly-Nolan, J. M., and D. E. Champion. "New Thoughts about Newberry Volcano, Central Oregon USA" (abstract). American Geophysical Union Conference, fall 2004.

Gardner, J., S. Carey, and H. Sigurdsson. "Plinian Eruptions at Glacier Peak and Newberry Volcanoes, United States: Implications for Volcanic Hazards in the Cascade Range." *Geological Society of America Bulletin* 110, no. 2 (1998).

Garrett, S. G. *Newberry National Volcanic Monument: America's Newest National Monument: An Oregon Documentary.* Edited by Bert Webber. Webb Research Group, 1991.

Jensen, R. A. *Roadside Guide to the Geology of Newberry Volcano.* 3rd ed. Bend, Oreg.: CenOreGeoPub, 2000.

Jensen, R. A., and L. A. Chitwood, eds. *What's New at Newberry Volcano, Oregon.* Guidebook for the Friends of the Pleistocene Eighth Annual Pacific Northwest Cell Field Trip, 2000.

Kuehn, S. C. "Stratigraphy, Distribution, and Geochemistry of the Newberry Volcano Tephras." PhD dissertation, Washington State University, Pullman, 2002.

Larson, C., and J. Larson. *Central Oregon Caves.* Vancouver, Wash.: ABC Printing & Publishing, 1987.

——. *Lava River Cave.* Vancouver, Wash.: ABC Printing & Publishing, 1987.

MacLeod, N. S., and D. R. Sherrod. "Geologic Evidence for a Magma Chamber Beneath Newberry Volcano, Oregon," *Journal of Geophysical Research* 93 (1988).

MacLeod, N. S., D. R. Sherrod, L. A. Chitwood, and R. A. Jensen. *Geologic Map of Newberry Volcano, Deschutes, Klamath, and Lake Counties, Oregon.* U.S. Geological Survey Miscellaneous Investigations Map I-2455 (1995).

Sherrod, D. R., L. G. Mastin, W. E. Scott, and S. P. Schilling. *Volcanic Hazards at Newberry Volcano, Oregon.* U.S. Geological Survey Open-File Report 97-513 (1997).

Williams, H. "Newberry Volcano, Central Oregon." *Geological Society of America* 46, no. 2 (1935).

THREE SISTERS

Calvert, A., and W. Hildreth. "Radiometric Dating of Three Sisters Volcanic Field" (abstract). Geological Society of America, Cordilleran Section, 2002.

Calvert, A., W. Hildreth, and J. Fierstein. "Silicic Eruptions of the Past 50 Ka at the Three Sister Volcanic Cluster" (abstract). American Geological Union Fall Meeting, San Francisco, 2003.

Chitwood, L. A. "Geology [of the Three Sisters Area]." In *Oregon's Sisters Country: A Portrait of Its Lands, Waters, and People,* edited by R. R. Hatton. Bend, Oreg.: Geographical Books, 1996.

Clark, J. G. "Geology and Petrology of South Sister Volcano, High Cascade Range, Oregon." PhD dissertation, University of Oregon, Eugene, 1983.

Grubbs, B. *Hiking Oregon's Three Sisters Country.* Helena, Mont.: Falcon Press, 1997.

Hopson, R. E. "The Arctic Alpine Zone in the Three Sisters Region." *Mazama* 43, no. 13 (1961).

——. "Collier Glacier—A Photographic Record." *Mazama* 42, no. 13 (1960).

Keen, R. H. "Collier Glacier: 1970–1978." *Mazama* 60 (1978).

——. "Collier Glacier: 1979, 1980, 1981." *Mazama* 63 (1981).

——. "Collier Glacier Report: 1966–1969." *Mazama* 51 (1969).

O'Connor, J. E., J. H. Hardison III, and J. E. Costa. *Debris Flows from Failures of Neoglacial-Age Moraine Dams in the Three Sisters and Mount Jefferson Wilderness Areas, Oregon.* U.S. Geological Survey Professional Paper 1606 (2001).

Scott, W. E. "Quaternary Glaciation and Volcanism, Metolius River Area, Oregon." *Geological Society of American Bulletin* 88 (1977).

——. "Temporal Relations Between Eruptions of the Mount Bachelor Volcanic Chain and Fluctuations of Late Quaternary Glaciers." In *Guidebook for Field Trip to the Mount Bachelor-South Sister-Bend Area, Central Oregon High Cascades,* edited by W. E. Scott, C. A. Gardner, and A. M. Sarna-Wojcicki. U.S. Geological Survey Open-file Report 89-645 (1989).

Scott, W. E., and C. A. Gardner. "Field Guide to the Central Oregon High Cascades: Part I: Mount Bachelor–South Sister Area." *Oregon Geology* 52, no. 5 (1990).

——. "Field Guide to the Central Oregon High Cascades: Part 2: Ash-Flow Tuffs in the Bend Area." *Oregon Geology* 52, no. 6 (1990).

——. *Geologic Map of the Mount Bachelor Volcanic Chain and Surrounding Area, Cascade Range, Oregon.* U.S. Geological Survey Miscellaneous Investigation Map I-1967 (1992).

Scott, W. E., R. M. Iverson, S. P. Schilling, and B. J. Fisher. *Volcano Hazards in the Three Sisters Region, Oregon.* U.S. Geological Society Open-File Report 99-437 (1999).

Sherrod, D. R., E. M. Taylor, M. L. Ferns, W. E. Scott, R. M. Conrey, and G. A. Smith. *Geologic Map of the Bend 30 by 60 Minute Quadrangle, Central Oregon.* U.S. Geological Survey Miscellaneous Investigations Map I-2683 (in press).

Taylor, E. M. "Recent Volcanism between Three Fingered Jack and North Sister, Oregon Cascade Range: Part I: History of Volcanic Activity." *Ore Bin* 27, no. 7 (1965).

———. "Volcanic History and Tectonic Development of the Central High Cascade Range, Oregon." *Journal of Geophysical Research* 95, no. B12 (1990).

Taylor, E. M., N. S. MacLeod, D. R. Sherrod, and G. W. Walker. *Geologic Map of the Three Sisters Wilderness, Deschutes, Lane, and Linn Counties, Oregon.* U.S. Geological Survey Miscellaneous Field Studies Map MF-1952 (1987).

Wicks, C. W., D. Dzurisin, S. Ingebritsen, W. Thatcher, Z. Lu, and J. Iverson. "Magmatic Activity Beneath the Quiescent Three Sisters Volcanic Center, Central Oregon Cascade Range, USA." *Geophysical Research Letters* 29 (2002).

MOUNT JEFFERSON

Begét, J. E. "Evidence of Pleistocene Explosive Eruptions of Mount Jefferson, Oregon." *Eos, Transactions, American Geophysical Union* 62 (1981).

———. "Pleistocene Pyroclastic Deposits from Eruptions of Mount Jefferson, Oregon." *American Quaternary Association Projects and Abstracts,* 1982.

Conrey, R. M. "Geology and Petrology of the Mount Jefferson Area, High Cascade Range, Oregon." PhD dissertation, Washington State University, Pullman, 1991.

Walder, J. S., C. A. Gardner, R. M. Conrey, B. J. Fisher, and S. P. Schilling. *Volcano Hazards in the Mount Jefferson Region, Oregon.* U.S. Geological Survey Open-File Report 99-24 (1999).

MOUNT HOOD

Ayeres, F. D., and A. E. Cresswell. "The Mount Hood Fumaroles." *Mazama* 33, no. 13 (1951).

Brantley, S. R., and W. E. Scott. "The Danger of Collapsing Lava Domes: Lessons for Mount Hood, Oregon." *Oregon Geology* 59, no. 4 (1997).

Bunnell, C. O. *Legends of the Klickitats: A Klickitat Version of the Bridge of the Gods.* Portland, Oreg.: Metropolitan Press, 1935.

Cameron, K. A., and P. T. Pringle. "A Detailed Chronology of the Most Recent Major Eruptive Period at Mount Hood, Oregon." *Geological Society of America Bulletin* 99 (1987).

———. "Prehistoric Buried Forests of Mount Hood." *Oregon Geology* 53, no. 2 (1991).

Clark, E. E. "The Bridge of the Gods in Fact and Fancy." *Oregon Historical Quarterly,* March 1952.

———. *Indian Legends of the Pacific Northwest.* Berkeley: University of California Press, 1966.

Crandell, D. R. "Recent Eruptive History of Mount Hood, Oregon, and Potential Hazards from Future Eruptions." *U.S. Geological Survey Bulletin* 1492 (1980).

Gardner, C. A., W. E. Scott, Jon J. Major, and T. C. Pierson. *Mount Hood—History and Hazards of Oregon's Most Recently Active Volcano.* U.S. Geological Survey Fact Sheet 060-00 (2000).

Grauer, J. *Mount Hood: A Complete History.* Privately printed, 1975.

Jillson, W. R. "The Volcanic Activity of Mount St. Helens and Mount Hood in Historic Time." *Geographical Review* 3 (1917).

Lawrence, D. B. "Mount Hood's Latest Eruption and Glacier Advances." *Mazama* 30, no. 13 (1948).

Lawrence, D. B., and E. G. Lawrence. "Bridge of the Gods Legend, Its Origin, History, and Dating." *Mazama* 40, no. 13 (1958).

Lundstrom, S. C. "Photogrammetric Analysis of 1984–1989 Surface Altitude Change of the Partially Debris-Covered Eliot Glacier, Mount Hood, Oregon, U.S.A." *Annals of Glaciology* 17 (1993).

Mainwaring, W. L. *Exploring the Mt. Hood Loop.* Salem, Oreg.: Westridge Press, 1992.

McNeil, F. H. *McNeil's Mount Hood: Wy'east the Mountain Revisited.* Edited by Joseph A. Stein. Zig Zag, Oreg.: Zig Zag Papers, 1990. First published in 1937.

Pringle, P. T. "A Circa AD 1781 Eruption and Lahar at Mount Hood, Oregon—Evidence from Tree-Ring Dating and from Observations of Lewis and Clark in 1805–6" (abstract). *Geological Society of America Abstracts with Programs* 34, no. 6 (2002).

Scott, W. E., T. C. Pierson, S. P. Schilling, et al. "Volcano Hazards in the Mount Hood Region, Oregon." U.S. Geological survey Open-File Report 97-89 (1997).

Sylvester, A. H. "Is Our Noblest Volcano Awakening to New Life?" *National Geographic Magazine* 19 (1908).

Williams, J. H. *The Guardians of the Columbia.* Tacoma, Wash.: J. H. Williams, 1912.

Wise, W. S. "The Geologic History of Mount Hood, Oregon." *Mazama* 46, no. 13 (1964).

———. "Geology and Petrology of the Mt. Hood Area: A Study of High Cascade Volcanism." *Geological Society of America Bulletin* 80 (1969).

———. "The Last Eruptive Phase of the Mount Hood Volcano." *Mazama* 48, no. 13 (1966).

MOUNT ADAMS

Byam, F. M. "The Mount Adams Slide of 1921." *Mazama* 6, no. 2 (1921).

Hammond, P. E. *Geochemical Analyses, Age Dates and Flow-Volume Estimates for Quaternary Volcanic Rocks, Southern Cascade Mountains, Washington.* Washington Division of Geology and Earth Resources Open-File Report 83-13 (1983).

Hildreth, W., and J. Fierstein. *Geologic Map of the Mount Adams Volcanic Field, Cascade Range of Southern Washington.* U.S. Geological Survey Map I-2460 (1995).

———. "Recent Eruptions of Mount Adams, Washington Cascades, USA." *Bulletin of Volcanology* 58 (1997).

Hildreth, W., and M. A. Lanphere. "Potassium-Argon Geochronology of a Basalt-Andesite-Dacite Arc System: The Mount Adams Volcanic Field, Cascade Range of Southern Washington." *Geological Society of America Bulletin* 106 (1994).

Mueller, M., and T. Mueller. *A Guide to Washington's South Cascades Volcanic Landscapes.* Seattle: The Mountaineers, 1995.

Phillips, K. N. "Fumaroles of Mount St. Helens and Mount Adams." *Mazama* 23, no. 12 (1941).

Scott, W., R. M. Iverson, J. W. Vallance, and W. Hildreth. "Volcano Hazards in the Mount Adams Region, Washington." U.S. Geological Survey Open-File Report 95-492 (1995).

Swanson, D. A., and G. A. Clayton. *Generalized Geologic Map of the Goat Rocks Wilderness and Roadless Areas (6036, Parts A, C, and D), Lewis and Yakima Counties, Washington.* U.S. Geological Survey Open-File Report 83-357 (1983).

Vallance, J. W. "Postglacial Lahars and Potential Hazards in the White Salmon River System on the Southwest Flank of Mount Adams, Washington." *U.S. Geological Survey Bulletin* 2161 (1997).

MOUNT ST. HELENS

Brantley, S., and B. Myers. *Mount St. Helens—From the 1980 Eruptions to 2000.* U.S. Geological Survey Fact Sheet 036-00 (2000).

Carey, S., J. Gardner, and H. Sigurdsson. "The Intensity and Magnitude of Holocene Plinian Eruptions from Mount St. Helens Volcano." *Journal of Volcanology and Geothermal Research* 66 (1995).

Crandell, D. R. *Deposits of Pre-1980 Pyroclastic Flows and Lahars from Mount St. Helens Volcano, Washington.* U.S. Geological Survey Professional Paper 1444 (1987).

Crandell, D. R., and D. R. Mullineaux. "Potential Hazards from Future Eruptions of Mount St. Helens Volcano, Washington." *U.S. Geological Survey Bulletin* 1383C (1978).

Criswell, C. W. "Chronology and Pyroclastic Stratigraphy of the May 18, 1980, Eruption of Mount St. Helens, Washington." *Journal of Geophysical Research* 92 (1987).

Decker, R., and B. Decker. "The Eruptions of Mount St. Helens." *Scientific American* 244, no. 3 (1981).

———. *Road Guide to Mount St. Helens.* Mariposa, Calif.: Double Decker Press, 1993.

Doukas, M. P. "Road Guide to Volcanic Deposits of Mount St. Helens and Vicinity, Washington." *U.S. Geological Survey Bulletin* 1859 (1990).

Hausback, B. P. *Geologic Map of the Sasquatch Steps Area, North Flank of Mount St. Helens, Washington.* U.S. Geological Survey Investigations Series Map I-2463 (2000).

Hickson, C. J. "The May 18, 1980, Eruption of Mount St. Helens, Washington State: A Synopsis of Events and Review of Phase 1 from an Eyewitness Perspective." *Geoscience Canada* 17, no. 3 (1990).

Hoblitt, R. P. "Was the 18 May 1980 Lateral Blast at Mt. St. Helens the Product of Two Explosions?" *Philosophic Transactions of the Royal Society of London* 358 (2000).

Hoblitt, R. P., D. R. Crandell, and D. R. Mullineaux. "Mount St. Helens Eruptive Behavior During the Past 1,500 Years." *Geology* 8 (1980).

Holmes, K. L. *Mount St. Helens, Lady with a Past.* Salem, Oreg.: Salem Press, 1980.

———. "Mount Saint Helens' Recent Eruptions." *Oregon Historical Quarterly* 56 (1955).

Lawrence, D. B. "Diagrammatic History of the Northeast Slope of Mt. St. Helens, Washington." *Mazama* 36, no. 13 (1954).

———. "The 'Floating Island' Lava Flow of Mt. St. Helens." *Mazama* 23, no. 12 (1941).

Lipman, P. W., and D. R. Mullineaux, eds. *The 1980 Eruptions of Mount St. Helens, Washington.* U.S. Geological Survey Professional Paper 1250 (1981).

Major, J. J., W. E. Scott, C. Driedger, and D. Dzurisin. *Mount St. Helens Erupts Again: Activity from September 2004 through March 2005.* U.S. Geological Survey Fact Sheet 2005-3036 (2005).

Majors, H. M. "Mount St. Helens Series." *Northwest Discovery* 1, nos. 1 and 2 (1980).

Moore, J. G., and C. J. Rice. "Chronology and Character of the May 18, 1980, Explosive Eruptions of Mount St. Helens." In *Explosive Volcanism: Inception, Evolution, and Hazards.* Washington DC: National Academy Press, 1984.

Mullineaux, D. R. "Pre-1980 Tephra-Fall Deposits Erupted from Mount St. Helens, Washington." U.S. Geological Survey Professional Paper 1563 (1996).

Pallister, J. S., R. P. Hoblitt, D. R. Crandell, and D. R. Mullineaux. "Mount St. Helens a Decade after the 1980 Eruptions: Magmatic Models, Chemical Cycles, and a Revised Hazards Assessment." *Bulletin of Volcanology* 54 (1992).

Pringle, P. T. *Roadside Geology of Mount St. Helens National Monument and Vicinity.* Rev. ed. Washington Department of Natural Resources, Division of Geology and Earth Resources Information Circular 88 (2002).

Schilling, S. P., P. E. Carra, R. A. Thompson, and E. Y. Iwatsubo. "Post-Eruption Glacier Development within the Crater of Mount St. Helens, Washington" (abstract). *Geological Society of America Abstracts with Programs* 34, no. 5 (2002).

Tilling, R. L., L. J. Topinka, and D. A. Swanson. *Eruptions of Mount St. Helens: Past, Present, and Future.* Rev. ed. U.S. Geological Survey, 1990.

Wolfe, E. W., and T. C. Pierson. *Volcanic Hazard Zonation for Mount St. Helens, Washington.* U.S. Geological Survey Open-File Report 95-497 (1995).

Yamaguchi, D. K. "New Tree-Ring Dates for Recent Eruptions of Mount St. Helens." *Quaternary Research* 20 (1983).

———. "Tree-Ring Evidence for 1842–1843 Eruptive Activity at the Goat Rocks Dome, Mount St. Helens, Washington." *Bulletin of Volcanology* 55 (1993).

Yamaguchi, D. K., R. P. Hoblitt, and D. B. Lawrence. "A New Tree-Ring Date for the 'Floating Island' Lava Flow, Mount St. Helens, Washington." *Bulletin of Volcanology* 52 (1990).

MOUNT RAINIER

Barcott, B. *The Measure of a Mountain: Beauty and Terror on Mount Rainier.* New York: Ballantine Books, 1998.

Byman, J. M., and J. W. Vallance. "An Early Holocene Eruptive Period at Mount Rainier, Washington" (abstract). *Eos, Transactions, American Geophysical Union* 82, no. 47 (2001).

Crandell, D. R. "The Geologic Story of Mount Rainier." *U.S. Geological Survey Bulletin* 1292 (1969).

———. *Postglacial Lahars from Mount Rainier Volcano, Washington.* U.S. Geological Survey Professional Paper 677 (1971).

———. *Potential Hazards from Future Eruptions of Mount Rainier, Washington.* U.S. Geological Survey Miscellaneous Investigations Map I-836 (1973).

Dragovich, J. D., P. T. Pringle, and T. J. Walsh. "Extent and Geometry of the Mid-Holocene Osceola Mudflow in the Puget Lowland—Implications for Holocene Sedimentation and Paleogeography." *Washington Geology* 22, no. 3 (1994).

Driedger, C. L., and K. M. Scott. *Mount Rainier—Learning To Live with Volcanic Risk.* U.S. Geological Survey Fact Sheet 034-02 (2002).

Filley, B. *The Big Fact Book about Mount Rainier: Fascinating Facts, Records, Lists, Topics, Characters and Stories.* Issaquah, Wash.: Dunamis House, 1996.

———. *Discovering the Wonders of the Wonderland Trail Encircling Mount Rainier.* Issaquah, Wash.: Dunamis House, 1992.

Hoblitt, R. P., J. S. Walder, C. L. Driedger, K. M. Scott, P. T. Pringle, and J. W. Vallance. *Volcano Hazards from Mount Rainier Washington.* Rev. ed. U.S. Geological Survey Open-File Report 98-428 (1998).

Kirk, R. *Sunrise to Paradise: The Story of Mount Rainier National Park.* Seattle: University of Washington Press, 2003.

Kiver, E. P., and M. P. Mumma. "Summit Firn Caves, Mount Rainier, Washington." *Science* 173 (1971).

Le Guern, F., E. Ponzevera, Y. France, W. M. Lokey, and R. D. Schroedel. "Mount Rainer Summit Caves Volcanic Activity" (abstract). *Washington Geology* 28, nos. 1–2 (2000).

Majors, H. M. "Mount Rainier—The Tephra Eruption of 1894." *Northwest Discovery* 2, no. 6 (1981).

McNulty, T., and P. O'Hara. *Washington's Mount Rainier National Park: A Centennial Celebration.* Seattle: The Mountaineers, 2003.

Molenaar, D. *The Challenge of Rainier.* 3rd ed. Seattle: The Mountaineers, 1979.

Pringle, P. T. "Buried Forests of Mount Rainier Volcano—Evidence for Extensive Holocene Inundation by Lahars in the White, Puyallup, Nisqually, and Cowlitz River Valleys" (abstract). *Washington Geology* 28, nos. 1–2 (2000).

———. *Geology of Scenic Byways at Mount Rainier National Park and Vicinity.* Washington Department of Natural Resources, Division of Geology and Earth Resources (in press).

Pringle, P. T., and K. M. Scott. *Postglacial Influence of Volcanism on the Landscape and Environmental History of the Puget Lowland, Washington.* Washington Department of Natural Resources, Division of Geology and Earth Resources (2002).

Schneider, H. *Hiking Mount Rainier National Park.* Helena, Mont.: Falcon Press, 1999.

Scott, K. M., J. L. Macias, J. A. Naranjo, S. Rodriguez, and J. P. McGeehin. *Catastrophic Debris Flows Transformed from Landslides in Volcanic Terrain: Mobility, Behavior, and Mitigation Strategies.* U.S. Geological Survey Professional Paper 1630 (2001).

Scott, K. M., J. W. Vallance, and P. T. Pringle. *Sedimentology, Behavior, and Hazards of Debris Flows at Mount Rainier, Washington.* U.S. Geological Survey Professional Paper 1537 (1995).

Sisson, T. W., and P. T. Pringle. "Progress Made in Understanding Mount Rainier's Hazards." *Eos, Transactions, American Geophysical Union* 82, no. 9 (Feb. 27, 2001).

Stockstill, K. R., T. A. Vogel, and T. W. Sisson. "Origin and Emplacement of the Andesite of Burroughs Mountain, a Zoned, Large-Volume Lava Flow at Mount Rainier, Washington." *Journal of Volcanology and Geothermal Research* 2518 (2002).

Vallance, J. W., and S. Donoghue. "Holocene Eruptive History of Mount Rainier" (abstract). *Washington Geology* 28, nos. 1–2 (2000).

Vallance, J. W., and K. M. Scott. "The Osceola Mudflow from Mount Rainier: Sedimentology and Hazard Implications of a Huge Clay-Rich Debris Flow." *Geological Society of America Bulletin* 109, no. 2 (1997).

Walder, J. S., and C. L. Driedger. "Frequent Outburst Floods from South Tahoma Glacier, Mount Rainier, USA—Relation to Debris Flows, Meteorological Origin and Implications for Subglacial Hydrology." *Journal of Glaciology* 41, no. 137 (1995).

———. *Glacier-Generated Debris Flows at Mount Rainier.* U.S. Geological Survey Open-File Report 93-124 (1993).

Warfield, R. *Mount Rainier National Park.* Mariposa, Calif.: Sierra Press, 1998.

Wuethner, G., and D. W. Moore. *Mount Rainier: A Visitor's Companion.* Mechanicsburg, Pa.: Stackpole Books, 2003.

Zimbelman, D. R., R. O. Rye, and G. P. Landis. "Fumaroles in Ice Caves on the Summit of Mount Rainier—Preliminary Stable Isotope, Gas, and Geochemical Studies." *Journal of Volcanology and Geothermal Research* 97 (2000).

GLACIER PEAK

Begét, J. E. "Glacier Peak, Washington—A Potentially Hazardous Cascade Volcano." *Environmental Geology* 5 (1983).

———. *Postglacial Volcanic Deposits at Glacier Peak, Washington, and Potential Hazards from Future Eruptions.* U.S. Geological Survey Open-File Report 82-830 (1982).

———. "Recent Volcanic Activity at Glacier Peak." *Science* 215 (1982).

———. "Tephrochronology of Late Wisconsin Deglaciation and Holocene Glacier Fluctuations near Glacier Peak, North Cascade Range, Washington." *Quaternary Research* 21 (1984).

Crowder, D. F., R. W. Tabor, and A. B. Ford. *Geologic Map of the Glacier Peak Quadrangle, Snohomish and Chelan Counties, Washington.* U.S. Geological Survey Quadrangle Map GQ-473 (1966).

Dragovitch, J. D., R. L. Logan, H. W. Schasse, et al. *Geologic Map of Washington—Northwest Quadrant.* Washington Division of Geology and Earth Resources Geologic Map GM-50 (2002).

Dragovitch, J. D., and D. T. McKay Jr. "Holocene Glacier Peak Lahar Deposits in the Lower Skagit River Valley, Washington." *Washington Geology* 28, nos. 1–2 (2000).

Mastin, L., and R. Waitt. *Glacier Peak—History and Hazards of a Cascade Volcano.* U.S. Geological Survey Fact Sheet 059-00 (2000).

Porter, S. C. "Glacier Peak Tephra in the North Cascade Range, Washington—Stratigraphy, Distribution, and Relationship to Late-Glacial Events." *Quaternary Research* 10 (1978).

Tabor, R. W., and D. F. Crowder. *On Batholiths and Volcanoes—Intrusion and Eruption of Late Cenozoic Magma in the Glacier Peak Area, North Cascades, Washington.* U.S. Geological Survey Professional Paper 604 (1969).

Waitt, R. B., L. G. Mastin, and J. E. Begét. *Volcanic Hazard Zonation for Glacier Peak Volcano, Washington.* U.S. Geological Survey Open-File Report 95-499 (1995).

MOUNT BAKER

Davidson, G. "Recent Volcanic Activity in the United States: Eruptions of Mount Baker." *Science* 6, no. 138 (1885).

Gardner, C. A., K. M. Scott, C. D. Miller, B. Myers, W. Hildreth, and P. T. Pringle. *Potential Volcanic Hazards from Future Activity of Mount Baker, Washington.* U.S. Geological Survey Open-File Report 95-498 (1995).

Frank, D., M. F. Meier, and D. A. Swanson. *Assessment of Increased Thermal Activity at Mount Baker, Washington, March 1975–March 1976.* U.S. Geological Survey Professional Paper 1022-A (1977).

Harper, J. T. "Glacier Terminus Fluctuations on Mount Baker, Washington, USA, 1940–1990, and Climatic Variations." *Arctic and Alpine Research* 25, no. 4 (1993).

Hildreth, W. "Kulshan Caldera: A Quaternary Subglacial Caldera in the North Cascades, Washington." *Geological Society of America Bulletin* 108, no. 7 (1996).

Hildreth, W., J. Fierstein, and M. Lanphere. "Eruptive History and Geochronology of the Mount Baker Volcanic Field, Washington." *Geological Society of America Bulletin* 115, no. 6 (2003).

Hyde, J. H., and D. R. Crandell. "Post-Glacial Volcanic Deposits at Mount Baker, Washington and Potential Hazards from Future Eruptions." U.S. Geological Survey Professional Paper 1022-C (1978).

Kiver, E. P. "Mount Baker's Changing Fumaroles." *The Ore Bin* 40, no. 8 (1978).

Majors, H. M. *Mount Baker: A Chronicle of Its Historic Eruptions and First Ascent.* Seattle: Northwest Press, 1978.

Scott, K. M., W. Hildreth, and C. A. Gardner. *Mount Baker—Living with an Active Volcano.* U.S. Geological Survey Fact Sheet 0059-00 (2000).

Tabor, R. W., R. A. Haugerud, W. Hildreth, and E. H. Brown. *Geologic Map of the Mount Baker 30 x 60 Minute Quadrangle, Washington.* U.S. Geological Survey Map I-2660 (2003).

MOUNT GARIBALDI

Evans, S. G., and G. R. Brooks. "Prehistoric Debris Avalanches from Mount Cayley Volcano, British Columbia." *Canadian Journal of Earth Science* 28 (1991).

Green, N. L. "Late Cenozoic Volcanism in the Mount Garibaldi and Garibaldi Lake Volcanic Fields, Garibaldi Volcanic Belt, Southwestern British Columbia." *Geoscience Canada* 17, no. 3 (1990).

Green, N. L., R. L. Armstrong, J. E. Harakal, J. G. Souther, and P. B. Read. "Eruptive History and K-Ar Geochronology of the Late Cenozoic Garibaldi Volcanic Belt, Southwestern British Columbia." *Geological Society of America Bulletin* 100 (1988).

Hickson, C. J., J. K. Russell, and M. V. Stasiuk. "Volcanology of the 2350 BP Eruption of Mount Meager Volcanic Complex, British Columbia, Canada." *Bulletin of Volcanology* 60 (1999).

Matthews, W. H. *Garibaldi Geology: A Popular Guide to the Geology of the Garibaldi Lake Area.* Vancouver, BC: Geological Association of Canada Cordilleran Section, 1975.

———. "Geology of the Mount Garibaldi Map-Area, Southwestern British Columbia, Canada." *Bulletin of the Geological Society of America* 69 (1958).

———. "Historic and Prehistoric Fluctuations of the Alpine Glaciers in the Mount Garibaldi Map-Area, Southwestern British Columbia." *Journal of Geology* 59 (1951).

———. "Mount Garibaldi, A Supraglacial Pleistocene Volcano in Southwestern British Columbia." *American Journal of Science* 250 (1952).

———. "The Table, A Flat-Topped Volcano in Southern British Columbia." *American Journal of Science* 249 (1951).

Read, P. B. "Mount Meager Complex, Garibaldi Belt, Southwestern British Columbia." *Geoscience Canada* 17, no. 3 (1990).

Souther, J. G., and C. J. Yorath. "Neogene Assemblages." In *Geology of the Cordilleran Orogen in Canada,* vol. G-2, edited by H. Gabrielse and C. J. Yorath. Boulder, Colo.: Geological Society of America, Geology of North America (1990).

Stasiuk, M. V., J. K. Russell, and C. J. Hickson. "Distribution, Nature, and Origins of the 2400 BP Eruption Products of Mount Meager, British Columbia." *Geological Survey of Canada Bulletin* 486 (1996).

Westgate, J. A., and A. Dreimanis. "Volcanic Ash Layers of Recent Age at Banff National Park, Alberta, Canada." *Canadian Journal of Earth Science* 4 (1967).

Index